One of Amazon's Best Books *i*

More pra

BILLIONAIRE WILDERNESS

"An eye-opening look at a specific element of economic and social inequality."
—*Kirkus Reviews*

"[Farrell] offers a challenge to the legacy of conservation itself, particularly as environmentalists work to reconcile ongoing errors of racism and exclusion while still protecting landscapes and wildlife that need protection. There are no easy answers in *Billionaire Wilderness*, but the book raises the question: When we protect the environment, whom are we protecting it for?"
—AUSTIN PRICE, *Earth Island Journal*

"Enlightening.... *Billionaire Wilderness* peels away a lot of pretty scenery to reveal things underneath a lot less pleasing to look at."
—MARK HUFFMAN, *Jackson Hole News and Guide*

"Eye-opening.... A great read for anyone interested in the intersection of conservation and inequality in the West."
—JENNIFER WEEKS, *Society of Environmental Journalists*

"[Farrell] renders a picture of how the ultra wealthy live, protect their wealth, and handle the stigma associated with being unbelievably rich.... Highly recommended."
—*Choice*

"*Billionaire Wilderness* is a thoroughly reported, measured account of what it's like to live in Wyoming's new Gilded Age, and a welcome addition to the national debate on the American West—what it's for, who it belongs to, and who gets to decide its future."
—NATE BLAKESLEE, *New York Times* bestselling author of *American Wolf*

"This important and innovative book offers a rarely seen glimpse into the lives of the ultra-wealthy, exploring the ways in which they think about status, social inequality, privilege, and the environment in a context where all of these factors collide on a regular basis."
—DAVID NAGUIB PELLOW, author of *Total Liberation: The Power and Promise of Animal Rights and the Radical Earth Movement*

"Justin Farrell explores a bold new understanding of nature and people in America's wealthiest county. This startling, provocative, and respectful analysis of conservation and the Teton community will ignite important future scholarship. A must-read."
—THOMAS E. LOVEJOY, George Mason University

BILLIONAIRE WILDERNESS

PRINCETON STUDIES IN CULTURAL SOCIOLOGY

Paul J. DiMaggio, Michèle Lamont,
Robert J. Wuthnow, and Viviana A. Zelizer,
Series Editors

For a full list of titles in the series, go to https://press.princeton.edu/catalogs
/series/title/princeton-studies-in-cultural-sociology.html.

Billionaire Wilderness

The Ultra-Wealthy and the Remaking of the American West

Justin Farrell

PRINCETON UNIVERSITY PRESS

PRINCETON AND OXFORD

Copyright © 2020 by Princeton University Press

Requests for permission to reproduce material from this work
should be sent to permissions@press.princeton.edu

Published by Princeton University Press
41 William Street, Princeton, New Jersey 08540
6 Oxford Street, Woodstock, Oxfordshire OX20 1TR

press.princeton.edu

All Rights Reserved
First paperback printing, 2021
Paper ISBN 9780691217123
Cloth ISBN 9780691176673
ISBN (e-book) 9780691185811

British Library Cataloging-in-Publication Data is available

Editorial: Meagan Levinson and Jacqueline Delaney
Production Editorial: Natalie Baan
Jacket/Cover Design: Faceout Studio
Production: Erin Suydam
Publicity: Kathryn Stevens and Maria Whelan
Copyeditor: Jennifer Harris

Jacket/Cover Credit: A distant view of the Tetons at sunrise,
Grand Teton National Park, WY / Getty Images

This book has been composed in Adobe Text and Gotham

Printed in the United States of America

In loving memory of my brother Josh.

CONTENTS

ACKNOWLEDGMENTS

During my childhood summers I would, along with my two brothers, Josh and Jordan, accompany my mom to the homes she cleaned. Depending on the week, she'd clean about seven different houses. They were all quite large, and my mom worked alone, so she'd spend a good part of the day scrubbing, bleaching, vacuuming, dusting, sweeping, mopping, and making sure things were tidy for when the owners returned home from work. We'd always have the volume of their television up loud enough to hear the *Price Is Right* game show, listening eagerly if the contestant struck it rich, or at least won a new midsize sedan.

At the time, it was strange and exciting to spend so much time in these expensive homes, and even though we were there with my mom to scrub toilets and change sheets, it gave us a small window into affluence.

My mom always seemed grateful for the work and mostly spoke well of the wealthier folks whose homes she cleaned. Back then, it all seemed so straightforward: these wealthy families chose not to clean their homes themselves, and my mom could use the money. Simple enough—a straightforward exchange. And before writing this book, I hadn't given these childhood experiences much more thought. But now looking back, I can see the imprint of these seemingly inconsequential experiences all throughout this project, beginning most importantly with the initial curiosity to think more deeply about who these people were, and their relationship to people like my mom.

Conducting scientific research on the wealthy is notoriously diffi-cult, and thus I relied heavily on, and am indebted to, a huge number of people. This book was far and away the most challenging piece of research and writing I've ever done (and likely ever will do), and I certainly could not have gone at it alone. What you're holding is the product of many, many individuals.

I owe my biggest debt of gratitude to the respondents who made this book possible, beginning with the fifty low-income interviewees. Many of these folks are recent immigrants, work multiple jobs, fear family separation, live in poverty, and have every good reason to decline being interviewed for a project like this. I sincerely hope that I have accurately represented the complexity of your hard-won views and experiences. I am also grateful for the local organization (who requested to go unnamed for fear of retribution from its donors) and interviewers who graciously worked with me to collect a representative sample and conduct interviews in Spanish. Your commitment to the community and to its working-poor and immigrant population was, and is, truly inspiring.

Of course, this study would be nowhere without the generosity of the hundreds of ultra-wealthy people who took the time to be interviewed and/or observed in your homes, at your private clubs, at fundraising events, on the phone, in cities on the East and West Coasts, at local restaurants, and on the local hiking trails. Throughout this long process, I met many wonderful people and made several new friends in Teton County and in Bozeman/Big Sky/Yellowstone Club. As I write in the introduction, I am especially appreciative for your willingness to participate, because researchers have had a very difficult time getting access to your population, which has led to a popular reliance on uninformed clichés and cheap exposés that perpetuate a hackneyed "rich and famous" stereotype. This study is certainly not perfect, but please know that throughout the years of research, I've attempted to honestly understand each of your lives with accuracy, generosity, fairness, and clarity. While some of the findings of this study are at times quite critical, my hope is that with your help I've collected reliable information and drawn conclusions with integrity that have improved our basic knowledge of a growing class of people in the United States, and their increasingly important influence on the environment and local communities.

I also owe a debt of gratitude to many locals who may not have been interviewed, but were indispensable for making connections, providing quantitative data, reading drafts, and keeping me abreast of local issues. First, I especially want to thank David and Cathy Loevner for their generosity and support, allowing my family to stay in their guest house during long periods of fieldwork. Because of the exorbitant housing costs in Teton County, I would not have been able to complete the fieldwork for this project without David and Cathy's generosity. Thank you. Similarly, I am grateful for the local support of community leaders, especially Lety Liera, Isabel Zumel, Rev. Mary Erickson, Jonathan Schechter, Charles Pinkava, and several organizations and individuals who have requested to remain anonymous.

I am grateful to my academic community at Yale University and beyond, made up of many people I now call friends. In particular, Kathryn McConnell was a truly fantastic research assistant in the early days of the project, was instrumental throughout the entire interview and data collection process, and has been a valuable conversation partner over the years. My dean, Sir Peter Crane, was very supportive of the project from its early stages, and provided additional funding for the fieldwork. Similarly, Mary Evelyn Tucker and John Grim have always been extraordinarily generous and kind colleagues. Pete Raymond, Mark Bradford, and Ben Cashore have been indispensable sounding boards as I have attempted to navigate the foreboding gauntlet of the Yale tenure track.

Chris Smith read multiple drafts, and at times talked me off the ledge in some of the darker days of the project. I remain so grateful for my training at the University of Notre Dame and to the community of friends and scholars there who continue to sustain me. James Leep did nothing, but selfishly requested that I acknowledge him.

I am grateful for the many other people who listened with sincerity and challenged me in various ways, including Paul Burow, Susan Clark, Jordan Holsinger, Dave Everson, Ben Robinson, Charlie Bettigole, Chuck Marshall, Liam Brennan, and the penetrating calls for peace, justice, and care for the earth in the homilies of the late Fr. Bob Beloin. My curious and critical graduate and undergraduate students at Yale have also helped me more than they know. I am thankful to have such a great editor Meagan Levinson at Princeton University Press, who has been with me since my first book and believed in this project from the very beginning. I also want to thank Michèle Lamont for sharing her interview guide, which was essential during the design of the research.

Finally, rather than thanking my family, I probably owe them an apology. At times, the fieldwork and writing of this book consumed me, and when I lost perspective, my wife, Ashley, was there to see through the pedantic academic nonsense and bring me back down to earth. Further, she incisively contributed to many of the book's main ideas, drawing on her own experiences in nonprofit development with wealthy philanthropists. My light, my love, and my moral compass, she's put up with me for seventeen years, and I truly do not know where I would be without her. And none of this would mean anything without our daughters, Ruby and River, who make it easy to see the big picture of why anything means anything.

I dedicate this book to my older brother Josh, who died in a car accident. In addition to accompanying my mom to clean wealthy folks' houses, we also spent our childhood summers exploring the changing landscapes and towns that make up this book. Revisiting these places during the fieldwork brought both immense pain and inexpressible joy, but it was so worth it to feel those feelings again, viscerally and unpredictably brought to the surface by the smell of the sagebrush, the sound of the whispering pines, and the crunch of the gravel where we used to pedal our bikes. Selfishly, doing research in this place transports me to times past, allowing me for a moment to revisit Josh's wild spirit and experience anew our most sacred memories.

Introduction

SETTING OFF INTO THE WILDERNESS

The sun was setting on the majestic Teton Range, its long shadow sweeping across the wilderness, slowly darkening the view as I steered my car up a secluded gravel road toward a large home nestled at the base of these craggy and picturesque mountains.

I arrived at the property and pulled through a big stone gate that led down a long driveway. Unsure of where to park, I crept forward and was eventually greeted by valet employees who welcomed me, took my car, and pointed me toward the main entrance. As I walked across the expansive property, I passed the open doors of a four-car garage attached to the residence. The first door held a Chevy Tahoe SUV with muddy mountain bikes strapped on the back; the next had a vintage convertible peeking out from underneath a blue tarp; the third was bustling with ten well-dressed workers cooking food and preparing drinks; and the last contained a collection of kayaks, winter ski gear, and old cowboy boots.

Walking through the house's front door, I was welcomed by Erika Raddler, the executive director of the environmental organization sponsoring tonight's event here at the home of Julie and Craig Williams.

"Welcome!" said Erika, handing me a name tag and a pamphlet describing this "grassroots meeting of local environmental advocates." She continued, "Feel free to make your way to the back deck, where there are drinks and hors d'oeuvres."

The name tag read "Justin—Yale Professor." While my job title had surely gotten me in the door at this exclusive event, it wouldn't allow me to play my preferred role of fly-on-the-wall while conducting my research. Slipping the name tag into my pocket, I headed toward the back deck.

As I left the entryway, I was struck by a photo of an impoverished Navajo girl prominently displayed on a four-foot-high marble base. Looking despondent, her face covered in dirt, she carried a burlap sack over her left shoulder. I walked past the display toward an enormous, colorful Navajo rug and stepped down into a grand living room. Its towering vaulted ceilings and multistory glass windows looked out onto Grand Teton peak, behind which the sun was dropping, the mountain's shadow now covering the entire valley 7,200 feet below. The enormity of this room easily accommodated a full-size bronze statue of a stoic-looking Lakota man, flanked by a mural of Western wilderness dotted with roaming cowboys, and three 8-by-8-foot acrylic paintings depicting a moose, a grizzly bear, and an elk, respectively. I made my way across the room and into a long glass hallway, through a cavernous white kitchen, and finally out onto the back deck.

Of the roughly thirty-five people in attendance, most were neighboring homeowners interested in learning more about environmental issues in the region and how they might be able to contribute to the cause. To that end, Erika gave a short presentation about various threats facing the area and offered ways to get involved. After her talk, I mingled with the crowd to get a sense of who they were and the nature of their environmental concern. As it turned out, the casual Western dress of many in attendance—Wrangler jeans and cowboy boots—belied the fact that these were people of elite social status and immense wealth.

And there was no shortage of local environmental concern among those in attendance. I chatted with a prominent tech CEO from San

Francisco who described his distress over the level of dissolved oxygen in the stream behind his house. I stood in the yard with a globally known political leader, making small talk about how this local community has changed in recent years. I sat on the deck stairs with the founder of a multi-billion-dollar oil and gas company and learned of his work as chair of the board for a wildlife art organization. I conversed with the heiress of a multi-million-dollar foundation in Texas about her efforts to slow housing and tourism development in this community. I ended the night over a craft beer with an affable hedge fund millionaire from Boston, who lamented the declining moose population in the national forest adjacent to his Wyoming property.

On the surface, these were friendly and informal conversations about water, animals, trees, and other natural things—but a closer look revealed much more.

———

These folks are members of what used to be a tiny class of ultra-wealthy millionaires and billionaires. But in recent years, this class has soared to unprecedented levels, in terms of both its size and the amount of wealth it commands.[1] In just one year between 2016 and 2017, there was a 13 percent increase in the ultra-wealthy population (255,810 people) and a 16 percent surge in combined wealth ($31.5 trillion), with no signs of slowing. And while the United States is home to the largest ultra-wealthy population (90,440), these staggering increases are a global phenomenon.

But surprisingly, nowhere is this global storyline seen more clearly, or perhaps with greater local impact, than in a little, overlooked corner of rural America. Teton County, Wyoming, is well known for its pristine and awe-inspiring natural landscapes. Boasting one of the largest intact ecosystems in the world, it is a crown jewel of the West and cradles both Grand Teton and Yellowstone National Parks. What most people don't know is that the grandeur of its wilderness is matched by the awe-inspiring concentration of wealth and a canyon-size gap between the rich and poor there: It is both the richest county in the United States[2] and the county with the nation's highest level of income inequality.[3]

This center of extreme wealth and wealth disparity creates a powder keg of intertwined problems, affecting both those who hold the wealth and those who don't, as well as the ecosystem that encircles the community.

Billionaire Wilderness offers an unprecedented look inside the world of the ultra-wealthy, focused on their increasingly significant relationship to the natural world. More specifically, *it shows how the ultra-wealthy use nature to resolve key predicaments in their lives.* Along the way, it reveals the surprising ways in which nature and wealth intersect in America, and the swelling impact of these relationships on the nation's social and environmental landscapes.

The first set of problems the rich seek to resolve are rooted in *economic concerns*: how best to enjoy, share, protect, and multiply the wealth they've acquired. The second set of problems are more *social in character*: how to wrestle with and respond to the social stigmas and personal guilt sometimes associated with great wealth. Nature comes to play a unique role in their struggles to deal with these ongoing financial, political, moral, and existential dilemmas.

Thus, investigating the ultra-wealthy requires a wide-ranging look into a number of compelling puzzles about money, nature, and the meaning of authentic community in the twenty-first century: Why did their lives turn out the way they did? Does great wealth actually make life more difficult? Why do they love and emulate the rural working poor? Why do they love Wrangler jeans? How do they define "community"? Are they aware of the fast-growing gap between the ultra-rich and everyone else? Do they feel criticized or have trouble sleeping at night? How do money and materialism contrast with the "innocence" and "purity" of nature? How do they conceptualize environmental problems, and by extension, philanthropy? How do they relate all of these issues to racial and ethnic inequality? And, moving beyond what they might *say*, how do their views actually influence their *behaviors*?

In writing this book, I set out on a journey to answer questions like these, moving beyond common presumptions about the rich toward a more open-minded and evidence-based account that allows the reader to see life from the perspective of the ultra-wealthy themselves. *Billionaire Wilderness* is not a sloppy finger-pointing exposé of greed and hypocrisy that some readers might assume exists (or hope to find). But nor is it an effort to defend or coddle my research subjects.[4] Rather, my goal is to gather facts that allow us to better understand a rarely studied and little known but highly influential group.

Along the way, *Billionaire Wilderness* will introduce this world and the growing number of people who inhabit it. We will engage its social nature from the inside out, and from bottom to top, revealing findings that have important implications—not only for improving our understanding of wealth but also for improving our understanding of how we should envision the future of our communities and the ecosystems that sustain them.

———

One reason we know very little about the ultra-wealthy is that this powerful social group is extremely difficult to access for close study. So our contemporary understanding of the topic remains empirically shallow.[5] Studies rely almost exclusively on reports of national economic trends that, while vital, are sterile and can distance us from the real-life experiences of actual people and local communities. Or we rely on popular stereotypes of the rich that oversimplify their lives, mask complexity, and discourage the empathy and objectivity researchers need to understand any social group from the inside. This current shallow understanding is especially disconcerting given the immense economic, cultural, and political power of the ultra-wealthy and their growing interest in and impact on environmental issues.

The final reason these problems are seldom studied is because rural places are too often written off as irrelevant, or just interesting bucolic sideshows. It is easy enough to view Teton County, with its spectacular natural scenery and its equally spectacular levels of wealth, as atypical, or as a relic of rich-and-famous consumer culture: amusing, but certainly not to be taken seriously by scholars studying places more representative of "real" wealth disparity that we have come to expect.

This view is shortsighted. The increased concentration of wealth is not only an urban phenomenon, but it also deeply and directly affects tens of millions of Americans living in rural areas. Overlooking this reality denies the struggles of the rural working poor and ignores an entire range of other effects on rural gentrification, environmental health, public lands, and massive socioeconomic change in rural communities. Teton County and thousands of other rural places are part of a larger story of wealth concentration and inequality in the United States that has been unfolding over the past four decades. Far from a rural oddity, we have much to learn about this national story by turning to how it plays out at the local level. Perhaps nowhere else on the planet are these issues seen in sharper relief than in Teton County, which is an ideal real-life social laboratory for research into these puzzles because of its nation-leading wealth and inequality, as well as its location in what is arguably the epicenter of American environmentalism.[6]

Developing this story required collecting a massive amount of data, based on five years in the community conducting in-person observation and in-depth interviews with 205 different people.[7] Interviews lasted between one and two hours, ranging from "ordinary" millionaires to billionaires. Counted among this group are some of the most powerful and well-known figures in business and politics.

I also collected a great deal of original quantitative data that provide unique insight into the shape and activity of ultra-wealthy social network interactions over two decades of time (based on more than 100,000 social connections), including information on philanthropic giving, board membership, environmental conservation, real estate development, and demographic and socioeconomic change, as well as compiling large amounts of digitized text for computational machine learning, These quantitative data informed the interviews and observations, as I fully immersed myself in the world of the ultra-rich, spending time at their exclusive clubs, homes, environmental meetings, ski resorts, charitable events, art exhibits, recreation areas, houses of worship, watering holes, restaurants, and other haunts.

———

Through my research, I found that nature takes on unique power for the ultra-wealthy, allowing them to confront the urgent *economic* and *social* problems they face—such as how best to enjoy, share, or multiply their money, and how best to respond to social stigmas and feelings of inauthenticity or guilt. They resolve these dilemmas in two corresponding ways, each of which has a sizable impact on themselves, the environment, and the wider community.

First, whatever their good intentions, those at the very top of the socioeconomic pyramid leverage nature to climb even higher. Ironically, environmental conservation becomes an engine for multiplying wealth and gaining social prestige for wealthy people and wealthy institutions. And seeking to enjoy their wealth, landscapes and wildlife are transformed into ultra-exclusive enclaves, where money ensures private access to the healing tonic of nature and a sanctuary from crass materialism. Importantly, all of this is entwined with—and often under the guise of—genuine concern for ecological science and environmental health, an unselfish commitment to environmental philanthropy, and an uncritical devotion to nature as an affluent storehouse of spiritual and therapeutic wellness.

Second, burdened by social stigmas, status anxiety, and feelings of inauthenticity or guilt, the ultra-wealthy use nature and rural people as a vehicle for personal transformation, creating versions of themselves they view as more authentic, virtuous, and community minded. They model their personal transformation on a popular idea of the working poor in rural, outdoors-oriented places in the West— people who, despite their low-status careers and lack of material comforts, seem free from the snares of wealth and power, and are thought to live a noble life of contentment, frontier authenticity, pastoral simplicity, community cohesion, wilderness adventure, and kinship with nature. Wealthy folks' outward performance of this social conversion includes friendships with moneyless people, sacred experiences enjoyed in untouched nature, professed environmental concern, appropriation of frontier art and style of dress, and love of bygone small-town character. By living in such rural and nature-oriented communities, they are literally buying into the idea and experience of a primordial America that offers salvation from the careerist rat-race and the moral temptations of high society where life is simpler, and the honest rural values of the dusty cowboy, noble native, and nature-loving bohemian prevail.

These two uses of nature and romanticized rural people allow the ultra-wealthy to effectively manage the economic and social dilemmas they face, often behind the *semblance* of good-faith commitments to the community, philanthropy, and environmental concern. Yet for many observers, these local commitments reek of hypocrisy when viewed in light of how some ultra-wealthy made their fortunes, often involving financial and industrial practices that have greatly contributed to global socioecological ruin.

This does not mean that all rich people are hell-bent on ruthless domination or live their lives in bad faith. Like most of us, they want to do good but don't always live up to it, and even the most disparaged fossil fuel CEOs or scorned hedge fund managers don't fully grasp the extent to which their lives benefit from larger social, economic, and ecological systems. These systems ultimately matter much more than sloppy or inaccurate stereotypes that cast individual rich folks as either greedy monsters or philanthropic saviors. Yet, while I avoid these stereotypes—and certainly give the ultra-wealthy a fair shake—their use of nature and rural people leads to what seems to be some unjust and regrettable outcomes.

In the end, love for nature and rural people can create a thick veneer that helps to morally justify vast natural resource consumption, romanticize the ugly reality of rural hardship as an idyllic choice—iconically modeled in the past by rugged cowboys and noble natives and lived out today by lovable white ski-bums and "van-life" bohemians—rather than the actual face of modern rural poverty as an overworked immigrant family living on razor-thin margins, deliberately conceal outward indicators of socioeconomic and racial and ethnic inequities, gain rewards for trivial acts of individual charity and selective environmentalism that hide patterns of structural harm, alleviate personal guilt, and ultimately disguise and foreclose the need for economic and political action to address pressing local and global problems.

Paired Experiences of the Rich and Poor

Once my research into the ultra-wealthy was completed, I recognized another important piece to this puzzle: It wasn't sufficient to study the "haves" created by decades of extreme wealth accumulation. This era had also created "have-nots." Who are they and what can we learn about the ultra-wealthy from their firsthand experience? The working poor of Teton County are often in close contact with or employed directly and indirectly by the ultra-wealthy. Most are Spanish-speaking immigrants from Mexico. Some are U.S. citizens and others are undocumented. Sometimes their relationships with the wealthy can be intimate, such as playing the role of home caretaker or providing childcare.

I talked at length with the ultra-wealthy about their views of what life might be like at the bottom of the socioeconomic ladder. But to complete the story, I wanted to know how those at the bottom view themselves in relation to such immense wealth, and to the ever-increasing dilemmas in the community revolving around race and ethnicity, immigration, affordable housing, and environmental protection.[8]

So, with a team of researchers from a community-based nonprofit in the area, we conducted fifty in-depth, in-person interviews with this mostly poverty-level population. In some cases, I was able to pair low-income interviewees with the ultra-wealthy persons for whom they worked. I was then able to interpret many of the *same* stories, events, experiences, and behaviors in relation to each other, and to explore questions such as: What do they say about one another? Do they think the rich deserve all the wealth they've accumulated? What do they make of ultra-wealthy's love of nature, their environmental philanthropy, or their attraction to rural culture as a means to transform themselves into "normal" authentic people?

Collecting these "paired experiences," as I call them, is a novel methodological advance that, to my knowledge, has not yet been done in recent social research.[9] It provides unique analytical insight—from the very top, the very bottom, and the direct connection between them—into the themes and questions earlier concerning the cultural logic of wealth, the character of communal bonds between the rarefied top and the bottom social strata, how money affects one's relationship to the natural environment, and political action within a community that is so top-heavy with wealth. As Plato wrote in Book Four of *The Republic*, "For indeed any city, however small, is in fact divided into two, one the city of the poor, the other of the rich; these are at war with one another." These are age-old concerns, and in a place like Teton County that is the modern prototype of Plato's idea of a city "divided into two," it is critical to consider both sides of the linked divide.

———

Let's return to the party at the Williamses again. One person at the event is ultra-wealthy, and the other is near poverty level. They interact quite frequently. One considers the other a friend. They epitomize the two main storylines in a grand narrative that has unfolded in this area, and around the country, over the last thirty years. In some ways, these two people could not be any more different, but they depend on each other to live their version of a good life.

JULIE WILLIAMS

Julie Williams sees herself as no different from anybody else. Reflecting on her life, she tells me "money hasn't really changed her." In my time spent with Julie and her husband, Craig—who had been fortunate enough to make more than a hundred million dollars during the 1990s and 2000s—it became clear that immense wealth hasn't made their lives any simpler. Julie admits that money "is certainly nice to have," but reminds me that "it doesn't remove the stresses that are common to any other American, and having great financial means can actually make life harder sometimes." She describes the disquiet running through her life, whether it's worrying that her kids are overburdened with activities or that Craig is working himself to death. Craig acknowledges that he invests a lot of time into his work, but absolves himself a bit, telling me that the meteoric rise of his hedge fund over these past twenty-five years would not have happened without his putting in long hours.

Lately, both Julie and Craig have been more involved serving on boards of directors for a handful of prominent corporations and nonprofit organizations. I can tell that they are proud to share a place on these boards alongside so many distinguished business and political personalities.

But all of this, too, can be quite stressful, says Julie. One solution to this stress, she explains, was building their grand home here amid the Tetons, and hosting conservation events like this one where her neighbors can organize for a good cause. Even though they decided to buy this $14 million property on a whim, in response to a "crisis moment," she says that looking back, it was "just what the doctor ordered." It pulled the family from their routines at their primary home in Fairfield County, Connecticut, and provided experiences that were, in her words, more "authentic" and "natural."

Joyfully, she tells me, "All our kids go out there in the summer. We would go out for a month at a time or sometimes more, and all of them fly-fished. They all ski, they all rock climb, mountain climb, so we just love it. It just feels like our souls are happy. That's kind of how we ended up there and we love it. We absolutely love it." Her neighbors share a similar sentiment, explains Julie. "They care about nature and love the peace and the beauty. I'm never happier than when I'm out in the middle of Grand Teton National Park, and I'm there all the time. It's my backyard. I just love that place."

Given their substantial wealth and professional financial acumen, I wondered if their part-time move from Connecticut to Wyoming might also have been influenced by Wyoming's lack of an income tax. Wyoming consistently ranks number one on *Bloomberg Wealth Manager Magazine*'s rankings of "America's wealth-friendliest states," and Sotheby's real estate and local elite clubs aggressively advertise this fact.[10] For example, all things being equal, a household making $10 million annual income could potentially save around $700,000 *every year* just by relocating at least part-time from Connecticut to Wyoming. When asked, Julie admits that much lower taxes are a "nice perk," but expressed with a genuine tone that the real reason they came is to be closer to nature and experience authentic rural community.

In addition to providing respite from the pressure-cooker of the finance industry and the kids' busyness, Julie has developed an identity as an environmentalist, becoming politically active in local conservation groups. She laughs as she tells me this, and her kids roll their eyes, saying, "Oh my God she just went on a rant about the environment . . . she picks recycling out of the trash!" Julie responds, chuckling, "Well, why did you put it in there in the first place!?" Continuing, she explains "Anyway, it's so funny, but I love Wyoming for that, because the people here are very green. They're very careful about the environment. People care. It's a community that really cares. I find also that the people who are drawn to that area are the same kind of people like us, people who care about the environment."

Julie is also aware that Teton County has America's highest per capita income, as well as the nation's most extreme income inequality. She reflects a bit, saying, "I don't know if you did any research on wealth here. But I think it was *Forbes* who came out with the two wealthiest counties in America, and at the time it was Teton County and Fairfield County. And my husband Craig goes, 'What is wrong with this picture? We live in both places.' [laughs embarrassedly]."

But in her experience, immense wealth inequality does not mean that the community is fractured, or that there is resentment among those way down at the bottom. She continues, "There's a lot of wealth here in Teton County, but the people are very under the radar. It's not showy . . . you wouldn't even know it was wealthy, because money is not important, people don't give a hoot." In fact, Julie describes the community in quite positive terms, as one where people are as laid back as the Western casual dress they sport. In her view, as long as people's basic needs are met and the environment is protected, members of the community just don't seem to "give a hoot" or get too worked up about who has immense wealth and who doesn't.

As evidence, Julie explains that she "has many friends who are not as financially fortunate . . . ones who struggle to make ends meet," citing as examples her caretaker, ski instructor, and the manager of their favorite local restaurant. When I asked if she feels guilty when she sees these people she calls friends, she says that money doesn't really come up. Certainly, everybody is generally aware of the financial gulf that separates the haves and have-nots. But as Julie describes this world—where people wear jeans, enjoy nature, and are simply too laid back to be resentful—feeling guilty just doesn't make too much sense to her: "By far, the best thing about the area are the laid-back people. I mean our friends are everything from ski-bums to people who are very successful with immense wealth, and you would never know it because we're all just in our jeans and flannel shirts. It's very casual, and money just doesn't matter to people like it does other places. I like to say that there is a 'no asshole' policy in the community."

HECTOR PADILLA

Hector Padilla is an undocumented immigrant from Mexico who arrived in Teton County about ten years ago with his wife Dolorita and their two children. At Julie's conservation event that opened this chapter, Hector was working in one of the four garages attached to the house, mostly cooking hors d'oeuvres and serving drinks. He typically works twelve hours each day, six days a week, laying brick for a construction company that specializes in elaborate homes, and then, to help make ends meet, he picks up a few more hours at night doing catering jobs for folks like Julie. Dolorita also works for Julie and a few other well-to-do families, cleaning and doing domestic odds and ends around their homes, as well as helping out with childcare. Between the two of them, they just barely cover rent for the small trailer they share with two other families, where they all take turns sleeping on the bed, couch, or floor.

During the course of our interview with Hector, he explains that he and Dolorita took a risk and made the long journey from Mexico to Teton County because they knew it was a safer place to raise their children, and because they had heard jobs were aplenty. Looking back, he knows it was the right decision—they love the area and the natural beauty, but with the skyrocketing cost of living, life is getting to be more difficult. Dolorita explains that people are crammed in tough living conditions, sometimes ten people to a trailer. Nevertheless, she and Hector continue to work hard, juggling multiple jobs to make it all work.

The previous month, the Padillas were unexpectedly and immediately evicted from their trailer to clear the way for a new upscale development called "Nature's Escape."[11] Despite pleading with the developers for more time, they were forced out in two weeks. Unable to find affordable housing in town, they were pushed forty-five minutes away into Idaho, on the other side of the treacherous Teton Pass, where a good majority of the working poor now live. Each day, both Hector and Dolorita make the dangerous and sometimes even deadly drive to work and back, up and over the steep 8,431-foot mountain pass. Living on razor-thin margins, Hector says he doesn't have time to bemoan setbacks that seem to be more frequent—instead, he mostly keeps his head down and focuses on his work and his family. He expresses gratitude to people like Julie who provide him with a second job.

Hector and Dolorita's daily lives are radically shaped by ultra-wealth. They live amid it every day, journeying in and out of ultra-wealthy life through their work at upscale homes, restaurants, construction sites, and social events. As we will see in part 4 of this book, perceptions of ultra-wealth and ultra-wealthy people can vary greatly among the low-income community. Even though from Hector's perspective, his relationship with Julie is a purely economic one—and would not approach the depth of "friendship" that Julie waxes lyrical about—he still speaks highly of her because she has treated him and Dolorita with respect and provides them with much-needed income.

When asked, he says that, sure, Julie mostly deserves her wealth because she and her husband, Craig, have likely worked hard for it.

He also sees Julie as philanthropic and environmentally conscious—noting that she makes sure that all workers recycle any plates and beer cans when holding social gatherings at her property. Altogether, Hector certainly didn't express any initial resentment of ultra-wealthy people that some people might expect or wish to find.

This is beginning to change, however. Lately, Hector and Dolorita have made an effort to attend civic events and meetings led by some advocacy organizations in Teton County, as well as at the local Catholic Church they attend. Like many low-income people, their views of wealth in Teton County are evolving as they connect their recent struggles to the explosion of all the money in the area, and some of the problems that have come in its wake. Hector is beginning to question his positive perception of wealth, philanthropy, and environmentalism—and even the genuineness of community relations between people like him and people like Julie. He wonders aloud whether wealthy people care more about saving a moose or a bear than helping him and other immigrants who are suffering.

Hector's ponderings are becoming a common refrain among the working poor in Teton County, pointing out what they view as the self-serving hypocrisy of affluent philanthropy and environmentalism and questioning the authenticity of their relationships with ultra-wealthy people. Yes, the ultra-wealthy treat them kindly, call them friends, and at times even dress down like them. Yet at the same time, people like Hector are seeing more clearly how these same friends who have so much extra money and power to help nevertheless support the status quo and perpetuate a system that is making it increasingly difficult for Hector and his family to live a decent life.

Shielded from Intrusion: Two Walls Blocking Up-Close Research

Given these two stories, the tendency among social scientists has been to write books about Hector rather than Julie. To research and write about poverty rather than wealth. To shine a light on those at the bottom rather than those at the top. To document cases of extreme inequality rather than extreme social advantage. Over the years, most social scientists and journalists have done just this, and done it well. Scores of books and articles have shed light on the people and communities plagued by incarceration, employment discrimination, gang violence, health disparities, economic anxiety, environmental harm, eviction, police brutality, rural poverty, and labor abuse, to name just a few problems.

This literature remains integral to understanding the causes and consequences of inequality, and the systemic struggles people face. We need more of it. But the gaping hole still remains: We know relatively little about the flip side of economic hardship—namely, the lives and experiences of those at rarefied heights who sit atop the socioeconomic strata. And while they may not be exposed to inequality and harm at the same rates as others, their involvement in these processes is just as important, given their economic, cultural, and political power. Perhaps by focusing on people like Julie we can learn more about people like Hector.

My study is not the first to examine the top of the American class structure. Moving beyond the Marxian "ruling class" concept, the classic work of Thorstein Veblen and C. Wright Mills on the culture and structure of elite power set the stage for thinkers like E. Digby Baltzell, who first sketched what he called the American "WASP" establishment in Philadelphia and Boston. Within this tradition, sociologist William Domhoff has done more than anyone to teach us about the influence of the upper-middle-class power elite, with his 1967 classic *Who Rules America?*, his 1974 study of Bohemian retreats, and numerous books and articles in the decades since.[12] Also beginning in the 1970s, the now defunct Boston College Center on Wealth and Philanthropy provided important insight into charitable giving among the affluent.[13] Since the 1980s and 1990s, the work of Pierre Bourdieu has become a theoretical cornerstone for the study of elites. And we have recently witnessed a revival of this area, spanning such topics as the influence of gender,[14] elites in educational settings,[15] religion and politics,[16] styles of speech among the upper class,[17] twenty-first century impacts on democracy,[18] elite status insecurity,[19] life on Wall Street,[20] class reproduction among the French bourgeoisie,[21] elite upward mobility,[22] lifestyle "down-shifting,"[23] and elite networks of political funding,[24] among others.

The Columbia University sociologist Shamus Khan, a pioneer in this recent revival of the study of elites, has called for more methodological diversity, especially of the kind employed in this book: interviews, ethnographic observation, social network analysis, and content analysis of administrative data.[25] An excellent contemporary example of this approach is Rachel Sherman's in-depth interviews with fifty affluent New York City parents to understand how they grapple with the stigma of wealth, their desire to be normal people, and internal conflicts about how they ought to spend their money and still remain good people.[26] Especially interesting is that the majority of these New York City parents identified as liberal, and thus were less reticent to discuss their wealth openly, given their general knowledge of, and concern for, increasing economic inequality. Similarly, Elisabeth Schimpfössl's recent book on wealthy Russians unpacks, from the inside, what it's like to sit atop Russian society, and their justifications for having such great wealth, as well as the civic responsibilities that come with it.[27] Hanna Kuusela has taken up a similar line of work among the super-rich in Finland, showing how these Finnish families construct meaning and moral boundaries that help to legitimize their economic position in Nordic welfare society.[28] Taken together, the work of Sherman, Schimpfössl, and Kuusela, along with the revival of research on elites more generally, reveals the fascinating diversity of wealthy culture, and highlights just how much more empirical work needs to be done to understand how the culture of wealth can vary by location.

The topics taken up here build on and extend Sherman's work in particular, by integrating her insightful diagnosis of the "anxieties of affluence" with the paired experiences of fifty low-income people like Hector and Dolorita, and the various perspectives of a more geographically diverse and politically representative sample of ultra-wealthy people who are among the several thousand to have congregated in this corner of the Rocky Mountains in hopes of using the natural environment, philanthropy, and moneyless rural culture to transform themselves, in search of salvation from the anxieties that Sherman so aptly describes.

Thus, while there is a small but quite robust tradition of interview and participant observation-based work on elites, we still need more—especially in locales beyond those typically studied (for example, Paris, New York). And we need more research not just on elites, but on the elite of the elite who sit at the lofty *pinnacle* of the economic hierarchy. In his recent book on poverty and eviction, Princeton University sociologist Matthew Desmond wonders why there is such a lack of contemporary research on the wealthy, asking social scientists and journalists who study inequality, "Where were the rich people who wielded enormous influence over the lives of low-income families and their communities—who were rich precisely because they did so?"[29] I agree. How could we be missing out on such an important part of the story? This research gap is especially troubling given the ultra-wealthy's immense influence, and puzzling in light of the recent flood of attention to inequality and to wealth concentration in particular.[30]

This scholarly shortfall did not happen by chance. Part of it has to do with particular discomforts characteristic of left-leaning academic social scientists. Conducting high-quality ethnographic or long-term participant observation research can require a great deal of empathy for one's subjects. Such research involves more or less taking on the perspective of the people and culture being studied. It means listening to their stories with honesty and, if only for a moment, giving their experiences and their explanations the benefit of the doubt. But most social scientists know the facts about inequality, wealth, and privilege, and thus find the empathy required for ethnographic research in short supply when it comes to the ultra-wealthy. Empathy is more naturally given to the people and communities obviously suffering harm, rather than, say, a Wall Street financier who struggles with the life complexities and social-psychological dilemmas that accompany immense wealth and power.

In her recent immersive study of the Tea Party, renowned Berkeley sociologist Arlie Hochschild describes these mental barriers as "empathy walls," "obstacle[s] to deep understanding of another person, one that can make us feel indifferent or even hostile to those who hold different beliefs. . . . In a period of political tumult, we grasp for quick certainties. We shoehorn new information into ways we already think. We settle for knowing our opposite numbers from the outside.[31]

Within the academic community, which tends to be left-leaning, these empathy walls can limit the people and topics we research. With best intentions of making a difference, qualitative researchers have focused disproportionately on stories that expose systemic inequality from the perspective of those who suffer it.[32] Like Hochschild, who chose a more difficult path and set out from her comfortable Berkeley enclave to deeply and charitably understand the Tea Party in rural Louisiana, scholars must scale the empathy wall that is currently limiting our scientific knowledge of ultra-wealthy culture.

Second, and perhaps more importantly in explaining the dearth of in-depth studies is the fact that ultra-wealthy culture has all sorts of ways of shielding itself from intrusion by scholars and journalists.[33] As one might expect, the first hurdle is the barrier to entry, as these people live within a tightly knit, elite social system with multiple layers of security and privacy. Physical barriers (for example, private clubs, box seats, isolated neighborhoods, pricey restaurants) and communicative barriers (for example, unlisted numbers, private personal assistants, layers of phone/e-mail screening) make it very difficult to obtain access to ultra-wealthy people. Then, if access is obtained, cultural barriers (for example, educational prestige, high art, elite forms of recreation) can create an uncomfortable and emotionally taxing power discrepancy between researcher and subjects.

Similarly, people of great wealth and power do not often expose themselves to vulnerability, which entails loss of control and is a complete reversal of their accustomed role. One mechanism protecting ultra-wealthy people from vulnerability is the remarkable level of deference they enjoy in their day-to-day lives, both from people at work (for example, administrative assistants and other staff) and from people they encounter as they go about their normal routines (for example, wait staff, salespeople, caretakers). This position of social dominance means that they are rarely subject to honest scrutiny, especially outside their workplaces.

Even when pressed, they are well-educated in the ways of public relations and political speak, able to deliver credible canned answers. Further, some researchers, such as Brooke Harrington, have been threatened with legal sanctions by the elites they research.[34] At best, this situation makes it tricky to obtain information. And at worst, it can mean never breaking through the shell protecting personal ideas and behaviors relating to wealth, community, politics, and morality.

Taken together, all of these barriers can become insurmountable. They are a major reason why most research on the ultra-wealthy tends to rely on impersonal, macro-level economic data, or mirror popular stereotypes such as John D. Rockefeller Sr., Bernie Madoff, or the fictional Jay Gatsby.

How I Gained Access: Yale Professor and Ignoble Westerner

My dual identity—as an Ivy League professor at an ultra-wealthy and prestigious institution and at the same time a seeming ignoble native Wyomingite—was essential to accessing this exclusive population. Like recognizes like. The status associated with being a Yale professor was very similar to that held by many of the people I sought to interview and observe. While I do not have a hundred million dollars in the bank, my professional identity largely leveled the playing field between my respondents and me. The elite cachet this group attributes to a place like Yale opened the door for my initial access to this exclusive world.

In many more ways, however, I was also an outsider, which proved to be critically important. As a native Wyomingite and first-generation college student, I symbolized and represented in good faith the role of the authentic, anti-aristocratic, rural Westerner that Teton County's elite found so attractive and often romanticized. I intentionally conveyed this identity through our many conversations, but also outwardly because of my clothing, Old West mustache, and penchant for the refined taste of Coors Light.

In addition to possessing the social currency of affiliation with an elite and ultra-wealthy university, I am also a white guy. My light pigmentation and masculine appearance implicitly and explicitly improved the access I was given and how I was treated, especially by some of the more intimidating and pugnacious white guy respondents (and there were many). For example, while my intention—to conduct accurate research—was in honest good-faith, I still expected to raise suspicions in those I studied. But to my surprise, other than one notable instance (described in chapter 2), I experienced very little distrust or questioning in my years of freely wandering through and observing ultra-elite spaces, including highly securitized private clubs, gated neighborhoods, and exclusive restaurants. These spaces are overwhelmingly inhabited by white people, who in the United States make up the large majority of the ultra-wealthy population. Sadly, the same unquestioned trust likely would not have been afforded to a researcher with even a slightly darker shade of skin, which would have made it nearly impossible to get the kind of coveted access needed to probe beneath the surface of ultra-wealthy lives.

But once these doors were opened to me, I found the über-elite culture foreign and often intimidating. My mother cleaned houses, ran an in-home daycare, and was a homemaker, and my father had been a lifelong railroad worker since his teens. I was entirely ignorant, therefore, of elite rituals such as attending exclusive summer camps in Maine, the social currency of graduating from an elite college, and the aristocratic legacy of mainline Protestantism. I had never before read the *New York Times'* wedding announcements, and I am still doing my best to enjoy red wine. As I embarked on this research, I began to think that I lacked the cultural capital needed to survive in this rarefied world.

While my own ignorance surely made things more difficult and uncomfortable for me personally, I began to use it to my advantage, and soon found my outsider status was my greatest asset. I began to notice subtleties that an insider might take for granted, and I became more confident relying on my naïveté to probe people about ideas or behaviors I found peculiar. So, while the privileged identity of Yale professor provided me unparalleled access, my role as the ignoble Westerner and my class-based ignorance of elite culture let me take on the identity of the "stranger in a strange land," to ask basic questions. Not only did this make me curiously confident, but it also created a blank slate upon which to form impressions and learn the ways of the culture on the fly, as I attempted to understand and decode it from the inside out.

Charting New Directions for Research: "Community" and Environment

Studying wealth can feel like studying everything at once and nothing at all. Everywhere we look, we see its influence. Yet paradoxically, money means nothing in isolation from culture, politics, and markets. I knew that I needed to ground my examination of ultrawealth in something concrete and specific—tied to and interpreted within real-life contexts. Thus, I chose to examine the nexus of two of the most critical and far-reaching issues of our modern era: the form and character of "community," and the natural environment. Just as these two issues cannot be separated from wealth, they also cannot be separated from each other, especially in Teton County, Wyoming, where environmental issues penetrate all aspects of the community.

RETHINKING "COMMUNITY" AND WEALTH IN THE TWENTY-FIRST CENTURY

What makes "community" has been a fundamental question for thousands of years, occupying most ancient philosophers and authors of major religious texts. It has persisted as perhaps *the* classical concern within sociology, playing a central role in the projects of early giants like Tönnies, Durkheim, Weber, and Marx. The early and mid-twentieth century produced several landmark studies about the character of American community, such as Robert and Helen Lynd's series of field studies on "Middletown" Muncie, Indiana, during the 1920s and 1930s; C. Wright Mills's *White Collar: The American*

Middle Classes; Riesman et al.'s *The Lonely Crowd*; and Robert Nisbet's *The Quest for Community*. These texts focused mostly on white, middle-class experiences in the era of modernization and postwar capitalism, highlighting the effects of loss of tradition, alienation, and communal disintegration. More recently, "community" has come to the fore through the work of thinkers like Robert Putnam, whose *Bowling Alone* explored the collapse of civic and community involvement; Robert Wuthnow's prolific series of books on the changing nature of community in middle America; Eric Klinenberg, whose *Going Solo* examined the choice of more Americans to live alone; and accomplished journalists like Bill Bishop, whose *The Big Sort* focused on how Americans are clustering themselves into homogenous communities composed of like-minded people.

Despite the importance of recent studies of community, one thing always seems missing: a deep, first-person ethnographic understanding of the wealthy. Without it, we lack a complete picture of community in the twenty-first century. There is a great opportunity here to learn something new, far beneath the usual top-down aggregate of economic statistics, at the intersection of community and wealth.

For example, I asked the ultra-wealthy how they think about and perceive "community" in this new era of income polarity. Perceptions are one thing, and reality is another. So I also studied how these cultural perceptions interacted with economic realities to actually *alter* the form and character of community itself.[35] Beyond the obvious fact that wealth concentration alters the economic makeup of a community, my aim was to uncover the ways wealth actually shapes the restructuring of community boundaries (for example, who is in, who is out?), the performance of authenticity (for example, romanticizing and appropriating Western rural struggle and/or closeness to nature), the meaning of social bonds (for example, confusing servants for friends), acts of community obligation (for example, altruism, philanthropy), status markets and community recognition, poverty and conspicuous consumption, and even conceptions of "community" itself.

In other words, in our era of increasing wealth inequality, what does a rural community with extreme wealth disparity actually *look like* and *feel like* according to those who live there? How does the community perceive of itself in the absence of a middle class? What are social bonds like between the top and the bottom? How does a community talk about, or justify, an extreme wealth gap? What are the perceived responsibilities of community members? Who is the ideal member of the community, and what individual personal qualities are esteemed the most? What are the primary boundaries of inclusion and exclusion?

I found that this approach, and these questions, were best answered by holistically examining an *entire* community—its history, people, culture, economics, and politics. All of this meant that one of the most important decisions I made for my research was selecting an appropriate community to study. Two important criteria went into this decision: First, and most importantly, the case study site needed to be somewhere that typifies the extreme wealth concentration that we have seen nationally. Second, it had to be small enough to allow me to examine the entire community from the ground level, but at the same time, be representative enough to allow me to generalize beyond the local specifics to learn broadly applicable lessons.

Teton County, Wyoming, proved to be an exemplary case study site because, as noted earlier, not only is it the richest county in the United States, and the county with highest levels of income inequality, but it is also a place where these patterns developed rapidly over the last thirty years or so, providing me a unique window into the unfolding of these dynamics over a relatively short period of time. Further, this community exists within the larger social context of Wyoming, a state in which, as a new report from Stanford University[36] has documented, 1 percent of the population owns the largest share of the wealth (50 percent). Thus, it is representative of national inequality and at the same time offers the opportunity to examine a distinctly rural locale, the type of place too often ignored in mainstream research.[37]

Also, the source of wealth concentration in this community mirrors national patterns in that it comes overwhelmingly from financial investments. Thus, this community was an especially suitable site for research because it exists outside the stereotypical halls of urban financial power (for example, Wall Street), yet it is intimately connected to this financial nerve center, given that many millionaires and some billionaires have relocated to Teton County not only for its rich natural amenities but also for its attractiveness as an income-tax haven. As such, a handful of interviews and observations with certain respondents were conducted in Manhattan and various Wall Street bedroom communities in Connecticut as well as in Teton County.

CARVING NEW AVENUES FOR ENVIRONMENTAL RESEARCH

In the same way that perceptions and realities of "community" provide a unique window into the various cultural boundaries and interactions between the ultra-wealthy and the working poor, the issue of environmental sustainability offers a lens into ultra-wealthy ideas and practices around altruism, philanthropy, financial accumulation, social prestige, rural exoticism, consumerism, escapism, and activism. Rather than engaging in abstract conversations about these topics that could be seen as agitating or threatening in isolation, I was easily able to raise and discuss them within the context of non-threatening, local environmental issues (for example, moose, bears, national parks, and so on), which most respondents were more than happy to discuss, given the primacy of these issues in Teton County.

Importantly, I was often able to examine their *actual behavior* relative to environmental problems, be it through their philanthropic giving, consumer choices, volunteerism, leisure and recreation habits, or local political engagement. Furthermore, I was able to segue from the discussions of nonthreatening environmental issues into the social problems connected to them, such as affordable housing, services industries, fair wages, and immigration.

In doing the interviews and day-to-day observations, I pondered such questions as: Does environmental conservation actually make wealthy people wealthier? Do the ultra-wealthy use "nature" to recapture a lost sense of authenticity? How do people reconcile their local love of nature with the ecologically destructive ways in which they made (or currently make) their wealth? Does nature offer salvation from the moral minefields of careerism, myopic materialism, and self-absorption? How does nature play into upper-class Americans' longtime love affair with the West? What counts as an environmental "problem," and why are some deemed more important than others? Are the poor and working class viewed as having a more authentic and direct connection to nature? Is it morally permissible to spend large amounts of money (for example, having a second home, hiring a private environmentalist tour guide) if it is for the purpose of enjoying nature? Which philanthropic issues receive the most time and money? Does wealth concentration create new environmental problems? Might the ultra-wealthy's interactions with the natural environment—whether through recreation, philanthropy, or spiritual encounters—serve to canonize and valorize a particular elite experience of nature for the rest of us to emulate?

Throughout, I argue that, despite the immense amount of attention given to environmental issues, we need to more closely examine the ways the affluent relate to and employ the natural world to achieve personal or political goals and resolve dilemmas they face. Certainly, similar dynamics have been revealed through historically important events such as the economically—and "scientifically"— motivated removal of indigenous tribes from their own lands to create the first national parks or, more recently, as documented in the seminal work of David Pellow and Lisa Park, the Aspen, Colorado, City Council's support of racist immigration restrictions as a means of preserving environmental and cultural purity in the region.[38] We know that the modern wealth gap presents new challenges and, unfortunately, the role of ultra-wealth is rarely a topic in today's deluge of public and scholarly discussions about the environment.

Granted, academia boasts a truly vast "environmental justice" literature documenting how and why some people (for example, the underserved and/or people of color) tend to suffer environmental risk, discrimination, and harms. This work is hugely important, but I concur with preeminent environmental sociologists Dorceta E. Taylor and David Pellow, who pioneered the study of environmental privilege through the lens of race, that we are missing critical perspectives by ignoring those on the flip side of suffering.[39] Unfortunately, the same barriers to studying the ultra-wealthy also help explain why there continues to be a shortage of ethnographic research related to wealth and the environment.

There is a growing body of macrostructural research on inequality and the environment, including recent work by Andrew Jorgensen, Juliet Schor, Tammy Lewis, Kenneth Gould, Liam Downey, James Boyce, and many, many others. This research reveals the intricate linkages among the high-level institutions, organizations, nation-states, and macroeconomic systems that create environmental inequality from the top down. In this book, I aim to complement this top-down literature by exploring life created by, and existing within, the shadow of these macrostructures. I narrow in on the powerful ultra-wealthy actors who live and work within the seemingly impersonal systems whose huge impact on the environment and society has already been demonstrated. And by narrowing the focus still further using ethnography, social network analysis, and machine learning, I hope to expand the public and scholarly conversation on wealth and the environment in new directions.

Setting Off into the Wilderness

Back at the Williams's house, the event was coming to a close, and I had gathered more than enough field notes for one night. Hector and the other workers were sorting the recycling, removing tablecloths, and transporting the trash to the bear-proof dumpsters on the edge of Julie's property. I worked my way back through the house, into the living room with the bronze statue of the stoic Lakota man flanked by the towering murals of cowboys and wildlife, past the marble base displaying the young impoverished Navajo girl, and joined a short line that had formed in front for the valet car service.

Waiting in line, I thanked Julie and Craig for their generous hospitality, and filled them in about my plans to spend the next few years researching and writing about the area. Excitedly, Julie asked if I'd be interested in having dinner with her and Craig at their newly completed country club. Selling me on the idea, Craig interjected, "It'd be a great place to meet other people who make up the community." He continued, "I'm not sure what types of people you want to meet and talk with, but many of them are also involved in the environment." We agreed that Friday night would work and exchanged phone numbers. Craig shook my hand, Julie gave me a hug, and I took my keys from the valet driver.

Leaving the property, I steered my car down that same gravel road into pitch-black darkness. Looking up into the starry night, I knew that the gigantic Teton Mountains towered seven thousand feet above me, but I could not make them out through the dark. It was a strange, and somewhat disturbing feeling. These massively important entities were right in front of my face, but they remained cloaked from view. Invisibly present, yet still immensely powerful as their tectonic plates kept pushing them upward, continuing to shape everything in their expansive range.

My journey into the heart and soul of the ultra-wealthy became much like this drive through shrouded mountain-peaked wilderness. I possessed the knowledge that something hugely important was out there, but despite strong indicators of its outsized influence, it remained largely unseen. This often happens when we fixate on the darkness itself—in this case, relying on blind stereotypes or impeded by elite barriers to access. But, curious to see what lay out there beyond the darkness, I set out on my ultra-wealth odyssey to shine a little light here in hopes of illuminating something important about everywhere else.

PART I

How We Got Here and What It Feels Like

1

New Nation of the Ultra-Wealthy

I met Jim Roselli over breakfast in the town of Wilson, Wyoming. Wilson is at the base of Teton Pass on the southwest end of Teton County, just fifteen minutes from its more famous neighbor, Jackson, Wyoming. Like many other people I interviewed, Jim insisted that we meet at his favorite breakfast joint, Nora's Fish Creek Inn. This old log-cabin turned greasy-spoon breakfast cafe is where many locals come to chew the fat, both literally and figuratively. Its rustic interior has an old-money feel consistent with this sleepy, but deceptively exclusive, town.

I arrived a few minutes early, pulling off the two-lane highway down into a mostly empty gravel parking lot in front of the cafe. It was dark, but the first light of the sun was beginning to peek over the mountaintops. Moments later, Jim pulled up in a worn-down Toyota Four-Runner. Hopping out, he smiled and cracked a joke. "Being a Harvard guy, I'm not sure what I'm doing up this early meeting a Yalie, but the breakfast here sure is worth it." By now, I had gotten used to these sorts of elite inside jokes, but appreciated his warmth and friendliness. Because even the summer mornings here can be quite chilly, Jim was wearing jeans with a Patagonia fleece sweatshirt. He was about six feet tall, white, and heavy-set.

We sit at a corner table next to the big stone fireplace. As we sip our coffee, we get to talking about his life, beginning with his childhood. Born in Pennsylvania, he had what he called a fairly routine childhood, the majority of which was spent on a farm in upstate New York. He excelled in school and then attended Harvard for college. From there, he went to Wall Street. I know from my own research that Jim is worth more than $90 million, but he talks about his career in unspectacular terms. "I was an investment banking guy in New York—did stints with Goldman Sachs, Lehman Brothers, and ran a private investment operation in London." No small task, I think to myself. Certainly, Jim feels a sense of accomplishment from the businesses he's built and the money he's made, but he doesn't dwell on it.

We both order omelets, and Jim continues to tell me about his career, and the decision he made to retire early. "I didn't want to be one of these guys that retired at 65 and you couldn't do anything, so I stepped down in my 50s." Jim admits that some of it had to do with how fast the finance industry was moving, and I got the sense that he felt it was passing him by.

The waitress interrupts us to top off our coffee, and asks if we are enjoying our omelets. For a split second, the waitress had me wondering absurdly to myself what a nine-dollar omelet tastes like to someone worth $90 million? Probably the same as mine, I suppose. Jim continued, reflecting that at fifty-seven, he "felt like there's no room for a guy like me in the investment banking business." With the finance industry being as mercurial as it was, and the fact that he, in his words, had become "quite financially secure" during the 1980s and 1990s, he sensed that it was time to move on with his life.

At first glance, Jim's story may sound surprising and unique. Over the course of a few decades, he rose from the dirt of a middle-class farm to the pinnacle of Wall Street. But Jim's story is *not* all that surprising, especially when viewed in light of recent economic gains among the very top in the United States, the ways these gains are generated, and the speed with which these gains can happen.

What we see here simply reflects—and is made possible by— broader trends in the nation's economic and political system during last thirty years.[1] Set against this backdrop of dramatic socioeconomic transformation, the number of ultra-wealthy people in the United States has grown precipitously in the last decade (growing at a near 10 percent annual clip), with few signs of slowing.[2] The majority of new folks joining this rarefied group make their money from finance, banking, and investments, which as we will see, is also true of wealth accumulation locally in Teton County. Thus, this community, and the meteoric rise of folks like Jim, are not as unique as we might think. Each are simply products of these broader winds of change and emblematic of this new era of wealth concentration in which we all—including Jim—now live.

Creating the Richest Community in the Richest Nation

SKYROCKETING INCOMES

When I was a kid, my parents, two brothers, and I would drive through Teton County on our way to my grandfather's home in nearby Idaho. We would never stay in Teton County—just stop for gas and keep moving an hour and a half northwest through the potato fields and small Mormon towns of eastern Idaho. Even though Teton County was just ninety miles away, it might as well have been, according to my extended family at the time, a different world—or worse, the East Coast.

Through the many pointed wise-cracks, I learned that this was the other side of the tracks, and increasingly so, with each year that passed. My family was right. Not only was Teton County changing dramatically relative to its neighboring communities, but it was distinguishing itself from every other county in the nation. And now most Wyomingites don't even consider Teton County to be part of the "real" Wyoming. Certainly, for the locals, it didn't take a sophisticated understanding of financial markets, real estate trends, or any other aspects of macroeconomics to see that this community was being entirely transformed by wealth.

According to the U.S. Department of Commerce,[3] Teton County has the highest per capita income of all 3,144 counties in the United States, at $194,485. In a distant second is New York County (Manhattan) at $148,002, and the lowest in the nation is Wheeler County,

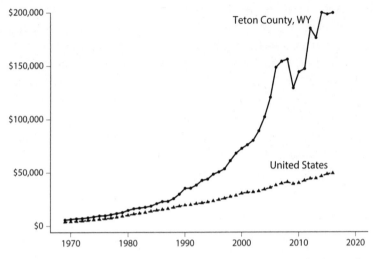

FIGURE 1.1. Per capita income, 1969–2016, showing growth over time compared to the rest of the United States. As noted in the text, median income (not pictured) is similarly high. *Source:* Bureau of Economic Analysis.

Georgia, at $15,787. Median family income in Teton County is also sky high at $96,113, putting it in the top 2.6 percent of all U.S. counties. Figure 1.1 provides a nice visual picture over time, comparing Teton County to the rest of the United States, demonstrating that this place was not always so wealthy. You can see that it was fairly average up until the mid-1980s, when from there, local incomes began to skyrocket. There is a dip just after the recent great recession, but things pick back up considerably.

Even though Jim has owned a very nice home in the area for many years, he grumbles about the escalating costs of real estate, and tracks the markets as a hobby in his spare time. "The number of houses in this county that trade for less than a million dollars are not very many anymore." Jim is right. Real estate here has become one of most expensive markets in the United States, with median home values hovering around $1 million. Jim laughs, and recounts back in 2011 when the most expensive residence in the United States was listed here for $175 million. This was just one day after another local property was on the market for $100 million. Skyrocketing incomes, untouchable real estate, along with booming population growth, has dramatically transformed this community from its historical roots as a pastoral region for rustic tourism and hardscrabble agriculture. Instead, it has become a storehouse of wealth.

THE ASCENDANCY OF FINANCIAL INVESTMENT INCOME

But almost as important as the *amount* of wealth pouring in, are the *sources* of wealth. Where was this money coming from, and how was it being made? Data show that the majority came from financial investments, rather than wages or salaries people take home from a typical 9-to-5 job. It was not always this way. During the early and mid-twentieth century, income from investments in Teton County mirrored that of the rest of the United States. But come the 1980s, investment income began to climb, making up 30 percent of all income in the area. It accelerated further, hitting the 40 percent mark in the 1990s, and still even further in the 2000s, when investment income made up *more than half* of all income in 2004.

Unrelenting, income from finance refused to slow. Surging further, in 2015, nearly *8 out of every 10 dollars of income made here was coming not from traditional wages or salary*, but from financial interest and dividends. Put in real terms, in 1970, only $52 million in annual income came from investments, but by 2015, this number grew to $3.4 billion—an increase to the tune of 6,500 percent. These local numbers are astounding, yet they fit within data on national and global trends, where the finance, banking, and investment industry has created more billionaires than any other industry.[4] In other words, we see skyrocketing income levels in this community because people moving in are leveraging wealth they have already made to create more.

Thus, the rush of wealth to this community has a particular source. It was not the result of broad-based economic growth or rising wages and salaries, but was gains from one particular sector of the economy. There are, however, an abundant number of low-paying jobs to provide services for folks like Jim. In other words, the large majority of *income* comes from a handful of people who have

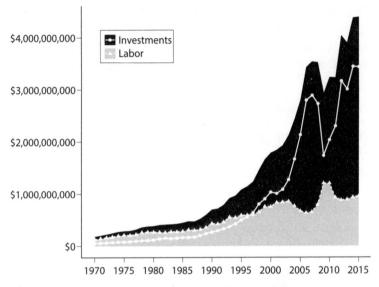

FIGURE 1.2. Growth of investment earnings compared to labor from traditional wages or salaries, 1970 to 2015. Investment income (that is, financial interest and dividends) makes up less than labor income (that is, earned from traditional wages or salaries) until the mid-1990s, when investment-related income skyrockets, and by 2015 makes up about 80 percent of every dollar earned in Teton County ($3.4 billion dollars of income). *Source:* U.S. Department of Commerce, 2016, Bureau of Economic Analysis, Regional Economic Accounts, Washington, DC, and Headwaters Economics.

investments, but the large majority of *jobs* are low-paying services (for example, food, retail). Figure 1.2 demonstrates this quite clearly, showing the rise of income from nonlabor investments, compared to the relatively static growth of annual income from labor (wages and salaries).

Astoundingly, while this community became the richest in the nation because of investment income, the wages or salary from an ordinary job remained shockingly stagnant: *in 1970 the average earnings per job was $39,943, and by 2015 this number had climbed only to $41,052—an increase of just $1,109 in 45 years,* making it difficult to survive amid inflation and now untouchable home prices.[5]

What all this means is that while the rapid population growth in this community over the last forty years is certainly unique, it is not what makes this area distinctive. What makes it unique, and why it sits atop so many county rankings regarding wealth, investments, and economic inequality, is that the people who are moving here are unusually wealthy *and* earn a good deal of their money from investments.

PRIMARY CAUSES: TAX SHELTER AND TECHNOLOGY

Were these skyrocketing incomes in this community just the result of sheer chance, or are there particular reasons why wealth accumulated in the spectacular way it did? The evidence points toward two main causes. The first is driven by specific political decisions by the state of Wyoming, and the second concerns larger forces of technological change. Of course, these two underlying causes are bolstered by the fact that this place has unique natural amenities. Scholars have written a great deal about Americans' romanticized love affair with the "West," with more recent attention on natural amenities and the rural gentrification of the "New West."[6] I focus attention here on what I think is actually at the root of the income and population growth, because there is much more at work than just the fact that this is a nice place to live and recreate. Certainly, natural amenities play a part, but there are many nice natural places to live in the United States, and not all became the richest in the nation.

To the first main cause, it is well-known that the state of Wyoming does not collect personal income tax. Nor does it levy a corporate income tax. It also has one of the lowest sales tax rates in the country. In addition to its cultural and political aversion to taxes, Wyoming has not needed to collect such taxes because, more than any other state, it has long enjoyed record windfalls from oil, gas, and coal production. But these windfalls are fewer and far between in recent years, and point toward an uncertain future, and even potential crisis, for the state. Nevertheless, income tax is not being levied, even with skyrocketing population and income growth among the very wealthy here, almost all of whom are nonnative Wyomingites—some genuinely contributing to the community, but many others who have simply parked their personal money, or created a corporate shell,[7] beneath this lucrative tax shelter.

For better or worse, specific governmental policies have contributed to the local changes that we have seen. It is not the cause of random market forces, but *deliberative* choices for one tax policy over another. And even if these choices result in staggering wealth inequality, or cost the state dearly in much needed tax revenue, policies remain unchanged because of Wyoming's longstanding antifederalist cultural streak that has created an all-out aversion to new taxes, even if it means cutting off your nose to spite your face. This aversion is inflamed by the state's marriage to a powerful fossil fuel industry that itself is facing insurmountable odds moving forward.

Jim sums things up rather well when discussing his best friend from college, who never really liked Wyoming too much, but "for tax purposes" bought a place in the area, despite "only spending four weeks a year out here." Others I've interviewed told myriad similar stories. No doubt, Wyoming consistently sits atop *Bloomberg Wealth Manager Magazine*'s rankings of "America's wealth-friendliest states."[8] The personal and corporate tax benefits of the state are advertised widely by local brokers seeking to attract the wealthy from high-tax environments like Connecticut, New York, and California.

One prominent broker's advertisement makes it very clear:[9] "Wyoming offers homeowners nearly as many financial benefits as it does outdoor activities and amenities. Learn about residency requirements in Wyoming so that you can take advantage of the state's shelter from income tax, corporate tax, estate tax, capital gains tax and trust tax, as well as some of the lowest excise, sales and property taxes in the United States." On top of all this, they remind potential transplants that with no "formal set of residency requirements for tax purposes," Wyoming makes it easier than ever to "legally" qualify as a Wyoming resident, which is why Teton County regularly has the nation's largest discrepancy between the number of people *claiming* to live here for tax purposes and those who *actually* live here as reported by the U.S. Census Bureau.[10]

Beyond the state-level benefits provided by Wyoming, waves of economists and political scientists have shown that the ultra-wealthy have also enjoyed an especially large drop in their *federal* tax rates. For example, Internal Revenue Service[11] data show that the 400 highest-earning Americans (some of whom were interviewed and observed for this book) paid 27 percent of their income in federal taxes during the mid-1990s, but by 2012 this number tumbled down to 17 percent. So, in conjunction with these lower federal tax rates, the ultra-wealthy flocking to income-tax-less Wyoming have it especially good, explaining why the community has grown so rapidly, both in both population and investment income.[12]

The second major cause has less to do with local decisions in Wyoming, and more to do with larger technological shifts in our society that have allowed people to work remotely. These technological changes are especially beneficial for professional careers where most work can be accomplished online. With development of new software, it makes no difference for a financial investor if she is sitting in an office in Manhattan or on her deck beneath the Tetons. In a previous book, *The Battle for Yellowstone*, I described in great depth the causes and consequences of this footloose economy in the New West, which has triggered a wave of wealthy in-migrants seeking tax breaks *as well as* "noneconomic quality of life factors associated with aesthetic values and recreation opportunity."[13]

Jim is now retired, but many other ultra-wealthy in the community maintain active careers by telecommuting. For example, Sam Adelmann, a very prominent media mogul from New York, describes to me his typical workday here:

I get up at probably 6:00, which is the best time of day. I have my coffee, I do my stretching, I check my e-mails. I get on the phone and talk to my office in New York from maybe 7:00 to 8:00, which is 9:00 to 10:00 New York time. Deal with whatever crises and emergencies I have to deal with there. Then I go out probably four days a week and play golf from 8:00 to noon. Come back at noon, which is 2:00 New York time, people are just coming back from lunch. I check my seventy e-mails that have piled up, maybe get on the phone. I make calls from 2:00 to 4:00, whenever New York closes, and deal with whatever I need to deal with. And then I either take my dog for an hour and a half walk or go for an hour bike ride at 5:00. It's so perfect for what I like to do, meaning I'm outdoors probably six hours a day, and I can get my work done and keep my dog happy and be in a beautiful place. I never put on a tie. I mean that's the best part. I can be sitting on my back deck in shorts and a t-shirt with a headset on doing a conference call, and nobody knows the difference.

Even the basic improvement of cell-phone reception has had a huge impact, meaning that one may not even need to be in their home office. For example, Derek Ganz, a medical device investor I met from Boston, describes how he can even get work done at 12,000 feet elevation while backcountry skiing the slopes of the Tetons: "I wake up between 5:00 and 6:00 and read the papers, and then about 7:00 I do my East Coast e-mail and phone calls. . . . At 9:00 I get on the first ski lift [chuckles] and ski for two hours. Do a hike out of bounds, from the top of the tram." Even hiking in the snow at the top of the mountain doesn't stop his productivity. He continues, "If I'm hiking off the top, with my skis and boots on my back at 12,000 feet, there is no one the wisest. My phone rings, and I can stop to take a conference call, and I can even take a rest [chuckles], which is always appreciated."

These are common work-life stories for many ultra-wealthy in the community, made possible by changes in information technology. Flexible work-life opportunities for nonlabor professional sectors like these that rely more heavily on investments, in conjunction with the appeal of the Wyoming tax shelter, has led to the skyrocketing growth of wealth and people here in the last few decades.

The Dawn of Extreme Inequality

By now, the morning sun was flooding through the window of the cafe, every table was filled, and Jim and I had polished off about as much of our oversized omelets as we could. We had talked a great deal about Jim's background, and about the recent influx of wealth to the area. But now I sought to steer the conversation away from the ultra-wealthy, toward others in the community who may not have the benefit of recurring investment dividends or the work-life flexibility enjoyed by highly educated nonlabor professionals. Reflecting a bit, Jim sums it up, "Our biggest problem as a community is that there's a bifurcation there. We're hollowed out, you know, we've got a high end in terms of wealth and income, and we've got a low-end group which is primarily Latino, and barely gets by. We don't have as much of a middle class living here as we should have. So it's a barbell distribution across the income spectrum."

The income distribution is so skewed here that Jim's view of who is "middle class" is probably different from most people's view. At the top, Jim says, are "people like me that have done well enough, or very well, in business to finance their lifestyle out here. In the middle, there are lawyers, doctors, and a few hedge fund managers, some bankers that have carved out a niche . . . and they're in the middle. But the guys who are banging nails and busing tables, there's a big gap there."

For Jim, a community so top-heavy with wealth means that lawyers and doctors are middle class, and even *they* are rarely able to make it work in Teton County. Like many people I interviewed and observed, Jim is very informed and knowledgeable about economics and politics, but how accurate is his assessment of Teton County as a "hollowed out" and "bifurcated" community—so extreme that doctors and lawyers become middle class? For answers, let's turn to some socioeconomic data.

These questions concern levels of economic inequality, or in other words, the extent to which there is a gap between the wealthy and everyone else. The most straightforward measures compare the income and total wealth of the top 1 percent to the bottom 99 percent. The topic of economic inequality itself has become a hot-button issue in the United States, increasingly subject to politicization and partisan politics. Like the issue of climate change, the facts tend not to matter, and are easily ignored in favor of distorted messages reverberating inside partisan echo-chambers. So let's look at the facts.

To give away the punchline: Jim is right. The community is indeed bifurcated, the middle class has been completely hollowed out, and the gap between the ultra-wealthy and the rest is the largest of all

3,144 U.S. counties.[14] What does this mean in real numbers? Rather than relying on one singular statistic, here are a range of data points that paint an astounding picture of economic inequality in Teton County and Wyoming:[15]

- The average income for the top 1 percent in Teton County is $28.2 million. This is by far the highest for all counties in the United States. To put in context, the lowest is Quitman County, Georgia, where the 1 percent makes $127,425 a year.
- The top 1 percent in Teton County make 233 times more than the bottom 99 percent. This is the highest income disparity of all counties in the United States.
- Median income in Teton County is in the top 2.6 percent nationally, and average income is the highest in the nation.
- 90 percent of all income in Teton County is earned by 8 percent of households.
- The metro area of Jackson, Wyoming, has the highest income inequality of any metro area in the entire United States. The top 1 percent make $19,995,834, which is 213 times more than the bottom 99 percent.
- From 1979 to 2011, incomes for the bottom 99 percent in Wyoming actually declined (–2.5 percent), while incomes for the top 1 percent did not decline, but grew enormously (+172 percent). Only three other states saw rising incomes among the 1 percent at all, much less such a large increase.
- The average income of the top 0.01 percent in Wyoming is $368,823,036. This is by far the highest of all fifty states (Connecticut at $83.9 million and New York at $69.9 million).
- The top 1 percent in Wyoming control 50 percent of total income in the state. This is the highest of all 50 states.
- The top 10 percent in Wyoming control 65 percent of total income in the state. This is the highest of all 50 states.

However you slice it, one thing is clear: this is the richest area in the United States, but is also the most unequal. Economists, sociologists, and political scientists have provided various explanations for why, in the richest nation in the world, we still see such high levels of inequality. Or, to put it differently, why there has been such a concentration of wealth only at the extreme top. Most theories agree that this has been a long time in the making, beginning in earnest as early as the 1970s and continuing to present day. Scholars point toward, among other things, the decline of tax rates on the top 1 percent, the erosion of unions and collective bargaining, Wall Street deregulation, soaring executive salaries and bonuses, new trade agreements, and transformations within real estate markets.[16] My goal in this book is not to corroborate these explanations locally, or to offer additional ones. Instead, I am seeking to understand how changes in great wealth and great inequality actually *play out on the ground in a real-life community, in the lives of real people, especially through the lens of the ultra-wealthy themselves.*

Introducing the Local Impacts

Stuffed to the brim, Jim and I continue to drag out the morning with even more coffee, and I do my best to guide our conversation toward the *consequences* of all this wealth on the environment and local community—topics that became central as I sought to understand how the ultra-wealthy use nature and rural people to solve unique dilemmas they face.

Digging into these by-products of wealth are where the rubber really meets the road. It is where the most interesting and most important conversations were to be had. Even over breakfast, I found that talking about wealth in the abstract reveals little about Jim's views on the issues, nor does it really reveal anything about what things look like in the nitty-gritty details of everyday life. The forces of wealth, environment, and community are deeply entwined, resulting in a unique set of local consequences.

LOCAL ENVIRONMENTAL IMPACTS OF ULTRA-WEALTH

Just as important as immense wealth, the other fundamental fact infusing nearly everything here is that 97 percent of all land in Teton County is public, owned by the federal government and restricted from development. The land and wildlife in Teton County are an important component of what is one of the last large, intact ecosystems in the world, spanning two national parks. This means that every square inch of remaining developable land is extremely valuable. Within this context, how are the conflicting pressures of great wealth, private land scarcity, and ecological risk resolved? As we will see in the people we meet and stories we encounter, it is complicated, and raises all sorts of interesting puzzles.

Most notable is that the majority of the ultra-wealthy here support further restrictions on development—either out of stated concern for the environment and/or concern for the character of the town. In later chapters, we will unpack the complex cultural, political, and economic meanings of environmental "concern" and town "character." Not going unnoticed by most, however, is the fact that restricting development, either through private conservation easements or otherwise, creates even greater scarcity, maintains the scenery for the wealthy who already have homes, continues to drive real estate prices even higher, and creates roadblocks for building affordable housing.

As for Jim, he tells me that he favors policies that keep the community the way it is, by setting aside what few private lands remain, limiting further housing development, and preserving small-town character. "Well, 97 percent of Teton County is owned by the government. There isn't that much more land to buy and build on. So conservation easements here, whether you like them or don't, are the principle way that open space is protected and not subject to the kinds of real estate development that has happened in so many other places." The way Jim sees it, the "county commission and town council should restrict development to places where they don't threaten small-town character and wildlife values." On the whole, he is happy with what the Jackson Hole Land Trust—a local environmental nonprofit—has done to close off more private lands from development. Not only is it the right thing to do, but it's what most people out here want. "I think we're pretty respectful of wildlife out here and open space and vistas and so forth. That is why we elect the people we do."

The self-serving and hypocritical appearance of this brand of environmental concern is not lost on Jim, or the many other ultra-wealthy I spent time with. Some readily admit that yes, they came here, built or bought very large properties, and now they want to close the door behind them. They often recognized the ulterior motives behind this seemingly altruistic approach to conservation. In later chapters, I will recount in-depth discussions about these issues, and the cultural logic the ultra-wealthy draw on to define their views and behavior as selfish on one hand, or altruistic on another, or worthy of guilt or worthy of praise. My goal as a researcher is not to get inside their heads to fully uncover their "true" motives, but instead my goal is to understand how they think and talk about these complex issues, and measure how closely their behavior aligns with what they say.

One of the most important examples is their participation in what I come to call a "charitable-industrial-complex" that has emerged here in the wake of wealth concentration.[17] As I will show, the community is now home to a staggering number of nonprofits relative to its size. Jim, like many others, talks quite a bit about his nonprofit work, telling me that he is on the board of several conservation organizations, some of which he was asked by friends to join for social reasons, and some others because he cares deeply about their environmental mission. I unpack this ultra-wealthy charitable-industrial-complex by examining the issues on which they focus (for example, environmental versus poverty issues), measuring just how much money they have, which ultra-wealthy people are involved, how different organizations are connected, and how all of this impacts the link between wealth, community, and environment.

Last, the influx of wealth has affected not only the scarcity of land, and the subsequent growth of a charitable apparatus to protect that scarcity, but it has also influenced a certain *cultural experience* of the environment, often made possible only by wealth. For example, in addition to owning a disproportionate amount of income, the ultra-wealthy in this community also enjoy much more free time than their low-income counterparts. As discussed earlier, this luxury is partly due to technological advances, and their nonlabor investment income, which allows them more free time to develop certain skills (for example, fly-fishing, skiing, technical mountaineering) and to enjoy nature, and then in turn work to protect and normalize these experiences through various environmental efforts. As Jim describes, "I'm kind of an outdoors guy, and whether it's skiing or hiking or biking or fishing or hunting, I find I have more than enough to fill up my day, and I just love the life that I lead right now."

The luxury of free time, and the ownership of land, has allowed avid recreators like Jim to cultivate high levels of what we might call "nature capital." Similar to other noneconomic forms of cultural and social capital, it is a particular way of experiencing nature, and involves the right combination of wealth, land, free time, recreation capability, romantic attachment, and gilded environmental concern.

LOCAL COMMUNITY IMPACTS OF ULTRA-WEALTH

Given the staggering economic statistics earlier, what does a community actually look and feel like when there is no middle class, and a nation-leading gap between the billionaires and those pulling in $12,000 a year? In the absence of a middle class, how do these two very different groups of people get along? When do they interact? Are they friends? What role does money and power play? How genuine are their social bonds, and are these bonds a one-way street, or reciprocal? In what ways do they rely on each other to live the life they want, and to be the person they think they ought to be? Is each group aware of the other's extreme financial situation?

For someone like Julie Williams, whom we met in the book's introduction, this extreme economic gap is not that problematic, and can even be viewed positively, because she reports great relationships with working-class folks whom she would otherwise not interact with. She especially likes these relationships because these types of rural, low-income, and nature-oriented people are, in her view, not so materialistic like some of her old friends back in Connecticut.

As I will show throughout this book, Julie and many other ultra-wealthy people I spoke with view these cross-class relationships as authentic and enriching, and even providing a solution to overcome social stigmas and guilt that can plague the ultra-wealthy. Connecting with "normal" rural working-class people—who are perceived to have an innate and genuine connection to nature—can provide a model and means by which people like Julie can transform themselves into better and more virtuous people. Outwardly, this affects everything down to how the ultra-wealthy dress, what they drive, and the artwork they display in their homes. Beyond these individual personal transformations, these dynamics also create a larger perception that this is a healthy rural community based on genuine relationships, old-time Western virtue, and authentic small-town character.

But digging deeper and considering my research of the ultra-wealthy in light of the low-income interviews, these dynamics raised interesting puzzles about what constitutes true authenticity in relationships between the top and the bottom, and what impact this has on the meaning of "community" itself. Along the way, I develop a concept I call "class confusion" to understand and explain these ultra-wealthy ideas about authenticity, and how they can create a veneer of community in unequal social contexts.

A second puzzle has to do with what the ultra-wealthy *say* about the community, and how they live as members of it. For example, unlike Julie, who is more overt about her positive feelings, Jim actually laments the bifurcation: "I think it's wrong that you have a community where people fly in on Learjets and Gulfstreams. There's no community there. But the people that work in this town are the people that you meet, you know, from other walks of life, and so forth. I think that's critical. To me, that's how you define and build a community. I'm not a guy that says, 'Well, I was here first, and goddammit, you're not allowed in.' I like those people. I like seeing them; I like being around them. That's how community gets formed, I think."

We will hear from other ultra-wealthy who feel similarly to Jim, and we will compare what is being said, to what, if anything, is actually being done. With immense wealth and social capital in the community, what efforts are being undertaken to slow skyrocketing housing costs, repair social safety nets, and promote the vision of "community" that people like Jim have for the area? And, what role does environmental conservation play in this process?

Certainly, almost every ultra-wealthy person I spoke with wants what is best for the community. Yet, somehow, in the richest county in the richest nation in the world there are homeless kids who attend the local high school, multiple families living wedged into a single motel room, a quarter of all kids receiving free or reduced lunch and breakfast, kids too exhausted for school because lack of bed space means taking turns sleeping, families being forced to choose between paying high rents or buying food, affordable trailer parks being torn down for new luxury construction, and in general people facing dim prospects for upward mobility, despite hard work and plenty of hope.

2

Mount Billionaire

Imagine zooming through the Rocky Mountains upside down in a Russian fighter jet. No, you're not in the Kremlin's military, nor are you in a scene from the latest summer blockbuster movie. You're Jack Martin, an ex-Silicon Valley mogul, and member of the ultra-exclusive Yellowstone Club. Jack made his fortune as a computer scientist and early investor in more than 150 tech ventures. But after burning out on the Silicon Valley grind, he decided to build a house in the mountains. For Jack, there is just more freedom out here, not only because he can park hobby toys like his JetRanger helicopter in his backyard, or fly his Russian fighter jet around, but also because he can connect to the great outdoors through biking, snowboarding, hunting, and fishing. He chuckles, telling me, "It's funny, about ten years ago I bought this Russian fighter jet. You know, a little air-to-ground attack fighter. So, it's been a lot of fun out here."

Gregarious and friendly, Jack reflects that at first he didn't know what other ultra-wealthy folks out here would make of him being so rambunctious and free-wheeling with his time and money. "You know, not a lot of the East Coast blue bloods are gonna be hanging out with a Jack Martin, because he's loud and obnoxious, and he's always flying his jet upside down over the golf course . . . coming down and knocking flags down on the driving range." He reckons that people "used to get a little pissed off," especially when he kept his helicopter parked in his backyard. "I guess I've got a little bit of a reputation here, but I've been having fun," he says. Jack often donates rides for charity and is especially proud of his work taking wounded veterans on fly-fishing trips. Overall, being able to enjoy life up here in the mountains has been very rewarding for Jack. "I mean, I'm looking out my window right now at the mountains, and you know, it's just where I want to be."

Most Americans have never heard of the über-private Yellowstone Club, an ultra-wealthy enclave where Jack and a few hundred families are members. Located about fifty miles northwest of Teton County, it is not hyperbole to say that it is perhaps the most exclusive private club in the world. Owning an entire mountain to itself, larger than most ski resorts in the United States, it is the only entirely private ski and golf resort on the globe, and it counts some of the richest in the world as its members. Among these are billionaires like Bill Gates and former Google CEO Eric Schmidt; top executives of corporations like Citigroup, Comcast, News Corp., and Apple; politicians like Dan Quayle and Jack Kemp; sports stars like Phil Mickelson, Tom Brady, and Greg LeMond; A-list entertainers like Justin Timberlake and Ben Affleck; and many other titans of the pharmaceutical and finance industries.[1]

The club opened in 1997, right in the midst of the massive increase in wealth that flooded this region, detailed in chapter 1. The club filled a growing niche, aiming to attract the wealthiest of the wealthy, the elite of the elite. Optimism was high. So much so, for example, that several years ago the club set out to build and sell the most expensive home in the world, a $155 million, 53,000-square-foot mansion made of stone and wood that included its own indoor ski-lift and ice rink. According to billionaire founder of the club, Tim Blixseth, "You can't believe the number of people interested in this [house]. . . . And the guys who are calling aren't going to have to borrow any money."[2] Average single-family homes in the club cost much less, hovering between $10 and $18 million. All come with the advertised promise of "security and open space, luxury and wilderness."[3]

Club members also benefit professionally and financially from living amid such a concentrated network of ultra-elites. As one member Gary Kline put it to me, ski-lifts aren't just good for skiing. Gushing, he says, "I've not met one asshole in the Yellowstone Club. They are unbelievable fucking people, every one of them. You ride the lift with them, and [laughs] you're just blown away by who they are and what they do . . . riding up the lift I just did a deal for a gas pipeline; [laughs] they financed the pipeline for billions."

———

The Yellowstone Club represents the pinnacle, or inevitable *telos*, of the trajectory of extreme wealth concentration in the United States. The endgame, so to speak. Focusing on an institution like the Yellowstone Club is important because it allows us to get inside the numbers—to drop down 30,000 feet, to see what life at rarefied heights really looks like, on the ground, from the inside.

Based on my firsthand experiences inside the gates of the club, and in-depth interviews with club members, my aim is to accurately record what this pinnacle of wealth actually *feels like* for those who live it. In order to fully understand these dynamics, I also conducted additional interviews with small businesses owners who derive work from the club, and often have close relationships with its members, such as builders, architects, consultants, concierge, caretakers of homes, personal assistants, and longtime residents of nearby towns who have watched the rise of ultra-wealth in their community.

The particular uses of nature and rural people uncovered in this book do not emerge out of thin air. *Instead, they are often the product of ultra-wealthy institutions—such as the Yellowstone Club—that actively construct, sell, and manage these interactions and experiences.* When it comes to nature, they have created the appearance, both for the club's members and for the general public, that what they are selling is rooted in the responsible enjoyment of wilderness and a commitment to the region's ecological health. And when it comes to its relationship to rural people and the local community just outside its walls, they have drawn on popular American stereotypes to cultivate and sell the notion that members who buy into the club are granted access to an institution par excellence of a bygone time where frontier communities were more tight-knit, nature was a humbling force for even the most ruthless business titan, people were "normal," and folks looked after one another. This promise of authentic community also extends beyond the confines of the club, to include the experience of social solidarity with the local community just outside its gates, as evidenced by public acts of charity by the Yellowstone Club Foundation.

Yet, looking more closely, contradictions abound, and reality looks much different from these cultivated appearances. Beneath the veneer, the reality of this institution and its use of nature and rural people involves raw economic interest, lasting environmental harm, and an intense culture of rural exclusion and militarized privacy. Nature itself becomes a vehicle for economic gain through privatizing a huge swath of ecologically sensitive public land for billions of dollars in desirable land development and real estate construction, and providing private recreation services to those able to pay the exorbitant price. And despite romantic praise and emulation of the small Western community outside its gates, the reality is that their connections with these rural people are often motivated by economic exchange and services rendered, and actual levels of charitable giving by the Yellowstone Club Foundation are relatively minuscule, and day-to-day relationships with rural people are colored by affluent feelings of distrust and chronic paranoia that the rural working class might unfairly take advantage of the rich.

Building a Private Nirvana

EARLY YEARS

The Yellowstone Club was created on a whim—almost by accident—from a billionaire timber baron with time on his hands, and a savvy (and eventually fraudulent) knack for bending tax and land policies to his benefit. This billionaire, Tim Blixseth, who came from poverty in rural Oregon, made his fortune buying and selling timber lands. By the age of forty, he was retired in Lake Tahoe, but mostly bored because "there was no one to play golf with during the middle of the week."[4] For fun, he took up an invitation from a real estate broker to come check out 164,000 acres of land for sale just to the northwest of Yellowstone National Park. Blixseth and two partners ended up purchasing much of the land, planning to log the timber, despite its close proximity to the world's first national park and its ecological importance for threatened wildlife. There was considerable uproar from environmental groups, so he switched strategies, and convinced the federal government to agree to a series of complex land swaps, which ultimately resulted in his gaining permission to develop the pristine land.

His original plan for this unspoiled mountainous land was to develop it for the private enjoyment of his family alone. Spending nearly $100 million for this initial development, he cleared land for his family's ski-lifts and golf course.[5] But he soon sensed a demand for an ultra-rich enclave that could offer what he himself wanted in the land: supreme privacy, other-worldly amenities, authentic Western charm, and private skiing. Certainly, this demand was due in large part to the local and national forces of wealth concentration, as we saw in chapter 1.

After continued development and business planning, Blixseth officially opened the Yellowstone Club in 1999. With the motto "Sometimes you have to pay to play," he successfully targeted America's ultra-elite, with ski runs like "Learjet Glades" and "EBITDA" (Wall Street lingo for a company's performance), and aggressive marketing, with full-page ads in the *Wall Street Journal* and outreach to ultra-luxury magazines like the *Robb Report*. In 2005, the club trademarked the words "Private Powder."

As for early criticism that he was closing off an entire mountain from the public, to be enjoyed only by a gilded few, he saw no reason to feel ashamed. As he put it, "There's no hiding that there are people in the U.S. who have tremendous wealth, and that's the American dream. . . . It isn't in my book to be ashamed of wealth."[6]

Blixseth ran into significant legal trouble relating to alleged financial embezzlement, and as a result, the club crashed spectacularly hard—made worse by the great recession. After bankruptcy in 2008, the club has managed to rise from the ashes after being purchased by a private equity firm owned by a fellow club member. The club is now thriving, selling billions in real estate, and has doubled its membership. In 2009, there were 260 members, but it now boasts more than 500 households (membership is capped at 864 households to protect exclusivity). As of 2017, the membership deposit was $400,000, with $41,500 in yearly dues, in addition to the requirement of purchasing or building a multi-million-dollar property.[7] Private jet service, and a recently completed helicopter pad, make for convenient travel to the club, especially because the majority of members come from the Northeast, California, and Florida.[8]

ENVIRONMENTAL IMPACTS

All of this development and growth, and the rural enjoyment of nature at such a large scale, has not come without impacts to the surrounding natural environment. For example, early on, the club settled a lawsuit, paying a $1.8 million civil penalty (but not admitting guilt) related to the Environmental Protection Agency's Clean Water Act. In 2010, a club employee shot and killed a black bear that was on club grounds—an illegal act that not only infuriated local communities but also led to a strong response from the Montana Department of Fish, Wildlife, and Parks (FWP), wherein they sharply criticized the club in a written letter, for its "high level of negligence and disregard for public safety" by illegally managing wildlife on its own terms. The FWP further criticized the club's self-protective response in the wake of the shooting, claiming that the club was much more concerned about controlling negative public relations than the harm caused to wildlife and local ecology. Scolding the club, the FWP stated, "Your staff first stated concerns about whether FWP would issue a press release, rather than focusing on the critical wildlife and human safety issues at hand."[9] More recently in 2016, the club had a significant, and highly publicized, wastewater spill where 30 million gallons of wastewater that were used for the golf course irrigation spilled into the pristine Gallatin River.

What does an entire mountain look like when it is developed so rapidly, even if only for a small handful of people? Figures 2.1 and 2.2 illustrate these ecological changes using before and after satellite photos. To give a sense of scope, these aerial shots from 26,543 feet capture 10.8 square miles of development (4.5 miles across, and about 2.4 miles top to bottom). The club privately owns about 13,600 acres in total. The top photo is from 1995 *before club development,* and the bottom photo is from 2014. The many ski-runs and new roads are all visible in lighter colors, cutting down from the peak of the mountain from the far left to the right. The main village and clubhouse development are visible in the center of the photo, with the golf course and its wastewater pond visible toward the bottom right. Many new homes to the north are not pictured.

Most club members view themselves as environmental stewards rather than, as some local environmental groups described them to me, a gilded few who have plundered an entire mountainside for their occasional enjoyment. Certainly, high-level employees I spoke with had more sophisticated ways of touting the environmental benefits of the club, citing the land easements, and warning that the land could be in much worse shape if it were fragmented into smaller parcels.

Club members I interviewed, like the tech CEO Larry Samuel, believe that the environment and wildlife are actually *better off* because of the club's strong presence on the land. "Surprisingly, animals thrive where people are. They feel safe around the Yellowstone Club because there are humans around. Wherever there are humans, animals thrive and feel safer." This approach is what Larry calls "European" forest and wildlife management, by which wildlife feel safer when forests are heavily managed, which, according to Larry, is "just like the Nature Conservancy—the club locked up land and now preserves it."

The socioeconomic impact of the club on the local communities is less clear, and can become quite complicated depending on one's perspective. From the short-term perspective of many builders, architects, and others associated with the construction industry, the club has provided a steady stream of business, with the design and

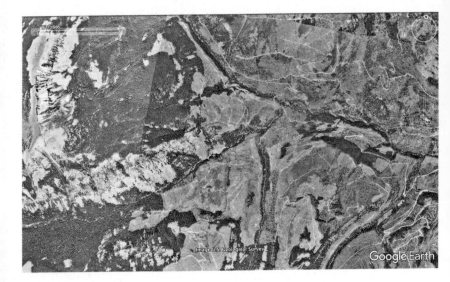

FIGURE 2.1. Aerial photo of the ecosystem in 1995, showing very minimal ecological disruption.
Source: U.S. Geological Survey and Google Earth.

FIGURE 2.2. Aerial photo of the ecosystem in 2014, showing significant ecological disruption.
Source: U.S. Geological Survey and Google Earth.

construction of massive homes, a new village core, as well as a new ski mountain in the works. No doubt, these development activities have poured hundreds of millions into the local economy, creating opportunities in the construction and low-paying services sector.

But like other Western boomtowns, jobs and income can be volatile. After the multi-million-dollar embezzlement and eventual crash of the club, many small businesses were hung out to dry—unpaid for work (and materials) already completed. Knowing the importance of these small businesses for the future development of the club, the new owners attempted to repair community relations by repaying all small businesses who had lost out because of the hundreds of millions in fraud. Many small business owners I spoke with were very pleased that the club repaid them in full. While this improved relations with construction workers, the relationship with other people in surrounding communities is still tenuous. This has in part to do with specific interactions that have rubbed people the wrong way, general resentment about changes to the character of the area, perceived entitlement to seclusion, and most importantly, skyrocketing housing costs brought on by high-end development in the area. This has meant that the majority of workers cannot afford to live nearby, and are forced to drive or ride a shuttle roundtrip two hours each day to and from Bozeman, Montana, on a harrowing two-lane canyon road.

Two Short Stories

LIFE AS A CLUB MEMBER: SECLUSION, PHILANTHROPY, RACE/ETHNICITY

What is it actually like in the world's most exclusive club? On a sunny spring day, I drove up a long winding road, riding a ridge that crests at 7,600 feet, leading up to the gates of the club. As I pulled up to a massive stone structure, which looked more like a lavish lodge than a gate, two uniformed guards stepped out and signaled for me to slow, until I was fully stopped beneath the shade of an arched stone overhang. I knew, of course, that I had permission to enter, but the seriousness of the guards, and the symbolic weight of the edifice under which I was now sitting, were all too intimidating, seeding doubts in my mind about whether or not this research and book were a good idea. After some questioning and verification, the guards gave me the green light, and off I went toward the base of the club.

I spent the afternoon with employees from marketing and sales, getting a tour of the club, meeting upper-level management, and interacting with club members. I was met with suspicion around every corner, but suspicion often subsided after I explained that I was from Yale, and was not here to write a poorly researched, or unfairly written, exposé. Certainly, all of the outside criticism, jealousy, resentment, and finger-pointing toward the club and the ultra-wealthy had created an internal club culture trigger-happy with suspicion.

I had to work hard to calm suspicions, and found that the best way was to emphasize my dual identity as a Yale professor *and* a native Wyomingite. The combination of elite status or wealth on the one hand, complemented by the appearance of Western "authenticity" on the other was the exact identity projected by the club itself, and the reason why many members find it so attractive. Using this dual identity of prestige and authenticity to my advantage, I was able to put people at ease and build trust inside an institution so prone to misgivings.

I also offered something else. In recent years, the club desired to change negative perceptions, wanting desperately to convince those outside these walls that they were a caring bunch, especially to nearby communities. Many at the club point to the biased media as the root cause of negative public perceptions, believing that the press has sought to "align [the club] with the excesses of the era."[10] Speaking to me anonymously, one employee disclosed that the club "rarely takes media requests," but they were optimistic that my writing would promote their philanthropic generosity.

After these initial meetings, tours, and mingling, I was escorted to the sales office for the weekly happy hour, where prospective members socialize and learn more about their real estate options. The mood was light, the staff was gregarious, and the beer and wine were flowing. In the middle of the room was a gigantic, and incredibly detailed, three-dimensional model of the entire club property for prospective members to envision at full scale the potential of authentic mountain living.

I stood gazing at this impressive 3D model, beer in one hand, and fieldwork notebook in another. An employee walked over, looking at the map. "Pretty crazy, huh?" she said. Not entirely sure what she meant by "crazy," I smiled and nodded. Continuing, unprompted, and making her intentions known, she confessed to me quietly that this map makes her feel guilty for working here. For her, seeing it at scale with this map made the whole thing feel all too real. Normally, she was able to keep out of her mind the huge scale of environmental impact on pristine land, relative to the tiny number of wealthy users. "I have this ongoing internal struggle," she continued quietly. "My family is completely opposed to the club, but it provides me with a great career." And standing here faced with the 3D model of gilded land ownership made it difficult for her to come to terms with the aftermath of such environmental opulence. I listened compassionately and jotted notes as she unloaded her guilt.

Time had flown by, and looking down at my watch, I knew I needed to head up the mountain for the annual Yellowstone Club Foundation dinner that was happening this evening. I hopped into my car and drove up the winding road toward the spectacular Rainbow Lodge, where the dinner was being held. The Rainbow Lodge was perhaps the most stunning setting in the entire club, with awe-inspiring vista views and palatial Western decor. It certainly made this annual dinner feel as important as the foundation had intended, with forty-five select people in attendance, including some of the most prominent club members, guest musicians like Lyle Lovett, as well as the governor and first lady of Montana.

Before the dinner and presentation by the club foundation, I mingled with many of the guests and members, gently probing about the club, community, and environment. Over and over again, I was surprised to hear the same refrain, no matter what member or employee I was talking to: *The club is special because the people are so "normal" here.* Contrary to popular stereotypes, they wanted me to know that money hadn't turned them into out-of-touch monsters.

Over and over again, I heard: we're just "normal" people who need (and especially deserve) somewhere nice to relax.

Longtime members Sharon and Tom Hayes—private equity financiers from California—spoke with me at length, mostly aiming to demonstrate to me the fundamental "normalcy" inherent to club culture, which applies to all members, whether one is a CEO, a celebrity, or just a financier. Tom excitedly told me two stories.

The first was the time he saw a nationally famous club member setting his ego aside. "There he was, bent over on one knee, tying his own kid's shoe. Not his nanny nearby, but himself. It was unbelievable to see." The second story was about an unnamed member who, he says, "is such an asshole outside of the club, but when he comes here, he's the nicest guy. Our paths sometimes cross outside of the club, but I just avoid him. But here, he's great. Love being around him." Continuing, after grabbing a second glass of wine, Tom tells me that normalcy is achieved because other members simply aren't impressed by what you've accomplished outside the club, because everyone here is already immensely successful. People don't need to put on airs, and instead can just be themselves—be "normal." Driving home his point, he chuckles, and recalls the time that he sent a prominent celebrity club member an e-mail telling him that he enjoyed his work in Hollywood. And proudly, laughing, Tom tells me that this guy actually "took the time to write me back, with an e-mail saying 'thanks!'"

The dinner itself was an opportunity for the club foundation to celebrate its support of local nonprofit organizations. It was the precursor to the grand white-tent fundraiser that was to come tomorrow evening, with a concert by Lyle Lovett (last year by James Taylor and Emmylou Harris). Over the course of the dinner, the executive director and members of the foundation board expressed enthusiasm and optimism about the huge impact of the club's philanthropy on local education, conservation, and community services.

The genuine enthusiasm and optimism were certainly impressive, but I had yet to look at the actual philanthropic data. The common view, as described by one member I spoke with, was that "what the club is doing for the community is nothing but positive." The club membership is among the wealthiest in the world, so the club members and the club foundation's optimism about their financial impact in the community is certainly something to be excited about. Digging into the data, IRS 990 reports show that in 2014 the club foundation gave a total of $493,890 in grants and sponsorships, and incurred $255,914 in fundraising expenses. The year before that, the foundation gave a total of $388,046 in grants and sponsorships, and incurred $215,732 in fundraising expenses.

Several local nonprofit executive directors I interviewed were overtly critical of the foundation for patting itself on the back for giving, what they viewed, was relatively little money. They often pointed out that the club foundation donates only slightly more than the equivalent of just one member's initiation fee and annual dues (~$441,500). Or viewed from another angle, *the average club member household donates about $571 annually to the community*, despite the billions owned by many of its members, and the billions the club has sold in real estate.

Back at the Rainbow Lodge, the dinner had ended, and people began funneling out, some to their cars and others into the black Yellowstone Club SUVs that chaperoned members around the property. "What are your plans for tomorrow?" I was asked by one of the higher-level employees. Continuing, he pressed, "You should really get out on the slopes. I'll set you up with some skis. You gotta experience the freedom firsthand." He was not the first to insist on this, and I agreed that it would be a useful experience (even if I had a hard time later explaining to my wife, my colleagues, and my dean that, yes, research involved skiing).

Early the next morning, I found myself riding a lift up to the top of the mountain. Their legally trademarked phrase "Private Powder" certainly proved to be true. The lifts traveling up this giant mountain were completely empty. There were no other people on the slopes. No people at the top except employees running the lift, and I saw only a handful of skiers on the way back down (figures 2.3 and 2.4). At one point, I ran into the boundary separating the club from the

FIGURE 2.3. Photo illustrating seclusion and privacy. *Source:* Photo taken by author.

FIGURE 2.4. Photo illustrating seclusion and privacy. *Source:* Photo taken by author.

outside world, posted with a sign: "YELLOWSTONE CLUB SKI AREA BOUNDARY VIOLATORS WILL BE PROSECUTED." This was a strange and eerie feeling compared to the majority of bustling ski experiences in the West. It felt like sneaking into a theme park after hours. Eventually, I stopped in one of the "snack shacks"—a sort of ultra-wealthy version of a 7–11 convenience store, only smaller and more opulently rustic. Longing for some food and bit of human contact, I popped off my skis and headed in, pleasantly surprised to find four others I had met at the foundation dinner the night before, and their guest of honor, Lyle Lovett.

Over the years, I have done thousands of hours of participant observation for various research projects, some of which have involved dangerous encounters with grizzly bears and memorable experiences with all sorts interesting people, but two hours of skiing in this securitized club, with slopes like a ghost town, was perhaps the most fascinating, and instructive, case of observational research I've ever done, giving me a tangible sense of the magnitude of differences between the ultra-wealthy and everybody else.

The remainder of the day I sought to more deeply observe something that rarely, if ever, came up voluntarily in my participant observation at the club, or in the formal interviews I conducted later: How are racial and ethnic boundaries constructed and maintained? What I discovered is consistent with recent research on rural immigration, gentrification, and racialized divisions of labor.[11] I found, through firsthand observation at the club and through interviews with club employees and outside small business owners (for example, contractors, architects), that people of color are more likely to be placed in the back-of-the-house spaces out of the view of members (for example, kitchens, housekeeping, construction labor), while non-Hispanic whites are placed in front-of-house spaces where face-to-face interaction and socialization with members was necessary (for example, bartenders, wait staff, ski-lift operators, ski-rental technicians, gift shop cashiers). In later chapters, I consider reasons for these stark racial and ethnic differences, which are certainly not unique to the Yellowstone Club, but are part of historically entrenched conceptions of nature—particularly with regard to how whiteness is associated with nature (for example, idealized purity of rural landscape) and rural Western culture (for example, mythology of the white explorer and cowboy).

Chronic Paranoia and Attempts to Bust Three Myths

Fast forward to summer at the club. The snow has melted, and the slopes—now just huge empty fields of grass etched into the forest—flow down from the mountaintop like green rivers. Vacant ski-chairs hang above, swinging in the sun, and everywhere wildflowers are poking through the dry ground. Summer is the most popular time of year in the area for hiking, biking, rafting, fishing, and touring nearby national parks.

I was at the Yellowstone Club to grab lunch with and interview Colin Stewart, a white middle-aged corporate investment executive from Connecticut. Colin specializes in raising money for a handful of hedge funds that invest primarily in oil and gas extraction, and given the domestic growth of this industry over the last few decades, Colin has done quite well for himself, riding the lucrative wave of the U.S. energy boom. We met near the clubhouse, and upon Colin's recommendation, we decided to soak up the sun, and grab our lunch poolside, where according to Colin, one can find the best burgers in the entire state. I hopped into his black SUV, and off we went down the winding mountain road toward the pool and spa.

From the moment I got into that SUV, Colin was on a mission. He was a mythbuster. More than anyone I interviewed, or had yet to interview, Colin aimed to dispel what he perceived to be stereotypes about the club, and about the ultra-wealthy in general. I was less concerned whether or not these stereotypes in Colin's mind mirrored reality (some do, some don't), because I was more interested to uncover the ways people like Colin *think* they are being perceived by others, how this feeling of being typecast *affects their behavior* toward outsiders, and their *rationale* for why these stereotypes are wrong.

I found that this all leads to a mild, but pervasive, sense of paranoia and persecution complex among the ultra-wealthy, symptomatic of Colin's defensiveness about three particular myths: (1) the ultra-wealthy aren't deserving people; (2) the ultra-wealthy aren't integrated into the community like other "normal" people; (3) the ultra-wealthy deserve to be taken advantage of.

BUSTING MYTH 1: THE ULTRA-WEALTHY ARE NOT DESERVING PEOPLE

We parked and walked down to the pool area, grabbing a table near the grill hut. "I'll have what he's having," I said, with no time to look over the menu, and instead furiously jotting down notes and quotes as Colin continued to spill his feelings, unprompted, aiming to open my eyes to the *actual* realities of having immense wealth, rather than the stereotypes he assumed that I, and others like me, had. One of the biggest misconceptions out there, according to Colin, is that the ultra-wealthy are not deserving people, and that the vast wealth they've accumulated is not commensurate with the work they've put in.

As an illustration, he told me a story about a recent float trip he took with some friendly locals on the nearby river. One guy, who despite liking and getting along with Colin during the course of the trip, was not aware that Colin was actually an ultra-wealthy club member. Colin explains that toward the end of the trip, unknowingly the guy started cracking jokes and being critical of the Yellowstone Club. Colin responded, defending himself and the club, saying, "Hey! I'm a member, and we've gotten along, so do you still think we are all assholes?" Colin is frustrated by the fact that people like to criticize wealth without knowing the stories of "how we worked our asses off to get it." They jump to conclusions. In his view, popular criticism is based on jealousy, but also because people just don't take the time to get to know the ultra-wealthy to truly understand how hard they've worked.

The ultra-wealthy have become victims of unfair accusation, especially when, according to Colin, many ultra-wealthy people came from "dirt," rising above their circumstances through hard work, ambition, and courageous persistence. To be jealous of wealth is one thing, but to criticize merit is another. According to Colin, this isn't a case of being born on third base and thinking he hit a triple. He swung hard and hit that triple. He proudly explains that his parents came from nothing, so don't criticize him as some trust-fund baby. "That's not the type of people who are here [at the club]. My wife's family came from nothing . . . they were dirt poor."

Continuing this line of thought, and questioning local criticism of the club itself, Colin reiterates that 90 percent of the club members are self-made, full of folks who have worked tirelessly—80 and 90 hours a week he says—and need desperately somewhere to relax, and to enjoy the fruits of their labor. "You know, work hard and then play hard," he says. Colin makes room for one exception, admitting that there are some club members who have benefited from the tech bubble, and these members aren't as respected by other ultra-wealthy people because they haven't put in the time to steadily earn their wealth.

All of this is even more frustrating for Colin because locals who unfairly criticize the wealthy don't realize that they are biting the hand that feeds. They come off as ungrateful for the jobs that have been created by the club, and the influx of tax revenue enjoyed by the community. Even if they don't want to be friends with the ultra-wealthy, Colin believes that they should at least temper their criticism, given the economic debt he says they owe to the ultra-wealthy.

At this point, I probed Colin about some of the well-known negative economic effects of ultra-wealth and wealth inequality in the community, such as exorbitant housing costs and lack of middle-class jobs. Responding, Colin acknowledges the growing gap between the rich and the poor, but does not see it as a problem, especially because from his perspective, wealth inequality is the result of a disproportionately high population of baby-boomers in the United States, and once they retire, he says the top-heavy income distribution will even out.

BUSTING MYTH 2: THE ULTRA-WEALTHY ARE NOT "NORMAL" PEOPLE

The burgers were average, but the pool area was unforgettable—something straight off the cover of a luxury lifestyle magazine. The other club members at the pool were mostly middle-aged women, some sprawled out on chairs soaking up the sun and mountain views, and a few other younger mothers in the water teaching their toddlers how to swim. Colin ran to grab a few extra napkins, and sitting back down, he begins another unprompted line of thought, this time explaining that contrary to popular opinion, the ultra-wealthy are actually just "normal" people. "We're all just humans," he says. Continuing, with an honest seriousness, he explains that the only difference is that people like him can buy whatever they want, when they want. From his perspective, this difference shouldn't be as big of a deal as nonwealthy people like to make it.

For Colin, it is unfair to judge people based on the material goods they have. A person's wealth shouldn't distract us from the fact that all of us are, at root, just fellow humans. Just because someone can purchase this or that doesn't change their innate personhood. Rather than focusing on wealth, we should focus on what we have in common, which is our shared human nature. *In other words: wealth is all just relative, and we shouldn't judge others based upon it.* "Sure, this [club] is a bubble . . . but we all live in bubbles anyways. Our other homes are in bubbles, so what's the difference?" Interjecting, I asked Colin to expand on this idea that, sure, some have more, some have less, but it shouldn't get in the way of seeing everyone as fellow humans. Responding, he exclaimed "What makes a man happy? . . . Relationships!" Continuing, he made plain, with vague references to scientific studies of happiness, that the club itself is based on the premise that relationships, not material wealth or social status, are the key to happiness, and this is the foundation upon which the club is built.

Colin repeatedly justified that he is just a normal guy by pointing out the fact that he has many good friends in the nearby community who are not ultra-wealthy. "I am very close with all sorts of people in town," he says proudly. I probe for a specific example, and excitedly, he reckons "I know one guy really well," and waxes on about an employee at the local fish market who gives Colin the inside track to the best cuts of halibut. "It's just a really tight-knit little community," he reiterates.

Colin views these relationships as authentic and equitable, yet looking more closely, one cannot help but notice that his friendships are often based on economic exchange and uneven power dynamics, such as his halibut fishmonger, or friendships he's developed through philanthropic giving in the community, or his local rafting guides, or the staff at the Yellowstone Club. He points me toward his "friends," who are down-to-earth guys who work at the outdoor shops in town and provide excellent fly-fishing guidance. Later, he describes the close relationship members have with club employees. "We are very close with the staff. With the waiters and pool girls. They are the closest of friends. We invite them to parties and get together with them." In providing evidence of these seemingly authentic social bonds, Colin aimed to show that the ultra-wealthy are just fellow humans, who like anyone else, find happiness not in material goods, but in the relationships they create with normal folks in the community.

BUSTING MYTH 3: THE ULTRA-WEALTHY DESERVE TO BE TAKEN ADVANTAGE OF

As our long lunch continued, the afternoon sun began to slump down toward the mountaintops, and our conversation turned toward another myth that was somewhat different from the others, and a bit subtler, but nevertheless is a source of chronic paranoia for some ultra-wealthy like Colin. The myth is that ultra-wealthy are deserving targets of exploitation. By "exploitation," I mean people thinking they can, and should, take a slice of people like Colin's wealth just because he has too much of it. For example, supposed friends duping them and treating them as a means to an end; the government taxing them at higher rates than those who have less; or contractors unfairly charging them more for the same work. By "deserving" exploitation, Colin points out that just because they are wealthy, people think that it is more ethically permissible to take advantage of the wealthy than to take advantage of a middle- or low-income group. He disagrees. This is just another way, according to people like Colin, where having immense wealth somehow means that they are not viewed as "normal" human beings, further justifying this myth that they can and *should* be exploited.

This chronic paranoia can condition the ultra-wealthy to feel isolated and distrustful of the people and communities around them. I found that this myth plays out at two different levels: (1) paranoia about national politics, with the Western United States becoming a refuge from the impending threat of socialism; and (2) paranoia about local folks targeting them, exacerbating a persecution complex and resulting in the downplaying of social markers that would identify them with wealth.

With regard to the first, Colin talked at length about the current assault on the rich within national politics, propelled by a secret, but growing, movement toward socialism.[12] High-tax environments like Connecticut, California, New York, and others are, for Colin, essentially "communism," subscribing to the myth that the wealthy deserve to be exploited. Predicting a dire future, and speaking to me prior to the unexpected results of the 2016 presidential election, Colin says, "I tell my kids that after Obama and the inevitable [socialist] revolution where all hell breaks loose—with Texas and others seceding—head for Montana!" Talking with Colin, I can tell that his decision to buy a place up here is not simply about escaping from high-tax environments, but it's also about being in what he perceives to be a more friendly "Wild West" *cultural* environment where he feels more insulated from exploitation by the federal government. "We needed a place where we could live among like-minded people. . . . Besides marrying my wife, it's the best thing I ever did."

At the local level, this paranoia manifests itself in different ways, and Colin describes how people like him defend themselves against exploitation from locals looking to make a quick buck. First, some members choose to disguise social markers that would identify them with wealth, or the club in particular. For example, whenever they drive five miles into the nearby town, many club members make sure to remove the large membership placard they are required to keep in their windshield while inside the gates. For most members I talked with, removing the placard allowed them to avoid the perceived stigma of having wealth, and to improve their chances of blending in as the "normal" people that they believe they are, and believe they ought to be perceived and treated as. One club member told the story of when he saw a newly minted member wearing his Yellowstone Club ball cap in the local grocery store, and promptly warned him to remove it if he wanted to be treated as a normal "local," rather than to be taken as a sucker, or a potential target for higher prices, fraudulent friends, and other forms of ultra-wealth exploitation.

Local small business owners tell of more formal ways that this paranoia manifests itself, noting that some club members have forced them to sign nondisclosure agreements even for very small and noninvasive home repair projects. Certainly, this sense of paranoia described by Colin and others can lead to a circling of the wagons among ultra-wealthy people, creating distrust and cementing group-boundaries, isolating them from the local community, and casting doubt among locals that they are indeed the "normal" people they strive to be.

Breaching Affluent Privacy

SECURE WILDERNESS

Immense wealth can provide unending material goods, but it doesn't always guarantee the luxury of privacy. From the beginning, the promise of total privacy has been a central selling point for the club, protected by an almost mythic, military-grade security team, which was led early on by a twenty-eight-year veteran of the U.S. Secret Service and former special agent to President Gerald Ford. Over the years, and with the early marketing savvy of Blixseth, the legend of this security outfit grew to include stories about whole teams of undercover secret service agents guarding the property, and routine patrol of property borders via helicopter. Part marketing and part reality, the club continues to sell the privilege of complete privacy—reassurance that many members find to be priceless.

What we generally think of as "privacy"—especially here in the case of the Yellowstone Club—is a set of *physical* boundaries marking off the ultra-wealthy from the rest of society. Physical boundaries in this case are clear: Those who can drive onto the gated land, and those who cannot. Those who can ski private powder, and those who cannot. Those who can meet and network with fellow millionaires and billionaires, and those who cannot. These physical boundaries are straightforward enough, and while important, they offer only limited (and predictable) insight into the ways ultra-wealthy institutions create and manage privacy.

Instead of focusing on these obvious physical boundaries that tend to rub nonwealthy people the wrong way, I dig deeper to show one of the ways that privacy is infused all the way down to the core culture of this institution. My experience gaining access to the club and its members revealed sacred boundaries that were not so much physical as they were deeply moral. These immaterial elements of privacy deserve our attention because they often go unnoticed and unanalyzed, despite being at the root of the enterprise of ultra-wealthy institutions like the Yellowstone Club. The difficulty, especially for in-depth research, is that immaterial boundaries like these are less clear, so one discovers only after-the-fact that sacred privacy has been breached, as signaled by the response that it elicits.

CROSSING THE PRIVACY LINE

I knowingly and unknowingly crossed these sacred boundaries at different times. The club management and some members reacted with shock and outright paranoia, citing a breach of privacy, respect, trust, and protection from outside exposure that, in their view, the ultra-wealthy inherently *deserve*.

The club was initially very friendly and accommodating in my initial contact with them, in large part because they are used to granting access to magazines (for example, *Bloomberg, Fortune, Forbes, Experience Magazine, Robb Report*) that have written articles positively promoting the club. They took me as such, rather than a more neutral academic researcher, and thus, these early conversations eventually led to my gaining access inside the club. From their perspective, my initial visit was permitted because they viewed me as a positive marketing opportunity, and thus my visit was organized around different meetings and dinners to show me not just the grandeur of the club experience, but its seeming role as generous benefactor in nearby communities.

Because I unexpectedly gained this inside access, and was at times able to participate as if I were a club member, I decided to expand my project to include research on the membership base itself. To do this, I acquired a list of all members based on publicly available tax and real estate data. I drafted a letter to every member, inviting them to participate in my study, and sent a physical copy to their club address and to any other addresses in the public record. The letter, like the research, was nonintrusive and guaranteed complete anonymity and privacy. Here's an excerpt:

> In recent years, the Yellowstone Club has become an increasingly important member of the community, and as part of my book, I will be chatting with all sorts of folks, including Club members, non-members, employees, and others who live nearby. All conversations will be anonymous, and the aim of the book is to share the experiences of these different people, including yourself. . . . Most people really enjoy the conversations. . . . I am happy to fly to meet wherever is most convenient for you. . . . I've provided a few ways to connect. You can give me a call or send me an email.

After several months of productive interviewing with club members, word of the research traveled to club management. What followed were phone calls, e-mails, and veiled threats from some employees and members that quickly revealed an unquestioned presumption of total privacy. Their shock was *based on the assumption that I should obviously know better*. Motivating the shock was a sense of entitlement, or assumed privilege of privacy that was, for them, self-evident given the high-profile nature of their careers, the threats that come with being ultra-wealthy, and that given how hard they work and the publicity of their lives, they deserve to relax in peace and quiet with their families, especially considering how much they've paid to an institution that promises such.

The reaction was visceral and became an important piece of evidence in my search to understand how ultra-wealthy institutions work in practice. One high-level employee accused my research of taking money out of the pockets of local charities, suggesting that members would stop donating if my research examines the philanthropic behavior of the club and its members. Another high-level employee insisted that even though I used public records, it was still "morally wrong" and "disrespectful" to "compromise the privacy of Club members," and suggested that I had stolen a member list during my time at the club.[13] Another member of the management wrote in an e-mail that, "our Member's privacy is one of the touchstones of Yellowstone Club. I have received many emails since your letter went out from Members who are extremely upset and feel that the Club breached their privacy." The club management then sent a notice about my research to all club members, which was later passed on to me by a supportive club member I had interviewed. In the wake of this notice, I was contacted by members who rescinded their interview appointments because they were led to believe that I had stolen a member list.[14] Another member wrote me, accusing me of being in "violation of the rules and general spirit of the Club," and further, asserted that I was not legitimately a professor at Yale, but had only said I was in order to gain access.

Other members still participated, but some were closely guarded, or refused to address the club at all, opting to toe the company line, repeating the same simple message that the club is a fantastic member of the community. One member I interviewed initially refused to acknowledge that he was really a club member (despite him responding to my letter requesting participation in the research project on the club). I gently probed him about the public record of the property he owned inside the borders of the club, and he begrudgingly admitted, "I'm a little leery [long pause] well, I'm a member. But I'm a little leery to talk about the club, because the club contacted us and said obviously they don't endorse any of this [study] and that we all are inclined to protect our privacy at the club. And not wanting to be very forthcoming as to what the club is, other than to say it's a terrific place."

LASTING RIPPLE EFFECTS

My research politely probed the unquestioned right to total privacy, and the immediate reaction of shock and moral outrage revealed a great deal about the function of ultra-wealthy privacy in this particular case. From top to bottom, the entitlement of privacy was an institutional product that the club worked hard to create, commodify, manage, and instill in its members as an inherent right. Of course, there were several members I studied who did not believe and act in ways consistent with this culture of entitled privacy, but they were outliers.

It is important to remember that the effects of this institutional culture have far-reaching impacts *beyond the institution itself*. I've provided one example here, documenting how it impedes the enterprise of honest and impartial research—which, in this case is especially important, given that we know very little about an entity in the community that owns a huge chunk of the local ecosystem, and affects the economy to the tune of hundreds of millions of dollars. A culture of total privacy also affects how the institution views the environment and its resources, as noted earlier with the illegal killing of a bear, and the knee-jerk plea for privacy when government officials investigated the killing. And last, the insulated culture in which the ultra-wealthy live can distort their perceptions of the romanticized outside world and fosters a naïve and overly optimistic understanding of what people outside of the gates really think of them. As one member put it to me, "many of us members were *shocked* to learn that the perception of the club and members is that we're a bunch of snooty people who don't really care about anyone . . . we just didn't realize we had such a perception issue."

But more generally, the culture of ultra-wealth privacy in this case fundamentally alters the relationship between the American people and access to gilded lands like these. Members of the public, and working-class Westerners in particular, are locked out of large parcels of private land that they once routinely enjoyed with the trust and permission of the owners. These are the same working-class Westerners whose way of life was used as the cultural building blocks for the club, and its members and the club itself still romanticize, venerate, and emulate this culture because of its perceived authenticity and rugged connection to nature. Of course, many locals have benefited, in boom and bust fashion, from the club members building new mountain properties and purchasing local goods and services. But, as I will explain in later chapters, I found that the problem many low- and middle-class people have is not that a billionaire is allowed to purchase this private land, but that this pristine land is then locked up and overlaid with an elite culture of privacy so intense, so anxious, and so entitled, that it requires highly securitized protection *from* the public by former U.S. Secret Service agents. Unsurprisingly, this sows seeds of distrust and resentment within communities, who fear that they are losing control in this new gilded age, where huge swaths of cherished land are being purchased and closed off, for the occasional enjoyment of a select few.

PART II

Using Nature to Solve Economic Dilemmas

Environmental conservation is at root a battle over the control of resources. These resources have material and symbolic value. Popular stories about these conservation battles—as told in movies like *Erin Brockovich, Avatar,* or *WALL-E,* books such as *The Lorax,* and scores of academic accounts—tend to follow a common storyline that goes something like this: *an underdog, but passionate and publicly minded, conservation group stands up to powerful and greedy interests who seek to plunder the land for their own economic gain.*

I will tell a much different story here—one that rarely gets told because it flips this common narrative on its head, challenging the popular assumption that environmental conservation is an altruistic public good, and suggests that conservation itself can become a tool for economic gain, social prestige, and exclusion.[1] The ultra-wealthy are not the only characters in this new story, but in our age of environmental tumult and wealth concentration, they certainly play a leading role.

Their role emerges from key economic predicaments they face: how best to enjoy, share, protect, and multiply their wealth. Nature provides a unique outlet for resolving these dilemmas, both through philanthropy and conservation of nature but also through using money to access and experience the healing tonic of nature, whereby landscapes and wildlife are transformed into exclusive rural enclaves.

Throughout the next four chapters, I'll unpack this new story. Each chapter shows from a different angle, and reveals in great detail, the implicit and explicit ways that nature is put to use by the ultra-wealthy in an attempt to address these economic dilemmas.

Chapter 3 presents a concept that I coin Compensation Conservation to understand the counterintuitive puzzle: Can conservation of nature actually make ultra-wealthy people even wealthier? Might this benevolent activity actually be a mechanism intensifying wealth inequality? In chapter 4, I lay out what I call Connoisseur Conservation as a helpful framework for summarizing affluent personal relationships to nature, showing how this unique connoisseur approach guides therapeutic outdoor experiences, and leads to unquestioned assumptions about the virtues of conservation.

Chapters 5 and 6 examine the philanthropic worlds of the ultra-wealthy, focusing on the social structure and activity of affluent philanthropy in Teton County. Using data spanning two decades' time with more than 100,000 social links—such as nonprofit board memberships—paired with information on individual philanthropic giving, I examine whether environmental philanthropy is as straightforward as most typically assume. In other words, where does all the money and social influence flow in a place as wealthy as Teton County?

And perhaps most importantly, in chapter 6 I bring it all together to reveal the deeper reasons why environmental conservation can become so meaningful and so useful for the ultra-wealthy, focused on three primary reasons: conservation as a tool to recapture something they've lost on their morally treacherous march toward economic triumph; conservation as a vehicle for gaining social prestige by modeling themselves after towering ultra-wealthy conservation saints like John D. Rockefeller Jr.; and last, how noncontroversial environmentalism can become the du jour leisure activity providing social integration into elite circles, with the implicit assumption that such conservation activities are also wholly altruistic, publicly spirited, and ecologically progressive.

Taken together, the dynamics uncovered in these four chapters create and reinforce the veiled presence of what I call an Environmental Veneer—by which I mean *the simplistic popular assumption that environmental conservation is assumed to be, in a vague sense, an altruistic public good, rather than a vehicle for protecting wealth, achieving social status and integration, expressing group identity, sustaining societal advantages, and generally reinforcing many of the social mechanisms that give rise to environmental problems in the first place.*

3

Compensation Conservation

Far flung from the spectacular granite canyons of the Tetons, my research took me two thousand miles eastward, to the human-made canyons of Madison and Fifth Avenues in New York City. Bob James, a prominent CEO in the entertainment industry had made arrangements for us to have dinner at a high-end restaurant on Fifth Avenue, in glittering midtown Manhattan amid the world's top designers, finest hotels, and titans of business.

I sat waiting for Bob, thumbing through my lengthy interview guide on the soft white tablecloth, doing my best to look the part in a dining room full of regulars unfazed by the $75 entrées peppering the menu. Unlike some of my other research subjects, I knew very little about Bob outside his role as a CEO, and had not met or spoken to him. All communication was channeled through his administrative assistants. Bob arrived sporting a bold pin-striped suit accessorized with shimmering cufflinks emblazoned with his initials. He was just under six feet tall, white, and heavy-set. Cheerfully, he greeted me with a crushing handshake fit for a CEO.

For nearly two hours, Bob talked in great depth about his relationship to the natural environment. With my constant probing along the way, we discussed how his relationship to nature is shaped by his immense wealth and elite social status, and the increasing value of nature for him and his family.

Seeking a slower pace of life, where the sky is darker and stars brighter, Bob and his wife built a house out West. Nine bedrooms, nine bathrooms, and 6,000 square feet later, they now had a place to call home. Their three kids absolutely love it, he says. One "cherry on top," as Bob put it, is that their house has appreciated significantly in recent years, climbing from just a few million dollars when it was built, to nearly $10 million today. Bob explains that this steep increase is due in large part to the growing scarcity of developable land in the area, with many landowners opting to put their property under protected conservation easement rather than selling to developers who would build new housing. "Economics 101," he says: as housing supply is constrained, prices goes up.

Bob doesn't consider himself a bona fide "tree-hugger," in his words, but he does believe that protecting the environment is generally the right thing to do, citing the preserved easements adjacent to his property as one effective method. It's a "win-win," says Bob, given the millions of dollars in easement related tax deductions he and others in the area have received. "No growth is good. I'll be the first one on the phone to fight that." Because, humans have a "great responsibility to protect the *experience* of the natural world . . . let's not screw this place up."

Over the years living in beautiful Wyoming, Bob explains that he's cultivated his taste for nature, developing an appreciation for its sophistication and therapeutic remedy. He is proud to say that this area of Wyoming is "the finest and purest that nature has to offer." But that does *not* mean it should be completely closed off by environmentalists or the government, because that would prohibit it from being *enjoyed*. He asks, rhetorically, how does one become a connoisseur of the finest wine or the finest yachts if we don't *use* them? Or, put differently, and more philosophically, he riddles, "If there is a beautiful place, and no one has ever seen it, then is it still a beautiful place? No. If no one is allowed to see it, then the beauty doesn't exist."

But I probe, asking, how are we able to know when we cross the line from enjoyment to harmful overuse? Easy, he says: we rely on science to keep things in what he calls "healthy balance." Not just ecological science, but also the science of laissez-faire economics. And, in his view, the ultra-wealthy have an important and unique role to play in this process, from the top-down. Bob explains that the flood of ultra-wealthy folks to these beautiful areas in the past few decades has created thousands of local jobs. And, after arriving, these wealthy migrants—according to Bob—then wield their financial and political influence for good, protecting the area through philanthropy and supporting anti-development conservation. Everybody wins with this powerful combination of wealth and conservation, including nature. "It is important that a bunch of very powerful people get to experience the area so that it will ensure the area remains environmentally healthy and happy."

———

Conservation has become a lucrative mechanism profiting people like Bob James and his ultra-wealthy peers. While I do not doubt Bob's genuine love for nature, folks like him have put nature to use—both knowingly and unknowingly—to accrue disproportionate economic benefits *under the banner of environmental protection*. These economic impacts can be divided into three separate, but related, processes that are introduced in this chapter: (1) preservation of wealth, (2) the production of new wealth, and (3) intensifying wealth inequality.

Even in light of the following data, the findings in this chapter might appear overly cynical to some. Yet, I argue that they appear as such to many people because of the blinding influence of a larger "Environmental Veneer" that currently dominates much popular thinking about conservation. I use "veneer" here to describe how the idea and practice of conservation has been overlaid with the assumption that environmental protection is always an altruistic activity rather than a vehicle for protecting wealth, sustaining societal advantages, and reinforcing many of the environmental problems our economic and political systems have created.[1]

Three important clarifications are in order. First, remember from the introduction of this book that my approach here differs significantly from most social scientific accounts because it focuses on the top rather than the bottom. On those who use nature to benefit from our current economic and politics systems, rather than those who lose out.[2] On über-rich institutions like the Yellowstone Club and others that construct and sell these benefits. In doing so, the goal is not to place blame on one individual or another, to carelessly point fingers at the successful, to dehumanize, or to unfairly accuse people like Bob James for simplistic money-grubbing via conservation. Instead, it is to consider the socioeconomic advantages that conservation might knowingly and unknowingly afford the ultra-wealthy, and to begin to understand how it works, and why it matters.

Second, it is important to clarify what this chapter is *not*. This chapter is not a comprehensive quantitative analysis, but is meant to simply introduce counterintuitive pathways—and highlight correlational evidence—through which environmental conservation can be lucrative for the wealthy. My reliance on qualitative and descriptive quantitative evidence is sufficient for my purposes in this project and establishes a general framework for much-needed future study on these economic issues.

Third, it is also important to remember that despite what is shown here, there are immense public benefits and intrinsic values from environmental conservation, such as access to public lands, protecting clean water, preserving biodiversity, safeguarding wildlife, just to name a few. Public land conservation also provides essential economic benefits for many rural communities, because rural areas with more conserved public lands perform better on a wide range of economic indicators such as per capita income and job growth.[3] But it is overly simplistic to think that these dynamics work the same in all areas, or that the economic and environmental rewards of conservation will be the same for different social groups. Thus, in any community, the key question is: who is conservation really for?

Preserving Wealth

"Financial advisors are a huge influence when it comes to new land conservation in Teton County," remarks Carolyn Jones, a three-decade employee of various environmental organizations and federal agencies in the community. "Really?" I ask, puzzled. She explains, "Most people with money usually aren't aware that investing in conservation can be an effective financial strategy, and all realtors and financial planners are keen to point this out to their clients." Curious as to exactly how this works, I probe for an example. She continues, "Well, for example, a lot of times it's somebody who's made a killing in the stock market, and now needs to offset their income with a huge tax deduction. Conservation easements are one popular way to make this happen. In some cases, we're talking about millions of dollars in deductions from federal income taxes."

Property owners receive such compensation—usually as a charitable deduction to their adjusted gross income for up to fifteen years or a cash payment from a land trust based on the appraised value of the land—in exchange for agreeing to put their land under easement, meaning that it is closed from any further developments, such as new housing or commercial construction. In some cases, this is viewed as a win-win, where land is conserved for its environmental values, but in other cases, experienced people like Carolyn Jones point out that it is a straightforward way for the wealthy to lock away their land and preserve their wealth through millions of dollars in tax deductions.

Certainly, not all easements are created equal, and deciphering landowners' hidden motivations might seem trite when there are significant environmental and public benefits to be gained. But according to Dave Unrein, who has seen it all as a longtime land trust expert, state employee, and resident, the "wealthy people out here tend to do land conservation easements as a financial tactic, rather than out of necessity or because of their genuine commitment to conservation values." By "necessity," Dave is referring to cases where putting land under an easement becomes the only way for middle- and lower-income families to stay afloat, or keep their familial land despite increasingly astronomic land values and property taxes in

Teton County. He suggests that this is a good-spirited use of easements by middle- and lower-income folks, in comparison to many ultra-wealthy who are taking advantage of conservation to "get even richer."

Of course, many ultra-wealthy people with whom I spent time, such as Bob James, often espoused uncritical views of conservation. They overlay a veneer of altruism—assuming that conservation is always and everywhere a positive activity—despite the fact that, for many of them, they and their financial advisors view it primarily as an effective means by which their immense wealth can be preserved. But of course, there is certainly nothing illegal about capitalizing on these million-dollar tax deductions. And there is considerable encouragement from local organizations. For example, the Jackson Hole Land Trust does its best to sell these benefits to landowners, specifically noting that land conservation is an effective financial strategy for wealth preservation. In its recruitment materials, it makes clear that

> a conservation easement donor can enjoy significant income and estate tax savings, which can help offset the acquisition costs of a new property. . . . Conservation easement donations can have four potential tax advantages: (a) the value of the easement may be considered a charitable gift and be deductible from your federal income tax, (b) the easement may reduce estate tax, (c) the easement may reduce your property tax, and (d) some expenses related to a conservation easement donation may be deductible.[4]

From a bird's-eye view, just how popular have these conservation easements become, and what effect have they had on the remaining supply (and demand) of developable land? The Jackson Hole Land Trust alone has conserved 55,000 acres in the region, and 25,000 in tiny Jackson Hole alone. This is a staggering amount in a county that was already made up of 97 percent federally protected land. Nearly all of the remaining 3 percent of private land is now developed or under easement. The small slice in the middle of both maps shown in figures 3.1 and 3.2 are the available private land in Jackson Hole

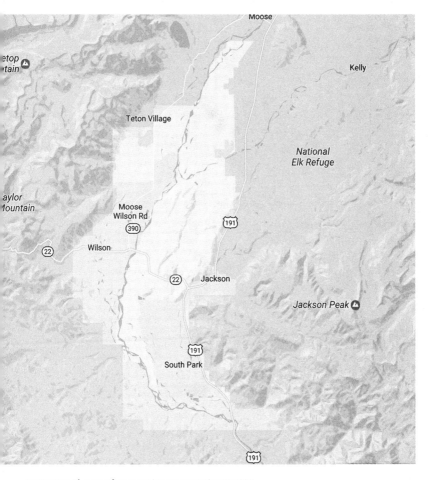

FIGURE 3.1. Absence of conservation easements in year 1980.

at two different time points. Clearly, when comparing the map from 1980 to the map in 2016, one sees a dramatic growth of newly minted conservation easements (shaded in black). These figures do not include other uses of private land over this time period (for example, new home construction), making the extensive coverage of land easements over this timespan all that more extraordinary, showing how more and more landowners—many of them very wealthy—took part in this environmental and financial strategy.

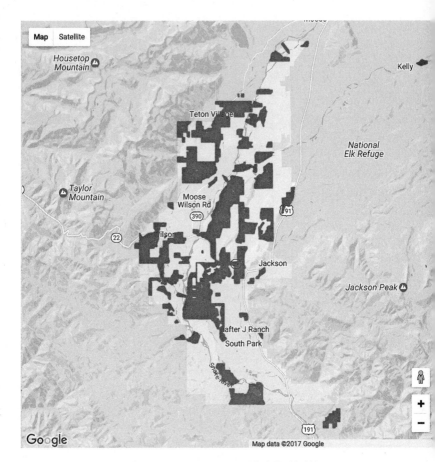

FIGURE 3.2. Growth of new conservation easements (shaded in black) by year 2016.

Conservation easements can become an instrument for what social scientists call "cumulative advantage" or the "Matthew Effect."[5] In layperson's terms, this phenomenon is illustrated with colloquial aphorisms such as "The rich get richer" or "It takes money to make money." In other words, aside from the select few who have inherited family land, there is a built-in cumulative advantage to the practice of conservation easements in Teton County—meaning that people who reap the million-dollar tax deductions are those who had the economic capital to purchase the land in the first place.

Again, this does not negate the ecological values of these actions, or condemn them as inherently greedy, which might regrettably discourage future easements—but it does reveal one important way that conservation itself becomes a tool for the wealthy to preserve their wealth.

Let's consider how people actually talk about these issues in real life. I have hundreds of quotes that I could include here, but in an effort to be concise, I present only a handful of the most representative ones that accurately depict these dynamics. These quotes are from separate ultra-wealthy respondents, either from an interview or participant observation at their homes, clubs, organizations, events, or around town, and were part of larger discussions we had about land conservation.

A lawyer, originally from northern California, but now a longtime permanent resident of Teton County, summarizes the economic incentives quite clearly, acknowledging that "There's a group that wants to put up affordable housing somewhere," but dismissively recounts, "But nobody wants it in their area, you know. People are afraid it'll lower the property values."

Similarly, a young financier from New England draws the connection quite clearly between conservation, philanthropy, and economic incentives, responding to my general question about whether he'd like to get more involved in philanthropic issues. He admits that conservation can be self-interested, but reassures me that he has the best of intentions. "Part and parcel to [philanthropy] would be land conservation, which preserves some of the habitat. If you want to be self-interested, it's also good from a property owner point of view, but I wouldn't do it for that. I would do it just for the land benefits and the community benefits."

Likewise, a London banker I interviewed reflected, pensively, "I guess that it's an easy answer for me from a personal, from a selfish individual point of view, to limit development. But I think there's also, you know, when looking at the whole community, I think there's also an argument for limiting development too in terms of, at some point, it kind of just brings down the whole thing. Like, from a selfish point of view."

Most people were hesitant to discuss their economic motives for conservation. They danced around the topic, using less overt language about preserving natural uniqueness, community character, and the like, and often invoked the Land Trust as the most effective means toward this end—an organization that provided the best return on philanthropic investment. An über-affluent elderly man in his eighties put it succinctly, "Well, we're great supporters of the Land Trust . . . to preserve nature and what we have, and not let development overgrow the community as it has in many other places."

A wealthy Silicon Valley transplant places some of the blame on self-absorbed people from the East Coast who have a distaste for mobile home parks, "Well, it's because you come from back East, and you want it to be the way it was the first day you came . . . you don't want it to be changed. At the same time, I spent this kind of money. . . . I don't want the zoning to be so that my next-door neighbor is in a house trailer."

Ironically, Teton County has a way of transforming even the most growth-oriented businessperson, illustrated by a commercial banker I interviewed. "Actually, I would hit the pause button on growth. You know, I was a commercial banker for years, so I believed in expansion and growth and development and all of that. But Teton County is so unique. . . . We've come to really enjoy the wildlife. We have deer, elk, and moose. We've had some bears come through, and we love living where this wildlife is such a critical part. . . . And so you know, I think maybe a pause in growth would be good."

As another example, a committed free-market advocate from San Francisco believes that some places in the United States should be off limits from this type of free-market thinking. For this reason, he has become involved in local environmental conservation, especially through the Jackson Hole Land Trust. He explains, "I'm already probably showing my cards with my involvement in the Land Trust and my environmental views. I believe that there ought to be places where . . . somebody advocates for no development or no growth. . . . You know I have a career that is very much free markets and allocating capital where it is best employed, you know that's deeply embedded in the way I think but as I said earlier there has to be overrides, there has to be limits placed on that otherwise we will chew up every available square foot of this country and exploit it."

Another centimillionaire I interviewed, who has homes all over the world, has spent much more time in Teton County in recent years, becoming quite involved in local nonprofits, both with the Land Trust and with organizations specifically focused on affordable housing. "I've been on many boards of organizations in the community. The Land Trust walks on water and the housing authority was despised, because you were bringing people in [to town]. People would contribute to [the Land Trust] and support it, and you know, make a big, *big* deal out of it." Despite his criticism of the Land Trust and the wealthy who donate to it as a means for social prestige or to restrict housing, even he seems to be having a change of heart, admitting that, "You know, there's a segment of the community that really doesn't want growth. Uh, and I'm personally starting to kind of join that segment."

Multiplying Wealth

As our Fifth Avenue dinner began to wind down, Bob opened up and joked, wisecracking, "What's the definition of an environmentalist? [pause] The guy who bought his place last year!" I chuckled, but knew that the joke held some truth, even for Bob, who seemed to be admitting that much. The subtle, but powerful, candor contained in this joke lays bare the ways environmental conservation can—directly and indirectly—become a tool not only for preserving wealth but also for multiplying it.

But what exactly is the connection between environmental conservation and the production of wealth? Just because Bob's home equity skyrocketed several million dollars in such a short time doesn't have anything to do with environmental conservation, does it? All things being equal, there are two simple economic factors to consider in this case. The first basic element of value is demand, meaning that as more people desire property, the value steepens. The second is scarcity, meaning as fewer and fewer properties become available, the more valuable properties become.

Of course, by its very definition, one main goal of environmental conservation is to *limit* development that might threaten the well-being of land, water, and wildlife. This is especially true in Teton County, which is situated in one of the last large, intact ecosystems in the world, containing Grand Teton and Yellowstone National Parks, and home to some of the most abundant and historically native wildlife in the world. Conservation increases demand for housing by improving the natural amenities and resources that make this area desirable in the first place. The staggering population growth in this cold, remote corner of the West is no coincidence. The health of the ecosystem, abundance of wildlife, and ubiquity of protected land are all a product of vigorous and ongoing conservation efforts.

More importantly, myriad conservation groups in the area—an area that is among the highest concentrations of nonprofits in the United States—continue to work tirelessly on anti-development efforts. New residents to the area, like Bob, often join in on these efforts, which have a direct effect on increasing scarcity. The dramatic growth of the aforementioned conservation easements is one important medium, as are other actions related to constraining commercial development, and working through legislative channels to secure new public lands with tighter protections. No doubt, these conservation activities are critical to the future health of the ecosystem, but less appreciated is the leading role they play in skyrocketing home values in the community, creating economic windfalls for people like Bob, who is among the select few Americans who have the economic capital to make such a profitable investment.

Historical data on increasing housing scarcity, as well as soaring real estate prices, provide evidence to confirm this story. U.S. Census data and a housing report published by Teton County show that scarcity has dramatically accelerated in recent years.[6] New housing units grew rapidly with each passing year, but in recent years they have come to a screeching halt (for example, only 3.2 percent since 2010, compared to 25 percent just a few decades ago). And, as

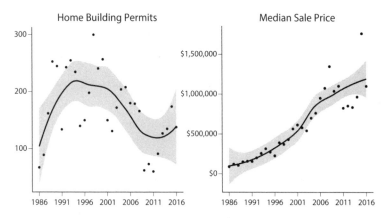

FIGURE 3.3. Comparison from 1986 to 2016 of the rise and fall of building permits for single-family homes (left) with the skyrocketing median home sales price (right). *Source:* U.S. Bureau of the Census, "Building Permit Estimates—U.S., State, and Metropolitan Areas."

housing demand and scarcity increased, mean and median list prices for homes soared to more than $2 million.

These dynamics are plainly illustrated in figure 3.3, charting these two important, and related, phenomenon: On the left showing the rise, and more importantly, *the precipitous fall* of building permits for single-family homes, meaning that home supply is being severely constrained. And, linked to this, in the figure on the right, the skyrocketing median home sale prices over the same time period.

Local real estate broker Tayson Rockefeller concurs, with his own on-the-ground experiences of these macro-level changes shown in the chart in figure 3.3, telling *Forbes* magazine that "The truth is, inventory is at historic lows and that's driving prices up. . . . That's good for sellers but bad for home buyers because the low inventory is making it very hard for even wealthy buyers to find available property."[7] Basic supply and demand. In just the last few years, these pressures are reaching a fever pitch, and will continue to accelerate so long as the conservation values of anti-development are sustained, and likely even ratcheted up. This means that those who own or can afford a scarce home in the area will see staggering annual gains, such as were witnessed between 2014 and 2015, where *home values increased a stunning 31.2 percent* in just 12 short months.

Now, let's look at how the ultra-wealthy actually talk about the relationship between conservation and wealth production, beginning with a retired CEO, who during the course of a breakfast in downtown Jackson, was very open about his economic motives, and criticized wealthy liberal people who tried to hide behind altruism or conservation. Snidely, he comments, "I think that there are a whole bunch of people that feel like Jackson Hole ought to remain the way it always was. And a lot of those people are the guys that bought last year, and of course, want their property value to go up."

In another interview, one oil and gas executive, who tended to espouse a more libertarian perspective, spoke in similarly naked terms, noting how he chooses to support conservation groups that serve his "selfish" ends. "So there's the conservation groups, and we've spent time getting to know those guys a bit more given that it's kind of right there in our back yard, sort of next door; and so they're doing different types of preservation projects. . . . I mean selfishly you gain from supporting some great organizations like that, so, that's been the thing that we've spent the most time with."

A wealthy doctor from Tennessee explains that even though the wealthy benefit economically from conservation and anti-development, it is ultimately good for the community, preventing it from being overrun by low-income people taking advantage of the system. "We don't want to get too developed. You do that, you got a lot of people, you make it too attractive, people are going to go, 'Hey, we get cheap housing here. It's subsidized. Let's come down here and live down here. We can work a little bit, all you have to do is show you make less than $40,000 a year and we're good.'"

Still another interviewee, this time from Philadelphia, who identifies as more liberal, sarcastically remarked, "So [Teton County] is where we built. And then of course, you know, we don't want anybody else to build there. We should be the very last people to arrive in this place! [chuckles]"

Others I interviewed wrestled with moral dilemma of skyrocketing property values, yet would nevertheless settle on supporting the current policies. As a lawyer from California explained it to me, it is "Super complicated, really complex. I have conflicting feelings about it. One of my feelings is that I would like Jackson to stop growing, period. I think that any further population growth is going to demand . . . greater infrastructure. . . . Every incremental bit of human development is a zero-sum game. It takes away from that side, so that's what Jackson is for me and my family. That's what Wyoming is for me and my family, and I very strongly believe that it should stop."

He realizes though, that stopping human development will largely benefit *his* pocketbook and quality of life, while making it more difficult on others in the community. Nevertheless, he reflects, "So probably while this dilemma will go unresolved in my mind forever, I would tend to err on the side of preserving Jackson at the risk of it just pushing up the cost of being there. . . . As much as I hate that outcome too. I would probably choose that over having it be a giant strip mall and no fishing, no hunting, and yea."

Intensifying Wealth Inequality

"Income inequality" has become a hot-button issue of late, taking on emotion and politicization extending far beyond the cold crunching-of-numbers about the gap between the rich and poor.[8] The swirling tornado of emotions impacting the issue, as evident in ongoing campaign rhetoric or previous movements like Occupy Wall Street, made it more difficult to candidly raise the matter in my discussions with the ultra-wealthy.

With that said, what is the relationship between conservation and the intensification of inequality? First, we must understand the taken-for-granted macroeconomic theory that I found operating beneath the surface. My dinner partner Bob sums it up well with an aphorism and a story. The aphorism is a popular one: "A rising tide lifts all boats." In story form, Bob tells about his friend who recently purchased a 200-foot yacht. With a price tag of $42 million, Bob notes that a cynic might view this purchase to be a selfish act that benefits only the privileged few who get to enjoy such luxurious ocean escapes. But, he argues, somewhat forcefully with an emotional tone to his voice, that these critics fail to realize just how many jobs this creates. "It provides a job for an entire year for a lot of different people."

In the same way, he says that spending money for the purpose of enjoying nature—an activity that was often lumped in with conservation itself—provides a hell of a lot of jobs in the community: as the logic goes, for example, building a 7,000-square-foot house with local construction workers, hiring housekeepers, dining at expensive restaurants, employing exclusive fishing guides, and so on, all have widespread economic benefits to the general economy, especially to middle- and lower-income groups. This does not even begin to include the philanthropic giving to local conservation groups.

But data reveal that this economic thinking is misguided, *especially in places where ultra-wealth and inequality collide with pervasive land conservation*. What this means is that the "rising tide lifts all boats" approach can have the effect of intensifying economic differences. More specifically, and following the same logic as earlier with the protection and production of wealth, I consider the effect of land conservation on which job sectors are growing or declining (that is, available jobs and total income), and as a result, the staggering decline of reasonably priced housing.

First, conservation has directly and indirectly intensified wealth inequality by making the area uniquely attractive to the ultra-wealthy, creating intense housing demand *and* land scarcity that has dramatically reshaped who lives in the community, and how people make their money. As documented in chapter 1, data from the U.S. Census and Bureau of Economic Analysis overwhelming show that this county has become the wealthiest in the United States because of investment income (for example, remember that in 2015, nearly 80 percent of personal income in Teton County came from investments). As more and more ultra-wealthy people move to the area for the natural amenities (for example, protected lands, abundant wildlife), it dramatically restructured the socioeconomic hierarchy—becoming both a cause, and a consequence, of conservation values. Conservation became a form of elite cultural currency, and conservation organizations benefited from the financial flow-down,[9] all while it became harder for middle- and lower-income people to survive there.

As evidence, local socioeconomic expert Jonathan Schechter sums it up well, noting that "In just four years, Teton County Wyoming saw a 10 percent drop in its population of people making under $50,000, and a 5 percent increase in those making over $200,000."[10]

Meanwhile, at the bottom, low-paying tourism jobs are booming, creating a large low-income immigrant population filling these jobs needed to accommodate the growing ultra-wealthy population who require services to enjoy nature. While more and more money from investments flowed into the community that became the richest in the nation, the average earnings per job remained stagnant: In 1970, the average earnings per job was $39,943, and by 2015 this number had inched up to $41,052—increasing only $1,109 over the course of 45 years.

Because of the community's commitment to conservation values, the only thing as scarce as a middle- to upper-income job is the dearth of available land for housing. This scarcity has led to what is now the key crisis posed by wealth inequality, which will be explored in part 4 of this book. Namely, to afford a median-priced home in the community now requires a down payment of $225,000 and no less than $125,000 in annual income. For half of the community, this is a drop in the bucket of their annual investment dividends, but for the other half, it remains far out of reach, meaning that they have to live at a distance requiring long commutes, often over the treacherous Teton mountain pass.

Meanwhile, the middle class is largely gone, and left over is a socioeconomic situation that our ultra-wealthy friend Jim Roselli from chapter 1 called a "barbell" community of two contrasting, but linked, groups: either ultra-wealthy people at the top with abundant time and money to enjoy (and further conserve) the natural resources that have hitherto been preserved, and their low-income counterparts making nearly the same wages/salaries they made in 1970 despite home values jumping 15–25 percent every year. In other words, intensified wealth inequality.

———

Indeed, while this link between land conservation and wealth accumulation is deeply important and interesting, there remain unanswered questions that go beyond simple dollars and cents. We have not yet gotten to the root of ultra-wealthy conservation values, in terms of both how they are *understood* by the ultra-wealthy themselves and how they are *enacted* in ways that perpetuate the mechanisms for economic gain we have witnessed in this chapter. To do so involves a cultural and emotional, rather than purely economic, analysis of how the ultra-wealthy use nature. In other words, there is so much more to the story.

4

Connoisseur Conservation

The lavish Fifth Avenue dinner with Bob James—the CEO we met last chapter—has ended, and he and I small talk before going our separate ways into midtown Manhattan. I get the sense that Bob feels a bit self-conscious about certain elements of our long discussion, especially concerning the ways that protecting nature can financially benefit wealthy people and wealthy institutions. He takes a moment to reiterate to me his genuine love for the natural environment, and for the West in particular. Again noting that he wouldn't necessarily consider himself a "tree-hugger," he expresses deep appreciation for the therapeutic value of nature, an indispensable tonic for his busy and stressful life as a prominent CEO.

While the scope of his environmental concern is quite narrow, and his acceptance and knowledge of myriad global environmental problems is questionable at best, I sense that he does feel a sincere responsibility to protect the health of the lands and wildlife in Teton County. Bob also sees people like himself, who wield significant wealth and power, as having a unique role to play through local environmental philanthropy and trickle-down spending in order to keep the natural resources, in his words, "healthy and happy."

Digging deeply into the mind and lives of people like Bob reveals a larger cultural worldview that shapes ultra-wealthy relationships to the natural environment. In chapter 3, I showed how protection of nature can be a lucrative economic endeavor for the rich, despite the Environmental Veneer that perpetuates the taken-for-granted popular notion that conservation is an altruistic good rather than a vehicle for cumulative advantage.

But to stop there—leaving only a story of economic gain—would be to miss out on a big part of the story concerning the deeper motivations and cultural worldview of the ultra-wealthy. Economic reasoning only goes so far, and centuries of philosophy and social science have shown[1] that all of us make decisions based on a complex mixture of factors that extend far beyond simple dollars and cents (for example, cultural, moral, spiritual).

There are a host of noneconomic reasons *why* the rich are drawn to nature and conservation, even if those reasons seem to be overshadowed by what appears to be pure economic self-interest. But economic self-interest is the easy part. For most social researchers, isolating other noneconomic motives presents the real challenge.

So we need a deeper understanding of ultra-wealthy *motives* that shape how and why this group relates to the natural environment. What cultural resources do they draw upon to make decisions related to enjoying or protecting nature? These are complex issues, and while it is impossible to get inside the heads of the ultra-wealthy, I uncovered illuminating evidence when my interviews and observations with the ultra-wealthy were focused on questions such as: How do they think about and justify their actions using cultural, scientific, emotional, or spiritual values? When it comes to protecting and enjoying nature, where do they draw the line between altruism and selfishness? Between modesty and opulence? Between moral and immoral?

More specifically, how does conservation—or even more broadly, just the enjoyment of nature—provide a rationale for decisions that otherwise might be viewed as greedy or overindulgent?

———

I found that nature provides a special dispensation for purchases and practices that may otherwise be viewed as morally suspect, opulent, or greedy. Nature is priceless, but priceless experiences can be quite expensive. In communing with nature we experience something much deeper, honest, and True than our everyday experiences in society that are seen as inauthentic, morally hazardous, or just the product of selfish economic exchange. Thus, for the rich, the amount of money spent is a secondary concern—both practically and morally—not just because they have plenty to spend, but because the purity of this realm that we call "nature" offers *invaluable* joy, goodness, and groundedness to protect against the crass materialism rampant in a world of social corruption and elite competition. The many flawed human elements guiding our lives and society melt away in the face of the cosmic, the mountainous, the spiritual, the ecological.

I was fascinated by the power of this nature/society dualism for shaping the worldview of the rich, given their high-stress and sometimes morally hazardous professional histories. As my study unfolded, this dualism became more and more foundational for understanding how they relate to and use nature. For example, is it morally permissible to build an 8,000-square-foot house *if the home is meant for reconnecting with nature, or if you've set aside part of your property as an easement for wildlife migration?* Or, is ordering a $75 steak less ostentatious, *so long as it comes from an ecologically progressive rancher?* Are people like Bob James, who work long hours in extremely high-stress professions, *perhaps more deserving than others of the therapeutic benefits that nature can provide?*

All of these questions concern the ways that the nature is used to justify the choices people make, often reframing these choices in a positive moral light. This is made possible by a veneer of nature that casts nature-related activities (including conservation) in a positive light, being altruistic rather than greedy, as clinically medicinal rather than self-indulgent, and as ecologically healthful rather than scientifically ignorant.

And the irony, especially for those respondents who made their money in industries that are ecologically destructive, is that conserving nature in Teton County is a drop in the bucket relative to their global environmental impacts as members of an economic and political system that has left a trail of natural destruction. While I focus my analysis here on the local social and environmental challenges, it is important to distinguish between their local love of nature here in Teton County, and their role as leaders in economic and political systems that have incurred much global environmental harm.[2] But this ironic incongruence is precisely the point, perhaps summed up best by the story in chapter 2 about the Yellowstone Club member who, as his fellow club member put it, "is such an asshole outside of the club, but when he comes here, he's the nicest guy."

———

Through all of this, I discovered a worldview I call "Connoisseur Conservation" to define how the rich relate to and use nature. More specifically, this worldview is made up of three interconnected aspects: (1) Feel Good Altruism, meaning the vague feeling that purifying and protecting nature is a selfless act of virtue, and that land conservation is a primary way this happens; (2) Conservation Therapy, meaning that conservation preserves nature for its medicinal therapeutic benefits for stressed out hard-working professionals, where nature is akin to other highbrow experiences enjoyed by the ultra-wealthy; and (3) Selective Science, meaning that what is best for nature is based on a vague "everything in balance" approach to environmental science that aims to preserve a local Garden of Eden, yet tends to ignore the rest of environmental science about the realities and systemic causes of global environmental problems.

By unpacking these three interrelated aspects, the cohesive picture of this underlying worldview begins to emerge, revealing how it works, and why it actually matters. It is helpful to note that no ultra-wealthy people actually call themselves "Connoisseur Conservationists," nor would they necessarily be able to articulate the presence of the Environmental Veneer that coats local ideas about nature with a layer of uncritical positive assumptions. These are my terms, and are meant to accurately summarize reality, based on evidence from hundreds of hours of interviewing and observations, where myriad beliefs were espoused, opinions expressed, and ideas explored until this discernible whole began to take shape. Of course, there are nuances, and not every ultra-wealthy individual will fit neatly into these broad categories, but nevertheless they represent the best social-scientific account summarizing how the rich relate to nature.

I conclude by considering how this worldview produces a watered down and apolitical way to be "pro-environment," and second, how this behavior—from apolitical conservation efforts to the therapeutic and aesthetic experience of nature itself—are an important currency in the local market for social status and prestige.

Feel-Good Altruism: Purify and Protect Nature

There exists a persistent but vague feeling among the ultra-wealthy that they ought to look out for nature, and doing so is an altruistic contribution to the greater good. This popular assumption provides conscious and unconscious justification for the use of nature for economic gains that we saw in chapter 3, but its effects also transcend the economic sphere. I found that environmental conservation for the ultra-wealthy is almost always associated with selfless behavior (for example, giving money, donating land easements, volunteering time), and despite what they say is only the *appearance* of economic self-interest, environmental outcomes are generally viewed as positive because they benefit their vision of constantly improving and purifying nature like a connoisseur does a fine wine or art. There is little consideration of conservation beneath the veneer that it is a taken for granted *good*, and even when probed, folks had a difficult time deciphering the potential self-serving and even violent effects of environmental protection (for example, removal of indigenous peoples to create national parks).

Of course, these feelings varied across a spectrum, but on average, there was a latent sense that we humans ought to work to purify and protect nature. Altruism, by definition, involves selflessness, and indeed this sentiment was present among the ultra-wealthy— especially for those who were politically active—but for most, it came in a watered-down form, stripped of any sort of radical sense of responsibility or call-to-action. In Teton County, this vague commitment to environmental altruism often manifested itself in discussions related to a handful of best-loved wildlife (for example, moose, wolves, bears), complaints about traffic congestion or crowded national parks, and praise of private landowner conservation. At times, this unquestioned assumption of altruism was difficult to uncover because it is more of a taken for granted feeling—in the water, so to speak—rather than an overtly stated preference or philosophy.

Again, there are hundreds of quotes that I could present as evidence and illustration of these findings, but to be concise, I present only a handful of *typical* quotes that accurately depict what I discovered through years of interviews and observations.

The sense of unquestioned altruism described earlier is illustrated in a discussion I had with a CEO who lives in Teton County but commutes to Minnesota for work. He describes his general love for the environment, "I'm, you know, I'm pretty close to a tree-hugger." He continues, telling me "generally, I think it gets back to paying my respect and love of the environment. I mean, that's a priority to me over commercialization of the environment. You know, I understand the economic or the commercial side of it, and you know, choices have to be made. But, you know, from what I have learned and understand, I'm biased toward doing all we can to, you know, keep it the way it was, is." In just one short response to my question about how he determines what is right or wrong for the natural environment, he used the phrase "you know" eight times, and had an assuming tone to his voice that indicated to me that he considered what he was saying to be generally accepted by any reasonable person.

Similarly, a hedge fund manager who runs his business from his home espouses taken-for-granted "general rules" relating to the "common good" that are "accretive" to the environment. But these rules, moral goods, and environmental outcomes are not well-defined. "The general rule I'd say is you wanna do something that enhances the common good. So you're trying to balance whatever private or corporate interest is presumably influencing that . . .

[but] hopefully you're doing something that's overall accretive to the environment."

The feeling that, because it was altruistic, conservation is generally viewed as a positive thing, manifested itself most clearly during interviews when I inquired into "who is most looked up to in the community?"

An interviewee from Philadelphia, who described herself as a "stay-at-home mom that does a lot of volunteer work for urban education," and ended up coming to Teton County in the early 2000s, answers, "I think [the community] looks up to people that try to preserve the beauty, preserve the wildlife. . . . I guess one of the real benefits of wealth is that the Land Trust will come along, and these super wealthy people put down millions of dollars and buy the land to be able to protect it from being developed, so that's a very positive thing."

Similarly, a single, forty-something investment banker from Boston has a typical response to my question about who is most respected in the community, reflecting that, "Well, the folks who are philanthropic, as in any place, I imagine get a fair bit of accolades. And those are people who have put large swaths of land under conservation . . . folks who donated a lot of time and money especially to the Land Trust. They are out here generally trying to put non-conserved land under conservation at this point."

In an interview at the world-famous Amangani Hotel, overlooking the Grand Tetons, a laid-back Californian who runs an investment management firm puts it rather succinctly: "People who are respected are those who have been involved in land conservation."

Relatedly, a common strand running through these quotes, and the hundreds of others not included here, is the sense that land conservation—and especially via a private organization like a Land Trust—is a *safe* way that the ultra-wealthy can get involved in environmentalism. Land Trusts conserve land by working directly with private landowners, which is viewed by most as a safe and noncontroversial activity[3] in comparison to more "political" or "extreme" environmentalist approaches that might challenge deeply ingrained commitments to private property rights or neoclassical economics.

The preference for a safe and politically comfortable form of environmentalism was evident in an interview I had with a retired woman named Laura. After earning their immense wealth in the DC area she moved to Teton County with her husband in 1985. While she has no previous environmental experience, she senses that it is generally a "good" thing to do, and so they recently attended the annual summer picnic put on by the Jackson Hole Land Trust. I asked her very generally about the type of philanthropic efforts in which she has been involved. After a few moments, she recalls, "I guess the only thing would be in Jackson Hole with the Land Trust. We've been sort of involved with that." I wondered to myself about the extent of her involvement, and what led her to the Land Trust and not another organization or philanthropic issue. I ask, and she recounts halfheartedly, "Well, we just went to the picnic. But we've also supported some artists who in turn give part of their money to the Land Trust."

Another interaction, with Tom, a corporate banker who bounced between large banks in New York and Boston and has lived in Jackson since the 1970s, illustrates again the common view that the multifaceted enterprise of environmental conservation has become synonymous with, and limited to, the narrow and safe issues of easements and land conservation. As we discuss philanthropy, I ask him to reflect on the ways that the wealthy are involved in the community. Eagerly, he interrupts me, "Absolutely. I think they're really involved with the Land Trust and the Nature Conservancy . . . it's a pretty cool thing, and so I think that there's a lot of people that appreciate some of those elements and are involved in lots of different ways that hinge around conservation."

The involvement in this brand of conservation ranged from something as small as attending a Land Trust picnic, all the way up to huge pet projects, like Matt Simpson's, a financier from London, who hadn't previously been involved in any environmental issues, but time spent in Teton County got him interested in land conservation. Feeling called to contribute something positive to nature, he recently chartered a helicopter in search of a huge piece of land to purchase for conservation.

Philanthropically, I don't know, uh, I mean am I interested in the stuff [of conservation], yeah because I spent the summer looking to buy a piece of property in Wyoming or Montana from a conservation perspective. . . . So I chartered this helicopter and spent the summer all over Wyoming and Montana with the idea of buying one of them and putting a conservation easement, and at some point, I probably will. I found one place in Montana that was just spectacular . . . it's 49,000 acres and there's big horn sheep and there's herds of elk and antelope the whole thing and it is fabulous and perfectly suited for that. . . . So, am I interested in this stuff? Yeah.

I inquire about what motivated him in the first place to purchase a large piece of property "from a conservation perspective," as he describes it. Matt pauses for several moments, and reflects, "I wanted someplace. I wanted a big piece of property. I don't want a ranch, you know. I'm an investment banker, private equity guy . . . you don't want me running a ranch, but I wanted a piece of property which had the sort of a sense of purpose to it, and you know if I thought about it and I talked to people and I did some investigating . . . so I've been working with a group that specializes in this, and they take me back there by helicopter and provide the places to look at."

Conservation Therapy: Safeguarding the Medicinal Storehouse

The second major component of Connoisseur Conservation is a specific cultivated *experience* of nature focused on its therapeutic benefits, and mirrors other high-taste aesthetic experiences enjoyed by the ultra-wealthy. Nature becomes a medicinal storehouse, tapped for its health-giving mental and physical rewards, administered by immersion in its aesthetic beauty. Of course, many nonwealthy people relate to nature in this same way, but what is unique here is that, from the perspective of the ultra-wealthy, many of them have, since college, thrown themselves into intensely stressful careers that, according to them, can result in overexertion, greedy materialism, preoccupation with power, and moral and spiritual hazard. In other words, what they view as the opposite of a romantic and benevolent nature. They have made sacrifices and worked to get to a point where they now come to realize that they need—*and especially deserve*—the tonic that a certain *experience* with nature can provide.

As an example, let's look more closely at how Bob James described his relationship to nature in chapter 3, and why he believes that we must protect it: in his words, humans have a "great responsibility to protect the *experience* of the natural world . . . let's not screw this place up." Bob unknowingly draws a distinction between "the *experience*" of the nature and the actual "natural world" itself. For him, "not screwing up" the experience is primary. These experiences have a strong aesthetic component, meaning that nature is akin to other experiences savored by the ultra-wealthy, such as fine art, wine, or cuisine. Like a famous painting, nature is best experienced in its most pristine condition, and given its delicacy, we need to guard against actions that threaten the perpetuity of that experience.

Importantly, this therapeutic experience of nature requires affluent goods and services. As we have seen in the last few chapters, these goods and services might come in the form of a $15 million home in the mountains, a heated driveway, a private fishing guide, a home concierge service, a private helicopter, $600 ski pants, or a membership at the world's most exclusive private mountain club.

Most interestingly, *I found that because these goods and services are purchased with a practical aim to access the therapeutic benefits of nature, they are not as likely to be considered impractical opulence or crass materialism.* Money spent on nature can be a moral loophole. Opulence with an ethical twist.

Where some critics might point to the contradiction between environmental sustainability and vast resource consumption like massive mountain homes or über-private ski clubs, the contradiction doesn't apply here for the ultra-wealthy because they tend to judge their actions using a different moral rubric when these actions involve therapeutic enjoyment of nature.[4] One cannot put a price tag on self-care and the nurturing of the soul. And, why must a person—especially a person who has worked so hard in his or her career—forgo personal pleasure, or suffer austerity just to enjoy nature? When money or resources are used for the purpose of enjoying the aesthetic tonic of nature, the typical contradictions or moral hazards no longer pertain: excessive consumerism doesn't pose a threat to personal character or to the sustainable future of the globe.

Let's consider how this actually works in practice, by illustrating the pervasive belief that nature has restorative benefits, especially via aesthetic experiences. A very friendly woman from the Deep South, who now splits time between a $30 million house in Massachusetts and a sprawling property in Teton County, gushes over nature, praising it as "restorative for the soul." Soul enrichment happens in practice, through specific recreation activities. She gets a rush even talking about it, proclaiming, "Everybody is fit. Everybody is out exercising. They're out riding their bike, they're running, they're fishing, they're hiking; you know, they're doing all the activities. They're kayaking. It's just a very healthy, and natural kind of environment . . . it's just very restorative for the soul. I think its restorative on every level when I'm there."

Another woman describes it as "feeling whole," in response to my question about how she would describe her relationship to nature. "Oh, I just feel so happy when I'm in it! I just, I feel whole, and close to nature."

Aesthetics are key, and many ultra-wealthy do their best to orient their homes and properties toward the most stunning local aesthetic attractions. Asking another person, this time a gentleman from the Midwest, about how he would describe his relationship to nature, he exclaims "Blessed! Blessed! Blessed!" Continuing, he describes for me the way his property, which he refers to as "Teton Masterpiece," is oriented toward these popular therapeutic benefits. "We have seven acres, and from most of the rooms in our house you cannot see another habitation. The house is oriented toward the Grand Teton which fills the window which goes 30 feet in height in our great room. The whole thing is oriented around the Grand Tetons and we call our property Teton Masterpiece . . . we just love it. It's something we created for ourselves and it partakes and brings in the beauty of the surrounding nature, and we live in the midst of our nature park."

Many times, ultra-wealthy relationships to nature were presented as a split personality of sorts. These often mapped onto the classic dichotomy—between polluted society and the purity of nature—that is ubiquitous in American culture, emblematic in the classic romantic works of Thoreau, Emerson, and Muir. Especially strong in my respondents was the sense that they fear that they have, or will in the future, get too caught up in the "unnatural"—which for them means being beaten down by seemingly shallow and stressful career pursuits. But the better person in them knows that they can, and should, revitalize themselves in natural and purer quests, guided by a romanticized view that nature possesses the power to offset all the unnatural ills of civilization.

In some cases, this was described as "escapism." For example, one couple I interviewed, medical professionals from the Midwest, were attracted to the area many years ago, because, as he puts it, "I guess we had a dream, and maybe it was a dream of escapism from daily life." Sometimes these feelings were more explicitly tied to the polluted society versus pure nature dichotomy. One New Jersey man I interviewed used this language, and then interestingly referred to nature as something more static and passively experienced, rather than the active and unnatural construction of civilization. "You get the feeling that it's incredibly big and beautiful and it wasn't created by anything man-made. And it's isolated from, you know, the hustle and bustle of civilization. Nature's a lot bigger than I am—I'm just looking."

Another East Coaster described this dichotomy in similar terms, romanticizing the "simple" way of life in rural Wyoming and in nature itself. "[Wyoming] is really a neat place and very close to the earth, very close to the nature. I think living on the East Coast we get away from that and it's nice to be closer to it. It's just a simpler way of life."

The unnatural ills and noise of urban areas are contrasted with the simplicity, quietness, and purity of these "neat" rural places that are ostensibly so "close to the earth." The remoteness of many ultra-wealthy properties affords them these experiences. As one respondent originally from Boston described it, "For me, it's in my DNA. . . . I just want to be sitting in a very quiet place and you know, um, staring out at whatever I'm staring at. Whether it's the river or the mountain, and so to me it's very connected, it's going to lead to recharging my battery." Reiterating this contrast, he continues, "I want to be sitting still. I want to be in that quiet place where there's not a lot of noise and not a lot of crowd confusion."

Putting your body in these natural places is usually sufficient. Nature will do the rest. Like the New Jersey man earlier who says that when it comes to nature, "I'm just looking," humans are passive in the face of nature, but *active* in urban areas where careers are aggressively built, money is made, and moral hazard must be dodged at every corner. But in nature, humans do not act. Nature acts. Or, as one woman put it to me, again in the passive voice, "You're out there in nature and it's just so pretty. . . . There's something about being surrounded by it that is just very, it just recharges me."

Finally, there exists a sense that *the amount of money is not an obstacle when it comes to nurturing one's soul in nature*. As noted, the ultra-wealthy do not judge consumer spending or resource consumption by the same moral yardstick as other areas of life, so long as purchases have the practical aim of allowing a person to enjoy nature.

In the words of Amani Benton, a middle-aged real estate financier, "As long as you enjoy what Teton County has to offer, you're totally welcome. The money doesn't do you any good. It doesn't really matter." But, of course, money does matter—especially for those who don't have it—because it requires immense money to live amid the priceless grandeur of nature in Teton County, and nearly every ultra-wealthy person I interviewed has spent many millions on homes, services, and other goods. What Amani was getting at, and what others relayed to me, is that money simply opens the door to these experiences, which are themselves viewed as priceless.

Recognizing something as priceless is what Amani means when he claims that in this community, "money doesn't do you any good. It doesn't really matter." Those who understand this point are here for what another ultra-wealthy person deemed as the "right reasons." He explains, "People want to be in Teton County for the right reasons. Define 'right,' I suppose. I mean if they like winter events, there's reason for them to be there; if they like the beauty of the mountains in the summer, there's reasons to be there; if they want to go fishing, it's great. If they want to float, they can go float. . . . The area attracts a lot of people for these right reasons."

The rightest of reasons, and the most priceless of experiences must be cultivated and even protected. And this takes money. Sometimes a lot of it. Homes like the "Teton Masterpiece" described earlier are good examples of how the ultra-wealthy compete for these experiences, showing that even at rarefied heights there is an economic competition for the "rightest" of reasons or the most priceless of aesthetic experiences.

A surgeon from South Carolina who owns a home in the Yellowstone Club describes how his aesthetic and therapeutic experience of nature is "safe" in perpetuity, because "the way my house is, you can't see a cell tower, you cannot see the golf course, you can't see a ski lift. All you can see is the very southern aspect of the Gallatin National Forest, and the northwestern aspect of Yellowstone National Forest [*sic*]. That will never be developed, and when my daughter is a grandmother, it will look the same. It's perfect for me . . . it's absolutely perfect for my desire because its views of nature are *safe*. I've got that, I can give it to my friends."

Selective Science: Save the Moose and the Status Quo

These deep connections to nature raise a critical question: what standards do the rich use to make informed environmental decisions? How do they determine if something is healthy or unhealthy for nature? What role does science play?

First, among the ultra-wealthy, I found that *there is a strong but exceedingly vague and selective commitment to science*. Especially ecological science. Their decision making does not often originate from scientific evidence, but from an informal and sometimes hollow ecological commitment to keeping "everything in balance." Nature is viewed as a pure Garden of Eden that should be kept at equilibrium.

This vague "everything in balance" approach means that environmental problems are more open for interpretation. Science is applied when this balance is under threat, but one person's "balance" might not be another's. It varies widely based on individual conscience and self-interest. What they defined as threats to "balance" varied greatly, and involved everything from the stream quality on their property to exhaust emissions from buses of Chinese tourists. The problems tended to be relatively minor and localized, rather than systemic global environmental problems such as climate change.

Because "balance" is mostly a matter of personal conscience, it allows folks to pick and choose which ecological problems are most important, and which issues deserve their financial support for scientific investigation (most often by giving to local and noncontroversial environmental organizations).

Additionally, the notion of "balance" implies maintaining a delicate equilibrium that discourages drastic changes that might disrupt the status quo. Change should happen carefully and incrementally, but not through radical or disruptive actions advocated by some environmental groups that might interfere with private property rights or laissez-faire economics.[5]

Second, and building on these points earlier, this approach to environmental science also includes an assumption that improving nature, or maintaining "balance," *affects only the nuts and bolts of nature itself, in isolation from associated societal impacts*—such as how conservation might impact the low-income community, or affect downstream political decisions. These alternative societal impacts were ignored or went unmentioned, and when I probed about them, most people had a hard time thinking outside of their vague ecological "balance" paradigm.

When environmental problems do arise for the ultra-wealthy (for example, concerns over moose populations, new housing developments, light pollution), these problems appear to be straightforwardly scientific, meaning that only credentialed scientific experts—usually from noncontroversial organizations—have the authority to recommend decisions.[6] This can create a false assumption that all problems of ecology should be addressed solely through impersonal, procedural, and technical solutions. In other words, there is little awareness about the deeper *social* causes and consequences of ecological problems.

This neglect is not entirely unique to the ultra-wealthy, but certainly has broader impacts, given their resources and power. While applying these technical standards might make an area more ecologically pristine, it might also come at a cost for other people in the community. A prime macrohistorical example being the removal of indigenous peoples from national parks based on the notion that indigenous tribes were deemed "unscientific savages," and modern scientific standards were used as evidence to remove them under the banner of "protecting" nature. Environmental problems may appear to be straightforwardly rational based on physical evidence (for example, water quality, wildlife carrying-capacity), but there are deeper motivations and social externalities that are often ignored, and can be used for ulterior purposes in the march toward protecting and improving the balance of Eden.

Let's now hear how the ultra-wealthy describe it in their own words, beginning with a handful of representative expressions of the "everything in balance" approach. Many of these responses come from a question in the interview guide asking them to reflect on how they determine what is right or wrong for the natural environment.

According to one bank CEO, it's quite simple, although still somewhat vague. "Well, I mean I think everything has got to be in balance." I probe further, and he continues, "I mean you've got to listen to science. You can't deny science. At best it is objective science, or the science designed to promote some particular interest that you may or may not have."

Another respondent similarly invokes the ubiquitous "balance" language. "It's a balance. The environment doesn't win wholly. If it did, you'd tear all the houses down and send all the people away. So, you know . . . it's a balance . . . it's so simple, and people are making it so complicated." Still another person insists, "Well, it's all got to be in balance," and six months later over lunch, another interviewee says, "It's a balance between what is there . . . it's the classic question how do you balance it?"

For some people, this "balance" means adjudicating between two artificially constructed extremes. The middle road between these two extremes, is by definition, most virtuous. This view was summed up well by a lawyer from Houston. "I would say I am realistic about the kind of conflicts between development and preservation. I don't think my views are very extreme in one direction or the other. I'm active with the Land Trust. I think they do a great job of preserving open space . . . but I think people are acting in good faith and all come motivated by that same goal, which is to maintain the unique character of Jackson."

These quotes shed light on the importance of science, but through an amorphous and individualized "everything in balance" approach. I would also ask about other yardsticks people might use to make decisions about the environment, such as cultural heritage or religion. These mostly fell on deaf ears. One respondent shot back, "Well, certainly I approach environmental issues like virtually any issues, kind of evidence-based. . . . I try to evaluate things based on science and evidence and proof. I would not say my approach is completely emotional."

In a tense lunch conversation at a cafe in downtown Jackson, another respondent bristled at my question about the role of cultural heritage, religion, or even personal experience as a basis for the "balance" that so many people preached. "Well, religion has zero importance to me, so I don't interface with that community at all. . . . Here in this wildlife, nature, science community, there is some component of an anti-science ignorance community, what can I say?" I asked him to explain what he meant, and how science might play a role. "It's not my community, but let me give you an example of an anti-science ignorance community. When you studied the reaction to wolves, I assume that you came across a great many people whose financial self-interests benefited from the forest being operated as a farm instead of a natural community and for whatever reasons, are just very eager to punch all critters, kill all critters. This is an anti-science ignorance community. I suspect that it has some association with the religion community."

So science still plays an important role, but again, its importance fluctuates depending on personalized and flimsy definitions of "balance." Additionally, how we decide to keep things in balance often has little connection to cultural heritage (for example, practical or familial knowledge) or formal religious considerations (for example, Pope Francis's climate change encyclical *Laudato Si'*).

The unsophisticated invocation of "science" and "balance" is also influenced by a certain *economic* naturalism, by which I mean an unquestioned commitment to fixed economic laws of private property rights and laissez-faire economics. One respondent, a leader of a local nonprofit who works closely with ultra-wealthy people, burst out in laughter when I asked him about recent moral critiques made by some working-class people that it is wrong for such a small selection of ultra-wealthy to own so much of the private land here. After laughing, he continued, "I'm chuckling because that to me is just utter nonsense and socialist drivel. I mean these people have paid for it. . . . I mean it wasn't as though the wealthy have kicked out the lowly construction workers and those sixth-generation residents. . . . I mean, come on. That to me is just absurd."

Similarly, in a discussion with a prominent retired Silicon Valley executive, he engages in environmentalism using the laws of private property rights and the free market, even if science itself may sometimes necessitate more of a "top-down" approach. Over a French toast breakfast, he explains that the best way forward is "just general market forces. I certainly don't think it ought to be mandated. I think that part of the American dream is the right to buy property and do what you will with it. I think it's ridiculous all this stuff that, you know some group of people are trying to keep some other landowner from doing what he wants to do."

Thickening the Veneer

Connoisseur Conservation describes the cultural worldview through which the rich relate to and use nature. To conclude, I more explicitly outline the consequences of this worldview, and the ways that it further thickens the prevailing environmental veneer whereby protecting and enjoying nature is seen as an unquestioned good.

APOLITICAL ENVIRONMENTALISM

First, taken together, the three themes (Feel Good Altruism, Conservation Therapy, Selective Science) unpacked earlier create the impression of conservation as a *safe and noncontroversial activity*. Conservation becomes a watered-down way to be "pro-environment," supplanting critical or disruptive ideas and behavior that might lure one into turbulent political waters.[7] No doubt, I found that among the ultra-wealthy, there is a feeling that looking after nature is the right thing to do. Yet, their assumptions that it is virtuous or altruistic is often undercut by the fact that their environmental concern is circumscribed to issues that benefit people with wealth. Further, because these activities are so vague and undemanding, it creates a façade whereby conservation is seen as an apolitical activity.

This approach also corresponds with the view that nature is a much needed (and deserved) therapeutic cure-all, enabling the ultra-wealthy to remain sane amid the stress-inducing powder keg of a high-profile career, great wealth, and family demands. This safe approach to conservation, which emphasizes a vague "everything in balance" use of science, is aimed to preserve and purify an imagined Eden *for the purpose of* providing health-giving aesthetic beauty. In the end, this veneer prevents engagement with many of the most pressing, contentious, costly, self-demanding, and "unsafe" environmental problems that we face today (for example, energy transition, climate change, modern consumption, drought, deforestation, and so on).

HIGH-STATUS TASTES AND THE SOCIAL REWARDS OF NATURE

Second, these three themes converge to *create a market for social and cultural rewards*. Because conservation is seen as unequivocally altruistic and honorable, there are social rewards to be gained for involvement in conservation, such as status, distinction, prestige, power, exclusivity, respect, recognition, and other forms of social, cultural, and symbolic capital that impact a person's position within a community. In Teton County, the exchange market for social status is most lucrative around issues of land conservation. This means that those with money to own or purchase land are in the best position to earn the highest rate of return for altruistic behavior.

So in addition to the economic benefits of engaging in ostensibly altruistic environmental behavior, there are also important social and cultural benefits. And, of course, cultural and economic capital often go hand in hand, with each being exchanged for the other. Engaging in conspicuous conservation not only signals high-social status, but because it is viewed as especially honorable here, it can also be used to obtain social status and recognition.[8]

Beyond involvement in conservation, social and cultural rewards are also bestowed on those who have cultivated the right skills, tastes, clothing, credentials, and recreation abilities that are required to properly enjoy the therapeutic benefits of nature. In a setting like Teton County, where there is a great disparity between ultra-wealthy and low-income folks, this market creates a stratified grouping of cultural winners and losers. As our friend Bob James from our Fifth Avenue dinner reminds us, nature is there to be *experienced*, and similar to learning how to appreciate fine wine, one must acquire the proper tastes and skills to fully enjoy nature's remedy. These tastes and skills don't happen naturally. Developing these skills takes time, and often requires leisure time, professional training, and expendable income—all of which the ultra-wealthy have in spades relative to their low-income counterparts.

These high-status forms of cultural capital, which I've referred to throughout this chapter as "therapeutic," "connoisseur," and so on, have great symbolic value in the community. They signal a highly coveted association with the high-status leisure class, which is in stark contrast to other groups in the community who are time crunched by multiple low-paying jobs. The development of such skills and practices (for example, birding, wildlife art, fly-fishing, skiing, other *non*motorized recreation) symbolize an authentic and morally enlightened attachment to nature, creating social group bonds of collective identity among the ultra-wealthy. This particular "connoisseurship" relation to nature then becomes canonized in the community, and certain skills and experiences are valued over others. Connoisseurship of nature becomes not just an outward signal of social status, but a producer of it.

5

Gilded Green Philanthropy

George Butler met his wife, Annie, in Ohio in 1945. They were married soon after, and found themselves headed east toward New York City, where George would make their fortune as a banker and an investor in the emerging telecommunications field. After a few decades of incredible financial success, they made the big decision, like so many others in this book, to pack up, retrace their steps back west, even farther west to remote Teton County. They've now lived in Wyoming for more than 30 years, and looking back, George boasts like a proud local. "The people are wonderful, the weather is nice. It's a safe place to live. It's philanthropic."

The large parcel they purchased in the 1980s was dirt cheap relative to the exorbitant prices we see today. "The land was very, very cheap. But, uh . . ." George pauses, thinking of the right way to phrase his next point that we both know is coming, "today it is worth quite a bit of money . . . and the tax rates here are wonderful." Today, their 10,500-square-foot home is worth more than $6 million.

Yet, as time went by, George recognized that there were problems in paradise. Problems brought on by the recent influx of the ultra-wealthy folks like himself and Annie. Things just aren't the same anymore, he laments. "I wish we could go back to the way it was when we came." The socioeconomic hierarchy is now completely bifurcated, with virtually no middle class to speak of, and a mounting set of social problems. Fortunately, for George, and the many other ultra-wealthy people I interviewed, there is a clear solution: *affluent philanthropy*.

George sums it up, "So, we have problems that we didn't have when we first moved here. You've got a housing shortage in Jackson . . . houses are priced rather highly. It's just a more prosperous community. *But I would tell you that we have a very philanthropic operation, and so a lot of people are attracted to come out here just because of [philanthropy]*."[1] In other words, problems created with the left hand can be solved with the right.

Another resident—a longtime financier from Boston, who is more politically left-leaning than George, but similarly involved in philanthropy—rehearses this common theme about the faith in ultra-wealthy philanthropy for overcoming the issues pertaining to wealth inequality, "there are over 200 not-for-profits in this community of 20,000 people, which is a pretty amazing number! On a per capita basis, *I would bet that it's the most philanthropic community in the country*."

———

This important philanthropic paradox—*can wealth solve the very problems wealth creates?*—has implications far beyond Teton County itself, in a nation increasingly defined by wealth imbalance. Are George and so many others I interviewed right? Is the concentration of wealth among a select few actually quite effective at solving problems that extreme wealth creates, so long as the ultra-wealthy are philanthropically aware and generous? Might extreme disparity actually be a *good thing* for those at the bottom? Is plutocracy—meaning a society controlled by a small minority of its wealthiest citizens—not getting the credit it deserves? In other words, are those perceived to be the villains really the heroes?

Among the ultra-wealthy, I found that there is a widespread *perception* that their philanthropy indeed makes up for, and even has the power to solve, social problems that arise in bifurcated contexts like Teton County. In other words, there is a perception that plutocracy can indeed work, and work well. Often subject to widespread criticism, there is the sense that the concentration of wealth among a very few actually has the potential to transform a community for the better, so long as those at the top loosen their grip enough to allow portions of this great wealth to voluntarily flow down from rarefied heights, to the charitable organizations laboring at the ground level. George explains, "It's become a very philanthropic place. We've given several million dollars to the community for various charities."

But perception and reality can differ. This puzzle about whether the perceived villains are actually the heroes is an open empirical question, answered only with philanthropic data. As the wealthiest county in the nation, including billionaires and world leaders in business and politics, there certainly seems to be enough economic and social capital to be transformational. Yet, on the other hand, we know that, like any social group, individual charitable giving can vary greatly. People like Bill Gates and Warren Buffett have pledged their entire fortunes to charity, while others give little to none.

So, we must ask, in the wealthiest community in the country, where exactly is all this money and social influence flowing? To alleviate suffering and promote greater equity, as is the assumed purpose of philanthropy? And, more broadly, how can we use this real community setting—this ideal laboratory of immense wealth and economic bifurcation—to move beyond detached rhetoric and sloppy accusations, to a local data-driven understanding of plutocracy, that includes the voices of the ultra-wealthy alongside the reality of quantitative evidence?

———

Working with, but moving beyond my interviews and observations, I examine these popular perceptions of George and other ultra-wealthy people regarding the positive impact of ultra-wealth, using a substantial amount of quantitative evidence. I comprehensively map out the entire system of philanthropy in the area using social

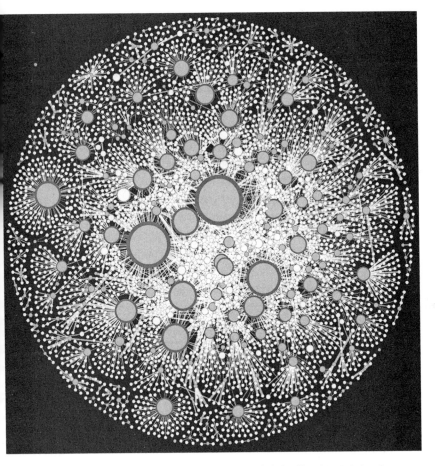

FIGURE 5.1. All organizations (larger gray circles) and individuals (smaller white circles), and the connections between them (light gray lines). The size of the circle represents centrality in the network, meaning their overall influence (the larger the size, the greater the influence). *Source:* Internal Revenue Service 990-PF forms and GuideStar.

network and financial data, including the full scope of connections between philanthropic organizations and the ultra-wealthy (figure 5.1). Collected from digitized Internal Revenue Service tax forms dating from 1997 to the present, the data include information on all nonprofit organizations and private foundations, including all board member links, as well as all links between individuals themselves.

Combined with interviews and observations, they provide comprehensive evidence to untangle the paradox and puzzles posed earlier.

People like George and Annie, who have established their own private foundation in Wyoming, who have given millions to local organizations, and who sit on boards of organizations, are a helpful *individual* indicator of the impact of ultra-wealthy on philanthropy. In talking with them, their perceptions about the positive influence of ultra-wealth indeed seem warranted. But we must move beyond individual perceptions to develop a clearer picture of the *entire scope* of financial and social influences of ultra-wealth philanthropy in the community. Zooming out from George and Annie, we see that they are part of a much larger philanthropic ecosystem pictured in figure 5.1.

More specifically, if, as perception has it, ultra-wealth is the primary source of a great philanthropic river trickling down from great heights, then to which organizations and causes do its tributaries flow? And, why?

This is the first of two chapters on philanthropy. Here in this first chapter, I focus on the "what," and in the next chapter, I focus on the "why." Beginning with this chapter, I will present a variety of important patterns pertaining to organizational finances, board member networks, and the overall structure of philanthropy over time to address the main puzzle described earlier concerning plutocratic power and the role of charitable giving in an age of extreme wealth concentration.

Just the Data, Please: How Money and Social Influence Are Allocated

CREATING A MARKET FOR PHILANTHROPY

Before jumping into the data, I want to very briefly contextualize why there is such a demand for philanthropy to meet human needs in Teton County, and why it carries such prestige and social currency. *Ironically, and somewhat counterintuitively, the influx of immense wealth actually created a greater need for charitable giving*, and I document these social problems in great length in chapter 1, noting the impact of ultra-wealth on housing, wages, and the collapse of the local middle class. Because there are now essentially two polarized socioeconomic groups left living in the community—those at the rarefied top and those at the bottom—philanthropy is largely, by necessity, an ultra-wealthy enterprise.

As wealth in the community skyrocketed to new heights, organizations with disparate goals scrambled to compete for the billions in potential philanthropic dollars. But, as with any aspect of social life, philanthropy also became about much more than simple dollars and cents. *Philanthropy became a valuable form of social currency in the community, and a status market emerged that conveyed higher prestige on some charitable issues, but not others.*

Importantly, the social-status hierarchy of philanthropy came to mirror the socioeconomic hierarchy, bifurcated between the high prestige of environmental conservation, and the low prestige of addressing basic human needs like food and shelter. And generally, the more pressing an issue is perceived to be, the more prestigious and heroic it is to respond. Organizations who have more resources are more successful at strategically framing their issue as critically important, publicly celebrated, and thus most deserving of ultra-wealthy attention.[2] It is within this context of organizational competition, issue framing, and social prestige that we should interpret the following data about where the money and social influence began flowing.

BOOM OF NONPROFITS AND PRIVATE FAMILY FOUNDATIONS

As immense of amounts of money poured into Teton County—the majority of which was through personal investment income—the number of philanthropic organizations also grew steadily over time. As I've noted, this was in part a response to the problems that were created by that money itself (for example, housing crisis, environmental pressures), but it was also because wealthy people took on personally meaningful pet projects that resulted in new nonprofit organizations.

The president of the esteemed Community Foundation of Jackson Hole, Katharine Conover, recently lamented the high turnover of nonprofits in the area, writing that "it makes me want to stick my head in the oven" when she hears about someone starting a new nonprofit organization. Continuing, she commends the passion, but "their naivety leaves me suicidal. We need to deal with the challenges to our existing extremely important nonprofits before we incubate new ones."[3]

The growth of nonprofits was not spread evenly among philanthropic sectors, but was strongest among groups tied to environmental and wildlife issues. There was a dramatic increase in environmental nonprofits between 1990 and 2000, coinciding with the steep increase of wealthy people to the area.[4] Even these organizations are no less susceptible to turnover, however. In the experienced words of Conover, "Charities enter loudly and leave quietly." She also notes that in addition to turnover of organizations themselves, there is also incredible turnover even *within* some of the most prominent conservation groups. "Already there has been a rapid turnover rate in nonprofit leaders in Jackson Hole. Of our 13 conservation groups, 12 had three or more directors in the past four years. Only one director has held her job for more than four years."[5]

On the surface, as more and more charities "enter loudly," it creates the perception that Teton County seems to be what our ultra-wealthy friend earlier regards as, "the most philanthropic community in the country." But, in my interviews and observation, people tended to see only the "boom" and not the "bust," and often confused the founding of a nonprofit as a victory, rather than what in reality is at best a starting point to solve a problem, and at worst an attempt to throw money at a pet project in hopes of a quick fix.

Digging a bit deeper, and especially relevant to this examination of ultra-wealthy philanthropy, is the growth of private foundations in the area (nonprofits who file an Internal Revenue Service Form 990-PF). This growth is shown in figure 5.2, charting the increase of new private foundations over time. In 1997, there were fewer than twenty-five private foundations, but by 2014 the number had swelled to nearly two hundred. One ultra-wealthy interviewee I spoke with, who has his own well-endowed private foundation,

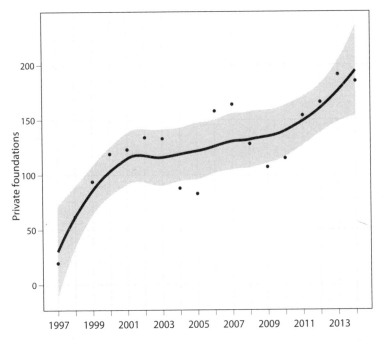

FIGURE 5.2. The growth of private foundations in Teton County, 1997–2014. *Source:* Internal Revenue Service 990-PF forms and GuideStar.

calls Wyoming "the best onshore version of an offshore trust," referring to Wyoming's notoriously loose and unregulated advantages for wealthy people looking to shield their assets, both from taxation and from public view.

Local financial services companies are popping up to assist with, and encourage the establishment of, family foundations and trusts, advertising specifically to those families who come to Wyoming in search of the next best thing to an offshore shelter. As a common example, consider the pitch materials from Willow Street Trust Company of Wyoming:

> In addition to its physical beauty and numerous recreational amenities, Jackson Hole has become a haven for wealthy families and a top trust situs location.
>
> Wyoming is a top trust situs due to its favorable tax environment, strong asset protection and privacy laws. It is an efficient,

flexible and cost effective jurisdiction in which to domicile trusts. Wyoming trust situs can be created by utilizing a Wyoming trustee even if beneficiaries or grantors reside outside the state.

Wyoming is one of only two states that sanction both regulated and unregulated private family trust companies. These unique structures enhance privacy, flexibility and continuity over generations.[6]

Certainly, these private foundations, especially in Wyoming, have encountered their share of criticism, mostly in response to the sort of ultra-wealthy admissions made earlier about Wyoming allowing de facto "offshore" accounts. Because of the amount of money that private foundations and trusts command, and the influence of the people who endow them, they are important to the landscape of local philanthropy, having an effect both in their action and inaction. Some are more active than others, and as we will see later, some are deeply connected financially and socially to nonprofit organizations working in the community.

For example, George made no mention of his private foundation in our hour and a half conversation about his involvement in local philanthropy, but from easily attainable public IRS records, I found that he and Annie put several hundred thousand dollars into a private foundation during late 1990s, named the George and Annie Butler Family Foundation.[7] Small donations ranging from $1,000 and $3,000 were made to various conservation organizations, before the foundation was liquidated and transferred to a donor-advised fund through the Community Foundation of Jackson Hole.

Given this growth of private foundations, and the emergence of scores of new nonprofit organizations, let's take a look at where the actual money is flowing.

WHERE DO THE RIVERS OF MONEY FLOW?

Each year, billions of new dollars in personal income flow into Teton County—$4.5 billion to be exact, in 2015.[8] Of course, this single-year figure is just a sliver of the cumulative amount that has accrued in this remote corner of the country over the decades—for example, there are individual residents living in this community whose net worth is alone more than $4.5 billion. All this is to say that, compared to any other community in the nation, there is unique *potential* for transformative change through charitable giving.

But how much money is flowing to local nonprofits, and to which causes? To get a sense of the overall picture, let's first consider whether money is dished out evenly among the 200-plus organizations, or whether it is concentrated among a select few.

In 2000, the top 1 percent of nonprofit organizations owned 23 percent of all charitable assets, and the top 20 percent of organizations owned 91 percent of all charitable assets. *This means that the bottom 80 percent of organizations made do with the scraps of the remaining 9 percent of assets.* By 2014, assets have become somewhat less concentrated (the top 20 percent of organizations own 85 percent of all assets, and the top 1 percent own 20 percent), but a handful of organizations still command the bulk of available charitable assets. The organizations commanding the most assets are private foundations, despite private foundations being fewer in number. Only 37 percent of local nonprofits are private foundations, but they own 65 percent of the total assets in the community, meaning that the bulk of the resources for the community might be locked away, or not even go toward many of the local needs.

Who sits at the top of this philanthropic heap? It is made up of a small mix of well-to-do private foundations and local conservation and arts-related nonprofits. Private foundations like the Lynn and Foster Friess Family Foundation, who at their peak commanded $175,607,290 in 2008, as well as the George B. Storer Foundation ($73 million in 2014), a private foundation focused on conservation issues in Wyoming. Aside from private foundations, the most economically powerful nonprofits include organizations broadly related to environmental issues, such as the Jackson Hole Land Trust and the Teton Science Schools, as well as arts organizations such as the National Museum of Wildlife Art, the Community Center for the Arts,[9] and the Grand Teton Music Festival. When it comes to assets in the coffers, these conservation and arts-related nonprofits sit head and shoulders above most others.

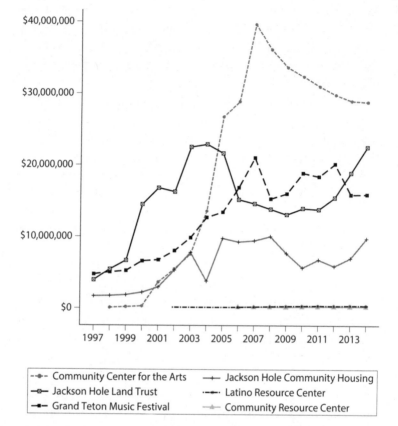

FIGURE 5.3. Comparing nonprofit organization assets between 1997 and 2014 for the most prominent nonprofits in environmental, arts, and social services. *Source:* IRS 990 forms.

How do these types of organizations compare to human services organizations, who assist with basic needs that have arisen in the wake of such stark wealth inequality? Let's take a look at these dynamics over time, in figure 5.3. This does not include private foundations, many of which saw incredible asset growth over this time period as well. As we can see, organizations like the Jackson Hole Land Trust and prominent arts organizations took off in the late 1990s and 2000s, while the most prominent organizations that focused on the housing crisis, community services, and the like, saw microscopic growth.

Digging deeper, just how big are these differences? We can see that, for example, the Community Center for the Arts, which recently built a magnificent new building in downtown Jackson Hole, had very little back in 2000—just $268,158—but a short seven years later they had nearly $40 million, an asset increase of nearly 15,000 percent. In 1997, the Jackson Hole Land Trust recorded $3.9 million in assets, but by 2014 that number had increased sharply to $22.5 million, driven largely by the cultural shift toward "compensation" and "connoisseur" conservation I presented in chapters 3 and 4.

Compare these dramatic increases to the Latino Resource Center—a prominent human services organization during this time period—which in 2005 had a little more than $126,438, and by 2014 this number had grown to only about $355,452—which is less than 1 percent of the assets of some other conservation and arts charities.[10] In other words, assets for health and human service organizations remained stagnant, especially when compared to other organizations that enjoyed an economic bonanza over this same time period, all while the needs of the working poor continued to escalate in scope and intensity.

So money is certainly flowing to organizations and foundations, but it is largely flowing to those in conservation, wildlife, and the arts. At one point in our conversation, George sums up this main finding well. "The community is philanthropic. People here are very interested in the community and contribute to the community. For example, we built in the last seven or eight years, maybe 14 to 15 million dollars' worth of bike paths for people to come out to Jackson and just ride bicycles." Indeed, ultra-wealthy optimism about the charitable spirit of the community holds some truth, but these perceptions assume charity of a certain kind for a certain purpose, benefiting a certain people.

The Importance of Social and Human Capital

For all the attention this community gets as the wealthiest place in the country, the astounding amount of *social and human capital* often goes unnoticed and underappreciated. A community full of some of the world's most prominent and powerful figures in business and politics means that nonprofit organizations directly enjoy the fruits of these social connections, most often through board memberships. And, in turn, this often has a positive impact on the economic health of an organization. If an ex-leader in world politics, a CEO, or a billionaire philanthropist are active on your board, chances are that your assets and social influence will be dramatically improved.

Here in this section, and in the next, I draw on comprehensive social network data to examine which organizations and people are most influential, and why.[11] These data are based on Internal Revenue Service 990 forms that report all board members for an organization. My analysis focuses on which people sit on which boards, and what that means for relationships between all the different organizations, as well as for all the different people. First, I will provide a bird's-eye view structure of the world of philanthropy, focusing on which organizations are most influential within the social network. From there, I will take a deep dive into specific organizations, including comparisons of "influence" in the conservation, arts, and human services sectors.

WHERE IS SOCIAL INFLUENCE FLOWING?

Looking more closely into the historical connections between organizations and their board members gives us a window into the social landscape of philanthropy, and to which issues social influence flows. Influential people are often on multiple boards for multiple organizations, which means that social influence is not isolated to single organizations, but often happens in a web of entangled relationships. Untangling these relationships can help us pinpoint the sources of philanthropic power in the community.

Figure 5.4 displays the structure of all relationships between individuals and organizations between 1997 and 2014.[12] The sizes of the circles represent the influence of the organization within the network—the larger the circle, the more influence. The lines between the circles represent a documented relationship (person to organization) based on IRS 990 forms. There are 280 organizations, 4,060 people, with a total of 17,848 connections between a person

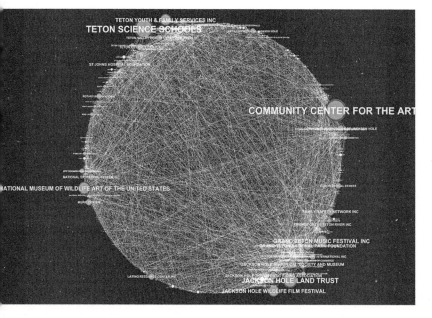

FIGURE 5.4. Plotting the structure of all relationships between individuals and organizations between 1997 and 2014. The sizes of the circles equal the influence of an organization within the network. The lines between the circles represent a documented relationship (person to organization)—showing 280 organizations, 4,060 people, with a total of 17,848 connections between individuals and organizations. *Source:* Full-size vectorized images of these graphs are available at JustinFarrell.org.

and an organization. This bird's-eye view perspective is useful for identifying broad patterns, and noticing different clusters of influential organizations.

The five most influential nonprofit organizations are the Teton Science Schools (conservation and education), the Community Center for the Arts (arts), the Jackson Hole Land Trust (conservation), the Grand Teton Music Festival (arts), and the National Museum of Wildlife Art (arts and conservation).[13]

Digging a bit deeper, let's look at the relationships *between* organizations themselves. Figure 5.5 displays the landscape of relationships between all organizations.[14] Organizations are linked if they shared a common board member (for example, Jane Doe is on the board of Org1 and Org2, which would result in these two Orgs now having a

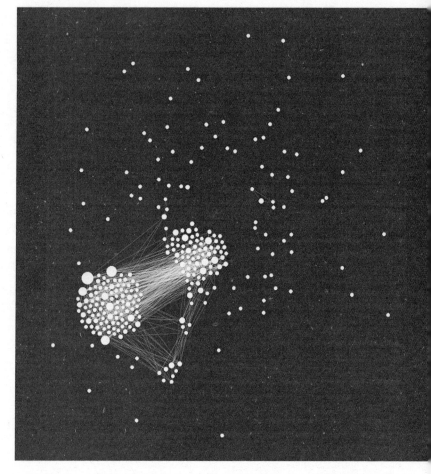

FIGURE 5.5. Plotting all organization-to-organization relationships, revealing two dominant clusters of organizations in the community, and the linkages between these two dominant clusters.

relationship). As is readily apparent, there are two main clusters of organizations, with the rest orbiting around the fringe, largely autonomously from one another. All of the top five organizations listed earlier are in the left cluster, suggesting that there is significant overlap, and coordination, among the area's most influential nonprofits.

In fact, similar to the concentration of assets among a select few organizations, there is also a concentration of social influence

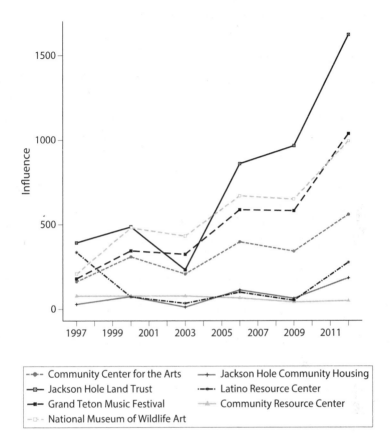

FIGURE 5.6. The growth of social influence among conservation and arts nonprofits, as compared to human and social service nonprofits, from 1997 to 2012. The amount of social and human capital accumulated much faster over this period of time for conservation and arts organizations.

among these organizations.[15] The top 10 percent of organizations (twenty-eight nonprofits) account for half of all social connections. *In other words, nonprofits at the top—conservation and arts—enjoy a disproportionately large slice of social and human capital that all organizations rely on to raise money and carry out their mission.*

How have these dynamics changed over time, as more and more wealth flowed into the community, as the middle class collapsed, and the housing crisis ensued? Figure 5.6 shows how the social influence of the four most prominent conservation and arts nonprofits grew over time, compared to three prominent human and social services nonprofits. During this period of time, the number of people getting involved in nonprofits increased, but this new surplus of social and human capital accumulated only among a *specific* handful of conservation and arts organizations.

DO ASSETS IMPACT SOCIAL INFLUENCE?

What does the landscape of philanthropy look like for just the upper echelon of organizations? Indeed, we've seen that there are a handful of organizations who command the majority of the assets, so it is worth taking a closer look at how these assets affect their level of influence. Let's take a look at the entire network again, but limit this look to nonprofits with assets topping $500,000 (figure 5.7). The number of connections corresponds to the thickness of the lines between the organizations, and the amount of assets corresponds to the sizes of the circles. The densely connected inner core of the network (toward the left side of figure 5.7) once again shows that these same conservation and arts organizations are at the center of the action, wielding the most social influence over the philanthropy sector.

As is also apparent, the majority of private foundations are on the periphery of the network, meaning that despite their wealth, and their professed mission as a philanthropic entity, they are far less plugged into nonprofit work in the community. In fact, *private foundations only account for less than 10 percent of all social connections*, meaning that they have far fewer people making the decisions (typically, a handful of family members), and these people are not very well connected to any other organizations. Being closed off makes it more difficult, and less likely, that a tax-free private foundation fulfills its expected mission—beyond being an "onshore" shelter, as our ultra-wealthy friend described it earlier—to faithfully serve as a philanthropic grant maker in the community. But the reality is, is that despite owning 65 percent of all philanthropic

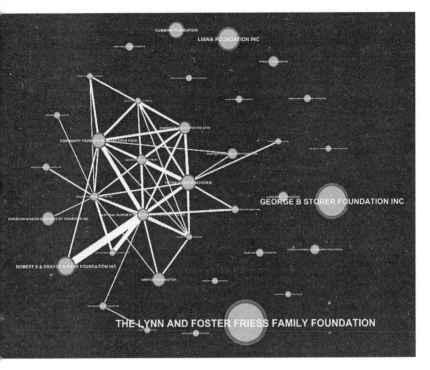

FIGURE 5.7. Social connections between nonprofits with assets topping $500,000, revealing again that conservation and arts organizations wield the most social influence.

assets available, private foundations remain socially, and therefore financially, isolated from the rest of the community.

So in terms of whether more money leads to more social influence, I found that yes it does, *except for private foundations*. Figure 5.8 provides a visual representation of this relationship, and shows the level of assets and social influence for a number of the most prominent organizations, most of which are the same handful of conservation and arts groups we've seen repeatedly in this chapter. Beyond looking at specific organizations, the general finding here is that as an organization's assets rise, it tends to become more connected and more influential within the nonprofit community.

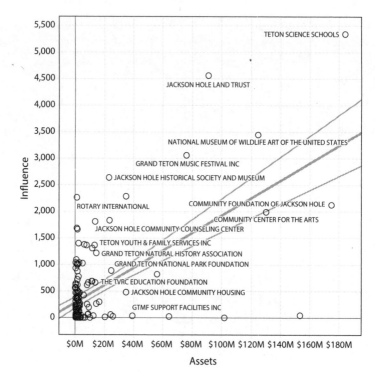

FIGURE 5.8. The positive association between an organization's assets and its social influence. As organization assets increase, so do the number of social connections in the community. Note: This analysis has been restricted to all nonprofits except private foundations. The same positive correlation between assets and social influence does not hold for private foundations. Influence is operationalized using the standard Betweenness Centrality measure from network science. This measure is especially useful for the purpose of this study because it quantifies which organizations have the most power within the network with regard to flows of information and resources, which often amounts to influence.

THE BRIDGE BETWEEN CONSERVATION AND ARTS

It pays to have friends in high places. And organizations often partner with other organizations, becoming close collaborators. But which organizations tend to associate with one another? Two findings emerged. First, I found that interorganization links are strongest across the sectors of environmental conservation and the arts, especially among the most well-connected and well-funded groups (for example, land trust, classical music festival, museums, art galleries).

At the very top of the heap, the lines between conservation and arts tend to blur, as these organizations share the same social and human capital. In other words, environmental organizations are not just connected to other environmental organizations. The same holds true for the arts sector. Moreover, their day-to-day activities and deliverables as organizations also tended to blend, as environmental organizations engage arts issues, and arts organizations engage environmental conservation. For example, the Jackson Hole Land Trust initiated a project to "unite art and conservation to cultivate a deeper sense of place in Jackson Hole,"[16] and local arts organizations frequently put on programs related to wildlife and conservation.

Second, I found that human and social services organizations tend to be narrowly connected to their own kind. They lack what is called "bridging" capital, which is enjoyed in abundance by conservation and arts organizations. Without bridging capital to different sectors, human and social services organizations are isolated and blocked from gaining entry into new parts of the network where the majority of money and human capital exists (that is, conservation and the arts sectors). Thus, not having a bridge to these different philanthropic sectors limits their access to an immense amount of social and economic resources. For example, I found that an organization like the Latino Resource Center or Community Resource Center has immediate access to only about 9 percent of people and connections available in the entire network, whereas their counterparts in conservation and the arts have immediate access to nearly 35 percent of total people and connections in the community because they often share connections across their sectors. Simply put, conservation and arts organizations enjoy bridges to one another, whereas the human services organizations are forced to operate in isolation.

A Tale of Two Humans

I've demonstrated that money and influence flows to certain organizations, but we also have reason to believe that these patterns will be reflected in the types of relationships we see *between individual people, explaining why some individuals are more influential than*

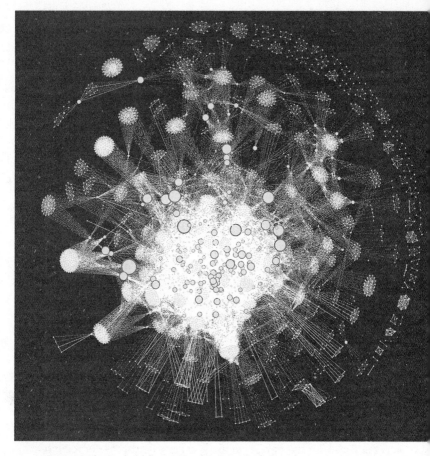

FIGURE 5.9. Plotting the bird's-eye view of 109,942 individual social connections based on shared connections to an organization.

others. Figure 5.9 provides a basic bird's-eye view of all connections between the 4,060 people who sat on nonprofit boards. Connections are defined broadly, based on whether two people sat on the same organization board between 1997and 2014, for a total of 109,942 different social connections.[17] The sizes of the circles depict the magnitude of their social influence in the network. Of course, we can see from this graph that not all individuals are equally influential, but some are isolated on the periphery, and some are much more connected in the dense middle of the network.

Let's consider how this looks in real life, at the ground level, by comparing two different people who lived life in this network. One is Clark Moore, an heir to a multi-billion-dollar business conglomerate, and the other is Abigail Smith, a longtime executive director of a human and social services organization.[18]

Let's start with Abigail. She was a longtime resident of Teton County, and worked for nearly two decades for a handful of non-profits focused on housing, mental health, and education. First, we'll take a look at her world of social connections, based on her work as executive director (figure 5.10). In Abigail's immediate network are 112 people, with connections that are mostly to people who are associated with other similar human and social service organizations.

Why does this matter? In 2009, her organization faced several hundred thousand dollars in government cuts, while at the same time the housing crisis and economic disparity led to an increase in people needing her services. What figure 5.10 shows us is that, unfortunately for Abigail and her organization—and for the increasing number of people in need of services—they had much less social capital from which to draw as they attempted to stay afloat as an organization. In addition to offering fewer inroads to new assets and human capital, this also made her organization far less resilient to inevitable threats like these funding cuts.

This is in stark contrast to a person like Clark Moore, who because of his economic power as the heir to a multi-billion-dollar enterprise, and the social influence that comes along with it, has become quite involved in local philanthropy. Conservation and arts organizations, as demonstrated earlier, are better suited to lure people like Clark to serve on their boards. When those organizations are in need, Clark is socially equipped to help mightily. Let's take a look at his world of social connections in figure 5.11. Looking closely at Clark's connections, we see that his network is not only farther reaching than Abigail's, but it is much more *concentrated* with connections. It is both wider and deeper. More specifically, Clark has immediate access to ten times more connections than Abigail, and these relationships are often with people who themselves are widely connected and well-heeled.

Certainly, Abigail has devoted her life to philanthropy, and has put in several decades' work to build relationships with people and

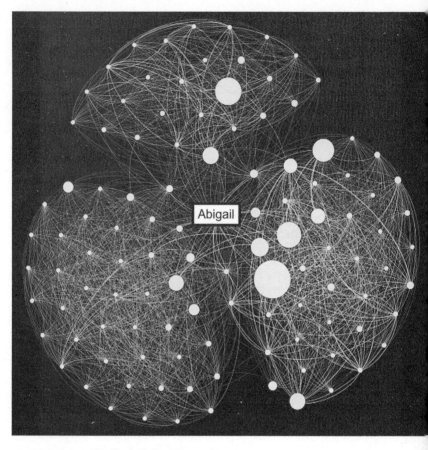

FIGURE 5.10. Abigail's world of social connections.

organizations, in addition to raising money and overseeing services for the working poor. Despite this work, Abigail herself, as well as her organization (and those like it), lack a broad or resourceful network from which to draw when they face problems. And on the flip side, we see these same dynamics work to the benefit of a small group of conservation and arts organizations that—with the help of people like Clark and his far-reaching connections to corridors of wealth and power—rose to local prominence, and currently command the majority of nonprofit assets and human capital in the area, while organizations at the bottom continue to struggle to address

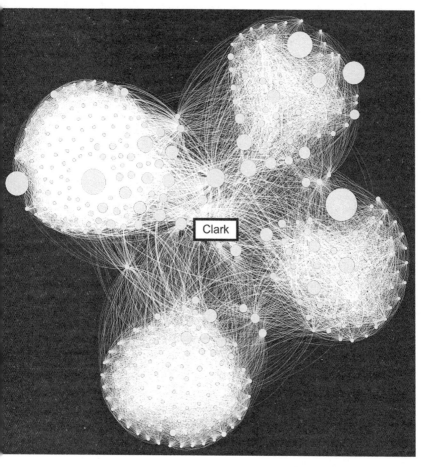

FIGURE 5.11. Clark's world of social connections. Ten times greater than Abigail's connections (shown in figure 5.10), and more importantly, with greater access to individuals who themselves are extensively connected like Clark.

the problems that have come in the wake of the housing crisis and local economic disparities.

These findings are the first important piece of the puzzle, painting a picture of the flows of money and influence, via organizations and board members, and within a larger social network of philanthropy in the richest community in the nation. However, these findings still leave one important question unanswered: Why?

6

Moneyfest Destiny

"Oh my God, what have I sacrificed in my life to get to where I am?" mourns Duane Carrington, an ultra-wealthy transplant from California I interviewed for two and a half hours one chilly fall afternoon. Duane's rhetorical question was more of a lamentation—a self-reflective admission that something important had been lost along the journey to economic success. It's not that Duane is looking to forfeit his economic triumphs, or to go back and do things radically differently. Instead, within his rhetorical question is buried a deeply personal dilemma and concern for the future. Fortunately, Duane sees a way forward: "But now I have the means, the resources, the time, the money to recapture what was lost."

For people like Duane, the solution is contained within the problem. Even though some have sacrificed time with their families, their health, their moral character, or their religious ideals, they now have plenty of money and time to recapture what was sacrificed along the way. In the face of this economic dilemma, it is the union of money *with nature* that provides the solution.

Three stories from three different ultra-wealthy people—as told throughout this chapter—provide a new window into motives for environmental philanthropy, and how nature becomes an instrument to help resolve these unique dilemmas they face as moneyed people. These motives, and their association with philanthropy, add an important layer to the Connoisseur Conservation worldview first introduced in chapter 4 that explains how the rich relate to and use nature in the ways that they do.

First, keeping with Duane Carrington, I consider what exactly some ultra-wealthy people believe they have "lost," and how they go about regaining it by supporting causes that connect to their vision of nature, as well as to their vision of a time when life was simpler and more authentic.

Second, we revisit Matt Simpson, who personifies what I call a "new Rockefeller" paradigm that has emerged from the legacy of John D. Rockefeller Jr., a local prototype and hero for some ultra-wealthy conservationists. Matt charters a helicopter each summer in search of huge chunks of land to purchase and protect. This brand of do-it-yourself philanthropy is attractive because it can make a big splash in a short amount of time, and its free-enterprise approach is a more politically comfortable form of conservation for many ultra-wealthy, as opposed to the perceived anti-capitalistic and litigious land grabs by far-left environmentalists or the government.

Third, I introduce Mary Wallace, an ultra-wealthy socialite with whom I ate way too many cocktail shrimp, and who personifies how environmental philanthropy becomes a leisure activity for the wealthy. Because philanthropy is an important venue for socializing and integrating into elite circles—especially through environmental leisure and the arts—this means that issues like poverty, affordable housing, or immigration are viewed as what I call "buzz-kill" issues that spoil the experience of paradise, and thus receive less charitable attention from the nature-loving rich.

———

Each of these stories illustrates from a different angle how the rich approach social and environmental problems, and how through the conversion of money to political power, they install a particular vision of nature and create the *veneer* of a charitable community that is altruistic, publicly spirited, and ecologically progressive.

Intimate insights like this help us move beneath the macro-level numbers from chapter 5 and take a deep dive into the lives of the ultra-wealthy to actually explain *why* they engage in philanthropy in the ways that they do. This approach reveals surprising insights that are often obscured by uncouth stereotypes, both negative and positive (for example, the villainous rich are real-life Ebenezer Scrooges, or the rich are heroic benefactors for communities). Certainly, it is impossible to isolate people's true motives, mostly because human motives aren't as singular as we like to think they are. Most rich philanthropists are neither entirely good Samaritans, giving altruistically for the purity of a cause, nor are they entirely evil colonialists with hidden self-interest or ideas of self-aggrandizement. In reality, ultra-wealthy philanthropy is often a *combination* of these clichés, a multilayered tapestry woven together by both altruism and self-interest, framed by the moral and political meanings they attach to their lives, their wealth, and their causes.

Thus, affluent philanthropy happens within a complex set of cultural entanglements—informed by their own ideas about how they acquired their money, what they gave up getting to the top, what it means to have a lot more than they need, what responsibilities (if any) come with life at rarefied heights, and whether they believe that individuals or the government should address social and environmental problems.

With all of the talk these days among scholars and journalists about where the wealthy's philanthropic dollars are flowing,[1] this community is the ideal living laboratory to understand these national issues in more depth, given its record-setting wealth and record-setting income disparity. As long as extreme wealth inequality in the United States persists, the need to understand the motives and methods of ultra-wealthy benevolence becomes all the more important, and questions about the impacts of plutocracy all the more relevant. How relevant? The top 10 percent of families owns 76 percent of all wealth in the United States ($67 trillion in 2013).[2] The bottom 50 percent—meaning *half of the entire population* of the United States—is left to divvy up just 1 percent of all wealth. Thus, it becomes incredibly important that we dig deeply into the experiences and worldviews of ultra-wealthy people like Duane Carrington or Mary Wallace, to truly understand the web of influences about if, how, and why money trickles down from rarefied heights.

Reclaiming Authenticity Using Nature

Duane Carrington's deeply introspective question that opened this chapter conveys that something important has been lost: "Oh my God, what have I sacrificed in my life to get to where I am?" he asks rhetorically. Fortunately, however, he finds assurance in knowing that he now has the time and money to "recapture" that which was lost. Duane is just one person, and the tone of his admission came off more dramatically than some others, yet nonetheless I found that this was a pervasive theme.

When the ultra-wealthy lament such loss and sacrifice, they are talking specifically about a lost sense of authenticity. Put differently, *they aim to regain a part of themselves that is more genuine, sincere, virtuous, and uncontaminated.* How have these perceived virtues of authenticity been lost along the way? Certainly, we humans are prone to be backward looking, nostalgically ruing the loss of a more "authentic" past, especially when faced with technological automation, racial and ethnic diversification, and so on. But the patterns of loss among the ultra-wealthy often focus on, in the words of Duane, what has been *sacrificed* to reach such levels of financial success. Three related patterns of loss emerged.

WHAT HAS BEEN LOST

First, there is a strong sense that they have scratched and clawed their way to the top, but that once they've arrived, there is a risk of losing the honor and dogged authenticity that motivated them on that journey to begin with. Indeed, there is honor associated with the success, but the deeper and more authentic honor—especially given American reverence for self-determination and myths about rags-to-riches—is in the *early* stages of the struggle itself, where individual will seems the only fuel for survival.

But what happens to your self-identity after this noble struggle is complete, and you've made it? Success can squash authenticity. *They are no longer the scrappy underdog, but the privileged aristocrat. They now play a different, and seemingly less honorable, role in the American story.* The question then becomes, how, if at all, do you reclaim that sense of scrappy authenticity, both for your own self-identity, and for how you are perceived by the rest of society?

Second, to varying degrees, the ultra-wealthy sense that they live in worlds more prone to corruption and moral hazard—a power-packed minefield of greed, myopic materialism, hyper-capitalism, and self-absorption. They've seen the darker side of incredible power and wealth, and some have faced these realities themselves. There is constant risk of losing your moral self, of being hollowed out and decaying into something lesser than you were at some earlier point in time. It seems that the higher you climb, the more risk of loss. To add to this reality, some people described that in addition to the risky pitfalls of this world in which they live, they are also unfairly *perceived* by society as corrupt and morally problematic, and out of touch from more authentic Americans on Main Street (for example, hedge fund managers; CEOs; oil/gas barons). Fair or not, these perceptions impact the ultra-wealthy's views of themselves, and created an urge to *prove* that they can relate to supposedly more "authentic" and morally uncontaminated Americans down on Main Street.[3]

Third, some expressed guilt about the fact that rather than spending their time on more supposedly authentic aspects of life such as kids and spouses, they were lured into the long hours, extended travel, and constant stress that comes with high-powered careers, all with the sudden realization that they already had *so* much more money and power than they would ever need. No doubt, these are life-balance questions faced by all working people from all social classes, but the guilt and loss in this case is unique because of the prodigious amount of money many had already made, and the diminishing life benefits of even *more*.

It's not that making money is felt as corrupting or inauthentic, but that at a certain point, some wondered what difference another $10 million or even $1 billion would make for authentic happiness?

Certainly, these conundrums are all relative, because such money would make a transformational difference for people and communities that are in poverty—but for these ultra-wealthy individuals, more money isn't necessarily transformative, but can be quite the opposite if more authentic aspects of life are sacrificed in exchange. Thus, when more money is viewed as superfluous, it can create feelings of guilt or loss because the tireless pursuit of wealth is viewed as a distraction from what many sensed were life's most fulfilling and authentic aspects.

NATURE THE REDEEMER

If Duane is right, that he and his ultra-wealthy counterparts now have the money and time to "recapture" these aspects of the authentic self that are lost, then how does it look in practice? In Teton County, there are two particular remedies to the moral risks and superficial pitfalls of living life at rarefied heights: (1) connecting to nature; and (2) connecting to the olden days when life was believed to be more honest and simpler. For them, Wyoming offers both in abundance. Establishing a connection to "nature" and these supposed "simpler times" becomes a vehicle for reclaiming the authentic sense of self that may have been sacrificed along the way.[4] Philanthropic organizations do well to channel these feelings and experiences into charitable giving.

Beginning with the first, there is a widespread view that connection to nature—the dirt, rocks, trees, animals, elevation, open air, and so on—are among the most *authentic* experiences we humans can have. These nature-experiences are in stark contrast to society, which is entirely unnatural and the product of flawed humans. Nature is viewed as intrinsically honorable, unselfish, and True. The expenditure of money and time on "nature" is part of the Connoisseur Conservation worldview that I laid out in chapter 4 to understand why nature is enjoyed as an aesthetic storehouse of health-giving rewards. Nature becomes a purifier, a source of goodness, and a protector from the shallow allure of crass materialism. Yes, nature "recharges their batteries," as people would often tell me, but much more than that, it is viewed as a realm of existence that is wholly separate from their world of social corruption, power, competition, and moral hazard.

We humans are capricious and distrustful, and thus nature becomes the only source so clearly authentic and True, where people can purify themselves in its primordial spaces, where our daily concerns are shown to be frivolous in the face of the cosmic, the geologic, and the spiritual. Or in the words of one respondent with whom I lunched in lower Manhattan, "Nature is good for the soul. It brings much-needed healing to us [affluent] people, who live such stressful lives and work so hard. We desperately need the healing touch of nature."

Sometimes this overwhelming feeling of attraction to nature, and to rural places in the West, can happen almost instantaneously, as it did for one very prominent political figure I interviewed, who was taken aback immediately upon arrival, "If I can interrupt for one minute to say that we landed in Wyoming for the first time, and got off the plane at the Jackson Hole airport, looked around, and said, 'This is where I want to die. Let's go look for houses.' And so we had this visceral reaction, that we had to be in Wyoming."

Salvation from the pitfalls of career and the temptations of money was sometimes described in overtly religious terms. A CEO from California explained that "When I go [into nature] I tend to be spiritually renewed, or just you know, I feel like I'm in God's country." A financier from London says that these spiritual feelings have grown in intensity as he's gained better perspective on his life. "Over the years, the environment has just become a lot more spiritual. That's really what is going on for me." The aesthetic beauty is central to these experiences, as illustrated by one woman I interviewed one late afternoon. "There's quite a bit of spirituality, just because you are surrounded by such beautiful scenery, and it's like, so amazing."

Even those who don't consider themselves to be formally religious often expressed a deeper "spiritual" connection. As one woman described it, "I think religion here is probably more like 'I'm going to go climb a mountain today, that's my religion, spirituality, we come here for that.' You know, to each his own." A wealthy medical executive from the East Coast explained to me that he wasn't very religious before coming to Teton County, and now, in his words, "my cathedral is the mountains . . . my wife is a good Episcopalian. And so yeah, I'll go with her to something in Jackson on Christmas Eve from a formal religion point of view. But the people that I spend my time with that I am most comfortable with, it's the mountains and the great outdoors that is the spiritual underpinning because it's so amazing."

This powerful relationship to nature stimulates philanthropic giving. In contrast to charitable giving to human and social services issues, which are mired in human failure, unintended consequences, and the complications of politics, this simple romanticized and spiritualized view of nature provides a more predictable return on charitable investment. Certain environmental causes become an especially good outlet for people like Duane, who in their mission to "recapture" that which was lost are able to sidestep the corrupting influences of humans, and instead give money to a realm that is viewed not only as deeply meaningful but also as steadfastly authentic.

Further, some who had made their fortunes in industries that directly exploited the natural environment described environmental philanthropy in the language of "giving back"—to make up for past sins, so to speak—in the mold of their ultra-wealthy counterpart John D. Rockefeller Jr., who used his family's oil money to underwrite a new national park.

LONGING FOR A PURER, RURAL WESTERN AGE

The North American West has always offered something deeply authentic and appealing to upper-class Americans, and there is a long tradition of wealthy elites engaging with the mythology surrounding indigenous peoples, rugged cowboys, and Old West communities and landscapes. The enduring legacy of luxury dude ranches is a prime example. Popular movies like *City Slickers* are another. The persistent popularity of expensive indigenous artwork, almost always from white painters depicting stereotypical "noble natives" locked in time, is still another.

Upper-class longing for this culture, and continued engagement with it, is not an amusing anomaly, but signals something important. The longing for Old West traditions—qualities like frontier grit, honest work, common sense, rugged symbolism of the cowboy, closeness to nature of native tribes, and material contentment in rural environs—are an especially appealing antidote to counteract the loss of authenticity felt by some ultra-wealthy.

This longing for cultural authenticity plays out in the ways they construct their homes, the books on their shelves, the art on their walls, statues on their floors, and the clothes on their bodies. Even though this idea of a lost Western age is based on half-truths, and is always an idyllic rural figure *of the past* (thereby erasing today's experiences of rural life lived by some indigenous people and the rural poor), it is nevertheless powerful because it opens up the possibility of access to a primordial America where life was simpler, and honest rural values of the noble native, the dusty cowboy, and the homesteader prevailed, all against the backdrop of untamed nature.

My claim here is simple: the engagement with these Old West traditions and nature is not just some fleeting cultural taste, but connects to, and can even mitigate, the deeper cultural and moral loss expressed in the words of ultra-wealthy people like Duane, "Oh my God, what have I sacrificed in my life to get to where I am?" Engaging, and even living in a community like this presents an opportunity to reconnect them to this seemingly authentic and rugged primordial legacy.[5]

Sure, trading stocks in front of a computer can involve long hours and have lucrative returns, but as one investor in his mid-forties put it, he was in search of something more "genuine" than just "buying stocks and bonds on behalf of investors. . . . I wanted to come back out West." Because, as we learned in chapter 1, within the larger context of the financialization of the economy, especially at the top, the majority of ultra-wealthy income is disembodied and nonphysical—the opposite of work in the rugged environs of the Old West. Thus, the labor practices built into these romanticized myths are appealingly authentic, especially in contrast to the dominant myths of the aristocratic East, where family blood is the currency for the affluent, rather than physical blood, sweat, and tears of the rugged individualist poured out in nature.

Furthermore, there is an ethic of *contentment* that is built into this Old West myth, which again, is an especially attractive antidote for the ultra-wealthy, who are constantly presented with opportunities to make even *more* money or attain *more* power. A prominent corporate lawyer I interviewed described what he called the "ethics of the cowboy," emphasizing that we're supposed to work hard, and take only what we need. He's applied these lessons since moving to the West, and in his home he has a prominent room dedicated to displaying his impressive collection of Old West memorabilia, books, and artwork exhibiting these values. These rites and rituals of the frontier are diametrically opposed to the rat-race mentality of high-profile careerism. Thus, the ultra-wealthy find unique meaning in Old West culture because contentment keeps our most dangerous ambitions in check, and counterbalances the problems and superfluous temptations they face in modern times.

Philanthropy can play an important role for ensuring the survival of this perceived way of life, fighting to maintain what people often described to me as the "Western character" and "small-town charm" of the community. This happens in all sorts of diffuse ways, from directly supporting organizations focused on cultural preservation, to more indirect means, such as supporting Western art galleries, museums, and playhouses that sustain the mythic Western culture. As we saw in the quantitative data in chapter 5, when it comes to charitable giving, there is an emphasis on environmental *and* cultural preservation, and in Teton County, the lines between environmental preservation and cultural preservation are blurred, especially in efforts to restrict population growth, which prices out the more diverse groups who do not fit the Old West stereotypes and thus threaten the purity of this powerful myth.[6]

New Rockefellers?

THE ULTRA-WEALTHY PROTOTYPE FOR CONSERVATION

The legacy of John D. Rockefeller Jr. looms large in the history of American conservation, and nowhere more so than in Teton County. As the only son, and heir to the nation's first billionaire, John Jr. found less interest than his father for being an oil tycoon, and instead devoted his life to philanthropy. Among his charitable accomplishments, he is perhaps best known for his pivotal contribution to what became Grand Teton National Park. Under the guise of another name (Snake River Land Company), he secretly agreed to purchase 114,170 acres north of Jackson Hole beneath the Tetons, for about $1.4 million, with the purpose of donating them to the federal government for conservation.

But this was much to the chagrin of locals. There were groups of armed ranchers staging protests on the land, and national newspaper columnists compared the establishment of federal land protections to Hitler's annexation of Austria. It was viewed by some as simply another example of billionaire colonialism from the East, aided and abetted by the federal government. Locals resisted what they viewed as the tyranny of outside control, whether it be the billionaires or the federal government. For example, a letter circulated by locals in the 1940s warned fellow neighbors that "your recreational privileges in Jackson Hole will be practically at an end. There will be 'don't' signs staring you in the face every mile or less."[7] In the long run, Rockefeller, with the help of several federal bureaucrats, as well as multiple presidents (Calvin Coolidge, Franklin Roosevelt, Harry Truman), eventually pushed through the establishment of Grand Teton National Park in 1950.

No doubt, his example still looms large here, especially for some of today's ultra-wealthy who, like John Jr., have immense amounts of money to go along with their newfound passion for the natural landscapes of the North American West. Rockefeller has become a modern prototype for ultra-wealthy conservation—a brand of philanthropy that is viewed as generally positive, relatively simple, and within reach, assuming one has the cash.

A mere sixty-five years later, virtually nobody looks back on Rockefeller as a billionaire outsider with colonialist ambitions. Instead, he is universally celebrated as conservationist par excellence who used his family's oil money for good, not evil.

BIG SPLASH

This "new Rockefeller" paradigm, as I call it, and as it plays out today, focuses on making a big splash through massive land purchases, rather than on less glamorous incremental change that typically characterizes environmental progress. I heard this over and over again throughout my research, best summarized by a well-known fundraising director in Teton County: "the ultra-wealthy tend to view conservation through the lens of simple romance, equating conservation with the purchasing of large tracts of private land to be set aside under protection." But we know from research in environmental studies[8] that successful large-scale conservation often requires a focus on a less romantic, and more complicated, set of processes that involve much more than purchasing expensive lands.

The new Rockefeller paradigm is personified today to varying degrees. Its fullest expression is epitomized by Matt Simpson, the ultra-wealthy philanthropist we met in chapter 5, who during the summer charters a helicopter to fly around Wyoming and Montana in search of large swaths of land to purchase for conservation. "I chartered this helicopter and spent the summer all over Wyoming and Montana with the idea of buying one of them and putting a conservation easement, and at some point, I probably will," he explained. Specifically, he is in search of what he calls a "big piece of property," but only for the purpose of preservation, rather than running cattle, agricultural production, or some other traditional usage. "I'm an investment banker, private equity guy . . . you don't want me running a ranch," he quips. But like Rockefeller, he'll provide the millions in order to achieve his vision of large-scale preservation.

Fixing one's name to a piece of private Eden is an incredibly attractive way to mark one's legacy in American history. Certainly, it worked for Rockefeller, whose name is etched into local conservation lore (for example, in 1972 Congress attached his name to the famous highway connecting Grand Teton National Park to Yellowstone National Park). Even today, after the violent removal of indigenous peoples and the still-ongoing and supposed "settling" of the West, it is still possible—with enough money—to inscribe one's name upon a large section of land, fixing a family legacy into time. As compared to the overpopulated and overdeveloped eastern United States with an already well-established philanthropic hierarchy, the West is still mythologized as wild, open, and free, and even offers the opportunity to be a big fish in a small pond, perfect for those looking to make their mark.

DIY CONSERVATION

The allure of the Rockefeller paradigm is its apparent well-meaning simplicity. First, it appears to be *ethically* simple, meaning that preserving large pieces of land is, like Rockefeller before them, viewed as an *unquestioned* contribution to the public and environmental good. This is part of a larger culture of assumed altruism that undergirds ultra-wealthy relationships to environmental conservation, as explored in the previous two chapters.[9] Second, it appears to be politically and pragmatically simple, where conservation becomes akin to any other real estate transaction—money is exchanged for land at market value. This free-enterprise approach to conservation is often contrasted to anti-capitalistic approaches, whereby land is forcibly and litigiously grabbed by environmental groups and government agencies.

This private solution is more politically comfortable, especially for ultra-wealthy philanthropists, many of whom come from enterprising backgrounds, where issues of market value and private exchange are in their wheelhouse. From this perspective, conservation is simplified, and what is often viewed as the domain of environmentalists or the federal government suddenly becomes attainable for those who have the money but don't want to deal with all the red tape.

Land trusts are especially popular for these reasons, and according to the leader of a prominent conservation organization, the success of the local Jackson Hole Land Trust is an indicator that the Rockefeller approach has been deeply infused into local culture. Large-scale land conservation remains the goal, but is accomplished through a more cautious, and politically safe, form of conservation that leapfrogs the advocacy arena and largely sidesteps the political snares of bureaucratic land management.

For some nonwealthy people, this brand of private conservation can bring negative side effects, such as sealing off the land from the public, forbidding access to these large areas for hunting, hiking, cycling, snowmobiling, and other forms of recreation. And in contrast to lands in the public domain (for example, state parks, national forests, Bureau of Land Management land, national parks), the owners of large tracts of private land can shield important information about the land itself, and their land trust dealings. As summed up by a local reporter when I asked her for information about the local land trust, she grumbled, "I'm not sure I can be much help, because whenever I've reported on the Jackson Hole Land Trust acquisitions, the financial specifics have been off limits."

Philanthropy, Social Status, and "Buzz-Kills"

One late afternoon, I sat with Mary Wallace at her country club on the deck of the clubhouse, eating oversize shrimp, and watching the sun dip beneath the Tetons. She eagerly introduced me to friends, waiters, and even the owner of the club—really, most anybody who passed by our table. She was genuine and friendly, and I hardly needed to probe using my interview guide because she was intent on showing me the ropes, especially when it came to philanthropy. Gushing, she sums it up, "there is just so much human capital here. So many dynamic people who live here and are committed to protecting this special place." No doubt, Mary is right that there is no shortage of personal commitment, as many ultra-wealthy donate their money and time out of genuine concern. Yet, personal commitment goes only so far, and I found that it is a poor predictor for understanding how and why people donate their time and money.

What matters most is how local organizations create a social and moral context to "pull" the ultra-wealthy into philanthropic activities. This "pull" dynamic explains why the ultra-wealthy would sometimes unintentionally find themselves sitting on a nonprofit board, heading up an expensive gala fundraiser, or tapping their networks for donations. In other words, there is much more going on than naked personal commitment.

I consider two important explanations, and both are related to the idea that philanthropy is a leisure activity. First, philanthropy is often *the* venue for socializing, and nonprofit organizations are keen to harness social networks in this way. Second, according to Mary (and other ultra-wealthy people), the purpose of philanthropy is, in her words, to protect "this special place." Any issues that are not related to the environment or arts are viewed as what I call "buzz-kill" issues, and receive less charitable attention because they cast the long shadow of reality on this rural Western paradise.

SOCIAL INTEGRATION

We've all heard the same line of advice from friends or family, especially when we've moved to a new community: get involved; volunteer; join a civic group; attend a religious congregation. Research has shown time and again how these avenues connect us to people and issues that we care about, integrating us into the social fabric of a community. With more involvement, our social networks may grow, and we may find ourselves caring about issues that had never been on our radar.

These patterns hold true for Teton County, with one exception: this is a community that has grown exponentially since the 1970s, and many of these new residents are among the wealthiest in the world, with plenty of money, time, experience, and connections to use as they integrate themselves into the community. Not all see this as a good thing, however, and the ubiquity of charitable concern and political activity can drive some ultra-wealthy crazy, such as one retired CEO of a Fortune 100 company I interviewed over breakfast in Jackson Hole town square. "My assessment of Jackson is that it's full of type A personalities with not enough to do, so there's [environmental/political] controversy because these people are sitting around, and they have opinions and they write letters to the editor, and they organize in various subgroups. It's just an interesting phenomenon."

Issues that had never been on their radar, such as wildlife migration corridors or stream ecosystems, become hot topics of conversation at elite cocktail parties. Among all these issues, environmental topics carry the most social weight, and to be ignorant is to risk embarrassment among one's peers, or to be exposed as an out-of-touch carpetbagger.

As one expert ecologist, who has lived and worked in the community for thirty-five years, described it, "the wealthy want to establish themselves in the community, socially and in terms of status. But they are also searching for meaning. The quickest way to do this is to start a nonprofit around some environmental issue that they believe is important."

While some choose to start their own nonprofit groups, most are recruited to connect through established organizations. I asked all interviewees about if, how, and why they got involved in environmental issues, and heard many of the same passive responses, almost as if they were lured into involvement, rather than through willful choice. One corporate lawyer, originally from Oklahoma, and never before involved in "environmentalist" politics, paused and stumbled out an answer that sounded to me as if he had no choice in the matter, "umm, well I guess, you know, I just met people in the community who, you know, *got me* involved."[10]

In other words, environmentalism does not come naturally to many ultra-wealthy people, and can even be uncomfortable, but there is a strong social patterning that *gets* people involved. The social pull begins with the nonprofit organizations who evangelize in fun social settings like picnics, cocktail hours, art exhibits, and so on, where problems can be introduced, solutions presented, moral meanings framed, and concrete opportunities to give their time and money provided.

This also means that local organizations incessantly compete for a slice of the ultra-wealthy pie, monitoring who has moved into the community, gathering intelligence on their social connections, their economic capital, and their potential interest in participating. Social events become the cornerstone of these recruiting efforts, such as lavish house party I described in the introduction of this book thrown by an environmental organization, or the annual Jackson Hole Land Trust picnic attended by our ultra-wealthy friend Laura from chapter 4.

But some nonwealthy people who work in conservation, such as the longtime ecologist quoted earlier, are critical of the tight alliance between wealthy socialites and conservation, and criticized these organizations as largely social clubs for the rich. Some of the more prestigious events held by the well-funded organizations attract everyone from the very rich to the very powerful (for example, U.S. senators, governors), but according to this same longtime resident, the events—galas, picnics, art exhibits, open houses, and so on—are merely elite rituals of patting peers on the back for what are at best marginal and politically safe accomplishments, and at worst, just philanthropic efforts to benefit their own financial bottom line or gilded experience of nature.

Certainly, not all organizations are the same, and there are many that have accomplished a great deal, but at the same time, I did discover a strong tendency toward politically safe projects that reinforce the status quo, especially when it comes to socioeconomic problems. Organizations are careful not to rock the boat, and because there is no sizable middle-class population from which to draw organizational support, the scramble to ingratiate one's organization with the ultra-wealthy becomes all the more important. These self-congratulatory rituals, and the prominence of social events, are necessary for organizational survival in a context where there is only one source of money, and it is held by a handful of people who tend to be politically moderate, and whose environmental activism is synonymous with socializing.

BUZZ-KILLS AND PARADISE LOST

Ignorance is bliss, and knowledge can be a buzz-kill. In addition to the inability of human and social service organizations to offer the kind of social prestige, fun events, and connections to power, they are also associated with what one Teton County employee called "buzz-kill issues." Over lunch at Cowboy Coffee in the Jackson town square, he explained that "people just don't want to believe social problems exist here. The addiction, the abuse, and so on. 'Don't tell me that because I want to believe this is paradise,' they say." He continues, explaining that "this is part of a larger issue contributing to the fact that social service nonprofits have a hard time raising money. They have a hard time recruiting smart people and paying them enough to stick around."

Ironically, extreme wealth disparity can render social problems invisible, creating the illusion that all is well in paradise. There is very little authentic interclass contact on a day-to-day basis, making it difficult for human services organizations to even convince those who hold the majority of the purse strings that the problems are real and could use more support. For decades, social scientists have demonstrated the negative effects of social-class segregation, poverty concentration, and settings with little intergroup contact.[11] No doubt, these dynamics have influenced the awareness of social problems and the philanthropic response, but that does not necessarily mean that they won't remain a buzz-kill in this context of extreme wealth.

I witnessed these dynamics very clearly as I was acquiring ultra-wealthy access and conducting my interviews. Most interviewees accepted my invitation because they were thrilled to talk about the rural West, because it meant talking about the beauty of the pristine ecosystem, their favorite recreation spots, Yellowstone Park, the small-town Western character, and their breathtaking properties and homes. In addition to the status appeal of participating in a Yale-sponsored study, I acquired access because people were eager to chat about this place they had come to love, and considered our interview to be a refreshing conversation, in contrast to the gloominess and depressing politics that consumed much popular conversation.

But the tone of the conversation would noticeably change when I moved to questions about Teton County being the most unequal community in the country, or the role of ultra-wealth in solving some of the known side effects of wealth concentration and the housing crisis (for example, homelessness, addiction, illiteracy). I had many great conversations about these issues, but the buzz-kill effect described by the Teton County staffer earlier was evident. Up until this point, poverty and inequality hadn't really been a buzz-kill for most people I interviewed, because it was associated with the stereotypical "ski-bum" just scraping by, rather than an immigrant family of ten living a tiny hotel room. Confronted with this information, there was a sense that an emotional boundary had been crossed, and that the interview had become something completely different. My questions conveyed more than they wanted to know—as if it now made them complicit. Through this process, I uncovered much more clarity about why the environment and cultural preservation had received the bulk of philanthropic support.

Converting Wealth to Power

There is no doubt that private giving can be socially and politically transformative.[12] The power of philanthropy is on display in this community, whereby the ultra-wealthy convert huge amounts of money to influence, shaping this place around their own vision of nature, albeit in ways that on the surface appear to be more altruistic, progressive, and pro-environmental. Certainly, the notion of "converting wealth to power" has a strong negative connotation, even drumming up images of violence, force, coercion, or outright deception. Yet, power is not always so overtly forceful or violent, but still its effects persist. Here in this community, power is exerted—many times with good intentions—in ways that appear on the surface to be publicly spirited and for the ecological benefit of nature. But as I've shown, ultra-wealthy power is born from a mixture of motives, and money disproportionately flows to nature and arts, both of which are taken as an *unquestionable* good benefiting the entire community.

But stepping back, we see that the flows of money and power have injected a *particular* view of the world favored by the ultra-wealthy, especially concerning the natural environment. Money is power in this community and across the New West because it promotes what I have called "compensation" and "connoisseur" conservation, and is more deeply motivated by an attempt to recapture what was lost, to preserve the myths of the Old West, to achieve authenticity, to make a big Rockefeller-type conservation splash, to be socially integrated into elite circles, and as a form of leisure. This way of seeing the world, and this brand of philanthropy, has become institutionalized, and taken for granted as *good*, despite the ways that it disproportionately benefits the ultra-wealthy, and neutralizes deeper issues of social and environmental inequality.

David Callahan, a foremost expert on American charitable giving, writes in his new book,

> Philanthropists indeed have more power than ever before . . . that influence is likely to grow far greater in coming decades. . . . Philanthropy is becoming a much stronger power center and, in some areas, is set to surpass government in its ability to shape society's agenda. To put things differently, we face a future in which private donors—who are accountable to no one—may often wield more influence than elected public officials, who (in theory, anyway) are accountable to all of us. This power shift is one of the biggest stories of our time.[13]

Nowhere in the United States is this power differential more on display than in Teton County, Wyoming, where there is very limited government, the nation's most favorable tax codes for the wealthy and private foundations, and a community where economic power is more concentrated at the top than anywhere else. In other words, in no other community is there greater potential for private sector control through the conversion of wealth to power.

As a result, local charitable organizations, who rely on immense amounts of economic and human capital from the ultra-wealthy, are prone to becoming captive to a particular view of the world promoted by their donors and board members, which tends to sustain the status quo, and nullifies efforts for more groundbreaking change to address the roots of social problems brought on by such wealth disparity.

Importantly, I found that all of this can happen with the best of intentions by all parties involved, and that the institutionalization and normalization of these patterns make them appear as the standard modus operandi. They have become the new normal. Meanwhile, organizations with agendas that challenge the status quo, either by promoting more dramatic political changes, grassroots organizing, or direct action, or pointing out the roots of social, economic, and environmental inequality receive drastically less charitable support, and thus wield relatively little power.

Peter Buffett, an author, philanthropist, and the son of billionaire Warren Buffett, has been an outspoken critic of late, and his words, worth quoting in full, ring true here in Teton County.

As more lives and communities are destroyed by the system that creates vast amounts of wealth for the few, the more heroic it sounds to "give back." It's what I would call "conscience laundering"—feeling better about accumulating more than any one person could possibly need to live on by sprinkling a little around as an act of charity. But this just keeps the existing structure of inequality in place. The rich sleep better at night, while others get just enough to keep the pot from boiling over. . . . I'm really not calling for an end to capitalism; I'm calling for humanism. . . . Money should be spent trying out concepts that shatter current structures and systems that have turned much of the world into one vast market. Is progress really Wi-Fi on every street corner? No. It's when no 13-year-old girl on the planet gets sold for sex. But as long as most folks are patting themselves on the back for charitable acts, we've got a perpetual poverty machine. It's an old story; we really need a new one.[14]

Thus, despite the good intentions of many ultra-wealthy bene-factors, things continue to get worse for everyone else in the com-munity, as the middle class has mostly died off, and the low-income immigrants struggle to hang on, all this despite near consensus among my interviewees that this is one of the most charitable com-munities in the nation. They aren't necessarily wrong, as charity continues to be the bedrock social currency in the community, moti-vated by genuine altruism, "new Rockefeller" benevolence, a long-ing for authenticity, guilt alleviation, social leisure, social prestige, and economic self-interest—but, as we've learned, this brimming river of money and influence continues to flow beneath a mountain of "buzz-kill" social problems that casts a long dark shadow of reality over nature's Eden.

PART III

Using Rural People to Solve Social Dilemmas

Was Jesus right? Is it really easier for a camel to go through the eye of a needle than for a rich person to enter the kingdom of God? In other words, do the ultra-wealthy really need to sell their possessions and give to the poor if they want to live a life defined by character, worth, and communal virtue? I decided to ask them.

This section of the book picks up where this famous biblical story leaves off, when the rich person, who hears that he must sell his possessions and give to the poor, "went away sad, because he had great wealth." The rich man fades from view, and we are left with this simple lesson about the moral jeopardy of possessing great wealth.

But moving beyond this time-honored lesson, I wanted to track down modern people emblematic of the rich man at the heart of this story, seeking to understand in detail the actual role of great wealth in the lives and minds of those who have it, and how it shapes the type of person they see themselves as, and the type of person they strive to become.

This journey into the heart and soul of the ultra-wealthy happens in two ways. In chapter 7, I examine *how great wealth affects their perception of themselves, how they wish to be seen by others, and their attempt to transform themselves accordingly.* Burdened by social stigmas, they use the natural environment and rural working-class culture to actualize a "normal" version of themselves rooted in authenticity, simple contentment, and old-time communal virtue.

In chapter 8, I ask a deceptively simple question that reveals a great deal: *Do they feel guilty?* I employ this question because, while potentially loaded, it reveals a lot about the ways people justify great wealth and excuse great inequality, but more importantly, I show how it raises bigger concerns about wealth and inequality that go right to the heart of one of the most critical questions of our time: what makes a community in the twenty-first century?

Engaging the ultra-wealthy for hundreds of hours on these intimate questions is a sharp departure from most popular and scholarly studies of wealth. The difficulty of gaining access to the über-rich has restricted the questions researchers could ask, and research tends to be limited to impersonal macro-level studies about social class and economic stratification.[1] In focusing on these impersonal dynamics, this common approach has revealed time and again how a small group of peoples' wealth is converted to power, acting downward on the rest of society, creating class-based advantages and widening the gap between different social groups.[2] To be sure, this bird's-eye view research is incredibly important and is consistent with the approach taken thus far in this book, where I've shown how acute wealth concentration has created the richest and most unequal community in the nation, and how the natural environment is used as a tool to for economic gain, private access to nature, and gilded philanthropy.

Yet, at the same time, this approach can sterilize us from ground-level experiences, and is limited in its ability to fully explain how great wealth actually functions *in the individual lives and minds* of those who have it. It leaves unexplored the rich cultural, social-psychological, and moral dilemmas that accompany great wealth. Beneath these class-based systems are actual living/breathing persons who, like many of us, navigate basic existential aspects of the human condition: seeking happiness, yearning for social acceptance and integration, striving to be a good person, caring for and socializing their children, searching for ultimate meaning, facing the specter of death, struggling against regret and guilt, just to name a few. Such an approach requires greater attention to individual and group reasoning, *focusing on how having such wealth might uniquely shape how they think, talk, and reckon with these issues.*

And more broadly, it requires moving beyond the popular and scholarly explanations that apply an overly simplistic model of human motivation to the ultra-wealthy—namely, that they are a class of people on a straightforward and seemingly robotic conquest for more power, more money, more control. And while it can certainly appear this way from the bird's-eye view, given the well-documented increases in economic inequality in the United States and the cumulative advantages enjoyed and protected by a tiny class of ultra-wealthy elites, the story becomes more interesting, and reveals new surprises, when we dive deeper into the lives and minds of the *human beings* that make up this increasingly powerful social class.

7

Becoming Rural Poor, Naturally

John Truett is a tremendously wealthy oil and gas CEO who, above all, prides himself on being a "normal person." Being a normal person can take some effort, however. "When I go into town, to the bars, I don't tell people that I live in a gated community. They accept me as a local, and I'm drinking beer with the locals," he says proudly. "And I'm dressed like a local, and I look like a local, and I say, 'I'm John, I'm from the Midwest.'"

In story after story, John fills me in on his social circle, composed *not* of fellow CEOs but of "normal" folks, as he describes them, who live a simple and stress-free life—working to live, rather than living to work. He gushes over his friend Karen, who "just works as an administrative person. She's a neat lady. She hikes during her noon hour. She doesn't even eat lunch, she heads up the hill [to hike], you know. She's quite a jock—solid muscle, fifty years old and not a pinch of body fat on her, and fun and local. You know, I know all the local people."

Has money changed John? Yes and no, he reckons. "Yeah, I've got the airplanes, a motorcycle, and I love driving my Beemer through the mountains . . . [but] remember that I think I'm a local, so I go down and drink beer with the guys that run the lifts, and I'm as much as a 'lifty' as they are."

At first, John's eagerness to wax lyrical about all of his working-class friends, and his taste for working-class clothing, seemed trivial to me. I wrote it off as insignificant, thinking that, like all of us, John was simply trying to relate to those around him, or alternatively, as a good upper-class cultural omnivore,[1] he had expanded his taste repertoire to include low-brow culture as a way to signal his cosmopolitanism. But these common explanations seemed too shallow and incomplete to account for why the theme of normalcy kept emerging as I interviewed and observed the ultra-wealthy. Something wasn't lining up—there had to be more to the story.

Probing more deeply, I found that their desire to assimilate into "normal" rural culture was hardly trivial, but signaled something fundamentally important, revealing anxieties among the ultra-wealthy about whether money had fundamentally changed them. Had it aggrandized their own self-perception without their realizing it, like a frog lingering in hot water until it boils? Had it impaired their ability to relate to these "normal" working-class people? Had it somehow diminished their moral character? And as a result of these anxieties, I wondered, *what was it about "normal" people that they found so appealing*, and why was identifying with these rural residents (and their presumed normal Western values) being used by some of the ultra-wealthy to reclaim what they might have lost?

There is much more going on here than expanding one's cultural palate to include working-class tastes. *It is about self-transformation.* It is about the creation of a new social identity.[2] The appropriation of romanticized rural frontier ideals and nature-oriented culture makes such a transformation possible, as they attempt to actualize a version of themselves that they view as more virtuous, authentic, and community minded.

In John's case, it was clear that he was burdened by the anxieties and social stigmas associated with being rich. In large part, this was because he wasn't born into a wealthy family and his sense of self is still shaped by what he believes normal folks think of him. "I put myself back to being nineteen years old, and seeing these rich people and big houses. I might have some misconception that these people are fucking assholes; rich fucking assholes from the East. You know,

members of the lucky sperm club. They've fucking inherited everything and I'm fucking working a ski-lift here, freezing my ass off. You
know, that type of attitude. But, it's *not that*. These [wealthy people]
are self-made people that have families that are out there trying to
do family things."

Whether or not these perceived stereotypes about "rich fucking
assholes from the East" or undeserving "members of the lucky sperm
club" are true, or fair, does not concern me here. What matters is the
effect of these perceptions on how the wealthy *see themselves*, and
how their self-image can *prompt efforts to reclaim virtues they associate with normal people* who have not, in their view, been polluted
by the pitfalls of wealth. As I will show, this is a complex process
whereby the ultra-wealthy attempt to reconcile their great fortunes
with the associated social stigmas of greed, elitism, and savage ambition, which place them at a social and moral distance from normal
people.

To bridge this gap, they attempt to have their cake and eat it too,
by both remaining ultra-wealthy *and* striving to attain the honorable
attributes they associate with normal people, such as authenticity,
simplicity, contentment, purity, tranquility, and closeness to nature.

The natural environment plays an important role in this process
because it is also viewed as a wellspring of purity and simplicity,
beyond the snares of money and careerism. Such a relationship
to nature allows even a stigmatized fossil fuel baron like John to
remodel himself into something he views as more socially and ecologically virtuous. Or in the words of a hedge fund executive from
Connecticut, "It's not about money here! We are all just deeply in
love with Wyoming. It has *completely changed* us!"

―――――

But changed how? And why? The transformation follows four dis-
tinct stages, each of which I will unpack in this chapter.

First, the *stigma* stage. Here, I briefly return to a theme from
chapter 6: how wealth can create social-psychological anxiety and
a crisis of authenticity. This point is informed by recent findings in

cultural sociology about how certain groups of people can become stigmatized.

Second comes the *lifestyle consumption* stage. Here, I show how wealth itself offers a solution to this problem by providing needed resources (for example, money, time, access to nature) for a brand of lifestyle consumption that seeks to be *self-transformative*. In contrast to previous American generations, wealth is no longer viewed as innately evil or corrupting, but is simply an amoral tool to be used for individual self-fulfillment, self-actualization, and happiness. This process of individual transformation has an important social function, whereby one refashions oneself into a person who is no longer stigmatized, and thereby gaining recognition as "normal" members of the community.

Third is the *romanticization* stage, containing the assumed ingredients that constitute a "normal" person. In this section, I delve deeply into my interviews and observations, showing that the qualities the ultra-wealthy strive to adopt, and find the most venerable, are rooted in a romanticized infatuation with the rural working poor.[3] These are people who, despite their low-status careers and lack of material comforts, seemingly live a noble life of honesty, goodness, passion, and simplicity. Ultra-wealthy stereotypes coalesce into a conception of the rural working poor, pieced together with popular motifs pulled from mythical dusty cowboys, native peoples frozen in the past and assumed to be one with the natural world, and modern-day penniless nature-loving types (for example, ski-bums, "van lifers," recreation guides) who have honorably *chosen* to relinquish the pursuit of wealth for a life of rugged survival and adventure in nature. The reality, however, is that the vast majority of the working poor in this community are anything but that. Rather, they are Spanish-speaking immigrants who are not living a life of romanticized poverty or nature-oriented adventure, but who narrowly survive by working two or three jobs in the services sector.

Fourth, and perhaps most remarkably, comes the *social performance* stage. I show how self-transformation based on these romanticized personal qualities is accomplished by (1) establishing and professing bonds of authentic friendship with normal members of the low-income and working classes, and (2) outwardly adopting Western rural culture (for example, style of dress, artwork in their homes, and consumer goods) that help the ultra-wealthy to reduce the social and symbolic distance between themselves and (what they perceive to be) the rest of the community, thus signaling their conversion to normalcy.[4]

What does this process of transformation look like on the ground? It is best summed up by Claude Rudolph, a real estate mogul originally from New Jersey: "Jackson has as big an economic gap as exists anywhere on the planet," he acknowledges, "but you usually don't ever see it. You can be at a party, and you don't know if the person that is there in blue jeans is a billionaire or a struggling tree-hugger."

This theme was echoed repeatedly throughout my research. As another ultra-wealthy interviewee put it, "If a guy is wearing cowboy boots and jeans and a plaid shirt, you don't know whether he's a hedge fund manager or a carpenter or a ski instructor. But if the fashions start to change, and the distinctions start to change, then I fear that there will become class strata."

But from the perspective of the nonwealthy—and especially the working poor we'll hear from in later chapters—the class strata aren't determined by taste in fashion or artwork, but by their daily struggle in the most economically unequal county in the United States. And these intentionally blurred class lines—what we might call "class confusion"—are not taken kindly to by the nonwealthy. Claire Drury, a disenchanted nonwealthy resident, sums up these sentiments, ribbing, "Yeah, yeah, yeah, the ultra-wealthy are befriending us savages while drinking a really nice 1976 Bordeaux. What's not to like? It is reminiscent of all the Buffalo Bill Wild West shows, [with] the noble savages sitting there stiff as a board while their photos are being taken in some sort of sepia-toned thing." Continuing, she reflects more deeply, "I just think that they realize that there's more to life now, and they've got the means to refashion themselves . . . to become a normal person, like some of the common folks. And they truly believe they can."

Social Stigmas and Anxiety: Evidence
from Neuroscience and Sociology

A large body of research from the neurosciences and psychology has shown that wealth can change how we see the world, altering even how our brain functions. For example, based on findings from experiments and brain imaging, there is a growing consensus among cognitive scientists that people with higher economic status are less empathetic than others. Having wealth affects the way the brain responds when someone sees another in pain: those with more money respond less empathetically, whereas those with less money respond more empathetically. Furthermore, one such study found that wealth can also inflate the wealthy person's self-perception of how empathetic they are, "suggesting that those higher in status may not realize that they are actually lower in empathy."[5]

One explanation for this phenomenon is that high-status people tend to be laser-focused on their own goals and desires, which blinds them from registering the concerns of those from lower socioeconomic groups. A simpler reason is that the wealthy can turn a blind eye to others' troubles because their power and status affords them that option. Lower-income people do not have this luxury, perhaps explaining why they have more sensitive mirror-neuron systems—the part of the brain that allows us to put ourselves in the shoes of another.[6] Beyond affecting our perceptions, behavioral science has documented repeatedly that wealth has a negative effect on pro-social behavior.[7]

Importantly, I also found that great wealth can affect people's minds in another way: *by producing intense social-psychological anxiety—and for some, a crisis of authenticity that goes to the heart of who they are as people.*

GROUP STIGMATIZATION

The Harvard sociologist Michèle Lamont has written extensively about the symbolic boundaries that separate groups of people, and the cultural processes by which these boundaries are drawn, resulting in the lumping and splitting of individuals into larger collectives. These boundaries are erected using myriad familiar social categories such as class, income, religion, race, ethnicity, and nationality. Individuals often self-identify with certain groups, but equally as often, *individuals are identified by others* as members of a particular group. As Lamont notes, these symbolic differences often involve a moral component: We draw boundaries between "us and them" to maintain our sense of individual moral worth, and to assure ourselves (and signify to others) that *we* are good people, worthy of respect and praise.

At the same time, social groups can undergo a process of "stigmatization," in which the group becomes negatively associated with qualities considered deeply unfavorable.[8] The ultra-wealthy have become one such group in the United States. Stigmatization of the rich has intensified in the last decade as issues of income inequality have become more visible via protest movements that have publicized and stigmatized such inequities (for example, Occupy Wall Street, with its "1 percenters"). Politicians such as Bernie Sanders and Elizabeth Warren have risen to prominence by incorporating this stigma into their policy platforms, lambasting the ways that the wealthy influence politics, and how policies benefit the ultra-wealthy.

Stigmatization is communicated through *stories and narratives* that we tell about a group, involving villainous characters that help to put a face on the entire group and reinforce negative perceptions. Stigmas on the ultra-wealthy are often embodied in the stereotype of the insatiable Wall Street banker who, despite playing a major role in the collapse of the U.S. economy in 2008, still reaped huge rewards. In light of the suffering incurred on so many middle-class and working-poor Americans as a result of the Wall Street crash itself, many Americans believed the bankers' success to be both undeserved and immoral.

Similarly, as younger generations have become more concerned about climate change, another symbolic character entwined with ultra-wealthy stigmas has emerged: the executive from an environmentally harmful industry whose company earns record profits at the expense of the earth. For example, stigmatization was created by the moral outrage against the fossil-fuel industry in the wake of the record-shattering BP oil spill.[9] Beyond such disastrous events, this outrage has been channeled into a growing chorus of activists seeking to stigmatize not just the executives or companies themselves, but also those who invest in them, directly or indirectly. This social, political, and moral pressure has created a divestment movement, led by a handful of universities, religious organizations, and investment funds acting in response to the stigma associated with the fossil-fuel industry. In this way, social stigmas can have significant consequences for all involved.

SOCIAL ANXIETY AND CRISIS OF AUTHENTICITY

The Wall Streeter and the fossil fuel executive characters are just two popular examples of the stigma associated with the ultra-wealthy, which asserts that *how* you make your money matters, in addition to how much of it you have. Of course, not all ultra-wealthy individuals earn their income from these stigmatized industries, although finance is certainly the most prevalent one. More generally, the stigma placed on the ultra-wealthy can cast them as garish, out-of-touch, environmentally hypocritical, selfish, inhumane, and undeserving people. In other words, the moral worth of this group has been discredited.

Many ultra-wealthy people wondered aloud to me whether these stigmas are fair and whether the majority of Americans actually view them in such a negative light, given the ways that popular culture simultaneously venerates the rich. These are fair questions, and at the same time revealed that the ultra-wealthy are, consciously or subconsciously, aware of the stigma they bear.

Importantly, I found that *this stigma creates a pervasive sense of anxiety among the ultra-wealthy about the extent to which they are viewed as deserving, virtuous, and authentic people.* Feelings of anxiety stem from their status as members of this stigmatized group, set apart from the rest of society. Other research has described similar findings, such as Rachel Sherman's recent study of wealthy New Yorkers. The British epidemiologist Richard Wilkinson reported that, "As status differences grow, we worry more about status insecurity, we get widespread anxiety about self-esteem, and that brings rising rates of mental illness and depression."[10]

Some of the ultra-wealthy expressed their anxiety to me directly in interviews. These people were hyper-aware of society's perception of them and worked to combat the stereotypes, going to great lengths to debunk the popular image of the rich. But most often (and more interestingly), I uncovered this pervasive sense of anxiety by studying the ways they *talked about and behaved toward other people.*

Ultra-wealthy anxiety about their money and how they earned it is part of the larger pattern I unpacked in the preceding chapter on the crisis of personal authenticity, perhaps best conveyed by the words of Duane: "Oh my God, what have I sacrificed in my life to get to where I am?" In this short quote, Duane sums up a *crisis of self-image,* but the anxiety I'm describing here adds another layer because it is driven by *how others see him* and his ultra-wealthy counterparts. After achieving immense success, Duane felt that he had sacrificed something important, and that something authentic had been lost. Duane can make the lifestyle changes necessary to try to recoup aspects of life he deems most important (for example, time with family, or philanthropy). But what he has less control over are society's opinions and judgments of him as a morally worthy person, and these negative stigmas have become sharper and more amplified as the rich have continued to get richer while the wages of the middle and working classes have remained stagnant.

Unless the ultra-wealthy lock themselves underground and ignore scientific findings about the anti-social impacts of wealth, there is no way to completely escape the reach of the prevailing anti-wealth stigma. The questions, then, are to what extent does it affect them, and what do they do about it?

Using Wealth for Inward and Outward Transformation

Returning to the biblical story earlier that opened part 3, we know that the rich man had become concerned enough about his own standing and character that he approached Jesus to ask what he must do. Jesus's famous response, to sell all he has and give to the poor, was probably not the answer the man was looking for. After all, he went away sad. Immediately, Jesus reminded his followers—using his peculiar but now famous line about a camel squeezing through the eye of a needle—that great wealth brings immeasurable problems that can only be fully resolved by giving it all away.

The majority of ultra-wealthy people I studied were not planning to relinquish their fortune. Many had an alternative plan: to have their cake and eat it too, perhaps at the peril of warnings by the likes of Jesus and other ancient philosophers and religious thinkers such as Aristotle, Buddha, and Confucius, which are supported by the recent findings from behavioral neuroscience showing the negative impacts of wealth. The ultra-wealthy implicitly and explicitly cope with the persistent stigma, anxiety, religious warnings, and scientific findings about the risk of their affluence by using their great wealth to transform themselves. This transformation is both internal and external. Wealth is used as a tool both to regenerate oneself by cultivating a lifestyle that leads to self-fulfillment and happiness *and* to facilitate greater social recognition from the nonwealthy, thereby gaining acceptance as authentic members of the community. Two birds, one stone.

HISTORICAL CONTEXT: WEALTH, INDIVIDUAL TRANSFORMATION, AND PERSONAL HAPPINESS

It is important to recognize the historical context within which this transformation is taking place. It is part of a larger shift in American culture in which the value of great wealth is less about status and more about the individual who has it and the extent to which she or he uses it for positive self-development, spiritual growth, and personal happiness.[11]

This perspective is a recent development. Three phases preceded it, which—while still lingering—have been displaced by the focus on individual self-fulfillment. First, early in American history wealth was viewed as a *positive sign of virtue rather than selfishness*. We might call this the "Protestant Ethic" phase.[12] Those who had wealth were thought to deserve it; it was seen as a reflection of their self-discipline, hard work, and moral and religious rectitude. During the second, or "Robber Baron" phase of the nineteenth century, Americans had come to judge wealth not as sign of virtue but as a *threat to civilized society*, due in large part to the extreme concentration of wealth among a few powerful families (for example, the Rockefellers, Vanderbilts, and Carnegies) and the monopolies, inequality, and corruption that came in its wake. In the third stage— the "Conspicuous Consumption" phase—the idea of using money for self-fulfillment began to emerge, but was rejected because of the *superficiality, emptiness, and ultimate tragedy of conspicuous consumption*—as explored in novels such as *The Great Gatsby* and films such as *Citizen Kane*.

In the fourth and current stage, finding self-fulfillment via affluent consumption is no longer seen as tragic or empty. *Conspicuous consumption is viewed as a legitimate path to individual happiness.* This view of wealth bridges the moral gap between those at the top and those at the bottom of the economic pyramid. They are separated not by purpose or goal, but only by how much money they have to consume. In other words, the nonwealthy are actually striving for the same outcomes as the wealthy, but simply have less to work with on their path to happiness.

As the literary critic Winfried Fluck explains,

> The criterion for justifying wealth is now whether and how it can make the individual happy. Self-development is radically "democratized." Films like *Pretty Woman* illustrate to what extent conspicuous consumption has become a commonly shared cultural ideal in contemporary society. For if wealth is defined primarily by lifestyle and consumption, then this provides the basis for successful mimicry. The more successful this self-fashioning becomes, however, the greater the problem of determining on what grounds the rich can be criticized, because either as professionals or conspicuous consumers, they are merely more successful in doing what everybody wants to do.[13]

So while there is indeed a stigma associated with being ultra-wealthy, there is also a strong current within American culture that venerates the rich because *they are doing what all of us want to do*: *consuming in ways that make them happy*. Perhaps one indicator of this cultural ideal is the election in 2016 of America's first billionaire president who, despite his many moral failings, was hardly penalized for having great wealth—quite the opposite—and rode his tycoon image to victory with the help of reality TV and a dominant culture that idealizes conspicuous consumption. Today, having wealth is no longer viewed as inherently immoral, as it had been during the Robber Baron phase. Wealth is now seen as amoral—simply a means to an end, allowing us all to pursue the ideals of personal happiness and self-fulfillment. The catch? This perspective implies that there are no grounds on which to judge the ultra-wealthy, because the rest of us are striving for the same thing they are.

SOCIAL TRANSFORMATION: SEEKING AUTHENTIC COMMUNITY RECOGNITION

In addition to viewing wealth as an amoral vehicle with which to regenerate themselves via a particular lifestyle (for example, working less, spending more time in nature or with family), the ultra-wealthy are driven by a desire to gain recognition as normal people. In interviews, they expressed a sense that they were not recognized by the nonwealthy as legitimate members of the community, in large part because they had been wrongly stereotyped and stigmatized by the media and politicians.

This feeling among many I studied led to an effort to transform themselves socially in ways that signal their worth as normal and authentic members of the community. This response is in line with prior research showing that individuals from stigmatized groups are especially hungry to rewrite their life script in order to rehabilitate their social identity in hope of gaining positive recognition from those outside their group who view them as illegitimate or otherwise discredit their societal citizenship.[14]

The anxiety induced by being the source and symbol of deep inequality in the community—and in the nation as a whole—led many of my interviewees to construct and promote a new version of their social self. This new person, so to speak, could be very different from who they were during their prior life on Wall Street, in Silicon Valley, or in the oil/gas industry, and could behave in ways that directly combat the stigmas associated with that life: inauthenticity, garishness, selfishness, and being out of touch with the nonwealthy.

While I believe that this effort to gain social legitimacy is generalizable to other ultra-wealthy people beyond Western communities like this, some distinctive aspects of Western culture do make it more difficult to be accepted there. Principally, the prevailing culture is still influenced by a mythic Western authenticity wedded to values such as bucolic simplicity, radical self-sufficiency, anti-aristocracy, working-class grind, ruggedness, and material contentment. In other words, a cultural milieu that can be the polar opposite of that from which many of the ultra-wealthy came. And although these ideals are rooted more in myth than reality, any community members who outwardly challenge them are looked on with suspicion.

The regenerative effort to become "normal" is not always explicit. As I mentioned in the introduction earlier, this process most often revealed itself to me in the ways that the ultra-wealthy would talk about and act toward their nonwealthy counterparts, as opposed to them telling me bluntly that they are consciously undergoing a process of social transformation in order to be respected and validated as normal.

Social regeneration often required disguising the fact that they had wealth, with some respondents going so far as to lie about, or intentionally downplay, their career or their origins. Recall from chapter 2 that some Yellowstone Club members I interviewed remove the placard identification from the window of their car when they leave the club and go into town, and others avoid wearing T-shirts or hats with the club logo when interacting with the nonwealthy.

Most talk of careers, social status, or wealth is reserved for their ultra-wealthy peers. But when it comes to the locals from whom they seek recognition, they mask their social identity by avoiding talk of wealth, inequality, or politics. Instead, they stick to their preferred topic: no matter how much they make, everyone is here because of their shared love of natural beauty and small-town character. As one hedge fund manager from Manhattan put it, "The locals are crazy about being out here, and then the people who come here like us just absolutely love it [too], and so I think it's this shared love of the place—shared set of interests. It's kind of an identity thing."

The Ingredients for Normalcy

At first, I was not entirely clear what it was about the locals that led my ultra-wealthy respondents to continually express admiration for them, as well as desire closeness with them, seek acceptance from them, and model their personal transformation after them. How had this normal person become the utopian human being—a prototype of the right values and lifestyle, which the ultra-wealthy could in turn commandeer to reconcile their great wealth with their own conscience and with felt social stigmas? I had some ideas, but I wanted to dig deeper into the specific attributes that compose this mythical normal person, and why they seemed so attractive. These attributes, which I discuss later, provide a road-map for the ultra-wealthy to reach moral equilibrium, and might allow them to finally gain recognition as an authentic member of the community.[15]

This social roadmap converges on two major themes: (1) romanticizing working-class life as stress-free, simple, and morally pure, composed of noble handiwork; and (2) using poverty and the natural environment as vehicles for escapism.

ROMANTICIZING THE MONEYLESS: STRESS-FREE, SIMPLE, AND MORAL

What exactly did the nonwealthy resident Claire Drury, quoted earlier, mean by "us savages"? In my interviews and observations with the ultra-wealthy, I found that the attributes that mattered most to them—but were out of reach because of their great wealth—derived from a romanticized vision of rural life at the bottom of the socioeconomic pyramid.

The ultra-wealthy are certainly not the first social group to romanticize life at the bottom—especially in the United States, which has a long history of valorizing the bucolic struggle and positive values of everyday folks.[16] But the specific attributes on which the ultra-wealthy focus are driven by their own unique struggle: both to manage great wealth and to move beyond the social stigmas that mark them.

First, and most importantly, the ultra-wealthy envision the life of the rural poor as stress free. This image stands in stark contrast to their own lives, which were defined by high-pressure rat-racing, careerist ladder climbing, high-stakes decision making, and the ethical temptations posed by great wealth. The implicit message being that the former life is better because it is simpler. Sure, this coffee-shop waitress pouring my second cup might not have millions of dollars, but her uncomplicated life is slower, less stressful, and presumably much happier. It is one filled with contentment and moral stability rather than pressure and high stakes. Here, simplicity can be confounded with happiness.

Let me sum up this dynamic more clearly with a hypothetical story.[17] It goes something like this:

A New York banker buys land in the mountainous West and builds a lavish new home, only to meet a poor resort worker who is "truly living" life and finds out that—gasp!—the resort worker is the "richer" of the two. The resort worker's life is simple, and isn't it just so darn beautiful the way he can take in the setting sun over the Tetons after a hard day's work, before heading home to his mountain family—which, is in stark contrast to this New York banker who regretfully spent his career in congested and polluted Manhattan working sixty hours a week selling overpriced derivatives.

Oh, but wait, the resort worker has untreated pneumonia because he can't afford good health insurance. And the "mountain home" where his family lives is actually a run-down hotel room thirty miles from where he works. He and his wife are constantly distressed about housing, and he's always anxious because he knows he will always struggle to feed his children. Days often end in fights, and the constant, crushing poverty seems too much to handle. Yet he wills himself to get up each morning, hoping and praying that he'll make enough to keep his family fed.

In some cases, the *physicality* of working-poor jobs supercharges this perception of simplicity and respectability, especially compared with the complex and immaterial ways that some ultra-wealthy individuals make their money. For example, the Wall Street financier who amasses great wealth through thousands of immaterial transactions, or the Silicon Valley executive whose net worth is based on intangible valuation, can imbue the materiality of working-class professions with positive meaning. Consider the construction workers building lavish homes through rugged labor with stone, wood, and concrete; the fishing guide navigating a physically imposing river; the short-order cook who chops and sautés in a cafe kitchen, producing sustenance; and the local rancher who, with his antiquated trade, stands above all others as an exemplar of romantic physicality par excellence.

Beneath all of these romantic ideas lies the notion that there exists a morally pure way of life free from moneyed temptations and from the standard definition of success that is measured in dollars rather than in happiness, simplicity, and the fruit of an honest day's work. Deep down, there is a sense that this is how life *should* be: working to live, rather than living to work. Of course, the irony of this conceit is that despite the fact that they live in the nation's richest community, the people being romanticized are hardly able to live on their meager wages, and the ultra-wealthy are not *actually* interested in working these low-paying jobs. Even so, the ultra-wealthy tend to construe them as paradigms of virtue and contentment—the presumed antidote to the darker sides of wealth, aiding them in their regenerative efforts to reach moral equilibrium, overcome social stigmas, and gain positive recognition in the community.

VEHICLE FOR ESCAPISM: NATURE AND POVERTY

It was puzzling to me that not once did the ultra-wealthy I spoke with wax romantic about the working poor in the large city where they had once worked or lived. The working poor in New York City or Houston were one thing, but the working poor in Teton County were another—even though members of both communities share a struggle to keep their heads above water, facing low wages, high rents, and dim prospects overall for scaling the socioeconomic pyramid. Why was one romanticized as a paradigm of virtue and happiness, and the other not?

The difference, it turns out, is that the working poor in Teton County have become a *vehicle for escapism* for the ultra-wealthy, in large part because their struggle takes place in a locale that is geographically remote and environmentally exotic. This is in stark contrast to the stereotypical image of American poverty and inequality, generally envisioned to exist in congested, large, and underserved urban areas that are racially and ethnically diverse. As we will learn in part 4, the workforce in Teton County is also somewhat diverse, but this diversity is rendered invisible in the face of the romantic and mythical West.

The remoteness of this community, combined with its pristine natural environment, seems to *transform* poverty into something very different. The daily struggle of moneyless people, and the earnest way of life it entails, becomes synonymous with the simplicity, purity, and ruggedness of nature. The mutual enjoyment of nature by rich and poor alike eliminates the importance of money and reduces the perceived social distance between those standing at rarefied heights and those below. To paraphrase the philosophy of John Muir and Henry David Thoreau, money, power, and material possessions only get in the way of communing with nature, whether through hiking, meditation, or simply taking in the spiritual and aesthetic beauty it offers. From this perspective, nature levels the socioeconomic playing field. It reduces humans to their primal and elemental connection to the natural world.

Sure, having a $15 million home adjacent to lakes and mountains can certainly help, but in the view of many of the ultra-wealthy, the natural world unites and touches us all deeply and in the same way, no matter your income or the lavishness (or humbleness) of your home (or trailer). To repeat the words of the ultra-wealthy executive from Connecticut quoted earlier, "It's not about money here! We are all just deeply in love with Wyoming."

It is in this way that poverty in this community becomes a vehicle for escape. Wealth allows the affluent to make a pilgrimage to an exotic land and to live among and befriend the working poor—people who have a (supposed) deep connection to nature, live a simpler life, and eschew the money worries and career ambitions that have plagued them. Natural places like the mountain West, which earlier may have been viewed as backwaters and therefore career suicide, have become gardens of Eden where the wealthy can evade the stress and moral pitfalls of living exclusively among their own social class and participate in a new way of life inspired by a romanticized association linking nature and poverty. This sense of escapism is heightened by the fact that the ultra-wealthy fly in and out as they please, detached from the everyday grind of working-class life.

How Self-Transformation Looks

To idealize and fetishize imagined working-poor values from afar is one thing, but to fully integrate these qualities into one's life requires something more. I found that ultra-wealthy self-transformation based on the attributes of normalcy described earlier is accomplished through two means: (1) establishing social bonds of friendship with moneyless people—bonds that the ultra-wealthy believe to be genuine, and (2) adopting working-class tastes (for example, dress, art, music) that reduce the social and symbolic distance between the ultra-wealthy and the rest of the community, thus outwardly signaling their conversion to normalcy.

MAKING FRIENDS IN LOW PLACES

I could fill entire chapters with excerpts from unprompted discussions with the ultra-wealthy about their bonds of friendship with moneyless people. Along with the next theme (adopting working-class tastes), perhaps no other topic was more prominent in our conversations. The joy with which they talked about these relationships is laid bare in the representative quotes that follow. Why do these relationships matter so much to the ultra-wealthy, and to my argument that they are part of a larger effort at self-transformation motivated by the moral and social challenges posed by great wealth? There are two important facets to consider.

First, these relationships are so special, and considered to be so genuine, because *money is thought to play no role in them.* Unlike other relationships with professional colleagues or with wealthy peers, their bonds with moneyless folks are free from the materialistic shackles that can plague relationships, create competition, and take the eye off the goal of stress-free living in communion with nature.

Consider Pat Norwood, a longtime corporate healthcare executive from New England. In recent years, he has become, in his words, an "authentic Westerner." Proudly, he tells me that his friends run the socioeconomic gamut, driving home the point that his circle includes people who are barely scraping by. People are just people, he says, because they all value living around nature for the same reasons as he. He has friends in low places because, as he sees it, the basis of true friendship is not social class. Instead, it is based on "what people's values are for living here. And you sit down next to some guy and he's just a regular guy and he's good friends with the waiter, and he's good friends with the ski patrollers, and he's good friends with this and that; you come to find out that he's worth five billion dollars somehow. You'd never know."

As further evidence, Pat cites a recent wedding he attended here in the community whose guest list included a poor construction worker ("He's still a good pal of mine," Pat boasts) *and* the former president of a European country.

Puzzled, I dug deeper, asking, "So you think that folks in Teton County are more likely to be friends with people of different economic means and different backgrounds than people in other places like Fairfield County or New York City?"

Pat responded emphatically, "Oh, definitely. Definitely. . . . They're all pals. Regardless of how much they make or what they do, it's what's in the person. I think that counts for a lot."

Or take Joe Adelberg, a fifty-something investment banker from the Manhattan suburbs who, despite being from aristocratic East

Coast stock and one of the more powerful fixtures in the philanthropic world of Ivy League education and finance, is deeply proud of his new friends in Wyoming. "I'm in a nice place, and I'm hanging out with dirt-bag climbers. They [dirt-bag climbers] want you there. As long as you respect one another, and you enjoy what Teton County has to offer, you're totally welcome."

What about the glaring fact that these "dirt bags" live at the poverty line, while Joe is worth tens of millions? He assures me that "*The money doesn't do you any good. It doesn't really matter. . . .* It's noticeable and it's obvious, but the people that I would be hanging out with aren't gonna make me feel bad." Continuing, Joe steps back and reflects. "You know, I was lucky enough that I worked for a long time and I had the capital to have a nice place, and that's cool. But there's nothing I can do about it, and they don't care. My buddies don't care."

We hear the same from Cheryl Beyerlein, a Southern Californian who came up in the tech industry, now worth more than $80 million. She is hyper-aware of the social lines that can separate moneyed and moneyless people. And while she had few working-class friends in California, after moving to the mountain West she has been able to build relationships that are not based on money. Today, her friends are "the kind of people that will build a barn with you"—by which she means people of a lower socioeconomic status. But why a barn, I immediately think to myself? Did she *really* build a barn with these new friends? Before I can ask, she continues, "I don't see the lines drawn the way I do in other places; certainly out in Southern California, for example. I just don't see it [in Teton County]. I think there's much less of it. I think people are valued for who they are, and much less for what they have."

Fed up with the fast-paced existence in L.A., she sought out this rural Western way of life. "It's something that I longed for. It's people I think that are very neighborly. They're kind. They're considerate. . . . People understand each other and there's a certain closeness there [in Teton County] that's hard to get in other places."

Sure, Cheryl recognizes that this is the richest county in the United States, and the most unequal, but that fact embodies the beauty of cross-class friendships: it doesn't spill over into social life. "I mean, you're looking around the hills and saying, 'Wow, those are expensive homes!' There's no doubt about any of that, *but I don't think that shows up in social interaction*. At least I don't see it. For me, I don't see it." She goes on: "I just don't think people out here really care. I just don't see it. Like I said, *you could work at fifteen bucks an hour or be a millionaire. Doesn't matter*. We're having the same conversation."

But, I ask, "How do you *not* know that that person is a billionaire when you're talking to them?" Driving home the point, she continues, "I think it's strangely much more egalitarian to me. I mean, look, you walk into a coffee shop, and the guy next to you is a billionaire, but you'd never know it. He's going to talk to you about the same things you're going to talk to anyone else about. He doesn't know anything about you, and you don't know anything about him, and frankly I couldn't care less. I don't care. Your opinion is just as valuable to me if you're making fifteen cents."

In addition to Pat, Joe, and Cheryl, many others I spoke with talked in similarly fascinating ways about the unique relationships they have with the normal and nonmoneyed members of the community. Some of these relationships are based on shared activities. For example, one Yellowstone Club member seems to feel more comfortable *outside* of the gates of the club, hanging with locals. "I go down, I ride mountain bikes with all the locals. . . . I go down and get drunk with them at the Lone Peak Brewery, you know? I do. . . . I really embrace the entire area, it's not just the club. The club to me is sort of like a basecamp for my explorations. . . . So, I've talked to those guys, and gotten to know them, and they don't talk down to me, they don't talk up to me, they don't care whether I'm a club member or not."

There is indeed something about rural communities in this corner of the Rocky Mountains that breaks down the traditional barriers between the working poor and the über-rich. Or, in the words of another club member I interviewed, "It doesn't matter whether you're a Bill Gates type who is a Yellowstone Club member, or someone who is bussing the table. There seems to be a respect for each other. There doesn't seem to be any kind of perception, at least by those who are maybe better off, that people are subservient to them. Which is why, again, we were so shocked and embarrassed when we learned that there was a perception that club members didn't care about others when the bankruptcy occurred."

A very friendly stay-at-home mother, who has lived on both the East and West Coasts and now resides in Teton County, put it in similar terms. She suggested that the rich should get to know even more "local people" (that is, working poor) in order to continue to improve community relations. In this community, "It's a cultural thing. . . . We all mix, and we don't care if you're a CEO of a Fortune 500 company, or you're, you know, a professional ski instructor. . . . People need to get to know more local people to be more aware of that dynamic. . . . We're all part of the community, and equally so."

One reason why so many wealthy people have been able to develop relationships with lower income people is because they intentionally hide their immense wealth, fitting in with what they perceive to be rural cultural styles. As another woman described, "I don't find among the more privileged people of Jackson a proclivity to flaunt their wealth. They enjoy being here because everybody is valued as to their person as opposed to their belongings."

Another facet of the friends-in-low-places theme, which went largely unnoticed by the ultra-wealthy themselves, is that they often *confuse servants for friends*. Despite the romantic belief that money plays no role in the cross-class friendships described earlier, I found that these social bonds often originated in some sort of economic exchange, often with the ultra-wealthy paying someone for a service.

Here, we return to Claire Drury, the nonwealthy Teton County resident who sarcastically remarked that the ultra-wealthy truly believe they are befriending the common folks. In another conversation, Claire remarked that the notion makes her "cringe" and questioned whether "going out for a beer with the guy who is doing the finishing work on your house" qualifies as genuine friendship, especially because money always seems to be involved.

Pushing further, Claire fills me in on her friend who for decades was a year-round caretaker for a wealthy family from New England. Despite the fact that this family viewed her as a genuine "friend," the reality was that "From the moment they arrived, it was clear exactly what her status was in the pecking order: *She was the hired help*. They didn't know they were being patronizing in the same way that people don't know that they are being racist. They're not overtly racist, but that's who they *are*."

Claire's experiences speak for themselves, but let's also hear from the ultra-wealthy. Colin Stewart, the corporate investment executive from chapter 2, perhaps best represents the self-transformation strategy of having friends in low places. Profoundly proud that he is just a normal guy, Colin has been able to forge what he sees as genuine friendships in Teton County. "I am very close with all sorts of people in town," he says, especially a local fishmonger who cuts his halibut exactly the way he wants it. "It's just a really tight-knit little community." But again, even in quite subtle ways, these relationships are based on uneven power dynamics and tend to involve economic exchanges between the ultra-wealthy and the nonwealthy, whether the latter happens to be a halibut fishmonger or Colin's fishing and rafting guide. "You should go down to the outdoor shop and talk to Joe," he says. "He is one of my closest friends here and is my fly-fishing guide. Just a really great guy." Or consider the wait staff at his private club. "We are very close with the staff. With the waiters and pool girls. They are the closest of friends. We invite them to parties and get together with them."

Of course, some of these friendships may indeed blossom beyond economic exchange and become truly genuine. Yet the pattern identified by Claire and other lower income locals I interviewed certainly bore out in my interviews and observations with the ultra-wealthy, as illustrated by the following examples.

One Yellowstone Club member was pleasantly shocked by the nature of these friendships. "You know, the older son of the guy who built my house, who I became friends with . . . now just *imagine that*, an owner becoming friends with the builder, the general contractor! His older son last winter was dating the daughter of a billionaire hedge fund guy who is my neighbor, and everybody was cool." Similarly, another club member boasted about these surprising relationships: "You know, it's interesting because some of the people I love *the most* are the people who *work* at Yellowstone Club." This sentiment was echoed by a Teton County interviewee, who said, "To give you a sense, my friends run the gamut from ski patrollers and fly-fisherman [to] ski instructors and lifties, and you know, a lot of people have . . . not what I call immense wealth."

These sentiments were conveyed in a way that was genuine. And, they often assumed that their low-income friends felt the same way about them. Said one, "I don't say this because I think we're wonderful, but I think because we are really friendly to the people that work there, and we are happy to see them when we come back and we're very, you know, we're polite and kind to them. They like waiting on us and they like talking to us."

To drive this point home, another club member directly addressed the genuineness of his interactions with rural, moneyless, and seemingly nature-loving locals.

I want to go back for just a second to the genuineness of the people. I can remember—and this was our first winter when we were out there skiing—and we got to talking to the server who was serving us dinner in the Warren Miller [Lodge] dining room. And we got to talking to her toward the end of the meal and we were talking about bears. . . . And I said, "Well, do you use bear spray?" And she goes, "Yep." And I go, "Well do you keep it in a holster or whatever?" And she just slaps one thigh and goes, "Yep, I keep my bear spray here," and slapped her other leg, and goes, "and I keep my nine mil [handgun] here." [chuckles] My brother and I just erupted in laughter. But, you know, that's just simply the kind of thing that purely spontaneously happens in terms of, you know, just having talked, chatting with [local] people out there.

Having spent many years observing and interviewing rural and low-income people for this project and others, I often pushed back against what seemed to be the shallowness of some of these ultra-wealthy folks' claims to friendship. For example, in a conversation with another club member, I asked, "Would you consider those folks who are working at the club to be friends? Or just more of a professional relationship?" Similar to many of the respondents earlier, he insisted, "No, no, the way we are, they're friends! Yeah, no, no, definitely. They're definitely [friends]. . . . You know, they're interesting, a lot of them have traveled the world, or they're really good skiers, or they're really good fishermen. And most importantly . . . they're nice people. I don't really care if they're the CEO of XYZ or they're helping us out over at the club or I met them on the mountain. . . . I don't really care."

"THE COSTUME OF THE DAY": ERASING OUTWARD CLASS DIFFERENCES

I certainly did not set out to study the fashion patterns of the ultra-wealthy, and in the early stages of this research I wondered why several of my first dozen interviewees showed up in jeans and cowboy boots. They looked more like my Grandpa Ray in his jeans and cowboy boots common in eastern Idaho than the East Coast financiers or Californian real estate moguls they were. Nevertheless, it quickly became one of the most prominent and important themes of my research.

Something as trite as what they wear, and why they wear it, revealed much deeper insights about their attempts to deal with the social and moral implications of having massive wealth and their desire to be recognized and accepted by the rest of the community.

Thus, the second way the ultra-wealthy seek to attain normalcy, which goes hand in hand with making friends in low places, is to disguise their wealth by curating a personal appearance centered on rural Western working-class attire, which distances them from the stigmas associated with having money and reduces the social and symbolic distance between themselves and the rest of the community.

Much theorizing over the centuries has focused on how aesthetic tastes are formed, beginning with the work of Plato and Kant, but it wasn't until the emergence of formative sociologists such as Georg Simmel and Pierre Bourdieu that academia began to appreciate the importance of social class, especially how the wealthy and power-ful shape what is defined as "good" taste in fashion, art, consumer goods, and other aspects of culture. Fashion is often used as a tool to draw distinctions between oneself and another group, but one can also adopt the tastes of another group in an attempt to collapse the perceived distance between oneself and that group while still maintaining one's economic advantage and elite standing.

What does this look like in practice? Claude Rudolph, the real estate mogul from the introduction of this chapter, summed it up well: "Jackson has as big an economic gap as exists anywhere on the planet, but you usually don't ever see it. You can be at a party, and you don't know if the person that is there in blue jeans is a billionaire or a struggling tree-hugger."

Of course, blue jeans signify very little by themselves, but blue jeans combined with a flannel shirt, Carhartt jacket, cowboy boots, and a pickup truck can signify much more. These styles varied by person and by occasion. It was an everyday thing for some, but others opted for more technical outdoorsy getup during the day, saving the cowboy boots and formal flannel for evening dinners and entertainment. This style—which mirrors their tastes in frontier and wildlife art and rustic architecture—is what one ultra-wealthy resident referred to as "the costume of the day" in the community, exemplifying community values of "friendliness, openness, and knowing everybody by their first name." From his sincere tone, I got the sense that he wasn't aware of the irony of referring to the outfit as a "costume," but his phrase captures the way that appropriating this style of dress is intended to signify a transformed identity.

Representative quotes and observations that illustrate this find-ing were aplenty. Harken back, for example, to Julie Williams from the introduction of this book, whose friends "are everything from ski-bums to people who are very successful with immense wealth, and you would never know it because we're all just in our jeans and flannel shirts." Over and over, I heard this same refrain: the lower income people and the wealthy look the same. As another person put it, "You go into town to the restaurant or bar, you know that many of the people that are wealthy and many of their workers are in town, and you can kind of identify them by the way they dress and their cowboy hats."

One ultra-wealthy person pointed out that this is especially true "for the people coming from California who are über-wealthy but want to feel like they're just like everybody else and wear jeans and hang out and like to be part of a community that's not flashy." Acknowledging that they may have private jets, or very large homes, two different ultra-wealthy interviewees still claimed the importance of wearing jeans and cowboy boots. "I don't think the wealthy flaunt it. . . . People still wear their Levi's. . . . On the other hand, some do have aircraft that they enjoy." And another person happily reminded me that "There's certainly not an ostentatious type of lifestyle that people have in Teton County. It is a great thing that you get to wear cowboy boots and blue jeans and that is perfectly acceptable dress code for any occasion anywhere. . . . And I think everybody loves that. We've got a Ford F-150 pickup truck out there, it's great!"

They seem to understand that, because there is great inequality, it's all the more important that a wealthy appearance be downplayed, creating an equal plane for relationships to develop with the lower income community. As one ultra-wealthy interviewee put it, "You hang your ego at the door, and everybody kind of hangs out in jeans and boots and stuff." This nonchalance doesn't come naturally. It takes a bit of effort, as described by another interviewee. "Generally, if you see [the wealthy] around town, they're wearing a Carhartt jacket and they're having coffee at the coffee shop and they're not making a spectacle of themselves and that's what people see. . . . Kind of makes you feel like, okay, they are making an effort to belong."

One woman I interviewed likes to use the local dress code to surprise her unsuspecting and well-to-do East Coast friends. "All my friends that come to visit, they're like, 'Okay what do I need to bring? What do I need for dinner?' I'm like, 'You just need jeans and a nice shirt, a nice top and some boots.' And they're all like, 'Oh my gosh, that's so nice.' I'm like, 'Yeah, just bring a pair of jeans and a bunch of tops to wear with it. It's all you need there.' Very relaxed."

Or, as another woman put it, "If you're wearing more than jeans, you're basically overdressed."

Proudly, some told me about how this style of dress erases outward class distinctions that might otherwise hinder cross-class relationships from developing, whether at bars, coffee shops, or other community gathering spots. "You could be at the Cowboy Bar or something, and the person next to you could be in jeans and a flannel shirt, and they could be a billionaire, but you wouldn't know it," said one New Yorker I interviewed. Similarly, another person instructed me that "The guy next to you could be in a flannel shirt and could be a billionaire; you'd have no idea." Because, as yet another person put it, "We wanna go into the local restaurant or grocery store with our jeans and flannel shirts. We want to experience Big Sky like anyone else." Which is why another gentleman summed it up so well, saying, "People who live here . . . pretty much dress and appear all the same."

Some respondents described how adopting these tastes allowed their true self to emerge—a self that is less egotistical, less self-absorbed, and more in line with how the rural Western locals live. As a doctor from Kentucky described it,

> You need to park your ego if you want to be a big shot, but I think the people who are truly big shots could care less about being big shots. I think that's the irony of it. . . . I mean that's the thing. It's like when I went in there and [name of famous person redacted] was there, he's wearing a sweatshirt and I was wearing my jeans and a T-shirt. That was cool. Like I said, this is okay . . . but you see him and he's down there in his sweatshirt, his hair is not combed and he's laughing, it really kind of breaks things down.

Similarly, a banker from the West Coast felt a personal "release that I don't have to dress a certain way, or I don't have to look a certain way, I don't have to talk a certain way. I don't have to kiss anybody's ass and I can just be myself, and maybe that's one of the comforts of the whole area is that you can really be yourself." To dress any other way, according to one other interviewee, would "not be consistent with the value system here. It's very understated."

This process of self-transformation also extends to the vehicles the ultra-wealthy choose to drive. Pulling up in a pickup truck or worn-out SUV at the local greasy-spoon cafe prevents one from sticking out as inauthentic (that is, rich), and additionally signals that one is conforming to the norms of modern rural Western transportation. Some interviewees were very explicit about the cars they chose to drive. As one put it, "You know, I consider myself wealthy, but don't show it. You know, I drive a truck. . . . But I would never—you know this is ridiculous—but I would *never* buy a Cadillac, just because I don't want the image of owning a Cadillac. Even though they are good cars, I would never buy a Mercedes because I just didn't want the image of [driving] a Mercedes."

In the words of one gentleman who splits his time between Wyoming, Boston, and Los Angeles:

> I mean, you're not going to be able to tell by the truck the wealthy drive [laughs], or for that matter the Maybach or the Rolls Royce that they drive. No one is doing that. Nobody cares, and quite frankly it wouldn't fit for obvious reasons . . . most people aren't getting themselves up and dressing differently. No one is going to work in a three-piece suit, that's not the environment. . . . To the extent that the financial community is there, they can go to work in jeans and boots, hence there's nothing wrong with that [laughs]. A lot of the customers you're going to go see those days are going to be obviously dressed the same way, so there's no outward delineation of where the lines are drawn visually.

Thus, even vehicle choices run deeper than practical concerns about safely getting around in the mountains, but can mark their authentic connection to the soul of the rural West. At the same time, these choices can involve attempts to downplay the "outward delineation of where lines are drawn visually" between the ultra-wealthy and those from other socioeconomic classes. According to one hedge fund manager from the East Coast, these lines are mostly confined to the collection of ostentatious private jets at the local airport. "Nobody's driving around in Rolls Royces or Bentleys," he says. "It seems like a relatively healthy thing to not have that conspicuous consumption [here]. I think here in Jackson, the conspicuous consumption, where you really see it is when you land at the airport and you look out the window and then you see all these private jets, but once you get past that, there's not a lot of it going on."

As noted, the process of ultra-wealthy self-transformation involves escapism from rat-racing, which can also extend very concretely to choices in dress and vehicles. One gentleman explained to me that "Originally, we were a little concerned about being a little pretentious. . . . In fact, it almost goes the other way; there's the clothing, how people dress, it's very relaxed, which is nice. . . . I think there's a certain component of escapism, where you can just kind of leave your high-pressure job where everybody is looking to you or demanding if you're the CEO of this or that. You just leave your tie at home."

Escapism often had a specific geographic essence, whereby the dress and romanticized lifestyles of the rural West are contrasted with those in high-pressure urban areas, as illustrated by one person who moved to this community from the Midwest: "So whether that's here or whether it's in Chicago or wherever—in Connecticut—you have people that are really successful and are a little more uptight and formal versus informal. We just like things to be a bit more casual. I don't really like, and we're not impressed by, much of anything besides being around good human beings."

ULTRA-WEALTHY SELF-CRITICISM: KIM WALKER AND "REVERSE SNOBBERY"

Some ultra-wealthy respondents were more self-aware than others, recognizing the irony of trying to be "normal," and even criticizing their peers for attempting to *disguise* the dark underbelly of poverty by ignoring the struggle of their newfound friends, pretending money doesn't matter, or by appropriating their fashion sense to purposefully blur huge socioeconomic differences.

I met Kim Walker at a cozy coffee shop in Boulder, Colorado. She and her husband Max had flown in on their private plane from Teton County to visit their children, who live and work in Denver. Kim and Max built an immensely successful business in the Philadelphia area, but now live full-time in Wyoming. I spent two hours interviewing Kim, and then later in the day met Max for happy hour and conducted my interview with him over a few of Colorado's famous microbrews.

Kim was unashamed of being ultra-wealthy, but she pulls no punches, and her honesty was not only refreshing, but also deeply insightful. "Don't you find it interesting that they [her ultra-wealthy peers] are so fixated on how casually everyone dresses? That is just so interesting to me," she marveled. The dynamics I have described in this chapter have clearly kept Kim up at night. She continued, "I'll tell you what, I'm going to say this: Some of those people can put jeans on seven days a week, twenty-four hours a day, and it doesn't change the attitude and the way they carry themselves. So they're all kidding themselves! You might have sweatpants on, or pajama bottoms, but you're still a snob."

On the surface, it might appear that the ultra-wealthy are just trying to fit into their vision of rural Western culture, but Kim sees something more dubious about trying to be "regular" while also still being rich. She and Max both call this phenomenon "reverse snobbery." She goes on, "Yeah, we've seen this all our lives. People that have money, they dress down almost so that it's like the antithesis of wealth, you know. . . . They overdumb it down to make it look like 'Oh, look at me, I'm just, you know, one of the regular guys.'"

As for the specific working-class "costumes" her peers have adopted to blur class lines and ostensibly put inequality out of sight, Kim emphatically states, "I can't tolerate it. I grew up with money, Justin, but I was so blessed to have amazing parents that kept everything in perspective." And as for the specifics of this fashion, Kim again questions her peers' motives. "There are [ultra-wealthy] people in Wranglers 'cause they love them . . . but it's really crazy. This is my take: They're trying to prove something to [the working class], and that's all they have to use to prove it."

Toward the end of the interview, Kim offered her final assessment of her peers, based on her years growing up wealthy and her adult experiences in the West: "I think these [ultra-wealthy] people, it all becomes just about money to them. It all becomes about who they are and what they have. They lose total ability to see the world around them in a clear fashion. It doesn't matter if they have jeans on!"

Anything but Normal

Let's end where we started, at the opening of part 3 with Jesus the carpenter and John Truett the oil-and-gas CEO, each of whom has developed a panacea for the perils of great wealth. Certainly, Jesus's solution to give everything to the poor is more straightforward, but requires willpower that few people on earth possess. But John's solution, which is also the approach many ultra-wealthy people take, is to deal with the moral and social problems of wealth by transforming themselves into a normal person.

Ironically, it is wealth itself that provides the means to address social and psychological problems that wealth often creates: by furnishing access to a romanticized way of life that is ostensibly more virtuous, authentic, and community-minded than one's previous life in the rat-race. In so doing, the ultra-wealthy seemingly avoid the innately evil or inevitably corrupting influence of wealth as has been warned about over the millennia by religious leaders and philosophers, and more recently, neuroscientists.

Yet, there is much more to normalcy than meets the eye. As Kim and Max Walker pointed out, it is an open question whether their ultra-wealthy peers actually achieve the transformation they seek. Does it really *matter* if you create friendships with, or dress like, your idea of frontier people or lovable naturalists unconcerned with wealth or status? Yes, it might go a long way toward outwardly disguising the biggest income gap in any community in the United States. And, yes, in the nation's richest community, you may not actually know who has all the money and who doesn't—as was claimed repeatedly. Indeed, you may never know if that regular person in the coffee shop is a billionaire or just a poor tree-hugger, rafting guide, or carpenter. And sure, it may appear that your newfound friend leads a romantic, stress-free, and morally straightforward life because they are working class and are spiritually connected to nature, and so remain disentangled from the snares of success, power, and wealth.

But in reality, your friend—whom you likely met because they served as your nature guide so that you could enjoy untouched wilderness, or more likely, they rendered services for your home—is probably living crammed into a run-down hotel room or apartment with another family, working three low-wage jobs, commuting daily over a dangerous mountain pass, and relying on the food pantry to feed their kids. This person may be on the brink of divorce, have no time for recreation in nature, and have just received a notice that rent will increase by 30 percent next month. So, when your friend has time to stop and assess the character of the community, what they see is anything but "normal."

8

Guilt Numbed

"I really struggle with guilt. . . . I really do. I've been a very lucky person. I've been able to do a lot of things the average person can't do . . . and then I'm looking at the prices here, and I'm like how is the average person supposed to afford this stuff? There's a real [socioeconomic] dichotomy that I struggle with on a deep personal level." Emily Bell, an ultra-wealthy woman from the Midwest who lives with her family just outside Yellowstone, confided in me this "deep personal" struggle with her privilege, as if I were a priest administering the rite of confession—a safe confidant in the wilderness of ultra-wealth.

Emily's description represents the way people typically think about guilt: *personal feelings* of shame, wrongdoing, or failure of obligation. So to know if the ultra-wealthy feel guilty about their great wealth or the poverty that surrounds them, we should just ask each of them, right? Straightforward enough, it might seem. And ask them I did.

But these personal accounts of guilt tended to be highly unreliable from person to person. We humans, whether rich or poor, are just not very good at reflecting in honest and logical ways about how we are feeling, or even why we do what we do. This led me to pursue something much deeper, more interesting, and more important than this typical way we think about guilt. *Moving beyond individual experiences, I sought to uncover the larger social environment in which guilt is experienced.* Guilt is not just an isolated psychological state going on in our heads, but is inherently *relational,* stemming from our experiences as members of different communities and moral tribes that impress upon us certain expectations. Were there broader social patterns about guilt that I could discern, even if individuals refused to give an answer, became defensive, or as was more common, were unable to coherently articulate a response to such a personal and taboo question?

For example, how does their view of themselves as "normal" people actually suppress or mute feelings of guilt, or anesthetize their ability to recognize guilt? Or are there certain talking scripts—perhaps informed by the partisan politics of our current age—that dictate their response to such a question? How do the populist criticisms of the "undeserving rich" or "1 percenters" in our era of wealth concentration sow seeds of guilt on one hand, or perhaps create defensiveness at the *thought of feeling guilty,* on the other? Or are personal feelings of guilt and moral failure actually explained away altogether by rational economic argument: what is there to feel guilty about if by freely spending money—even if in excess or extravagance—it trickles down through the economy benefiting those far below?

No doubt, guilt radically shapes the worlds in which the ultra-wealthy live, but in more subtly important ways than we might think. Their answers to my simple question "Do you feel guilty?" revealed puzzles that are much more fascinating and significant than a straightforward confession of personal guilt that some might expect or hope to find. Before jumping in, I'd like to share a few instances when the ultra-wealthy actually did reveal to me a stereotypical personal struggle similar to Emily earlier, as a way to show that *even these* infrequent confessions were fraught with complexity and contradiction, and pointed toward something larger and more important that needed to be uncovered.

———

Megan Delaney, a Yale graduate from many years ago who made her millions in finance, and whom I met on multiple occasions in Jackson Hole, told it like this: "I'm trying to think of the right word for it. Guilt? I don't know if it's guilt, but it's a little bit of discomfort." She continues, reflecting on how this discomfort manifests itself, using a recent example of a lavish party they threw at their house in Montana.

> When we decided to host this party, I was very uncomfortable with the notion of having this big fancy party, with three bands and all of this stuff, and it costing a lot of money. I was uncomfortable with it. I knew there'd be all of these fancy people and CEOs flying in on their private jets. Like, there was going to be quite the [economic class] divide at the party, and I was worried . . . just feeling a little uncomfortable, because I didn't want our neighbors to view us as people who were throwing this ostentatious party for all these fancy people who fly in and fly back, which is exactly what a lot of people do.

Chet Fisher, another Interstate 95 financier, described similar personal discomfort. He admits that his life is "more upscale than I think we would like or need . . . we sometimes get our monthly bill and go 'Oh my God, look what that costs!' We can obviously afford it, but it certainly doesn't fall in the frugal end of the spectrum. So I suppose there are things that culturally—from the expenditure perspective—rub me a bit the wrong way against my upbringing."

The burden of guilt can be emotionally hard for some, such as Brenda Fox, a single mother of three originally from Seattle, who felt so guilty about how much she was paying for her house and her property taxes, that she gave in to her shame, and moved to a different part of town. As we sat in her new cavernous living room with views of the Tetons discussing the concept of guilt and privilege, she admits that, "Well yeah, it's [emotionally] hard to pay the kind of prices that we do . . . my property taxes were most people's income per year. Just ridiculous. I finally just sold it and moved. I felt bad, thinking good heavens, look at the money I'm paying here! I could be supporting and helping somebody else." I asked her directly, "Do you felt guilty about it?" Pausing, she explains, "No, it didn't keep me up at night, but you know, it was ridiculous." But I probe, "what do you mean by 'ridiculous'?" Clarifying, she continues, "Just a lot of property. That's a lot of property. It was wonderful. I loved living there, but it was time to get a decent-sized home. I mean, I guess I kind of felt bad."

Or consider Laurence Wafford, who wonders if his guilt is actually just self-serving sanctimony—a way for him to merely feel good about himself despite his role in perpetuating the inequality all around him. Expressing guilt was just a way to prove to himself that he had some semblance of character. "So, you get to this housing [inequality] issue and I started to realize, I'm the problem! I'm the reason nobody can afford to live here." Interested, I asked him about his response, and whether he feels personally guilty. Quickly, he offers a frank reply, "I do." Continuing, I probe further, "How do you deal with these feelings?" He laughs somewhat awkwardly, "To be honest—and I can only be honest. I'm not sure if I [truly] feel guilty, because it makes me feel good that I should feel guilty about it."

A few months later, during the course of a very early morning breakfast in Wilson, Wyoming, I talked with Daniel Earl, a likable CEO from Pennsylvania, who lamented his role in driving such a huge wedge between the haves and the have-nots. "Absolutely I feel guilty. And, so why is a free-marketer like me writing a check to Habitat for Humanity? There are all kinds of charities I could write that check to." To my surprise, he answers his own question, "It's for expiation of guilt. I'm not gonna say I was conscious of that when I was writing the check, but it's not surprising; you don't have to probe very deeply." Unprompted, he continues with another example—this time about the size and cost of his property. "You know, this guilt manifests itself in other ways. I mentioned the property we live on has a guesthouse . . . although one of the ironies is that it is a story of incredible waste that would make old Westerners cringe. And really, well, it made me cringe. And, oh, I'll tell you the guilt, the guilt is that the guesthouse is empty most of the time."

As we will see in this chapter, the straightforward candor from respondents like Daniel is out of the ordinary, but that does not mean that his ultra-wealthy peers do not also feel these same feelings, even if they are hesitant or unwilling to talk about it, or if like Daniel, the feelings weren't always easily articulated or consciously above the surface. Daniel certainly doesn't believe he is alone in feeling guilty, despite the fact that it is a taboo topic among his ultra-elite social circles. "Well, is my family an outlier [in feeling guilty]? . . . No, I don't think of ourselves as being peculiarly special in that regard."

But that does not mean these feelings are always easily detected. Take Kari Paglia, for example. She and her husband, along with their kids, came to Wyoming about fifteen years ago, and just recently joined a Shooting Star country club, an upscale new development that has stirred controversy among some in the community. The club advertises itself as the exclusive place, "Where the Old West meets the New West . . . [with] one foot in Jackson Hole's rich ranching heritage . . . [it] is a place where you feel one with nature, and yet is a short drive to the galleries, shops and restaurants of downtown Jackson." Toward the tail end of our interview, Kari confessed rather profoundly: "I have to disclose to you that we do belong to that club. So we're *guilty* of enjoying that. . . . Sometimes there are some people I don't like to tell that we belong to it . . . we don't always divulge it depending on who we're talking to. . . . We were having dinner with neighbors [but] we just don't like to divulge that we belong to that club because it's very expensive to join it, we just don't want to look like we're privileged people."

It became clear to me that intentionally concealing elite club membership from her friends signified a complex inner struggle that revealed much more than just a simplistic feeling of guilt. No doubt, Kari had a difficult time peeling away the social and cultural layers that led to her keeping this a secret, even from her friends and neighbors. So, I decided to ask her bluntly. "Do you personally feel bad about it?" Struggling to articulate an answer, Kari revealed the contradictions that are at the heart of this chapter. "Um, I don't really feel bad about it, no. Well, I mean, sometimes I feel a little bit guilty about it, but on the other hand it's one of my favorite places to go when I'm there to relax."

———

In all the thousands of hours of interviews and observation, these seven stories were the *only* clear admissions of guilt I encountered.

And even still, contradictions and equivocations abound in these narratives: Aside from Emily who "really struggles with guilt," people like Megan feel what they call acute "discomfort" (for example, about her lavish parties), but isn't so sure she'd call it guilt. Chet's life is much more upscale than he is comfortable with, and his exorbitant monthly bills rub him the wrong way. Brenda says she does not feel guilty, but then admits that she felt so bad about the cost of her property that she moved to a new part of town. Laurence admits to feeling guilty, but wonders if it's just a way to make him feel good about himself. Daniel "absolutely" feels guilty, even if it is mostly subconscious, and suspects his ultra-wealthy peers feel the same way. Kari says she doesn't "really feel bad" about her wealth, and yet hides any sniff of privilege from her friends, and then concludes that, well, maybe she feels "a little bit guilty."

We will never know with certainty the extent to which anyone "truly" feels guilty, but this deceptively simple question brings to the surface many of the ways people account for having great wealth. Further, because this is such a small community, and because the ultra-wealthy interact with those at the bottom of the economic pyramid, digging into the issue of guilt can tell us a lot about how those at rarefied heights see themselves in light of their obligation to the rest of the community. And behind all this lingers the billion-dollar question: *What makes a good community in the twenty-first century?* This remains one of the most critical questions of our time. And, as wealth concentration persists, and continues to reshape social, economic, and ecological arrangements, we must more earnestly seek answers to these questions from all angles.

With all this in mind, this chapter is broken down into two straightforward sections, which together build a comprehensive picture of the ultra-wealthy's ideas about their own moral standards, their obligation to others in the community, and the social pressures that can suppress, mute, rationalize, and hide from view their guilt about having great wealth.

In the first section, I examine the extent to which the ultra-wealthy feel criticized by others. Guilt arises from standards of criticism or moral expectations placed upon us. Do the ultra-wealthy feel judged by the growing populist criticisms? Do they feel judged by people in their local community? Do they even sense these criticisms? Or are they unaware, or even numb to it? If, as we learned in chapter 7, they go to great lengths to be "normal" people, then how are these critiques received (if at all), and might their self-perception of normalcy extinguish any deep sense of guilt?

In the second section, I unpack six reasons why guilt is viewed by the ultra-wealthy as irrational and unmerited. Taken together, these six reasons tend to dampen any *deep* sense of guilt, and in turn, diminish a sense that their wealth places a special obligation on them as members of this community. Among these reasons are (1) modern consumption as a means for personal fulfillment, especially via nature; (2) naked jealousy and resentment by the nonwealthy; (3) trickle-down economics; (4) hard work, ambition, and being self-made; (5) displacing blame onto their peers; and (6) inevitable forces outside their control.

Do the Rich Feel Judged by Society?

Guilt is tied to standards of moral judgment. It is a negative emotion that we feel when we've done something that we perceive to be wrong. But the obvious questions is: Why are some things wrong, and others are not? This depends on the social units and communities of which we are a part (for example, family, religion, neighborhood, workplace, nation-state, and so on) that provide moral and ethical codes that shape our self-identities and the standards we ought to meet. Guilt can vary greatly because our communities and social units themselves vary greatly in these standards—explaining why the very same behaviors can make certain people feel intense guilt (for example, drinking alcohol, female genital mutilation, skipping church on Sunday, eating your dog, not giving away enough money, overeating, child sacrifice), while some people and communities may feel no guilt at all, and may even consider these behaviors to be virtuous.[1]

The growing public criticism of wealth inequality in America carries implied moral standards that apply to the ultra-wealthy.[2] These moral standards are even clearer at the local community level in Teton County, where great wealth and great inequality are seen in such sharp relief. But whether or not the ultra-wealthy feel guilty depends on their awareness of these standards, and the extent to which they view themselves as meeting or falling short of these communities' expectations. In other words, before asking if they feel guilty, we first need to know if they feel criticized.

What did I find? *First, the ultra-wealthy do believe (like most Americans) that greed and elite affluence is morally precarious, and they vaguely perceive that they are judged and ethically rebuked by the rest of society. But, despite these vague perceptions, they were largely unaware or numb to the true intensity of these criticisms, and the extent to which these criticisms were present in their own community.* Let's unpack this a bit, and hear from the ultra-wealthy themselves.

VAGUE, DISTANT, AND IMPERSONAL FEELINGS OF JUDGMENT

Judgment and criticism were something they saw on television or in partisan political speeches, rather than something that existed in *their* community among *their* nonwealthy friends and acquaintances. As a result, the type of judgment felt by the ultra-wealthy tended not to be the kind that induced any real sense of guilt. It was abstract, impersonal, distant, disembodied, and generally disconnected from any deep relationship to the people and community in which they live.[3]

One gentleman—whose last name is nationally famous and perhaps has exposed him to more public scrutiny about his family's wealth—describes this distant sense of criticism. He says that vilification of wealth is "ubiquitous now, but it's not just now. Let's be real. The '80s was the greed decade, right? So, this is hardly a novel concern and critique. It just seems to get more strident periodically, and that's the natural consequence of the kind of recession that we've had over the last several years." Like many other interviewees, moral judgment is mostly described in the abstract. In this case, it is described as a time period (for example, 1980s) rather than, for example, the current feelings of one of their working-class friends in Teton County.

He detaches criticism even further from concrete reality and relationships to specific people or a specific community by chalking it up to human nature. "In the absence of opportunity, people begin to lash out at those who have had opportunity and succeeded; that's not unusual. . . . But again, this is normal. This seems to me to be utterly normal, and human normal stuff." Thus, this allows him to downplay, overlook, or perhaps ignore, the criticisms from folks in the community. In response to my question about being judged, he reports, "I don't see it as being particularly acute in Jackson."

Unlike coastal activists railing against Wall Street, the people in the rural West are viewed differently. As one self-described "East Coast guy" put it, "I don't think there's a lot of income-redistribution feeling out here, like the riots down in Wall Street and so forth, or the 99 percent . . . but out here [in Wyoming] . . . there's still that expectation that you're gonna make your own way."

Circumscribing moral judgment to national-level politics, disembodied from the community in which you live or the poor you call friends, makes criticism less personal and easier to accept. Sometimes this was described in more negative terms, as "part of the entitlement society, which is a broader problem in our country," as one person suggested. But the distant sense of judgment, existing largely at the national level, can also make room for feelings of sympathy, because the sting of judgment isn't very potent or personal. It can be more "understandable," as another person put it. "I mean, I've even eluded [to the criticism] a little bit myself, but I think that criticism is understandable. I get it. You know, there is an income disparity in this country that is too excessive, and I get all that."

Finally, the media play an important role. For one retired CEO, who identifies as politically conservative, he mostly hears about criticisms of wealth via television. During the flow of conversation, over breakfast in Jackson, I ask him if he's encountered any criticism. He laughs, "I do politically every day!" Interested, I ask him what he means by that. "Well, I watch Fox [laughs]." Wealth inequality has become a hot topic for the likes of Fox News and MSNBC, albeit from different perspectives. For this retired CEO, he hears about these criticisms "every day," yet, as we have seen, these criticisms are vague caricatures of the hard-won opinions of his fellow community members who are facing the impacts of extreme wealth in their own lives. It is clear from the rest of our interview that he genuinely cares about these people and this community, but the legitimacy of his low-income friends' critiques are overshadowed and even delegitimized by his media exposure to impersonal and partisan generalizations.

NUMB TO CRITICISM

Certainly, the ultra-wealthy, like most Americans, are aware of the age-old and stereotypical criticisms of the rich, which have gained steam in recent years, taking center stage in political campaigns, Wall Street protests, and on cable news TV. They even hold some of the same views as other Americans but are able to reconcile these dilemmas by fashioning themselves into a "normal" person out West. The quotes earlier demonstrate this general awareness, and as we saw in the last chapter, they do quite a bit of work to transform themselves. *Yet, when it comes to the deep, personal, and localized criticism that is brewing in Teton County, the ultra-wealthy are mostly numb.*

Some ultra-wealthy were "shocked" to learn that such local criticism exists. Remember the Yellowstone Club member from chapter 2 who was taken aback by this very experience. "Many of us members were *shocked* to learn that the perception of the club and members is that we're a bunch of snooty people who don't really care about anyone . . . we just didn't realize we had such a perception issue." Or, as another ultra-wealthy respondent acknowledged to me, "Look, we're reasonably comfortable ourselves, so you know, sometimes you're the last one to know about criticism. It's all behind your back. So, you know, I hesitate a little bit [to deny that criticism exists] because there's probably some disenfranchised group in Jackson Hole that we're not aware of."

They're right. But this is not all that surprising, given recent neuroscience studies of the wealthy, which have shown that the wealthy tend to be less perceptive of people who are suffering.[4] And in this instance, these neuroscientific findings also extend here to a certain obliviousness—or perhaps subconscious denial—of the criticism and moral repudiation aimed at those at rarefied heights, which if recognized, may initiate a deeper sense of guilt.

This perspective that I have characterized as "numb" takes a few different forms, ranging from outright cluelessness to rationalized denial, convincing themselves of an alternative reality. Let's begin with some examples that portray the reasons they do *not* feel judged, which have to do with general cluelessness to the criticisms levied against them.

One respondent from New England demonstrates this point quite clearly. "There's no regret or resentment [among nonwealthy locals] by the way. . . . And they're very, very comfortable with it and they're not upset by that choice either, and boy I think that's very liberating. . . . And they're not pointing their finger at anybody. You're not saying this is your fault. This is you, blah, blah, blah; it's 'I got this. *I made this choice.* I like living here . . . there's no complaint about it' . . . to me it's some of the quintessential American Spirit."

In the same vein, another respondent says that money is a secondary concern to all in Teton County, even to those who don't have it. "I think the ethos of that group of people [local nonwealthy] isn't about drawing distinctions based on wealth. You draw distinctions based on how fucking great you are on skis, whether you understand snow safety, whether you have climbed the Grand Teton. That's the social strata in Jackson." In the eyes of many ultra-wealthy, the local working poor live a romanticized life connected to nature and recreation. Social-class warfare isn't possible because it's not money that separates different groups of people, like it might in other communities. Thus, when I probed about these local criticisms, I was often, in the words of another interviewee, told, "No, no, not at all. I mean I think people are smart enough to not waste their time being critical of the wealth."

Others thought that their adoption of down-to-earth rural lifestyles and seemingly down-to-earth rural friends would insulate them from such criticism. One woman admitted that while they are the stereotypical "affluent couple moving from the East Coast and building a beautiful home," their "simpler lifestyle" might be one reason why, in her words, "I certainly haven't seen criticism. . . . We haven't felt it. . . . There's certainly not an ostentatious type of lifestyle that people have in Teton County."

Over and again, I heard this same refrain, as evinced here by many different ultra-wealthy people: "I've never really encountered any real hostility or anything like that. No." "All in all, the vibe is not antithetical, it's not combative, it's not polarized in any regard." "No [criticism]. No, I would say, actually, for the most part, the people we've interacted with have embraced the [affluent] people that come." "I wouldn't necessarily call it animosity though. It's more an acknowledgement or people noticing that there's a huge bifurcation here. . . . You don't hear a ton about it even in the paper that much. . . . I don't sense resentment." "[Local working poor] are not critical of the wealthy people who live here, just critical of their own situation." "It's a very smart community. . . . I don't hear that kind of backlash." "Affordable housing does not exist here . . . so probably the worker class would look at it and say, 'These guys have got so much money it's just not fair.' But I haven't heard anybody really bellyache about it; I mean most people I know figure hey you know that's the way it is. We all worked our way up there and maybe someday you'll get to that point. So I've really not heard anybody gripe about that, so the thing that most of the people, as I said, in our neighborhood have got enough money to where they don't begrudge the fact that somebody else has got a hell of a lot more."

Second, and more difficult to detect, was a form of rationalized denial, whereby they were aware of criticism (to various degrees), but refused to accept that the nonwealthy actually condemned the amount of wealth they had. This denial served as a defense mechanism to avoid dealing with this criticism, and perhaps protected them from confronting any deep sense of guilt.

And importantly, if as I showed in chapter 7 the ultra-wealthy view themselves as "normal" people and go to great lengths to reconcile the vague guilt they might feel about elite affluence (normal dress, normal friends), then admitting and internalizing this criticism from your

nonwealthy friends and acquaintances is very difficult. It can poten-
tially crack the community veneer and "normalcy" that you thought
existed, thereby exposing an inverted version of the pristine natural
and social paradise that has been constructed.[5]

In some cases, this showed up in subtle ways through conversations about nonwealthy perceptions of the ultra-wealthy, especially
when these conversations ventured into terrain about inequality,
poverty, or affordable housing. Often times, it was more about what
they *didn't say*, or *how* they said it, or even a *refusal* to engage in the
conversation altogether:

> JUSTIN: So have you ever personally had conversations with
>   people about criticisms of . . . [cutoff by respondent]
> ULTRA-WEALTHY RESPONDENT: **No.**
> JUSTIN: OK. . . . Do you feel like you're being judged?
> ULTRA-WEALTHY RESPONDENT: **No.** [blunt inflection]

Yet in other cases, this theme emerged through long-winded
accounts, sometimes accompanied by considerable mental gym-
nastics, to deny the reality of any serious societal criticism. Consider,
for example, my long conversation with Stan Cunningham, a very
wealthy sixty-something banker from California, which serves as a
nice representative example.

Stan admits that there might be some initial criticism, yet he starts
in on a story to illustrate how local criticism is likely temporary and
fleeting, and how the nonwealthy are coming around to the meteoric
growth of wealth in the area.

> The guy who taught me how to fly-fish was a ski patroller and
> fly-fishing guide and we were up at Yellowstone fishing the
> Louis Lake Channel one day in late October and we were driv-
> ing back in the pitch-dark and he said to me, "You know, when
> I saw these wealthy people moving into Jackson Hole I thought
> it was time for me to move out." And I looked at him and he said,
> "You notice we've been driving for an hour and we haven't seen
> a light?" And he said, "What I came to realize is that the people
> of wealth have the same value system that I have." And that was

an important . . . that's an important characteristic of the people that moved here . . . this very substantial accumulation of wealthy people that move here.

I probed, pushing him a bit, asking, "It sounds like the fishing guide was critical of all this accumulation of wealth," and before I could continue, Stan jumped in, "Well, that was his *impression* when it started to move in, and then he said to me, 'then I figured out that these guys all have the same value system I have.' . . . The culture of this place is very special. . . . *He didn't see it initially*, but then all of a sudden, he figured it out. He said, 'Hey wait a minute, I've got a whole different view of this.' . . . These people have the same value system that I did, that's a really big deal."

Not satisfied, I asked him to expand a bit more, "So you're saying that somebody like this gentleman, who might initially be critical, sort of shifts or removes his criticism?" Excitedly, he again jumps in, "You got it! I mean, I don't know if I'd use the word 'remove,' but certainly mitigate significantly."

According to Stan, nonwealthy residents such as the fishing guide he employs, often come to recognize that they are misguided in their criticism, and it easily washes away—or is "mitigated significantly" in the words of Stan—after recognizing that the millionaire has the same values as the low-wage worker. We will never know whether or not that guide was being truthful to Stan that night in the car, or whether he was simply flattering the person who writes his pay-check. Nevertheless, it certainly made Stan feel better about his role in the community, and shifted the focus to shared "values" as the way to heal the socioeconomic wounds that exist in the community, and takes blame off people like Stan. No matter if you're a billionaire or working poor, what matters more than problems of affordable housing are shared values across classes in the community. No matter how much money you have, or what kind of housing you have, everyone shares the "realization of the uniqueness of the community," and the beauty of its natural resources.

What I have described here are the most important and preva-lent general patterns, but that is not to say that there weren't some ultra-wealthy who were very much in tune with local criticism, and told of these experiences. But these were certainly the exception to the norm. For example, I talked at length with one respondent about his experiences feeling judged and criticized. "Yeah, we encounter some resentment [sigh]. Well to be honest it's [hesitates], it's everywhere if you look . . . just the guys that do the ski patrols and the guys that work on the boats on the rivers, the fishing guides, it's the caddies, it's the golf pros, the tennis pros, the people that work in the restaurants. It's the legal assistants; I mean you know they all feel that way if you talk to them."

Quite a list, I thought to myself. Interested in the content of these criticisms, I ask him what they say to him. "Well, that they can't afford it there. Have you ever heard the really horrible expression about Jackson Hole, that it's where the 'billionaires chase the millionaires out of town' and I think there's a sense in Jackson Hole, I think it's just like the Hamptons that it's just too much. Anyway, I'm getting way out over my skis . . ." Others described it as "a real tension in the community" or that "there's a lot of naysayers there" or that there is "absolutely [criticism]" or that "Somebody will tell you . . . all the rich people are spoiling Jackson Hole. Well how are they spoiling it? [speaking in a sarcastic tone] Well, um, clearly it's hard to find low-income housing. And it's hard to find people to work at the grocery store, or to serve the needs of the wealthier people."

These were the only clear examples, in all the years of research, where the ultra-wealthy recognized and named the deep sense of criticism and judgment. Instead, as I've shown in this section, it was more common for the ultra-wealthy to be largely numb to the criticism that surrounds them. This leads us to an important question: Why?

Six Reasons for Not Feeling Guilty

We've heard from quite a few ultra-wealthy people, so let's step back and connect the dots thus far. First, I found that the ultra-wealthy do, in a general sense, view greed and elite affluence as morally unsteady, and they sense this criticism from society, but their perception of this criticism and their feelings of guilt are *vague and impersonal*. Second, they address these criticisms, and reconcile any shallow sense of guilt, by transforming themselves into "normal" people with normal friends, as we saw in detail last chapter. But, third, despite their best intentions, this only creates a veneer—a candy-coated shell—that covers over the deeper criticisms that exist, blocking them from view, and perpetuating the problems that give rise to criticisms in the first place.

And this brings us to the present section, where I dig beneath the veneer, and probe them specifically about the deep criticisms leveraged against them both locally and nationally (for example, rich get richer at the expense of middle class, stagnant wages but skyrocketing costs of living, how much is too much, and so on). How do they respond? Their responses, which I classify into six categories, are woven together into a common motif that goes something like this: *Yes, we should be generally cognizant of greed and affluent elitism, but most criticisms of wealth are irrational, unfair, and unmerited, and thus there exists no reason to feel any deep sense of guilt.*

Of course, not all ultra-wealthy respondents fit neatly into these categories, but they represent the most accurate general patterns that emerged: (1) modern consumption as a means for personal fulfillment, often via nature; (2) naked jealousy and resentment by the nonwealthy; (3) trickle-down economics; (4) hard work, ambition, and being self-made; (5) displacing blame onto their peers; and (6) inevitable forces outside their control.

CONSUMPTION AND PERSONAL FULFILLMENT: WHO IS TO JUDGE? ENJOY IT!

I opened this chapter with the important point that guilt tends to be wrongly viewed as an individual phenomenon—a singular psychological sensation that happens inside our heads, as opposed to being inherently social, and the product of the communities, narratives, and broader societal forces that collectively shape our thoughts and feelings. One of the most powerful forces, which I found has a direct impact on ultra-wealthy responses to guilt and criticism, is modern consumption as a means to achieve personal fulfillment.

The underlying logic of this view, which was often poorly articulated by the ultra-wealthy, is that all of us—rich *or* poor—are striving for personal fulfillment; and consumption is a primary way we achieve it. Despite the rich often being the focus of criticism, the broader American culture of consumption and personal fulfillment also, at the same time, idolizes the lifestyles of the rich and famous. As the logic goes, we are all consumers: the rich are doing the same thing as the poor, and the poor want to be rich. It is not a matter of moral categories, but is a sliding scale, and a matter of degree. Why then should those with the money feel guilty, if *everybody* is striving to consume?

This cultural dynamic is summed up well by David Grusky and Tamar Kricheli-Katz in their book on modern wealth concentration, reminding us that

> consumption is deeply embedded in our everyday behavior and is not easily shed, even when it's appreciated that it's ethically problematic . . . consumption is organically interwoven into our lives, rendering it more a style of life than some unit act, such as abortion . . . we believe, in other words, that we are entitled to the money we make because it reflects how much value we create in the economy . . . the commitment to this principle is so strong that it allows us to ignore the brute consequences of our actions (e.g., the death of a starving child) and insist instead on our right to spend on ourselves.[6]

Or in the words of one interviewee, Allan Fahringer, who is worth upward of $100 million, "It's all a matter of perspective." One person's mansion in Teton County may be another person's cottage—and one person's cottage may be another person's mansion. And people struggling at the poverty line in the United States would be considered well-off in a less developed country. Allan continues, "You can no longer build a 20,000-square-foot house [in Teton County], but there are some. You can fudge, and get a 14,000-foot one in the zoning, but even building an 8,000-square-foot house, you know, that's not exactly huge . . . that's a cottage in the Newport context of cottages. So, again, it's all a matter of perspective."

The matter of perspective applies the same in the richest county in the richest country in the world, as it does in the slums of Mumbai, argues one ultra-wealthy interviewee. "You know, the human part of nature. Interesting, I read a book—*Beyond the Beautiful Forevers*, it is about the slums of Mumbai. And, you know, [chuckles] *they would be jealous of someone who had found a few extra tin cans that day*."[7]

As the logic goes, we're all just spending what money we have in order to find happiness, so we shouldn't fault the rich for doing the same thing as everyone else. Thus, upon what grounds can they be critiqued or judged? And as a result, what is there to feel guilty about? Allan sums it up well: "Given my background, I'm hardly hostile to people displaying their wealth and enjoying their wealth. *Not at all. However they find that enjoyment.*"

In my discussions with some ultra-wealthy, it was as if they could not envision any other option for their money other than to enjoy it themselves. Perhaps the most interesting aspect of this finding was that our conversations were not as emotionally charged as some of the other issues explored throughout this book. Modern consumption as a means for personal fulfillment was simply taken for granted. It is just the water in which most of us in the United States swim. It was the obvious and uncontroversial course of action, revealing to me just how deeply embedded it is into contemporary American culture, even at rarefied heights. In the words of another interviewee, "You see some of the amounts of money and you sort of shake your head and go 'wow,' . . . [but] the government will get the rest one day, so you might as well spend it on what you want to," as if there are no other options other than consumption. Put emphatically from another interviewee, "Hey, we've got money, but it's not about the trophy—it's about just having a whole lot of fun while we can! You know? [chuckles]."

NAKED JEALOUSY AND RESENTMENT FROM THE NONWEALTHY

There is also the common belief that critiques of wealth are motivated by basic jealousy and resentment. Given this fact, why should the ultra-wealthy be made to feel guilty by those who are motivated by naked envy? Unlike consumption and personal fulfillment, which was baked into modern culture so much that it became second nature and thus less overt, this theme was one of the most talked about. The reasons for resentment tended to vary, and the ultra-wealthy provided several different theories, based on their own experiences. For example, they note that some people were jealous and resentful because unlike the wealthy, they did not work hard earlier in life to get to where the wealthy are now.

It is important to note that in this narrative of resentment versus hard work—as exemplified in the following quotes—the main character in the story tends to be the mythical "ski-bum," who has *chosen* to live a life of poverty, giving up the modern allure of wealth for a life of adventure. While these types of people certainly exist (less and less so), *the ultra-wealthy tended to view them as the face of inequality, used as a romanticized scapegoat to justify great wealth and great wealth inequality, and ultimately, to obscure the real face of people struggling in poverty.* The regrettable irony is that these are communities of Spanish-speaking migrant workers, who rather than choosing to live a life of romanticized poverty are actually working as much or more than any of the ultra-wealthy respondents, holding down two and sometimes three jobs, and contradicting the popular notion that resentment is rooted in laziness or naked envy.

"There's definitely resentment, when they see someone building a $15 million house. But in some ways the people are making a choice, 'I want to be a ski-bum and work for the ski area [chuckles],' you know," explained one ultra-wealthy respondent. Other interviewees spoke in similar terms. An investment banker from New York City told me that the working-class people are "probably jealous as hell that someone's worked harder than they have and gotten ahead." This is all very straightforward and simple. "I could see how somebody who is a ski-bum, or somebody who has maybe not spent as much time trying to figure out how to make a lot of money, could have some resentment or could have the perception that all these rich people are, it's easy money and they didn't work for it, etc., etc. How that might generate resentment," says another interviewee.

Digging deeper into the minds of the rural working poor, one ultra-wealthy respondent pondered, "You know, you see all this wealth around, and I would imagine that there are some of those folks that may be getting bitter about it . . . yeah, it could be envy, and it also—without getting into psychoanalysis—you know, it could be disappointment in themselves, right? You know, now they're in their forties, and they're still here, and they're still a ski patrol guy."

Some ultra-wealthy argued that it's not just money that stirs up jealousy, but it's envy of the *work ethic* of the rich. As one person put, there are many people who "resent the fact that people have in most cases *earned* their wealth . . . so I think that those who resent people who come here and have worked hard and made a lot of money, sort of have a visceral 'share the wealth' mentality."

The resentment of hard work is another reason why the ultra-wealthy tended to equate the struggle of the working poor with the personal choices of the mythical "ski-bum" living the dream of a permanent vacation *rather than* working hard and climbing the economic ladder. In the words of an ultra-wealthy woman from the DC area, who moved to Teton County eighteen years ago:

> From what I have heard pretty consistently, [resentment comes from] a lot of the people who have given up, have chosen to live in Teton County because they wanted to pursue an activity that wasn't going to pay them. . . . But I think sometimes when they see [affluent] people come in and are able to do all these things they love, and not have the stresses of having to make ends meet, it creates a little bit of resentment . . . there's nothing you can do to address that, that resentment exists with some people who have sort of chosen that . . . there's a little bit more resentment from some people who it's too late for them to have more of a typical, or higher paying career.

On occasion, a handful of respondents explained that the resentment is also rooted in a person's natural intelligence. "You know, that's just how it is, and some people are born smarter than other people and it's not their fault . . . some people just don't have the capability," said one respondent. Similarly, a different interviewee stressed that, "Gene pool is another element of it." According to another ultra-wealthy person, this can lead the nonwealthy to ask, "Why do you have it and why don't I have it? The answer in many cases might be one worked hard and the other didn't, or one has a much higher skill set and intelligence level than the other. That's the way the world is, you know. Everyone is not created with equal faculties. Some resent that, some who are on the lower end of that spectrum resent it." The apparent fact that some people are born smarter than others can stir feelings of indignation and jealousy. It is important to note that I did not encounter this sub-theme as regularly as some of the others, but sufficiently enough to include it here.

And last, many just wrote off jealousy and judgment to animalistic "human nature," or talked about it in general and unsurprising terms. It's what we do. Humans want what other humans have, and there is nothing surprising about that. Tracing jealousy to these natural human capacities was a common way to delegitimize these criticisms, and to perhaps justify and elide any deep sense of guilt. "Frankly, that's just human nature," says one gentleman, and another gives me more of an academic perspective, "I'm sure you're going to run into people that say Jackson Hole is all screwed up, look what's happened!? But wait a minute [laughs to himself] . . . you know that's human nature. You know, your field of sociology. . . . I mean there's nothing strange about that. It's called jealousy."

It's no surprise that people who "are living in mobile homes" are jealous of "people who are driving a Tesla," argues a real estate developer from New England. At the root of all this, according to a handful of others, including a real estate mogul from New Jersey, is "Well, obviously, folks that don't have it, I presume they think *they* themselves deserve it, or alternatively, that others *don't* deserve it. So, there's anger. You have to be angry, because there's nothing anybody can to do anything about that." Put similarly by another person, "it's part of the deal. There are certain groups that feel a certain entitlement. And I don't mean that as pejorative . . . the not-really-hidden subtext is 'I have a right to live here' . . . and that right doesn't exist anywhere."

TRICKLE-DOWN ECONOMICS

"Thank God for rich people," said one ultra-wealthy respondent, in his attempt to sum up the reason for why he doesn't feel guilty. He was alluding to the way wealth percolates down from rarefied heights to the lowest rungs of the socioeconomic ladder. One respondent—a CEO from the Midwest—made this same point crassly, explaining that the presence of extreme wealth disparity is "just the way life is. It's reality." But despite this harsh reality, he offers hope. "My answer to everything is jobs. We are giving you jobs, and you simply wouldn't be here without us . . . we understand and believe that the noblest thing a person can do is to give people jobs . . . so while [the wealthy] may not really need a massage or spa things, or their lawn manicured, they do it because they know it provides work for people."

There are of course endless debates raging about "trickle-down economics," but my intention here is not to rehash the pros and cons of neoliberalism. Instead, it is to move beyond political caricatures and abstract wars of words, and hear from actual people in a real community. And not just any people, but people who—as their trickle-down thinking goes—serve to make the largest positive economic impact of any group of people in the United States.

At the home of another CEO, I sipped iced tea and talked at length with him about what it is like to run a large business, and more specifically, how good it feels to provide people with jobs and to improve the local economy. "To give you an example," he begins, "I took over a company that never made any money and in six months I had it profitable, and so now it can pay people . . . and we could contribute to the community." Not only is this good for the workers, but "it feels good to be part of something that's profitable and successful and contributing to the community."

He uses this story—and his role as CEO of this benevolent employer—as a metaphor for the ultra-wealthy in Teton County. He continues, underscoring the different role of those at the top versus those at the bottom (whose survival is tied to CEOs like him). "I think I've got to be worth a lot more than the guy who's screwing in the bolts, you know. . . . I think that's one of the great things about our country is that we do reward people for what they do."

Thus, those who criticize the wealthy are the "people that don't know how much benefit someone with wealth is actually making in our society." As evidence, he gives another personal example. "I pay a lot of money to a lot of people to do a lot of work. I'm able to do that because I've made a bunch of money, but it isn't just sitting around. At all times, I'm figuring out how to make more, and improve things that are around. . . . I'd like [the world] to be better when I'm done than it was when I got here." He laments that this positive perspective is "not the view that's conveyed of wealthy people. You know the view that's conveyed is somehow they're all out there partying and drinking and, and just wasting money, and people that I know, none of them are like that. There are a lot of wealthy people, people that fly in on their own planes and that sort of thing but, gosh, it provides a tremendous amount of jobs and opportunities for people that are not rich, you know, the restaurants and the hotels and the other things that are there."

In all of my years of research, this was the most prevalent and straightforward reason given for why the ultra-wealthy should not feel guilty. It also was a main reason why some felt that local political attempts to address low-income housing, low wages, and economic inequality, would actually *hurt* the community. Or, put another way, it is why the state of Wyoming should remain a tax haven for the wealthy (that is, no personal income tax, corporate income tax, low sales tax)—and, not just so the rich can get richer, but so that the rest of the community can benefit from the rich getting richer.

Quite often, respondents expressed positive feelings about the ways their money flows down from great heights. Many also assumed that the working class shared these positive impressions. In the words of a recent transplant from Atlanta, "I think there's some gratitude [from the nonwealthy] for the chance to work and get paid well and to have the consistency of the work. . . . I don't sense resentment. I mean, the economy is doing well and they're all getting paid." Another interviewee echoed this message. "I think that the locals have come to love the trickle-down effect. It injects a tremendous amount of prosperity into the area." Still another, who put it more strongly than most people I interviewed, suggested that, because of the job creation, "What [the wealthy] seem to be doing for the rest of the community is nothing but positive."

Indeed, with all of the home building, high-end services, and environmental philanthropy, there is no doubt that the ultra-wealthy are "pumping money into this economy," as one financier transplant from Philadelphia described it. Most felt positively about this fact, and other typical responses went like this: "I think that there is an appreciation by most people of the fact that people of wealth have contributed so much to making this a better place to live"; "we're giving all these people a lot of business. . . . I mean, she's [the interviewee's caterer] so genuinely grateful for the work"; "we can afford what we're spending on, and they're [working class], in a certain sense, part of the beneficiary of the fact that we're willing to do so"; "the positive effect is . . . job creation . . . and there's a lot of contributions that go to conservation organizations that wouldn't be available otherwise. That, and certainly tax revenue that comes in"; "the community won't thrive unless you have people that can spend money . . . create this economy that creates jobs . . . financially successful people that are trying to do good things for other people."

HARD WORK, AMBITION, AND BEING SELF-MADE

If wealth is the product of ambition, self-motivation, and years of hard work, then what is there to feel guilty about? Any criticisms about your self-made wealth falls on deaf ears. Self-made wealth is the highest honor and the ultimate fulfillment of the "rags to riches" American dream that has fueled mythologies of rugged individualism and success. It is no surprise, then, that this theme was ubiquitous in the interviews and observation. Along with the trickle-down motif, this self-made narrative is as American as apple pie, and has received a great deal of attention from social scientists for many decades, if not centuries, beginning with the likes of Alexis de Tocqueville.

Throughout the course of this book, this theme has bubbled up just about everywhere. In chapter 2 about privacy and paranoia in America's most exclusive club, we heard from Colin Stewart, who responded to strident criticisms of the club by reiterating over and again that 90 percent of the club members are self-made, full of folks who have worked tirelessly—80 and 90 hours a week he says—and need desperately somewhere to relax, and to enjoy the fruits of their labor. "You know, work hard and then play hard," he says.

Similarly, John Truett from chapter 7, who was not born into an affluent family, but is now an extremely wealthy oil-and-gas CEO, reminds us of the flawed thinking that goes into criticizing the wealthy, or expecting them to feel guilty. "I put myself back to being 19 years old, and seeing these rich people and big houses. I might have some misconception that these people are fucking assholes; rich fucking assholes from the East. You know, members of the lucky sperm club. They've fucking inherited everything and I'm fucking working a ski-lift here, freezing my ass off. You know, that type of attitude. But, it's not that. These are self-made people that have families that are out there trying to do family things."

Others spoke in similar terms, underscoring exactly why they will not be shamed into feeling bad for working hard. It's a matter of personal choice, according to a real estate developer who moved to this community from San Francisco. "There are people that choose to goof off" when they could have spent their young adulthood "productively steepening their own income curve." And it's not like he didn't want to goof off like some of the rural Western working class do. "I mean believe me, every night that I was ordering Chinese food to [large bank name redacted] at ten o'clock at night, I would have much rather have been in Jackson at the Cowboy Bar with ski-bums having beers. But I didn't do that and so you know those guys who are sort of bitter and struggling in Jackson, there's a slice of them where I sort of say, 'well you chose to spend your twenties [laughs] skiing and living on your buddy's couch, and so you sort of get what you deserve.'"

Another person explained that their success is not about chance or sheer luck, because "luck is the residue of design. The harder

I work, the luckier I get. . . . Most people don't have the focus or the stick-to-it-ness to follow their own trail. All you gotta do is follow your trail. And if part of that includes financial recompense, you can make that happen. And if it doesn't, you might make it happen anyway." The ultra-wealthy are, according to another interviewee, exemplars of the "willingness to dedicate themselves to the world of making money rather than the world of skiing and camping out."

I had the privilege of interviewing an older gentleman one chilly fall afternoon who told me many stories of the sacrifices he made to get to where he is today, and not-so-subtly criticized the entitlement culture he thinks exists today among lower income people in Teton County. "When I first got married, I was fresh out of the army, bought a house for $20,000 on the GI bill. I didn't have any money to put down. I had a $296-a-month house payment that scared the shit out of me." Then, alluding to the housing crisis in Teton County, he retorted criticisms of the ultra-wealthy here, "I had an hour and a half commute each way in Los Angeles; I mean I was living out in Los Angeles. And I didn't think I had a right to live downtown. I think that we have created an entitlement culture. And all you have to do is interview your grandfather." Feeling guilty makes zero sense for folks like him and the people he respects, who don't feel "entitled to anything" and have made "incredible sacrifices to achieve the greatness that they achieved."

DISPLACING BLAME ONTO ONE'S PEERS

Research in psychology and sociology has shown that displacing blame can reduce guilt.[8] When the ultra-wealthy spoke of blame, or implied guilt, it was most often displaced onto their own kind, reserved for the rich who flaunt their money or act like entitled jerks. In their view, those who act in this way are shameful and *should* feel guilty, and they were quick to provide examples of their peers behaving in this way. By associating culpability with interpersonal interactions in the community (for example, not appearing to be modest or normal), it seemingly relieves them from guilt associated with the larger structural and impersonal effects of extreme wealth concentration of which they are a part. As long as they are "normal," nice, and unostentatious, there is not much to feel bad about.

Additionally, I sensed that there was a degree of self-righteousness operating, which is of course not entirely unique to the ultra-wealthy, but is a common way all of us deal with criticism. They were simultaneously able to acknowledge to me that their peer group deserves some criticism, but displaced blame away from themselves and the larger socioeconomic systems and local social problems. Blame and guilt is for individuals who flaunt their wealth and perpetuate the spoiled "rich fuck" stereotype they admit exists, but that they themselves shun.

Eric Alexander is an Ivy League–educated banker who after making a vast sum of money came to the rural West to get away from his rich peers on the East Coast. Even for a multimillionaire, he considers himself to be a pretty down to earth guy with a good head on his shoulders and feet on the ground. Throughout our interview, he complains about rich "assholes" who not only give the wealthy a bad name, but actively damage the sense of rural community. "I'd say the thing that bothers me most is what's going on down in Shooting Star," referring to the controversial new country club that Kari Paglia earlier wouldn't tell her friends that she was a member of, and that many people—rich and poor alike—view as more "Aspen" than Jackson Hole, more Prada than Patagonia, more Colorado than Wyoming, more Tesla than Chevy, more cosmopolitan urban than gritty rural, more "rich fuck" than wealthy "normal" person. "[Properties] are all being bought up by dot-com people or Wall Street people. Those are the people that I came out here to get away from. And they're following me."

I inquire as to why Eric wanted to get away from them, and what it is about them that might rub him the wrong way. "They will change the nature of living out here," Eric says, "because they're the kind of people who come out here with a different set of values and different set of tastes—where what you're worth defines how important you are."

As we continue our conversation, I wonder to myself if Eric recognizes the thick irony, and obvious hypocrisy of all this—that he is what he hates, having recently moved to the area from the East Coast just ten years ago, building his own multi-million-dollar home. I ask him about this, and he acknowledges the irony, but his criticism is not the wealth, but the shallow values of some of his wealthy peers— the bad apples, so to speak.

> I don't mean to sound like a curmudgeon that, you know, "OK we moved here and nobody else should move here afterward, because it's all ours." I don't want to sound like that. But, when you see these people buying three- and four-million-dollar town-houses without ever having seen them, you kind of wonder about that. It's a place to be if you're in San Francisco or Silicon Valley, or Fairfield County or Westchester County. And, I can just see it in every damned cocktail party back there, people are dropping the names of where they just bought a place out in Jackson and so forth. I don't like those people a whole lot.

Still I probe further, trying to peel away the layers of Eric's critique of his peers even more, who again, on the face of it, appear to be doing exactly what he did just ten years ago, with money made in a similar profession. He attempts to explain further:

> Well it's the culture that they bring in here. It's "if I build a house, it has to be bigger than the guy that's next door" and that kind of thing. If you get the sense of what I'm trying to say, it's that wealth is their defining quality. It's a free world and a free country, and there's nobody that says they can't do what they're doing . . . [but] there are lots of people out here that are very private that, if you will, sort of fly under the radar, that don't need to make splashy statements or drive BMWs or Mercedes. You know, people—shit, like me I guess—I drive a pickup truck.

This long discussion with Eric is characteristic of a lot of similar conversations whereby the ultra-wealthy would admit that there is indeed blame and guilt to go around, but that it is reserved for the people who flaunt their wealth or act like entitled "assholes." And this of course fits well within the main finding in chapter 7 about understandings of ultra-wealth "normalcy," and the process by which, despite their immense wealth, they use nature and rural Western culture to transform themselves into "normal" people who strive to be "normal" members of the community.

It is disheartening for these "normal" ultra-wealthy people to see that Carhartt jackets are being displaced by fur coats, and that pickup trucks are less common than flashy Teslas. Like Eric, others were also upset about the ways that their ultra-wealthy peers were creating a bad name, and ruining the rugged authenticity of this rural Western paradise. One interviewee told of long ago, "when we first moved here in '95 . . . people with wealth would live in a fairly nice, beautiful home . . . but vehicle-wise you had no idea [they were wealthy], and dressing-wise, you just didn't dress up here. And I'd say in the last ten years there is a transition." A multi-million-dollar house is within reason, but "good lord there's more Mercedes and Porsches and Maseratis . . . to distinguish them as you know, somebody a little wealthier or better."

But even the size of a home has tasteful moral limits. "Our house is six bedrooms, and so there is room for a lot of people . . . [but] I don't want to see Teton County become Aspen, where people show their money. Certainly, in the old days people didn't do that. There were no mink jackets or fancy cars. It was technical clothing . . . made for outdoor exercise . . . skiing, snowboarding, and pickup trucks." Frustrated, and implicitly conveying the modesty of their six-bedroom home, she reckons, exasperated, that down the road from their property a family is building a 14,000-square-foot house. "It used to be just locals or maybe from Texas, but now hedge fund guys from New York and entrepreneurs from Chicago and San Francisco and Newport Beach and New England." Another interviewee quipped that Teton County is "going to be really tested going forward. Given the amount of money that's coming in and backgrounds of these people, I think it kinda looks much more like the Hamptons."

And still another ultra-wealthy woman, getting visibly upset, says that her husband isn't too bothered by it all, but "I let that stuff get to me . . . the way they throw their weight around. . . . I mean, I really don't want your freaking autograph. I could care less what you do. Attitude. Attitude . . . these people, reality is very different for them than it is for me . . . their sense of regular starts out very differently than my sense of regular." Some groups of affluent people are worse than others, she says. "The people that we found a little more difficult to take were some of those that were involved in finance."

One cause of all of this change is the ongoing tax shelter that I described in chapter 1. In the words of another respondent, "The Wyoming tax climate is obviously a great attraction for people to come and establish a residence . . . and we started to see more and more people of very substantial means and experience moving here." That is all well and good, of course, especially for this respondent who did the same thing about fifteen years ago. However, he laments the fact that "we're seeing a little bit more of people who have a sense of their importance rather than being understated . . . my sense is that Aspen and Sun Valley and some of those places are a lot *showier*."

A woman I interviewed at her home just north of downtown Jackson complained about the recent construction of ultra-high-end hotels and private clubs, including the "Four Seasons hotel . . . and a very high-end gated community golf course built called Shooting Star that are these massive 8,000- to 10,000-square-foot homes, and then there was an Amangani Resort built." For her, these physical entities symbolize in a very concrete and highly visible way the shift toward "a wealthier individual . . . who are sort of arrogant or have hubris; sort of blowhards about who they are or what they've done. The walking resume sort of people."

The good old days were when outwardly "you don't know who has $5 in their pocket or $500 million . . . it used to be a community of millionaires, now it's a community of billionaires." This was according to another woman, who fears that out-of-touch billionaires are spoiling the relationship that millionaires like her have with the working class. The billionaires she describes "are people who feel entitled. They come here, look who I am."

Being flashy is one thing, but being flashy in the face of an authentic rural Western culture is another. And thus the criticism that some ultra-wealthy have of their affluent peers has more to do with the threat it poses to *their own* romanticized ruggedness and down-to-earth simplicity. If this new flashy culture of Teslas and mink coats wins out, then what is left of this rural place that has allowed many ultra-wealthy to transform themselves into more virtuous and authentic people? So, in displacing blame onto their peers, there is much more at stake than just saying that the rich person down the street is garish. It is that they have not properly assimilated to the rural life of noble contentment, pastoral simplicity, and community connectedness—and moreover, their flashy way of life may actually destroy it.

One ultra-wealthy woman from Delaware, who I interviewed over coffee on a rainy spring morning, still holds out hope for the survival of the down-to-earth ultra-wealthy culture and community they've come to love. Despite trying "not to be judgmental," she can't stand the "Silicon Valley crowd that's sort of new to Jackson, flying in on their jets and to Shooting Star or some of these other clubs." Even still, she's hopeful. "The town is pretty 'podunk,' right? It's a cow-town, really, still."

Ultra-wealthy people who fashion themselves by the "podunk" nature of this "cow-town" are, in effect, less guilty than those behind the wheel of a Tesla. This theme resonates with the imagery of Old West art and dress we've seen throughout this book, and behind that, the strong pining for connection to primordial nature and primordial small-town America that is in direct moral contrast to flashy affluence.

These contrasts were put most starkly by a gentleman in his sixties who made his fortune in both law and business, and says that the problem with his wealthy peers is that "they have no idea what it's like to be a cowboy or to have a ranch." Concerned that the cowboy culture is on the decline—a culture that he's fully adopted, in dress, vernacular, and the decor in his sprawling home—he says "I hope that it remains . . . but it's really hard, and I've become very friendly with people who are ranchers of different kinds, and they are people just like it was in the movies, and they are still around." He laughs, again mocking his peers, and legitimating his own position as an authentic rural Westerner, "I can take a person from Wyoming and put them in any city, and they'll survive. But I take a person from the city and put them into the mountains of Wyoming, and they're going to die. I'm serious."

INEVITABLE FORCES OUTSIDE ULTRA-WEALTHY CONTROL

There was a sense of economic determinism that also eased any feelings of personal guilt. If the economy is an inevitable tidal wave that cannot be easily thwarted or redirected, then any one individual is not necessarily at fault for the damage it leaves in its wake. This is sociology 101—the fixed forces of social, political, and economic nature, so to speak. But, as we have seen too often, this same tidal wave has conveniently created a winner-take-all economy, with a patterned set of winners and losers.[9]

One winner is Abraham Farfan, an ultra-wealthy investor I interviewed in the thick of a harsh Wyoming winter, asking him specifically about these economic winners and losers, and whether he feels guilty. From his perspective, community and economic changes are inevitable, "I think it's the inevitable march of progress. It may not be quite as rapid and rampant as it has been, but that's the way life is. . . . I don't think it's a matter of pros and cons. It's a matter of inevitability. I don't think we can stand in its way. It's gonna happen." In a similar way, this sense inevitability means that—like the ultra-wealthy— the lower income folks are also blameless cogs in a larger machine, such as his property caretaker working just outside his door during the interview: "those people, such as the person who is just outside my door at the moment, are wonderful human beings. They're very responsible and raising families and ordering themselves."

Other ultra-wealthy people spoke in similar deterministic language when asked about the problems that exist, writing them off to inevitable change over which individuals have very little control. "I mean, it's reality. There's nothing you can do about it," one gentleman argues. Another man reflected on the time when he wasn't affluent, accepting it as a fact of life, and not the product of opportunity, family advantages, education, and so forth. "I remember back when I had lots of friends who were wealthy. And it's not that you're bitter or envious about them; it's just a fact of life, right? And, you're on a path, and whether you end up being more financially successful or not, who knows?"

Sitting on the couch in a gorgeous home near downtown Jackson, one woman expressed similar determinism and hopelessness because the billionaires are in control, and the millionaires are left helpless to change things. "How do you change anything? . . . so then is it the millionaires battling the billionaires here? . . . and so sometimes you just can't do anything because you don't have the money to do it."

Whatever the causes, there was broad consensus that, in the words of another interviewee, there's not "really a whole lot that anybody can do about it . . . the town is quickly growing and becoming more popular. . . . And so in some regard there's not really anything you can do about it." The impacts of wealth are the result of impersonal, and seemingly deterministic forces. "That's the way of the world . . . that's the way it is," says another person. Several others echoed these feelings, lamenting that "It's just the evolution of our world here," or "Unfortunately, I don't think it's going to change," or "we would have liked to have seen the resort stop growing the moment we moved in and kicked everyone else out. But that's the way it is, the way it is," or "I agree that [ultra-wealth] is crazy, but you're not going to change it. And to be angry about stuff that you can't possibly affect is nuts. But there's nothing I can do about it."

Guilt and Moral Obligation to the Community

Asking a group of people if they feel guilty about something can reveal surprisingly deep insights. It can uncover larger patterns about how that group talks about and justifies themselves in relation to the moral obligations pressed upon them. These are critical questions, especially because in recent years the critiques of ultra-wealth have become more strident, as wealth has become concentrated among fewer and fewer people. As a researcher, I wondered what effect these critiques have had on this group. Thus, this chapter focused on whether they recognize these criticisms, and how (or if) they deal with it.

The seven clear confessions of guilt that opened the chapter—which were the only clear examples I encountered in thousands of hours of interviews and observation—were still fraught with contradiction and equivocation, revealing the complexity of studying this issue. We humans, whether rich or poor, are just not very good at reflecting, in honest and logical ways, about how we are feeling, or why we do what we do.

Like any other social group, the larger social environment in which the ultra-wealthy live shapes how they think about and respond to the criticisms leveraged against them. What is certainly unique about this group is that they have come under increasing public moral criticism in the wake of wealth concentration and growing inequality in America. These critiques are certainly not new, dating back thousands of years. But they have been amplified in the last decade, and have become central in partisan politics and polarization these last few years, and likely for many years to come.

The ultra-wealthy do sense that greed and affluence can be morally risky, and they are aware of public criticism, but only vaguely and in ways that are impersonal and disconnected from a deep sense of community obligation. One reason many of them remain numb to the true intensity of criticism is because they view themselves as (or are actively transforming themselves into, as we saw last chapter) "normal" people. In spite of their best intentions to reduce the distance between the rarefied heights at which they sit and the rest of society, it nevertheless creates a veneer that distorts what they see and don't see, masking the truth about the suffering in the community, and who or what is to blame.

This finding has great importance for the second, and more important question, which is the title and focus of this chapter: Do they feel guilty? Their responses, which varied from person to person, coalesced into the six main themes that explain why they, on the whole, do not feel guilty, despite paying lip service to the age-old perils of money and power. In the end, these six reasons tell us a lot about how the ultra-wealthy think about themselves in relation to their great wealth and power, and their sense of obligation to local communities.

And more fundamentally, from the top-down, these findings about guilt reveal larger patterns that permeate all of American culture, where wealth is associated with ambition, and where wealth is viewed as the primary vehicle to achieve self-fulfillment through consumption of material goods. It also reveals how, for stigmatized elites, wealth itself can provide a pathway for self-transformation (via a nature-based lifestyle described in part 2) into nonstigmatized "normal" people who are connected to nature and share values with the working class, thereby extinguishing any deep sense of guilt about class-based problems. And last, even when class-based problems are acknowledged, or in the rare case that deep guilt creeps in, individual responsibility to address problems are chalked up to the inevitable march of progress, despite their immense social, economic, and political power to improve the community.

PART IV

Ultra-Wealth through the Eyes of the Working Poor

One final piece of the puzzle remains. In a community defined by such extreme "haves" and "have nots," *what might those at the very bottom teach us about those at the very top?* Contrary to popular opinion, neither group exists in isolation from the other, and they each rely on the other to live the life they envision. And as the ultra-wealthy often see it, they are linked to the working poor through friendship, a shared sense of rural "normalcy," and connection to nature.

Yet, too often, their perception of the working poor is based on the stereotype of a mythical Western cowboy in dusty Wranglers or a penniless white ski-bum, both of whom have honorably chosen to forgo the corporate rat-race in pursuit of a life of authenticity, lack of material comfort, simplicity, rugged survival, and adventure in nature. Yet, this stereotype belies the true nature of the working poor, and their relationship to the wealthy. In this section, I finally peel back the layers, revealing the reality of these connections between top and bottom.

The "paired" approach taken here—introduced with Julie Williams and the Padillas in the opening pages of the book—moves social research beyond isolated case studies of just the rich, or more commonly, just the poor, toward a more holistic understanding of how these different groups interact. The Harvard sociologist Michèle Lamont, a leading expert on the culture of inequality, reminds us that "cultural processes do not solely depend on the actions of dominant actors . . . subordinates often participate in the elaboration of cultural processes as much as dominant agents do . . . from intentional actions or as an unintended consequence."[1] And, similarly, the novel work of Charles Tilly suggested that future research investigate in more detail instances of "paired" groups of people, rather than just those at the top or those at the bottom.[2]

Working with a team of researchers from a local community nonprofit, we conducted in-depth and in-person interviews with fifty individuals, most of whom are at the poverty line and are Spanish-speaking immigrants.[3] We asked them many of the same questions that I asked the ultra-wealthy. In some instances, I was able to pair these working poor individuals with the specific ultra-wealthy people for whom they worked. These paired interviews directly linked individuals from the top and the bottom, and I was able to examine what each group said about the other.

For example, based on their firsthand experiences, what does ultra-wealth look like through the eyes of the working poor? What does ultra-wealth *feel* like to the working poor, who often move in and out of this world of ultra-wealth, yet they and their families struggle to make ends meet by razor-thin margins? What did they make of the ultra-wealthy's peculiar love of nature (for example, "Compensation Conservation, "Connoisseur Conservation," "Gilded Green Philanthropy")? Or what do they make of other important issues I encountered regarding the supposed vitality of the community, such as ultra-wealthy attempts to hide their wealth and romanticize and adopt working-class tastes in an effort to become more "normal"; or whether the working poor are really friends with the ultra-wealthy as was proudly claimed in the last few chapters; or ultra-wealthy faith in charitable giving or trickle-down economics to solve local problems; or even deeper moral questions, such as whether the ultra-rich deserve all the wealth they've accumulated.

We focused our questions on these issues, and on what it was like to live within the shadow of such towering wealth, which not only provided an important window into the grueling lives of many of these working-poor immigrants but also provided a novel window into the lives of their ultra-wealthy peers.

Answers from the working poor were anything but straightforward. Contrary to what some might expect, there was not widespread resentment, overt jealousy, or naked antipathy. That does not mean, however, that they were uncritical, driven by some shallow state of false consciousness. Their criticism emerged more indirectly and organically, through the telling of stories and firsthand experiences that provided a new viewpoint through which to understand affluent uses of nature and rural culture.

At times, these stories were very positive, praising specific ultra-wealthy individuals who they assumed had worked hard to make their fortune, or expressing appreciation for providing them with work, or giving examples of ultra-wealthy individuals who treated them fairly and with dignity. But at the same time, many critically called into question the motives and behaviors of the ultra-wealthy, especially related to their purported environmental concern and commitment to normalcy, authenticity, and community.

I unpack these views of the working poor in two separate chapters, each of which provides insight into their lives, as well as shedding new light on the preceding chapters from inside the world of ultra-wealth. Make no mistake, the working poor are certainly inside this world as well—many of them every day—but their experiences are very different from mine, being more hard won, and filled with difficulties and complexities that a privileged researcher like me will never fully appreciate. For that, we must turn our attention to them, and let their own voices be heard.

Chapter 9 introduces the day-to-day life of the working poor, many of whom are working two to three jobs to pay skyrocketing rent; facing discrimination and barriers associated with their ethnicity, language, and immigration status; and just narrowly providing for their families. How does this daily struggle to survive in the richest community in the richest nation in the world shape their perception of immense wealth and those who have it?

Chapter 10 digs deeper into their personal interactions, stories, and experiences with the ultra-wealthy, most of which tend to be very critical, and call into serious question the perception many ultra-wealthy have of themselves, of nature, and of this community. These views are motivated *not* by raw jealousy or naked antipathy, but by arduous and authentic experience. A growing chorus of low-income folks are beginning to publicly challenge the sincerity and benevolence of the ultra-wealthy, rejecting their involvement in environmental protection and community philanthropy as sanctimonious hypocrisy, serving only themselves while at the same time deepening the struggles of the rural people and rural community the rich claim to love.

9

No Time for Judgment

The days are long and exhausting for Carmita Sanchez, who works full time cooking, cleaning, and providing childcare for one of the ultra-wealthy families we met back in part 2 of this book. She's worked for this particular family for nearly a decade, caretaking their home and helping to raise their children. Early each morning, she takes the drive out to their sprawling property. "I arrive and start cleaning, do beds, feed breakfast to the kids if they are there. Afterward, if the kids are at school I pick them up, take them to their activities, and pick them up from the activities. I prepare their dinner if they are not going out."

The nights provide little respite for Carmita, who with four of her own children to raise as a single mother, juggles a second job in the evenings to cover the costs of their small trailer, where they share living space with another family. Her experience is typical of how the other half lives here in Teton County, where is it common for people to work two to three jobs and cram multiple families into a two-bedroom trailer. Through this hard work, households like Carmita's typically earn an annual income in the mid-$20,000s (an estimated 40 to 50 percent live in federally qualified poverty), compared to the those at rarefied heights in Teton County who earn an annual income of $28,163,786.[1]

But Carmita doesn't wallow in the struggle. There's no time for that. She remains positive. And, from our interview with her, it is clear that the margins are too thin, and the consequences simply too dire, to be distracted with anything else but survival. And survive she has, by first escaping a crumbling marriage and dim prospects fifteen years ago in Mexico, to build a life for her family here in Teton County, all despite the demands of four children, a meager education, scant English, and the initial risk of immigrating here on the thin word of those who "told me there was a lot of jobs here."

Through all of this, Carmita believes that the struggle is worth it, and views herself as a successful person, despite yearning for more free time to pursue an education. "As far as goals, I would like to study something, because I don't want to work just cleaning . . . [but] I think I am successful because, even though I am alone, I was able to buy my car and my small trailer home."

———

This last part of the book examines what ultra-wealth looks like and feels like through the eyes of the working poor. But, of course, not all working-poor experiences are the same, and in this the first of two chapters on the topic, I focus specifically on people like Carmita— and the scores of others like her in amenity-rich communities across the mountain West—who are living on especially thin margins.[2]

When thinking about these issues, it is important to understand that their view of ultra-wealth is not, like many of us, come upon from a distance. For them, it cannot be separated from daily experience. It is less abstract or idealistic. For Carmita, and the other working-poor individuals from whom we will hear, their views are based on firsthand accounts, often from years of up-close interaction. Certainly, the day-to-day experiences caretaking ultra-wealthy homes, cooking meals, and raising their children provide a unique window into the world of ultra-wealth.

What is it like to live in poverty, while simultaneously spending most of your days working in a 20-million-dollar home? Many people, including myself, have the privilege of pontificating about wealth and the wealthy, but most of us have not been exposed to them in the same way, spending our lives working for them, and depending on them for our narrow survival.

The most important finding in this chapter is that *the immediacy of their day-to-day struggle, and the razor-thin margins they face, combined with lack of time for education or engagement, radically shapes their experiences with the ultra-wealthy, and renders them more positive than others we will encounter next chapter.* We know from sociological research that something as basic as having free time, and simply being available to develop human capital, greatly enables volunteering, activism, and other forms of civic engagement.[3] Building on this work, two main themes emerge, each of which leads to positive views of the ultra-wealthy, and should be understood within the context of their time-intensive and weary struggle to persevere.

The first theme is expressed best by Carmita, when we asked her to reflect on the impact of wealth in the community. She conveys gratitude for the ultra-wealthy, and responds with a question of her own, pointing to her immigrant community's attempt to sustain a life here. "I think rich people have a positive impact in Jackson because they give us jobs. How else would we be able to sustain ourselves? We are poor." When, like Carmita, you are living with multiple families to a trailer, or watching your friends and family wrought by hunger and eviction, there is a tendency to live in the present, devoting all energy to survival, and being grateful for whatever allows you to make it to the next day, even if you know that you are living in a vastly different universe than others in the community. Carmita explains that "Latinos and wealthy people are like two different worlds, except for the [amount we] work. I think it is a relation between patron and servant."

The second theme relates to whether or not the working poor believe that the ultra-wealthy *deserve* their extraordinary wealth. Why do some people have multiple homes and billions they'll never spend, while others tirelessly work two to three jobs and still cannot stave off eviction from their modest trailer? Who deserves what? Among the people who are struggling the most (the focus of this chapter), we heard the same refrain in the interviews, as expressed here by Carmita: "I think a person that has a lot of money, maybe their families were responsible and work very hard, and that is how they got their money. . . . I have known a lot of people with money and since they were a kid they work hard. I think they have had many nights without rest and that is why they have money. Because American people are very responsible and that is how they are successful."

This entrenched logic of working harder is then assumed to be the solution for fixing the problems that have come in the wake of wealth inequality, especially the housing crisis. "Maybe if there were *more jobs* . . . that would help people that are struggling."[4] Yet low-wage jobs are aplenty in Teton County, and some folks are already working three of them, with literally no time in the day to take on a fourth. The idea that the amount of work you put in corresponds with the amount of wealth you acquire is symptomatic of a culture of meritocracy that has long permeated popular American culture at all class levels. The working poor, who are the most overworked and yet still the poorest people in the community, recited similar cultural scripts (as did the ultra-wealthy, revealed in chapters 7 and 8). For the many who struggle so mightily, it is no fault of their own that they simply do not have the time or energy or access to education about the false truths and entrenched cultural scripts that directly equate hard work with affluence.[5]

———

The relationship between the working poor like Carmita and the ultra-wealthy is a complicated one, especially for those we interviewed who have a desire for deeper knowledge of the issues and civic engagement, but do not have the time or the energy, and thus tend to fall back on familiar mottos about hard work and meritocracy. The irony is that they *epitomize hard work*, with incredibly long hours and multiple jobs, yet *still* face eviction, food insecurity, and day-to-day stressors that come with economic uncertainty. Or as it was put to me by a leader of one of the most prominent nonprofits serving the immigrant and working-poor community, "there are many people here who are so poor that they do not have time to know what is going on in the community. They do not have the time to know why or how wealth is created. So, they pull from talking scripts they hear, rather than actual facts about wealth . . . they're just trying to make it, trying to survive."

Who Are the Working Poor? Sociodemographics, Eviction, and Discrimination

Let's first take a look at the general contours of this population, before diving into their view of the wealthy, and the stories they tell to make sense of living day-to-day in America's wealthiest and yet most unequal community.

POPULATION GROWTH AND ETHNIC COMPOSITION

The large majority of the working poor in Teton County are immigrants from Mexico. Their presence is often underestimated because they have, in the past, tended to be physically and politically inconspicuous in the community, on account of fears about their own or other family members' immigration status, in addition to their long hours cloistered at their various places of work, and the fact that they have been pushed farther and farther outside of town because of housing insecurity.

Yet, despite their invisibility to some, they make up nearly 30 percent of the population.[6] The majority of children in the community are U.S. citizens, having been born in Wyoming. Similarly, most adolescent and young adults who were not born in the United States have Deferred Action for Childhood Arrivals (DACA) status. The presence of this immigrant community is growing rapidly relative to other groups. For example, their population more than doubled between 2000 and 2014—a far cry from 1990, when a mere 1 percent of Teton County identified as Latin American. Today, they make up 35 percent of all babies born, and as a result, the Teton County School District has undergone a dramatic shift in its ethnic and socioeconomic makeup, with some grades split equally between kids from Latin American origin and kids from Anglo American origin. Although it is difficult to calculate because of fears around the application process, it is likely that about a third of students from the Latin American community qualify for free and reduced lunch.

Leaders from social service organizations, such as Sonia Capece—the former executive director of the influential Latino Resource Center—estimates that about half of this population are undocumented immigrants.[7] Sonia herself was recently forced to move out of the community because of insecure housing, and is another example of the difficulties of making it here, even with a middle-class salary. As middle-class people like Sonia are pushed out, the community is now increasingly made up of those people at the top that we've heard from throughout this book, and those at the bottom willing to endure struggle, or who come from such extreme circumstances in Mexico that they enjoy the relative improvement in living quality, safety, and security.

Nine out of ten people in Teton County's Latin American community are immigrants from Mexico—many from the same small state of Tlaxcala in central Mexico.[8] Like Carmita Sanchez earlier, who made the dangerous and uncertain trek, a whopping 60 percent are first-generation immigrants. Or viewed from another angle, only 4 percent of individuals have parents who were born in the United States.

Teton County is now filled with people with immigration stories similar to the following, as told by a Mexican gentleman we interviewed:

It all started twelve or thirteen years ago. I was working and studying in Mexico, but sadly the economic opportunities were not very good. I decided to come to this country, but I brought my wife with me. Together as a couple we crossed the border walking. You could say it was illegal and we are here. We came from the state of Tlaxcala, Mexico. I think we decided to stay because it was the first place where we knew and worked, and also because there is an inexhaustible source of employment here. We are country folk, we are humble and we like to be in nature and Jackson is close to nature.

It is estimated that about 30 to 40 percent of the Hispanic population in Teton County is living in federally qualified poverty, compared to just 7 percent of white non-Hispanics.[9] Relatedly, access to affordable healthcare is similarly lopsided. In 2012, a staggering 60 percent of Hispanics in Teton County were uninsured, compared to just 16 percent of white non-Hispanics. Of course, this affects more than just their physical and mental health, and creates a cascade of problems and risks that sabotage pathways to progress.

The most important pathway to progress is education. Unsurprisingly, folks from Latin American origin also have much lower rates of educational attainment. Teton County itself boasts a very high rate of residents with a bachelor's degree or higher, at nearly 50 percent. Among the Latin American community in Teton County, only 43 percent have a middle school degree, 27 percent a high school degree, and 8 percent a college degree.[10] These low rates are not because they shun education, or don't see the value in it for upward mobility. The interviews and survey data show very clearly that educational attainment is a top concern and primary aspiration, but it is impeded by barriers of poverty and long work hours, and a shortage of public funding for higher education options in the region.

Why did they come in the first place? The immigration story of this working-poor community is integrally linked to the migration of ultra-wealthy people who brought a lifestyle that required new service industries, especially environmental, recreation, food, retail, and construction. In the wake of this huge influx of ultra-wealthy people came a surplus of low-paying service jobs needed to make possible the idyllic mountain lifestyle and elite environmentalism sought by moneyed migrants.[11]

Throughout U.S. history, people from all backgrounds have always came to the West in hopes of a job and a new future, but oftentimes these job booms end in bust: when all the gold has been mined; or the railroad has been built; or the price of oil and gas dampens the market and devastates the town. But what separates Teton County from other examples of economic boomtowns in the rural United States is that there is likely no bust in sight, and the immigrant communities who have come are here to stay.

A recent survey of this community showed that most have lived here between ten and fifteen years, and a huge majority indicated that they fully intend to live here indefinitely if they can.[12] Despite most being first-generation immigrants, they are now happily rooted here. In the words of one Mexican immigrant, "I have lived here for more than ten years, I came from Mexico with my family so that my children have a better future. I have two jobs and I barely afford my personal expenses, but I feel happy and calm as it is a town where there is much respect, tranquility, and I would like my children to have a better future."[13]

PARADISE LOST: THE CHRONIC THREAT OF EVICTION

Housing insecurity poses the most lethal threat to their future survival in Teton County, and has already incurred real damage, as many families have been evicted, forcing them to either endure crowded living conditions with multiple families or face the reality that they will have to leave the community.

A perfect storm of environmental conservation interests and limited private lands (a mere 3 percent of all land in Teton County is private, and the rest is owned by the federal government, restricted from development) combined with the flood of ultra-wealthy people who wield unmatched economic power, has meant that the hope for affordable housing is proving to be an illusion, despite it being the number one concern of most community leaders.

Paralysis on the issue is not for lack of appetite or will among people like Carmita who need it. Instead, it is because of two main obstacles: (1) tremendous economic disincentives from the market, which is formally and informally controlled by those with deep pockets who seek to build their dream house inspired by their brand of what I earlier coined as "Connoisseur Conservation"; and (2) at the same time, affordable housing projects have clashed head-on with the environmental goals of some conservation groups (for example, anti-development and NIMBYism), many of which happen to be supported and funded by these same affluent individuals who are committed to what I described earlier as "Compensation Conservation" and "Gilded Green Philanthropy," to uphold their particular vision of nature and altruism, which neatly separates social problems from environmental ones.

As such, the crisis continues to take victims, while still remaining the most obvious, serious, and talked-about problem that has yet to attain any meaningful progress, slowing tearing strand by strand at the fabric of the community.

Rents can increase by double-digit percentages each year, and with virtually no affordable housing to speak of, nearly one in five low-income households will have to move, or face eviction.[14] For example, take Emilio, a landscape worker, who has lived here for a decade with his family of four. "I am worried about what is happening now. They are evicting us, and we cannot find another place to live. My worry is for my children and their school and their activities that are routine for them throughout the year. I do not want to break their routine to move to another town."[15]

Local laws offer little protection. In 2015, a 294-unit apartment complex distributed letters to its tenants—many of them low-income—notifying them that they would be raising rent by 40 percent. They gave renters just a few months to pay or move. People questioned the moral basis of this decision, which was essentially an eviction into homelessness for many residents. But with few regulations in place, they could not question its legality. After public protests, the owners agreed to split the rent increase over two years.[16]

Homelessness has now become a problem in paradise. One longtime community leader is still shocked and saddened when he hears about examples, especially children, "there are a handful of homeless kids that go to the high school here, in this the richest place in the country!"

Today, eight out of ten (82 percent) Latin American–origin households in Teton County are cost-burdened, and a third of them are overcrowded. Consider Emely, who is fifteen years old, and whose family was recently evicted after living in the community for nine years. "I feel worried and scared most of the time. This is a big transition. I never thought this could happen. It never even came into my mind."

Or consider Ella, a middle-aged woman who has lived here for sixteen years and is also facing eviction. "I work for a group of restaurant companies and prepare the desserts. Today, I feel sad and confused because I have nowhere to live. Now I live in a hotel and pay every week but cannot find an apartment. I'm on the waiting list in lots of places and I ask God for a miracle and that's my situation. I'll have surgery soon and I have nowhere to go. This is my situation."

ETHNIC BARRIERS AND DISCRIMINATION

To add to these difficulties, ethnic minorities in the community also experience much higher rates of discrimination, which tend to occur during the all-important quest for housing. One recent study that included interviews with local property managers in Teton County reported implicit and explicit discrimination during the search for tenants and the signing of leases. For example, nearly all rental advertisements are offered in English only, and just 20 percent of market-rate rental managers offer leases available in English and Spanish, making it difficult for Spanish-speaking residents to know exactly what they are signing.[17] This is of course just one example, albeit critically important given the scarcity of affordable housing in the area, and evidence of the power-differential between property managers and those at the whim of the market who may be taken advantage of because of their ethnicity or language proficiency.

Of course, history is filled with well-documented stories about the myriad obstacles and discriminatory barriers all new groups of people have faced (and still face) upon migrating to the United States in the nineteenth, twentieth, and twenty-first centuries. Immigrants from Mexico to places like Teton County face similar barriers that go well beyond the issue of housing, but it is over housing that the barriers are seen in sharpest relief and pose the largest threat, given the critical importance of housing to the survival of these families.

Finally, the seminal work of Lisa Park and David Pellow in their book *The Slums of Aspen*, along with many others who study issues of environmental equity, have rightly pointed out the ways that ethnic minorities and people of color have been excluded from idealized and "pure" landscapes. Trenchantly, they draw on the work of geographer David Sibley, reminding readers of the historical link between racism and "pure" ecological landscapes:

> Sibley catalogues ways in which whiteness has been equated with purity and hygiene in the colonial world, and how dark skin and people racialized as the "other" were equated with filth, dirt, uncleanliness, and therefore placed outside of civilized society (e.g., Roma, African Americans, Irish, Aborigines, and Jews as rats, and others associated with pigs, cock-roaches, trash, and sewers). This ideology extends itself to perhaps the greatest challenge for the environmental movement in the United States: the underlying cultural, racial, and economic elitism of environmentalism that often consciously and blatantly associates clean environments with whiter and wealthier people.[18]

UNDERSTANDING WORKING POOR VIEWS OF THE ULTRA-WEALTHY

The challenging experiences described earlier that make up the worlds of the working poor (for example, overwork, eviction, immigration, and ethnic discrimination) dramatically shape their views of the ultra-wealthy. Digging into this world, especially those people who are struggling, raised a puzzle: why were some from this immigrant community so positive about wealth and the wealthy, while there were others who were very negative, and sought to expose the veneer of community and environmental care? Positive views of wealth and the wealthy emerge from the experience of toil and struggle. Not all working poor share these views, but it takes a certain amount of privilege to be able to reflect on the questions posed in this book, and those that have more life-threatening concerns are less likely to have the time to concern themselves with such issues.

In the remainder of this chapter, I move down from the broader sociodemographic lay of the land, and let the working poor speak for themselves, based on our in-person interviews.

This section focuses on how their life on razor-thin margins shapes their responses to questions about wealth. Or in the words of Carmita, "I think rich people have a positive impact in Jackson because they give us jobs. How else would we be able to sustain ourselves? We are poor."

RAZOR-THIN MARGINS

Many interviewees lamented their long work hours and multiple jobs, but recognized that they had no other option for survival, especially if they are raising a family. Working oneself to the bone was an all-too-common theme in the interviews. "There are many difficulties, [especially] housing. If you used to work one or two jobs, now you have to work three," says one man who immigrated here from Mexico in the 1990s. Another person, who speaks only Spanish, asks rhetorically during our interview, "We come to look for a better life, a better way of living, but we end up working 20 hours [a day] . . . so where is the better life if we spend it cleaning for hours and hours, washing dishes? We don't even see our kids grow."

One woman describes this reality quite starkly, saddened that her community is defined by "work, work, work. And then they forget about themselves and we do that as parents. And it is a lack of value of other aspects of themselves. So they don't care about themselves and they have health issues, don't sleep, anemia, don't eat, two works [jobs], they drive a lot, they are tired, and then you have depression problems, because if you work seven days and work two jobs."

Similarly, a single mom with two children under the age of thirteen told us about her three ongoing jobs, as a cashier in a gas station, food service worker for a hotel chain, and then last, a house cleaner for several wealthy families. All in a day's work, yet she still struggles to cover rent. This is not unusual, of course. Others told of friends who work full time, yet are sleeping in their cars after the weather warms up in the late spring and summer. I could fill an entire chapter with story after similar story, because nearly every person we interviewed had a harrowing personal account, or knew someone very close to them who did, in spite of hard work and wealth of hope.

Earlier in this chapter, we heard from people like Emilio, a father and landscaper, whose family of four was recently evicted, and Emely, a fifteen-year-old student whose family was blindsided by eviction, throwing her life into uncertainty, and Ella, a middle-aged woman who has lived here for sixteen years, now temporary living in a local motel and facing a mountain of healthcare costs, asking "God for a miracle."

Thus, despite their tireless work ethic and strong desire to remain part of the community, many people nevertheless face the harsh reality of eviction. Less than a week before we interviewed a young woman named Marcela, she and her family were suddenly evicted from their Jackson trailer with just two and a half weeks' notice. "I lived in Jackson for thirteen years," she laments. They now commute every day from fifty-five miles outside of town. Misled by a landlord who "said we were going to be living there for a long time," they were abruptly told that they had to be out straightaway. "One day he just decided that he was going to kick us out of there and we were not going to have a home." Marcela and her family tried everything. "We called him, and he was very rude to us. I asked him if we could stay a little bit longer because they were just giving us half a month." Their appeals fell on deaf ears. Construction on a new development had to roll on, and thus he said, "No, we are not stopping our construction just because you guys don't have a place to live."

Eviction is a standard occurrence. "I have friends, and in a day they took their housing away and they don't have housing anymore," says another woman we interviewed. Given the thin regulations around housing and the absence of meaningful rent control, huge annual rent increases—which can sometimes be sprung on residents at the last minute—are also a de facto strategy to evict the working poor. One respondent, a man in his thirties, told us of a friend, who like many others, is working "two or maybe three [jobs], and they just don't even sleep or eat." This friend's family, which includes two teenagers attending the local high school, were recently evicted because of a sudden rent increase, and "right now they're living in a hotel room. They have no place to go." A common solution to this problem is the pooling of resources among these families, so that, as another interviewee described it, it has become more typical to see "two or three families sharing space."

We also interviewed teachers at the local schools, to get their unique perspective given their daily interactions, on how this struggle of working multiple jobs, or sleeping on the floor of a trailer, might trickle down to children in this community. One teacher explained that "in my classroom our Latino kids come in and they are exhausted. So I don't see routines at home . . . so I think our Latino children . . . they're exhausted. Starting at 8 o'clock in the morning is really difficult." Asking why they are so exhausted, she spells out that, "A lot of them are (A) sleeping on the floor; (B) sharing a bed with a younger sibling; (C) sleeping on a couch in a house that's exceptionally overcrowded; (D) staying up very late watching TV or playing video games. Those I know for sure, I have experienced, because I've asked."

Student homelessness is also a reality in Teton County. Another teacher notes that in "every level I had a homeless student . . . just picture parent-teacher conferences. One couple walks in with stilettos and Armani, and the next family walks in with no clothes."

NO TIME FOR JUDGMENT: JUST GRATEFUL TO SUSTAIN OURSELVES

The working poor in this boat who are struggling mightily were much more likely to be positive about the wealthy because they perceive them to be the drivers of a successful economy and their only hope for survival. In short, they were grateful for the work, and when we asked them to reflect on the wealthy in this the richest and most unequal community in the nation, they often pulled from what the community leader quoted at the end of the introduction earlier called "talking scripts." Of course, some people, like Carmita, have genuinely positive relationships with the wealthy people for whom they work, but these examples were fewer and far between, because most responded with canned answers, motivated in part by their desire to work more in order to survive.

One woman we interviewed, who had immigrated from Mexico to Teton County thirty years earlier, explains that "we have accepted the people that have a lot of money. . . . I do not criticize, they provide a lot of jobs when they build houses, construction, plumbing, air condition." She admits that, "some people complain that we have a lot of millionaires, but they also create jobs and donate a lot." Another woman, who came to Wyoming fifteen years ago, describes this theme clearly. "I think wealthy people have a positive impact in Jackson because they provide a lot of jobs." As the logic goes, the more money a person has, the more things they need, and thus the more work needs to be done. "If they have lots of money, they have more needs, and need labor." Thus, "I don't think wealthy people have a negative impact in the community."

Time and again, we heard this refrain from people who had little time, and were struggling to make it, as illustrated further by this small selection of quotes: "I always heard this from my grandmother: the rich man lives off the poor one and the poor one lives off the rich." "I think rich people have a positive impact. . . . When they are here they spend money . . . that helps us for work, seasonal or year round, and helps the community." "I think rich people have a positive effect . . . all this is a benefit because we have a lot of jobs." "Jackson has a lot of economic opportunities . . . even two jobs per person, it all depends on your disposition to work." "I think the effect of wealthy people is positive because they provide jobs." "What I have seen is that wealthy people employ Latinos and treat people in a nice way." "From my perspective, rich people have a positive impact in the community, the school benefits from them; there are many things that happen in Jackson because of rich people."

A recent scientific survey on the immigrant community in Teton County (figures 9.1 and 9.2) found that the lack of time—stemming from overburden of work—was the number one reason why they are not able to be more involved in local civic life. So even though many of the people we interviewed *wished* they had more time and energy to pursue formal education and be more involved in civic

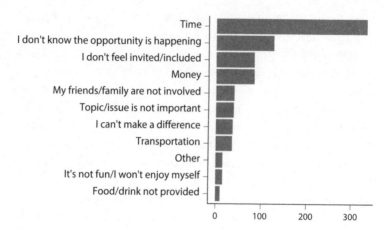

FIGURE 9.1. Lack of time is cited as the biggest restriction to civic engagement. The *x*-axis indicates the number of total responses to the question "What is the #1 thing that stops you from being involved?" *Source:* 2015 Teton County Latino Community Assessment Survey.

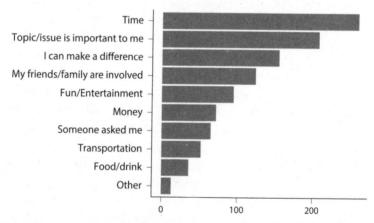

FIGURE 9.2. Lack of time is the most important reason for deciding whether to get involved or not in civic engagement. The *x*-axis indicates the number of total responses to the question, "When deciding to get involved or not, which of these affect your decision?" *Source:* 2015 Teton County Latino Community Assessment Survey.

issues, there are simply not enough hours in the day, and the urgency of survival takes precedence.

Take Miguel, for example, who is in his thirties and married, and who we interviewed one evening in late summer after he had finished one of his shifts working at a construction site. He is very optimistic about the local economy because of the number of jobs that come with the influx of wealth, yet at the same time he accepts that these construction jobs require working very long days. "There are a lot of opportunities to earn a lot of money, but it will take a lot of your time." And despite the fact that there "are jobs to go around," Miguel does recognize that people still "fall into poverty and many times have problems finding stable housing."

Or consider Carlota, who is a single woman in her twenties, and makes ends meet by piecing together various waitressing jobs. She too describes how time is the most important limiting factor in the lives of people like her. "I think in Jackson there are a lot of jobs available and the wages are good, but when you compare the living cost, it is hard here. I know a lot of people that need more than one job to live here, and then you are not able to enjoy, you have a lot of stress. There are a lot of people that need several jobs, and so they don't see their kids very often and they have a family, but they cannot be with that family."

Time has become even more scarce these last few years, as people run themselves into the ground to keep up with cost of living. Lolita, a woman in her thirties who enjoys the advantage of being bilingual, mourns her loss of time, especially with friends and family. "We used to see each other once or twice a week, but now it's like zero times a week because we're all just working. And, it's just like, what are you working for? Bills."

DO THE ULTRA-WEALTHY DESERVE THEIR IMMENSE FORTUNES?

Those with no time for family and friends certainly have little spare time for education, either formal or informal. They are less likely to be exposed to information beyond their immediate circles, and thus their awareness of broader socioeconomic issues can be limited, and as noted, they tend to rely on popular talking scripts when they are asked to share their attitudes about wealth, the wealthy, or how to address the obstacles they face for making a better life.

Using a number of different interview questions, we sought to uncover what they see when they look up at rarefied heights. Do they believe the ultra-wealthy deserve all of the wealth they've accumulated? Are they jealous or envious? What explanation do they give for why some people (like them) work tirelessly but still struggle mightily, while others (like their fellow community members) have millions and billions they'll never spend. We found that answers to these questions are not something they thought about often, and when we pressed for answers, they fell back on tropes conveying that the ultra-wealthy must have simply worked harder than everyone else, and largely deserve whatever comes to them.

One gentleman we interviewed, who came to Teton County about twelve years ago with his wife and two children, put it this way: "People with money have it because of their work, or their ancestors have worked hard for what they had, and I know people that are in this position are humble and kind." In his view, "I think rich people deserve the money they had because they have done things right. Gotten organized, they had an economic plan, and their money is more and more."

Another gentleman, who also came to the community with his wife and children just over ten years ago, was particularly shy during the interview, reminding us that not everyone we interviewed was interested in these issues, or had given them much thought. Or as one woman put it, "People are rich because of the work they have done . . . *[but] I don't think constantly about this. It is not my interest.* . . . I am not looking at what other people's wealth is, or if they have more than me." But back to this shy gentleman, we drew on our interview guide and pressed him a bit, asking "In general, why do you think in society there are people that are doing so well and others that are struggling?" From his perspective, "it might be because some people like to work, and some people expect things to be handed to them." It's all about hard work, he says. He continues, "I have never dealt with a person with money that is rude or arrogant . . . they deserve their money because they have worked hard and probably know how to manage their money, which is something we probably don't know how to do."

Many others expanded on this same point, offering their own unique diagnoses based on their experiences, and pulling from the popular talking scripts permeating the social ether of Teton County, Wyoming, and the broader United States. A sample of other people put it this way: "I am proud of people with wealth because they invested, started something and took risks and it worked for them. I don't take risks and I cannot complain to the person that is wealthy and invested to have their own money." "Wealthy people deserve their money because they already worked for it." "Of course rich people deserve their wealth, they have fought for it and worked to have it." "I believe that people with money have worked for it and have earned it . . . people deserve the money they have."

WEALTHY PEOPLE ARE GOOD FOR THE COMMUNITY

Finally, in the interviews, we asked members of the working-poor community to reflect on the impact of wealthy people in the community, beyond just providing jobs. We again discovered a theme that was, for reasons related to their time-crunched struggle, complimentary of the ultra-wealthy, and in fact echoed many of the themes we heard from the ultra-wealthy themselves (for example, hard work, earned wealth, job creation, trickle-down economics): *wealthy people have a positive impact on the community because they give away some of their money to causes that benefit us.*

Further, there is a sense that the working-poor community depends heavily on philanthropy, yet at the same time they are not as aware of the fact that wealth concentration has created many of these problems in the first place.[19] Similar to many of the ultra-wealthy in this book, there is a feeling that plutocracy can actually be better for those at the bottom, so long as the wealthy give to nonprofit organizations.

This positive assumption that the ultra-wealthy in Teton County are extraordinarily generous—a perception I found to be widespread across all social groups in the community—ignores many of the persistent social problems uncovered in this chapter. These perceptions do not account for the fact that environment and arts enjoy the lion's share of philanthropic assets, compared to cash-starved human and social services organizations serving the immigrant community.

Nevertheless, the time-crunched working poor picked up and used these cultural scripts in our conversations about the positive impacts of gilded philanthropy in the community. In some cases, their opinions were informed by their direct experiences because they've received support from one of these social service organizations, or because they hear about highly publicized gifts and events (for example, Old Bill's Fun Run).

One woman we interviewed, who has lived in Teton County for more than thirty years, believes that "Rich people are positive. They give money in Old Bill's Fun Run, or they are calling and letting us know that they have a bed, and want to pass that to the Latino community." Many of these stories were firsthand accounts, similar to this anecdote about the hand-me-down mattress. Another woman explained that "Wealthy people have a positive impact in the community, and I have seen this. They help a lot. There are events with auctions and people put down money for this. In that aspect, I think the rich people help for good things in Jackson."

Some were appreciative of the money given to environmental and lifestyle causes, such as the bike pathways. "I personally know very rich people that give money for the bike pathways, and there is this man that gives a lot of money for that, so I would say that I appreciate the work they provide and what they provide for these [bike pathway] organizations." Another example is philanthropy to cover the costs of downhill skiing, as explained by another interviewee. "I know that there is a program that during the winter gives money for low-income kids to learn to ski. I have also heard about donations for Latinos."

Many folks had worked as caterers or custodians for philanthropic events similar to the one that opened this book, and thus were uniquely exposed to the galas, auctions, golf-outings, and the various other events that are common in nonprofit fundraising. One woman, who came to Teton County twenty-three years ago, tells of one such cancer foundation event, and ties it more broadly to the positive impact of wealth in the area. "Rich people in Jackson have a positive effect . . . every week there is an event, for the cancer foundation, for the therapy foundation, and all the people that attend are the people with more money in the community. They help organize, and the jewelry supports as well, so that we can all see this, and it is for the community."

A younger woman we interviewed had received scholarships from a wealthy family. "I went to school here all the way to high school, and there I met people that give scholarships, and they don't have to do it, they just want to see Jackson students have other opportunities and advance their career." Excitedly, she tells us that she "met them, even after I received the help, they *still* check on me and ask how I am doing. It is very beautiful."

Specific examples like this were hard to come by, but they do reveal some of the bridges that have been built between the working poor and the rich. However, most others we interviewed were lacking specifics, and instead spoke in vague terms, often reciting some of the popular ideas about charitable giving that were revealed by the data in chapter 5 to be overblown or simply untrue. Often, it echoed these additional examples from our interviews: "I know two or three couples that are millionaires, and they are very humble, and they donate to a lot of foundations. If Jackson didn't have those kinds of people, it wouldn't be Jackson." "The rich community in Jackson has a positive effect in the community. . . . I don't think rich people can affect the community in a negative way." "Rich people in Jackson, in my opinion have a very positive effect in this town . . . rich people support [nonprofit] organizations." "I think rich people have a positive impact in Jackson, they help people. The donations when there are events, the food banks, and the celebration of May 5th that is about celebrating Hispanics. Many rich people donate food, space, and many other things." "Rich people have a positive impact in the community, the majority of the people I know are helpful and generous and do charities. . . . I don't think rich people can negatively affect the community."

"Just Trying to Make It, Trying to Survive"

The incredible day-to-day stress of living in poverty, being overworked, fearing eviction, experiencing ethnic discrimination, and seeing the cost of living continually skyrocket might tend to make some people jealous or resentful of neighbors who have more money than they'll ever be able to spend, and plenty of free time to go along with it. Surely, it must be difficult for people like Carmita or Miguel or others in this chapter, waking up every morning on the floor of a shared trailer or motel room, to drive to work for a family at their sprawling $20 million property, and then only to head home in the evening to your children, and then leave again for your second minimum wage shift at the gas station or grocery story. It is reasonable to assume that for any of us, negative feelings might fester—that the mind might wander toward thoughts of envy. On paper, at least, we might assume that the enormity of the gap between these two types of families might breed resentment or jealousy, if not directed at the individual wealthy people themselves, at least at the hand you've been dealt or the systems in society that enable it.

Yet, this is not the reality on the ground, and the interviews with people like Carmita, Miguel, Carlota, Lolita, and the many others, tell a much different story—one that tends to be more positive because they do not have time to attend informative civic events, participate in regular in-depth discussions over these issues, or have the privilege of formal education, as many readers of this book might. Thus, their positivity flows from the fact that when asked, they respond gratefully for what they do have relative to where they've emigrated from, and then recite familiar themes from U.S. culture that emphasize hard work, meritocracy, and gilded philanthropy.

This finding is summed up best by one of the most prominent nonprofit leaders in the immigrant and working-poor community, worth giving voice to again here: "there are many people here who are so poor that they do not have time to know what is going on in the community. They do not have the time to know why or how wealth is created. So they pull from talking scripts they hear, rather than actual facts about wealth . . . they're just trying to make it, trying to survive."

And survive they have. But this is only the first scene of an unfolding social, political, and moral drama. More recently, the second scene has been unfolding, as leaders from this community have risen up to become better informed and better organized, aiming to crack the thick veneer that has cloaked this community. To these voices we now turn.

10

Cracking the Veneer

María Guadalupe Flores journeyed to Teton County from Mexico twenty years ago with a baby, a toddler, and a husband in tow. Proudly, the first thing she tells us in our interview is not about this grueling migrant journey, or the two decades she's spent climbing out of poverty, but the excitement she has for her daughter's upcoming birthday on Saturday. "I am María Guadalupe Flores, I am from Mexico City. . . . I have two children. My girl is going to turn twenty-two this Saturday."

Throughout María's interview, it became clear that despite her typical immigration story, she has developed views, and had experiences, that differed significantly from many of the overworked voices we heard in the last chapter. Absent were the fatigue-induced talking scripts about hard work. Absent were the favorable assumptions about the wealthy. And absent was the unquestioned gratitude for low-wage jobs and philanthropic charity that trickle down from rarefied heights.

Like so many others, María arrived with little education, but importantly, over the course of two decades in Teton County she was able to carve out precious time for valuable skills training and exposure to civic issues. Over time, she became more informed about issues of the day, and more involved in local social service organizations and community discussions, rather than being confined to the grueling and time-restricted life of survival led by many of the folks we heard from in chapter 9.

Yet, despite her education and the fact that she doesn't live in poverty, money is still very tight, and becoming even tighter with rising rents and cost of living. "Ten years ago, we had more money and time. I think we work a lot now. I am going to compare it to Mexico; you know how we used to work full time in Mexico? A full day was from 8 am to 7 pm. I feel like we are doing the same now here and the salaries have not been raised. The hourly wage is not enough, now everything is more expensive." But she remains hopeful, and continues to develop her professional skills each day, including through online education. "In the morning I wake up and give thanks to God, I meditate and do yoga . . . then I have breakfast and I work on the computer on my workshops. . . . I am studying a career over the Internet, so I study for a while."

———

María is part of a movement that has arisen in recent years that is publicly exposing cracks in the veneer of affluent environmentalism and the ultra-wealthy's professed commitment to "authentic" community. This movement, spurred by the experiences of the working poor, is part of a process that social movement scholars call "cognitive liberation," whereby an aggrieved group of people organize themselves and "collectively define their situations as unjust and subject to change through group action."[1]

In doing so, they challenge the taken-for-granted ideas that have been so pervasive in this book among the rich and poor alike. To be sure, their sharp criticisms of wealth, and the solutions they seek, are not motivated by naked jealousy or raw resentment for the ultra-wealthy but originate in the hard-won experience of surviving as immigrants and a commitment to fighting for a community defined by fairness and dignity.

Perhaps most importantly for our purposes in this book, *people like María now call into question the perceptions that many ultra-wealthy*

have of themselves, exposing the ultra-wealthy's (often well-meaning)
engagement with the environment and community as green veneer.
They rebuff the purity of ultra-wealthy environmentalism, they dismiss
the authenticity of their professed friendships with "normal" people, and
they dispute the value of gilded philanthropy.

By moving past the popular talking scripts and positive assumptions about wealth that we heard from the working poor in the preceding chapter, this movement introduces a more critical approach informed by lessons from economics, history, politics, and religion. But this is not just a few individuals here and there, it is emerging from a handful of local civic organizations that have grown up with the immigrant population, providing valuable resources for educating people like María through English language instruction and opportunities for civic engagement.

Carmela Lopez, an interviewee with wisdom and historical perspective that comes with being in her seventies, reflects on the progress. "Things have changed a lot compared to ten years back. We didn't have agencies with Latinos, we didn't have teachers in the school that spoke Spanish, there were no resources for Latinos. . . . Now nearly all agencies have bilingual staff, we have a dual immersion program, we have lots of services, and thanks to that we are here now."

As a result, the imbalance of knowledge and political power is starting to change. A diversity of voices are now being heard, in contrast to how things used to be when—in the words of one Latino construction worker we interviewed—"Sixty-year-old rich white guys with lots of money can go to those [civic and political meetings] because they're not going to their job, and already own their third home here, and they can get up and complain about things. And that kind of creates an unlevel playing field to some degree."

Over the past twenty years, as María has learned English and become more informed about economic and environmental issues, she remains inspired and motivated by two people from her upbringing: "my Grandmother, rest in peace, and Pope John Paul II." As such, her concern about extreme wealth and local poverty is not simply about dollars and cents, or even about raw politics per se, but more deeply about how we human beings have come to see each other. "I think we have to see the workers as human beings, as people, as friends. . . . Jackson has grown and now we have people from New York, Los Angeles, Chicago, and they see their labor as only labor, not human beings. And that is where you lose your sense of community."

But María isn't averse to wealthy people, or even wealth itself. "I think [wealth] is great if you are wealthy," she stresses, in good faith. But at the same time, "the people who are super wealthy, I would love it if they would share more and really help those who don't have." Undergirding her view is a moral and religious idea that we all deserve to have enough to live with dignity. Wealth doesn't belong to individuals; it belongs to humanity itself. "Wealthy people do not deserve the money they have because the wealth of the world is for everyone, and *we all deserve it.*"

She continues, giving an example that starkly illustrates what she sees as the moral plight of the community, and the living laboratory of extreme wealth disparity that it has become." It is very sad to see rich people with five, six, eight bedrooms and only their dogs live there, and [at the same time] there are poor families with four, six people that don't have a house to live in, and then they have the power to increase rents and kick you out because they are going to rent to someone that has more money."

For María and this movement, the massive concentration of wealth and the extreme wealth disparity is as much an environmental problem as it is an economic one. Like many we'll hear from in this chapter, María is concerned with the hypocrisy of wealthy environmentalism.

They build huge houses and take down trees. I really hope that for every tree they take down, they plant five. That is my hope. . . . We all have to conserve the environment, because [our children] are going to inherit it, and we are going to pass it to the new generations so we need to preserve it, and take care of it, and we will still have trees, and flowers, and water and clean air, and it will depend on us and not throw garbage and not eating your 'neighbors.' Appreciate what we have and not destroy it.

———

Among the working poor, there is a growing chorus critically responding to what many of their ultra-wealthy counterparts think, believe, say, and do.[2] Remember that in our interviews we asked the working-poor community many of the same questions we asked the ultra-wealthy, and in some cases, these people know each other through work relationships (for example, nanny, property caretakers, construction), and so we can triangulate and compare what they say about one another. To foster comparison, I've organized the rest of this chapter into two sections, corresponding to parts 2 and 3 of the book, which were focused on the ultra-wealthy.

First, we will hear from the working poor about ultra-wealthy relationships to the natural environment. From these voices emerge the following puzzles: Do ultra-wealthy people really care more about nature than suffering people? Is the professed ultra-wealthy commitment to the environment that we witnessed in part 2 actually hypocritical, given their huge resource consumption (for example, large homes, private jet travel, and so on)? Is the purported success of local philanthropy, and the assumed generosity of the local ultra-wealthy, actually just a myth? Interviews and observations with people like María tell a different story from the one we've heard up to now.

Second, we will hear the working poor's critical response to how the ultra-wealthy romanticize the supposed purity and simplicity of penniless rural life, and ultra-wealthy attempts to transform themselves into "normal" people. What do people like María think of ultra-wealthy efforts to adopt working-poor tastes and working-poor friends as a way to shed the stigma of being rich, and resolve their crisis of authenticity?

Environmental Veneer: Empty Virtue of Conservation and Philanthropy

THE PERCEIVED HYPOCRISY OF AFFLUENT ENVIRONMENTALISM

"This is a community that prides itself on its progressiveness," utters David Toledo, a forty-something we interviewed, who has pieced together a few seasonal jobs to make it work in Teton County for twenty years now. No doubt, David is right that Teton County is a progressive blue island here in a staunchly red state. But David questions what "progressive" even means in the context of such affluence and wealth disparity, bemoaning that "'progressiveness' for this community is often about making sure that there's wildlife available for rich people to view." Sarcastically, but with seriousness, he continues, "and let's take care of the environment, it's really important that we recycle here, and we'll make sure that we do that on our way to the airport to fly out in a private jet."

David recognizes that the ultra-wealthy might be genuinely concerned for the natural world, but only in ways that are closely aligned with their personal interests and cultural styles—what I described as "Connoisseur Conservation" and "Gilded Green Philanthropy."

It's not that the environment is unimportant to people like David, but there is a sense that the ultra-wealthy population is only superficially progressive because they promote a selfish form of environmentalism at the expense of other people who are suffering from poverty and eviction. "You're not actually doing anything for the environment. You're destroying the environment, but you feel good about it . . . and being one with nature and all this stuff, but then at the end of the day the one thing that I don't see progressive politics doing is ever giving up anything of its own, ceding power or ceding resources or wealth, and at the end of the day that's what has to happen if you want to have social justice."

Issues of wealth, poverty, and environmentalism are deeply entwined here in Teton County, and increasingly, throughout the rural West. Low-income people we interviewed are frustrated that these issues are separated from one another, especially by the most affluent among them. David presses on, saying, "the thing that bothers me is the lack of self-awareness, and that we think we're this progressive town . . . but what does it do? It doesn't do anything for your town. It doesn't put roofs over people's heads or food in their mouths. At the end of the day, it's just bullshit platitudes."

And for David, the worst part is using supposed altruistic concern for nature to cover up, and even perpetuate, the exploitation of the working poor. "I just think it's mostly as it has always been: being rich and poor. You have [wealth], you want to keep it. And if you're progressive, you can deflect . . . people are starving while other people are flying around in jets . . . a great way to do that is to deflect what should be . . . [so] to me it seems that a lot of our politics is about making people feel good and making them say that, you know be able to ignore the real problems, and saying we've done something because we opened the greenhouse."

Carmela Lopez, the woman in her seventies we heard from earlier, echoes many of these same sentiments, based on her thirty years of experience working different fundraising events in the community. She explains that people with great wealth generally do not "want to be the center of attention, except some events, like the Paws [animal shelter] event, *where they give more money to dogs than humans.*"

This was a familiar refrain, pitting animals against human suffering. Echoing Carmela, an interviewee named Elias Sutton, an auto mechanic who we'll hear more from later, argued that the wealthy "take care of the wolves more than the Latino workers in this community." Another person characterized ultra-wealthy environmentalism as "flying around in a jet and talking about how much I wanted to save the moose."

And another critic, Antonio Galarraga, a landscaper in his early thirties, has noticed that, to the dismay of himself and his family, who have struggled in recent years, the ultra-wealthy tend to be more generous to environmental conservation rather than "human" conservation. He, like so many other people, view this as a grave hypocrisy that has great consequence for suffering people, and the planet:

[The ultra-wealthy] probably contribute quite a bit to conservation organizations that do things, and they certainly seem to be doing more of that anecdotally than to human conservation. But, on the other hand that's a very localized effect . . . but probably more impactful is, leaving aside, that they're flying in jets and driving around in Escalades and stuff. They are mostly supportive of the status quo and the status quo is planetary destruction. I mean that's where we're headed, and so they've got all of the power and all of the political power, and at a minimum . . . they're not doing anything about it, and they're the ones who can.

Let's hear from the host of others like David, Carmela, and Antonio, who reverberated this major theme based on their personal experiences with the ultra-wealthy, sharply criticizing what they view as the empty virtue of affluent environmentalism.

For example, one housecleaner we interviewed tells of "an experience with a lady that I work for many years ago. She saw me cleaning large windows with paper, and next time I went to her house, she had rags for me, and asked me if I could switch from paper to rags. She explained to me that we had to think about the trees, and she is one of those people that really loves nature. She has a huge lawn. So she made me think, and now I try to recycle." This story is similarly summed up in the words of another person, who told us that, "The rich people tell us to recycle to help the environment."

Another told us of his personal experiences working for one of the wealthiest people in the community, who was "a nice enough guy. . . . I think his place is valued at like $35,000,000 . . . [they] fly in on his jet and stay there for two weeks." It wasn't the amount of money that was the issue for this working-class respondent, but the fact that this ultra-wealthy oil baron was intent on saving the environment by making his employees print on double-sided paper. "He made all of his money running oil . . . or initially made his first batch of money running oil past the South African oil embargo in the '80s . . . [yet] he'd come back down to the office sometimes and he would say, 'Here let's use this again. Turn this page over, use the back side; we're going to recycle all of our paper.'" The hypocrisy was almost too much for him to take, he says, continuing, "I'm like, 'You just flew in here in a Gulf Stream. Why do you care?' [Recycling] just doesn't matter, you know, you're keeping this 15,000-square-foot mansion heated year round, and empty, and you're worried about *that*? But you know, I guess it made him feel better."

We had a long discussion with another person about what counts as an environmental problem, and in particular, how the ultra-wealthy focus on narrow and near-term problems relating to wildlife or recreation, as opposed to far-reaching global problems like climate change. "This kind of goes back to the feel-good, progressive conservation and environmental things, where you've got people who are so fired up about the environment, and then yet they don't have any problem with people driving old and relatively dirty vehicles 100 miles roundtrip every day to come to Jackson to mow their lawns." Exasperated and losing track, he pauses and asks, "wait, what was the question again?"

From here, we probe about how this relates to issues facing the working poor, asking them, "How does the affordable housing issue relate to the natural environment?" Knowing that the wealthy live on expansive properties spread out through the valley, he suggests "having people live close in a community is obviously going to reduce greenhouse gas, which is our biggest environmental threat at the moment." Continuing, he further highlights the hypocrisy he sees among the rich, "if you're talking about conservation in the environment and yet you're taking actions that are increasing the greenhouse gases, you're just full of shit." He concludes, "it just doesn't make any sense to me. I mean, why talk about conserving the environment for bears and moose if they're all going to be dead in eighty years?"

Beyond the carbon footprint of the ultra-wealthy's private jets and globetrotting lifestyles, a lot of working-class people focused on the local impacts of their prodigious homes. As one young woman noted, "when you build a huge home, you're not going to do that in town. You're going to do that out in the rural part of the county, and the rural part of the county is prime wildlife habitat, and so you're going to build your home right in the middle of an elk migration corridor." This, she says, contradicts their stated love and environmental support to conserve charismatic wildlife, because, in addition to obstructing rural wildlife corridors, "You're going to have grizzly bears come and mess with your garbage and then the state is going to kill them because they are messing with your garbage. So there is an enormous impact to the natural environment when people build large homes and roads and sewers to those homes, and everything that comes with that."

Thus, much of the local criticism concerns the ways that the ultra-wealthy consume resources to, ironically, live a life that is closer to nature—"loving it to death," as the popular saying goes. Over and over again, respondents echoed this theme, connecting these environmental concerns to concerns over housing. Cleaning windows with rags instead of paper towels, or printing double-sided, or donating to save some moose are not necessarily bad behaviors, but in light of their resource-intensive lifestyles—such as maintaining a $30 million property or getting around via private jet—folks like Antonio, Elias, and others view ultra-wealthy environmentalism to be rather trite and hypocritical.

Our respondents made this point over and again, as represented by these additional examples: "Big houses affect nature, because like I told you, they cut trees and plants. They open [roads]." "Because they have big houses and there's no more places here . . . when they build they cut trees and that destroys nature." "I think when rich people want to expand their wealth or monopoly, building hotels or restaurants in forests, that affects plants and animals." "The most expensive houses are close to the parks, so these houses affect animals, trees have to be cut and that affects the environment." "This nature is for everyone and if you build big houses, that affects the animals." "Rich people affect nature . . . by making bigger buildings they invade green areas, take trees down, so by growing their empire, they affect." "Probably in a negative way, I see a lot of big houses . . . big houses require more energy, more water . . . it is just consuming resources."

"YOU SEE A LOT OF CHARITY BUT VERY LITTLE JUSTICE": CONFRONTING THE MYTH OF PHILANTHROPY

If one spends any extended amount of time in Teton County, they will no doubt hear about all of the great past and present philanthropic efforts, led by rich folks who care deeply about the community. No doubt, many do care deeply about the community, and there is as much philanthropic potential—in both charitable spirit and in financial abundance—here as anywhere in the United States, but as I showed with data in part 2, popular positive perceptions about local philanthropy are greatly exaggerated. There is certainly money pouring down from great heights, but only to specific causes that tend to directly and indirectly benefit wealthy lifestyles.

This is certainly not news to informed people from the low-income community. They have experienced the personal sting of budget shortfalls firsthand from the nonprofits that provide resources and education for their families, while at the same they notice the surplus of wealth flowing unabated to certain arts and environmental endeavors. But perhaps those who notice it most are low-income people who are employed by these nonprofit organizations.

Take Margarita Dixon, for example, an English-speaking thirty-something who works for a local nonprofit, and is able to reflect on these issues through her own experiences. Eagerly, she proclaims that "The myth of our communities is that [the wealthy] have an incredibly positive effect. We just had Old Bill's Fun Run, an annual matching donation pledge drive, and it is one of the things I dislike most about this community. There is this feeling that 'oh we are so good and so generous.'" Old Bill's Fun Run is by far the most well-known philanthropic event in Teton County, and was almost unanimously cited by the ultra-wealthy as evidence that—in the words of our affluent friend George from chapter 5—Teton County is "the most philanthropic community in the country."

For Margarita, these one-off events do more for people's egos than they do for those who need housing. And what frustrates her most is that it is not for lack of money, or even lack of wealthy people who genuinely care about making a difference. In her view, philanthropy will not solve the serious problems faced by her community. Instead of relying on the voluntary generosity of caring people, she advocates for a state income tax. "If we had a reasonable sales tax or property tax, we would have so much more money coming in than has ever come in from these voluntary donations. So there's this huge 'pat ourselves on the back' myth that we're incredibly generous, and I just don't think it is true."

At times, Margarita holds out hope that the superabundance of money might find its way to organizations that need it, yet at the same time, she is wary that the money might come with strings attached.

> You know, the wealthy do give and support a lot of nonprofits that are doing good work . . . a lot of it is funding from philanthropists. I think that is very positive. The shadow side of that is that the donors have influence over what gets done, and so you see a lot of charity but very little justice. It's really easy to give money to charity, and to 'oh this person can't pay rent this month so we're going to give them a check this month,' but you don't see philanthropists giving money to systems-changing work, and trying to create a system where you don't need to do charity.

Margarita represents this general theme, summed up in her remark "you see a lot of charity but very little justice." Let's hear from other people we interviewed that share similar feelings and experiences, and accurately depict what Margarita calls the "myth of our community." Some straightforwardly called for redistribution of charitable funds. According to one woman originally from South America, if people "have money, they should support causes that don't get as much money. There should be more money distribution. If someone has money because they work, that is great, but money should be better distributed."

With all of the money flowing to sexy issues like environmental conservation and the arts, some working poor in the community wonder whether the wealthy see issues like poverty or housing as "boring"—or "buzz-kill" as I call it in part 2. For example, one woman we interviewed, who has done better in recent years, climbing just above the federal poverty line with her $22,000 annual income, remarks that the wealthy "just want to give to one special interest program, but maybe if they had a longer term view it would do better." She appreciates their charitable giving, but the problem has more to do with "what [they] choose to give to . . . maybe they would see other things [other than environment] that are more boring and grounded, but would help the community more if they gave their money toward these smaller things." She is talking specifically about housing, chalking up the inaction to short-term thinking and the "boring" nature of the issue. "If they got involved in housing, we have enough rich people that live here that have worked out very big problems in the world that housing in Jackson does not seem like [laughs] it should be overwhelming . . . billion-dollar companies, I mean come on . . . the brain power in Jackson could fix this one little problem, but it's a huge problem . . . it's crazy . . . with that amount of intelligence."

Community Veneer: Façade of "Normalcy" and Mirage of Authentic Bonds

The second pillar of this book, unpacked in part 3, dealt with ultra-wealthy ideas about community, and the ways that having great wealth can create a crisis of authenticity, which shapes the type of person they see themselves as, and the type of person they strive to become. The ultra-wealthy go to great lengths to reconcile their wealth with the insecurities and social stigmas of greed, elitism, and savage ambition. These stigmas create social and moral distance between those at rarefied heights and those at rarefied lows—a group of people the ultra-wealthy tended to associate with authenticity, closeness to nature, simplicity, contentment, purity, and slow pace of life. In order to reduce this distance, and improve their perceived standing in the community, the ultra-wealthy attempt to transform themselves first by establishing authentic social bonds of friendship with low-income people, and then by adopting working-class tastes (for example, dress, art, music) that outwardly display these romanticized attributes.

But are they actually friends, or are the ultra-wealthy greatly exaggerating the authenticity and reciprocal nature of these relationships? Or perhaps they are just honestly mistaking their servants for their friends? What do these "normal" people—of the likes we've heard from in this chapter such as María, Carmela, David, or Margarita—really think of the ultra-wealthy fixation with "normalcy," and attempts to be normal by adopting working-class cultural tastes and styles? Second, do these low-income people agree with the ultra-wealthy responses to guilt, and the justifications they give for whether someone deserves to own such a huge slice of the monetary pie? And building on these moral concerns about who is deserving and who is not, how, if at all, do they plan to confront such extreme wealth inequality?

"HE DRESSES LIKE US": CAMOUFLAGING CLASS DIFFERENCES

The eagerness of the ultra-wealthy to wax lyrical about their working-class tastes—especially clothing—had deeper implications than we might expect. A long line of research on elite cultural omnivores would suggest that they appreciate and appropriate low-brow culture because they are seeking social distinction by expanding their cultural repertoire. In other words, their obsession with "normal" dress is a signal of their cosmopolitanism. This may be true, but stopping here we would miss something much deeper that is going on related to their own moral self-appraisal, and whether money had fundamentally changed them as people.

It is about much more than taste in clothing, and thus during our interviews with the working poor, we specifically asked, "Other than having a large house, how can you tell if someone in Jackson is wealthy?" The results clearly show that the ultra-wealthy have been very successful at blending in by adopting an outward working-class appearance. Gloria Del Yando, a Spanish-only speaker in her forties, tells us just how hard it is to spot a billionaire from penniless worker on the edge of eviction, "It is difficult to say who is rich in Jackson, sometimes you can see someone and swear they don't have a penny and they are very rich. It is difficult to know who has and who doesn't have money in Jackson."

Let's hear from the voices of other low-income people who similarly confirmed the ultra-wealthy commitment to adopting "normal" cultural tastes, and further illustrate these interesting and important attempts to blur the outward class lines that would normally distinguish the rich from the poor. One gentleman described his boss as appearing outwardly to be "very simple. He has money [but] you cannot see it. *He dresses like us.*"

One woman described it as dressing like a "normal mortal," as opposed to her experiences with wealthy people outside Jackson who tend not to "dress like us." She explains, "I think here in Jackson [money] is not that obvious. I think it is easier to spot rich people from out of state, because they are always establishing wealth in the way they dress and act. Here in Jackson, they seem to camouflage."

Over and over again, our working-poor interviewees described this "camouflage" process, making it nearly impossible to see outwardly the nation-leading gap between those who have money and those who do not. "In this community, you cannot tell who is rich or not. The clothes are not fancy . . . they act the same as normal people," says one woman. Even at restaurants or events that "are $200 per plate . . . because this is a casual place, you can see them in jeans." One can identify them at certain events because "the event is to ask them for money. But if they are in the shop, or they are having a hamburger next to me, or we cross paths hiking in the mountains . . . you don't know who has more money," says one immigrant from South America.

Another immigrant named Diego—also from South America—described an encounter where a wealthy gentleman enlightened him, "I don't think in hundreds, I think in thousands." Diego's response was not anger or resentment, but he was simply puzzled by the fact that his gentleman looks just like him, despite their great financial gulf that separates them. "So, the difference is how they perceive money . . . but here you cannot identify them. It is difficult." Several others view it as simply impossible: "Truthfully, in Jackson you cannot know if someone is rich," says one woman. "I think you can notice it because of the education, but for that you need to talk to them. But just visually by looking, I think it is impossible," says another. And last, another, "You cannot know if people have money in Jackson. That is something very surprising. Rich people here behave in such a way that you cannot really know. You don't know who has money and who doesn't have money."

AUTHENTIC FRIENDSHIP? CONFUSING SERVANTS FOR FRIENDS

While people like Gloria agree that the ultra-wealthy have achieved outward "normalcy" by downplaying social markers that would identify them as rich, what do they make of the wealthy's enthusiasm for their purported friendships with "normal" low-income folks? They rejected the claim, and gave three reasons repudiating the authenticity and reciprocal nature of the purported bonds between the rich and poor.

First, the ultra-wealthy fail to remember the economic bases of these relationships. They confuse their servants for their friends. Despite all of the claims of the ultra-wealthy in chapter 7, the day-to-day relationship, as experienced by the low-income people, is not one of friendship, but strictly business. "I don't think Jackson has a strong sense of community; I think it has a strong sense of business," says one food service worker. "Latinos and rich people are mainly a labor relationship. They are the money and we are the workers," says another.

The working poor interact with the ultra-wealthy enough to get a sense of the relationship. As one housekeeper noted, "Rich people and Latinos interact a lot because the Latinos work for the rich people. They do the labor, they are the nannies, they do the landscaping. That is the main way they interact. And they interact *a lot*."

We often had to dig deeper for more on this topic because it was so straightforwardly obvious that their answers were often terse. What else was there to say? The relationships were "mostly because of labor. You do something for me, and I pay you. . . . I don't think there is any other relationship . . . that is the only relationship," says one line cook. "The interactions between Latinos and wealthy people are by cleaning their houses," says one housekeeper. Or, as another worker described it, the working poor "are essentially servants . . . that's the relationship. I don't know if there's any other one."

Some were quite negative about the relationship, going beyond describing it in sterile economic terms, offering critiques of how they are treated, which stood in stark contrast to any reasonable definition of authentic friendship. "The relationship of Latinos and rich people is distant. They don't want you near. The farther you are, the better it is." Existing as "the serving class" in the community, as one woman described it, can be very difficult, and is a more accurate description of the relationship between the top and the bottom. "When you are the one serving, you become invisible. There are a lot of people I see in an event, a wedding, a fundraiser in a beautiful place . . . the only Latinos here are myself and the people serving . . . the people doing the dishes."

A home caretaker and caterer we interviewed described it as a "one-sided," "dysfunctional," and "oppressive" relationship. He explains that, "when I first came here, I worked with the wealthy because I did some caretaking work, and I did private chef work. Well, you know, if you're serving them, they'll throw you goodies because you're taking care of their needs." Yet, it comes with a catch. "But it's a one-sided thing because if you have the tools to cater to their needs, you're good. But, uh . . . it's an unhealthy kind of dynamic. I think it's one-sided. It's dysfunctional. It's oppressive . . . when race and class comes up, it feels oppressive. I feel like I'm 'the other' and that's why I left serving them. I refuse to befriend them now. It's much healthier in my life to not have them around me."

AUTHENTIC FRIENDSHIP? FRIENDS DON'T IGNORE SUFFERING

Second, the low-income community challenged the idea of authentic friendship because there is so much unaddressed suffering in the community. In other words, real friends do not ignore the suffering of their companions, especially if they have the power to alleviate that suffering.

One gentleman who works at the airport explained to us that "there just seems to be no self-awareness among a lot of [wealthy] people that right down the road there's like thirty trailers with fifteen people living in them, sleeping in shifts." Part of the problem, he says, is that in Teton County, the wealthy "don't want to see discomfort . . . people move here because they want comfort—and probably more mental comfort and mental peace more than anything—but poor people shatter that." Poverty can be a buzz-kill, especially in romanticized rural environs where mountain water runs pure and magnificent wilderness lies undisturbed. This image is shattered by "people in dire straits, hungry people, and it's bad . . . maybe worse for people here than somewhere else where you're faced with it constantly, or you have self-selected to move somewhere to escape it."

Here in the rural West, where many of these wealthy people have come to escape and be transformed, one must intentionally *not* see the poverty around them in order to protect their romanticized veneer from being shattered. Poverty and hunger are "hidden in plain view, I guess. People don't see it and they're intentionally not seeing it." He suggests that conservation may play a role in promoting the veneer. "Maybe it's subconscious, but you don't see what you don't want to see . . . you don't want to use your moral view, and your sense of righteousness when you're busy fighting for the elk or the moose. You know you feel good about that, and it's hard if you go look outside and see . . . well, the other things that you're doing are harmful to other people."

One middle-class teacher, who is routinely exposed to these social problems via her students, described the veneer in similar terms. "So, it's either [the wealthy] put the blinders on, and they don't want to see problems, or they really honestly have no idea that it's even going on, because they would never socialize with the working poor outside of their setting." One nonprofit worker sums up the relationship between the wealthy and the working poor, noting that the wealthy don't "even know the reality of the workers . . . the awareness goes upward better than it goes downward. So to solve that, somehow we need more integration." She continues, responding to our follow-up question about solutions. "The only thing that comes to mind when you ask me that question is I see some of [the working poor] might be having ten to a home, but they love their families and they love their community, and they work really hard; and then I feel like there's the [wealthy] people that don't get it. *They don't want to get it.* They don't want to see it. They don't want to hear it."

AUTHENTIC FRIENDSHIP? EXCLUSION AND RACISM

Last, any thoughts of grandeur about friendships with "normal" people were hampered by more than just the extreme imbalance in power and wealth that low-income people have discussed earlier, but just as importantly, by the fact that those with little money and power happen to be immigrants and people of color, who continue to experience systematic exclusion and racism in Teton County. In such an environment, authenticity is often nothing more than a mirage.

In the following, we hear from a handful of low-income people who describe these experiences that have become the norm here, revealing once again the contours of the veneer that shrouds this rural Western paradise, and the rich's search for authenticity.[3]

Similar to the last theme about turning a blind eye to suffering, this theme of exclusion and racism was not a topic that came up easily in the interviews. We had to read between the lines, and probe deeper in places where folks had mentioned experiences of exclusion. To help, we adopted the analytical approach taken by Harvard sociologist Michèle Lamont, focusing on the symbolic boundaries that groups draw between each other. For example, in order to understand exclusion and racism, we did not ask directly about these topics, but instead asked questions such as, "What are the similarities and differences between the various groups that live in your community? Do you sometimes feel superior to certain people? Do you sometimes feel inferior to certain people? What kind of people?"[4]

A single mother from Mexico, who came to the community ten years ago, tells us that "I have not felt superior, and I think I have not felt inferior." She pauses, and continues, "But there are some people that want to make you feel inferior for being from a different nationality. Or that they have better pay or better job." Another woman, who has been living here for nearly two decades with her two children and her husband, similarly describes the racial and ethnic barriers to community integration. "No, I don't feel like part of the community. When you are Hispanic, you are not included. As Hispanic, you *can't* be included, or the activities are very expensive and you cannot do them."

Another person of color we interviewed described the discrimination he faced while working as a private chef for the ultra-wealthy. "Since they have the power and the wealth, the impact of racism is tenfold, and it's tough to toe the line being a person of color." Interested, we ask for a specific example. "Oh yeah, when I worked for some of these wealthy people doing private chef work, when they've had some alcohol in their systems all their prejudices come out, and they spew it out in front of me . . . they put me aside because I work. I do a good job for them, and they pay me, and so they feel entitled to say all these things to me." Alcohol helps to reveal their true colors, he says. Continuing, we ask what specific things they say that reveal these prejudices. "How they perceive of people of color, and how they put down when it's the very, very wealthy . . . I was called 'scum.'"

Many others described a general community environment that is as bifurcated by cultural and ethnic differences as it is by its nation-leading economic rift. But this too is hard to detect on the surface. Wealthy whites form the dominant culture, and interviewees who did not fit this mold often described Teton County as unwelcoming and exclusionary. As one young woman put it, "I see a lot of discrimination toward Mexicans. I went and applied two years ago to be a receptionist at the [ultra-elite hotel name redacted] and they just laughed at me, and I'm just like, 'Excuse me, I have education. Excuse me, I am well suited for this. I have amazing customer service. . . . I am well with technology.'" She describes her repeated struggles to get a foot in the door, especially in these elite spaces that can equate environmental purity with whiteness.[5] "A lot of times when I went to apply . . . they would be like, 'We don't hire illegal immigrants.' I'm just like, 'I have papers.' So I feel like a lot of places just look down upon a lot of Mexicans . . . that we're all illegal . . . that we are not smart . . . that we are not educated . . . and that we're kind of just work machines."

Let's hear briefly from a handful of others, who described these experiences in their own words: "When I first arrived in Jackson, I felt bad because some women stared at me, and asked me where I was from, and why was I so dark skinned, and I felt like they didn't like me." "Perhaps there are many people in this country that don't want to understand us, accept us because we have dark hair, we don't speak English, or we have an accent." "The worst part of living in this community is the racism. The latent racism in the community between cultures." "I feel like the majority—the upper rich class—do think that we are a minority, like we are kind of just here for work, and we're not really superior. They look down upon us." "I really do believe that there are certain people in Jackson that only want a certain type of person living here, and that has been stated, quoted, in our newspaper . . . they only want wealthy people living here. They don't want low income." "What I do not like is that there are some residents, some people that don't accept us as Latinos." "There is a lot of discrimination . . . and that just makes you feel morally down." "I still find people that are racists in this town, and that is something that I don't like." "I don't like the winter . . . it's hard for me to get warm. And I don't like the racism." "There are some people that don't like us, and they would love if we disappeared."

This all baffled one respondent, because the ultra-wealthy people he's encountered do a lot of international travel, and speak about how much they love the locals in places like Mexico, South America, Spain, and elsewhere. They love these cultures and people they encounter, so why don't they help their neighbors here in Teton County who came from these same places? "I think it's probably racial bias," he says. "I mean, probably, because it can't be just culture, because I know [wealthy] people that go to South America and hang out in Peru for a month and talk so much about how 'I met so many cool people in South America,' and then they come back here and there's no interest."

Are the Ultra-Wealthy Deserving People?

Gabriel Lucas is in his mid-fifties, and has recently started a small business that he hopes will be successful enough for him purchase a small home, or at the very least, not have to share apartment rent with several other families. Before this latest effort to launch his own small business, he gained work experience from a variety of nonprofits in the area. It was through this work that he developed his beliefs about why some people are so wealthy and others are so poor: "There is an enormous gap here. It is obscene. I mean, it is outrageous that people build 10-million-dollar homes and have people work for them, and the people who work for them, their kids are sleeping in shifts in one room. If there is any sort of human moral code, this is just obscenely wrong."

Of course, Gabriel isn't telling us anything we don't already know about this income gap. What we were really after in our interviews were their thoughts about *why* this gap exists, and by extension, whether those at such rarefied heights are deserving of their position. So we probed Gabriel for more, "Why do you think this gap exists, specifically here?"

With great conviction, he explains that "the American and global financial system allows for enormous accumulation of wealth, and treats labor as surplus and object, so you have people in America and in the world with a huge amount of money." From Gabriel's point of view, of course ultra-wealthy individuals do not deserve the *extreme* amount of money they've accumulated.

That is not to say that ultra-wealthy people haven't worked hard. But the question of whether the ultra-wealthy are deserving is a question about *the impersonal influence of larger economic systems, rather than assessing the merits of an individual person.*[6] Hard work and self-made ambition exists only within much more powerful systems of influence.

The second point emerging from this part of the study is the common belief that what is truly important, and how we judge whether someone deserves their wealth, is how they behave *after they get it*. Wealth entails a moral obligation to distribute it, especially if others are suffering because there is not enough to go around. In other words, one deserves their wealth only if they are a just steward, especially in cases where people around them are suffering.

So, once again, the amount of hard work and self-made ambition— which is often used as the metric for allocating deservedness—is divorced from the assessment of who is actually deserving. It's not how you make it, but how you steward it, that matters. In the words of one construction worker we interviewed, "I don't think that wealthy people deserve their money because they humiliate us. People that help others and worked hard and give jobs deserve their money."

Thus, even the hardest working self-made millionaire doesn't deserve her or his wealth if they are not willing to cede some of their financial power in the face of others who are unnecessarily suffering despite their hard work.

Even though people like Gabriel are critical of unchecked capitalism, they do not believe that having more wealth than others is necessarily a bad thing, just as it isn't necessarily an indicator of self-made virtue or deservedness. Gabriel explains, "The gap in itself doesn't matter. If everyone had a decent quality of life, who cares if some people have a lot more? But when people are living in unhealthy conditions, or they're not even able to live here and their kids can't go to school here, that's a moral problem."

It is not just Gabriel. Let's hear from the many others who typify these responses to the question of whether or not the ultra-wealthy are deserving. First, a selection from the many working poor who look up at rarefied heights and doubt the deservedness of individual people, in light of the impersonal economic systems that make wealth much more likely for some but not others: "Very wealthy people, no never [deserving], you could not have done it without society, which means you don't deserve it. And that's true of virtually everybody. That doesn't mean that I'm communist . . . communism doesn't work. . . . Humans aren't built that way . . . but essentially nobody earns anything. . . . It's just a lack of self-awareness." "If people are very successful, it is because of their history, they have had parents that were successful, or they had the support." "Primarily luck, genetic luck . . . you were born to the right parents . . . or you were born Caucasian in a country that glorifies white people." "Not everybody is deserving of everything. I think some people, it's like they're born with certain things that others are not." "In Jackson, we have billionaires, and we have people that earn ten thousand a year. The difference is . . . the capitalist system."

Second, and perhaps more novel and interesting, is that a person "deserves" their wealth only if they fulfill the moral obligation that comes with having it: "People that are wealthy and honest do deserve their wealth, but if you are rich because you paid your employees five dollars an hour, and you are now a rich millionaire, that is not morally correct." "They contract people and manage money and they avoid taxes. They don't pay well in big hotel corporations, and they are squeezing the most out of their workers." "Nah, they are not deserving of all their money. I don't think it's healthy for humanity. I think people should all have some kind of equity, some kind of [sigh] same amount of money so that there's more democracy. There's more give and take, as opposed to a few people having money and dictating the game." "Those that do deserve it are the ones that help other people that work, and the ones that don't . . . [are] the ones that sit and look pretty and get wealthy."

"Enough Is Enough, We Need to Do Something": Mobilization from Below

Since the early days of the rise of the richest community in the richest nation in the world, the prospect of any serious political organizing among the working poor had taken a back seat to the day-to-day realities of sheer survival, and the demands of being a new immigrant to this country. Among the working poor, there seemed to be two general approaches to politics, power, and civic engagement. First, the type of which we heard in chapter 9 that was too exhausted, uninformed, and relied on popular talking scripts praising wealth, hard work, meritocracy, and gilded philanthropy. There is very little awareness and even knowledge, of the prospects of political mobilization to improve and defend their interests.

The second approach is represented here by a handful of people who are better informed about the legitimate grievances of their own working-poor community, but without a critical mass, financial resources, or formal organizing, there was little confidence that anything could be done in the face of great wealth and great power. For example, conversations like the one we had with an auto mechanic named Elias Sutton, who voiced these feelings of political helplessness: "The trend is . . . there's a lot of growth in terms of businesses here that cater for the wealthy, and the politicians I think collude with them. . . . There are a lot of politicians in this community who serve the wealthy . . . based on the wealthy and not for the workers or not for the Latinos in this community, no."

And once again, folks like Elias point to affluent environmentalism as a reason for the persistence of such crass inequality: "[The wealthy] would care more for the natural environment then the Latinos or the community. . . . They will take care of the wolves more than the Latino workers in this community."

But this is changing. Many more people are now aware of the issues, and with the help of civic organizations, the general sense of their political power and efficacy is growing, and people are mobilizing.

Here in this section, I briefly chronicle this nascent movement through the eyes of the working poor who are calling for change, and describe how they define the problem at the level of political structures and systems, as opposed to blaming individual ultra-wealthy people. As such, the individual generosity of the ultra-wealthy, while sometimes appreciated, is viewed at best as a band-aid to these larger structural problems identified by the working poor. Central among these are nonexistent protections for tenants, unlivable wages, and Wyoming's tax policies that overwhelmingly favor those at rarefied heights.

POLITICAL SOLUTIONS BEYOND GILDED PHILANTHROPY

Despite the weight of pessimism in the face of the political and economic power of the ultra-wealthy, there is a growing sense that changes need to happen at the level of governmental policy, and not simply by raising more philanthropic dollars from the ultra-wealthy. Or in the words of one person, it is a realization that "housing is a problem of the government. We want more, and if they don't want to do anything, then logically nothing is going to change."

But changing public policy is much more controversial, and much more difficult in practice, than holding a fundraising gala or fun-run. They realize that it also involves challenging those in power who are, in the words of one person we interviewed, "influencing public policy to maintain the things that they enjoy the most, or influencing to keep what they have—even when doing that is going to limit the availability of vital resources to other groups of people."

One specific approach, which would require financial sacrifice on behalf of the ultra-wealthy, and perhaps have the widest reaching impact, is to remove the generous tax incentives enjoyed by the wealthy. Despite the political difficulty of such a proposition, this case was made by several interviewees. "There is a lot of money here . . . a lot of really caring people, so I think if we set up this structure differently, we could actually do really well, and I do think that means taxes," says one gentleman. Knowledgeable in this area, he continues, "We are the most tax-friendly place in the country pretty much, and 5,000 people tell the IRS they live here, and they tell the census that they live somewhere else, and they do that so that they don't have to pay income taxes anywhere, state income taxes. So we have people who are gaming the system, basically just taking advantage of the services and the workers and not really paying their way, so I think you know we should change the system so that there is an expectation and a law that you have to contribute more."

Data from the IRS and the U.S. Census Bureau back up this claim. In most counties in the United States, the population estimates from the census are similar to the number of people claiming residency for tax purposes. But not so in Teton County. It has the largest discrepancy between the number of people who actually live there and the number of people who claim to for tax purposes.[7]

The extreme economic bifurcation of the community is no accident, says another respondent. The income gap "has gotten worse over the last thirty-five to forty years because of specific policies; economic and political decisions that we've made in the country . . . and then the state of Wyoming has for as long as anyone can remember subscribed to the political theories that promote inequality." But what specific political theories, we ask? Answering, "Oh, that taxation is evil and that everything will be fine if we let the free market do its thing . . . the rich are crushing everybody else." Although all hope is not lost, he says. "I think people are starting to realize that the system doesn't work and isn't going to work for them . . . how that tension will be resolved is the question."

Or put simply by Margarita Dixon earlier, "As far as wealthy people, good for them . . . [but] I think there should be more money distribution. If someone had money because they work, that is great, but money should be better distributed."

A more modest and politically achievable proposal suggested by just about everyone we interviewed is to increase wages. For example, during one conversation about whether or not he likes his boss, a construction worker in his thirties, who happens to share a house with three other families, remarked, "My boss is a really good person. He is responsible. He helps a lot in the community, but the only thing is, is that we need a bit of a raise."

Other people were more deliberate, pointing out how the wealthy continue to take advantage of the desperation wrought by wealth inequality and by the fact that many of the working poor are vulnerable immigrants. This theme was expressed by another construction worker in his thirties, who also shares a home with a few other families, and has really struggled in recent years. "When [the wealthy] see the desperation of the Hispanics to get a job, they offer you a lower wage. They should pay you better, but they take advantage of this, and this affects your [pocketbook], so jobs that should pay higher, don't. And this affects you a lot." In a conversation with a person in a similar situation, she remarks on the "negative" impact of the ultra-wealthy who employ the working poor, noting that, "there is abuse from the side of the employers, they don't pay enough. Or if an employee gets hurt, they don't want to help."

We also wanted to understand the issue of fair pay from the perspective of a middle-class small-business owners who might be able to provide a different perspective from the extremes of the ultra-wealthy or the working poor. One gentleman we spoke with drew from his unique perspective as both an employee and an employer. "Uh, I mean there's a huge gap between the ridiculously super-haves, and people who are working three jobs to get by. Why does it exist? [sigh] . . . our pay scale here, I don't think it meets the cost of living." He continues, speaking as a small-business owner about the responsibility that weighs on him to alleviate some of these problems. "I also feel like as an employer it's partly my responsibility to pay people fairly, which I feel like I'm doing." He's been in the shoes of the working poor, and saw firsthand how "it comes down to greed. I feel like these companies are just maximizing every little dollar. You know that your employees are the people who make you money. Maybe you should treat them well, and it's just kind of disgusting."

GRASSROOTS POLITICAL MOBILIZATION

"For a long time, people just suffered as individuals. But there are a few organizers in the community who are in that situation who said 'enough is enough, we need to do something'" We know from research that there are all sorts of reasons why groups of people choose to organize,[8] but this quote reveals the motivations quite clearly. The working poor reached a tipping point. They were tired of suffering as individuals, and realized that they were not alone. In academic jargon, the working poor experienced "cognitive liberation."[9]

This quote earlier, from a longtime resident and budding community leader, describes the genesis of a movement: "We're trying to build an organization of the people, so the people most impacted by the housing crisis are basically getting together and saying, 'Hey, it doesn't have to be this way. There are things that the town could do. There are things that the county could do and really building a ground swell of community support and trying to get the town council and the mayor and the county commission to pass laws.'"

They started with practical and attainable issues like rent stabilization, as opposed to more unrealistic and thorny issues like fair wages or mammoth issues like Wyoming's income tax laws.

> For example, many communities have rent stabilization laws, which say hey it is a free market, you can raise the rent, but there has to be a limit. You can't hike the rent 40 percent or 100 percent . . . the town is not going to do that on its own, but if hundreds of renters get together and write letters and go speak at town council meetings, something could happen. So right now, we're trying to build the organization, you know, the backbone and all of the administrative side, as well as build hundreds of people into a movement to really push for political improvement.

One reason why this grassroots organizing did not coalesce sooner is because of the community's overreliance on the type of gilded philanthropy I laid out in chapters 5 and 6. According to one of the more experienced political organizers in Teton County, even if more money was donated from the ultra-wealthy to social services (as opposed to the environment and arts), it would still come with strings attached and stymie the grassroots energy and autonomy.

She explains, trenchantly, and worth quoting in full:

> I think one of the biggest reasons why we have the problems we do in Jackson is that there historically hasn't been ground up grassroots organizing . . . *so here we have more nonprofits per capita than pretty much anywhere, but those nonprofits are philanthropically funded, they are not grassroots funded,* so we have two hundred and some nonprofits, *but nobody who is advocating about housing and that's crazy. . . . So I think here you have a lot of individuals who individually are powerless and are getting screwed by the system.* If people got together in whatever groups, um, started by themselves, *not funded by wealthy donors,* but funded by themselves, then we could really have an interesting conversation and then you would see change [emphasis added].

Aside from specific goals, such as rent stabilization and tenant protection laws, there is a broader effort to simply spread awareness about the extent of suffering in the community. In my conversations with the ultra-wealthy, I found that they were generally aware of the housing crunch, but grossly underestimated its severity, or their role in perpetuating it. Of course, there are different approaches to getting the message across to those with economic or political power. For example, getting "lots of people camping on town-square or set up a cardboard house camp on town-square. Just ways to really raise that awareness, really clearly we have a problem. It's not going to stay in the shadows. I think from the perspective of people whose lives are going well here and own a home, maybe own a 10-million-dollar home, it is easy to look away. You know, you don't see the families living in shadows and if you don't know anyone who is like them, then maybe you just never even hear about it."

Others might take a more direct and confrontational approach, such as one low-income father who protested in the town square with a sign reading, "Fuck you greedy bastards. I can't feed my babies, and I work three jobs." Whatever form this movement takes, from something as basic as attending town council meetings[10] to these more confrontational protests, it is snowballing to include more and more people.

Perhaps most notably, the movement is beginning to comprise people who have never been involved in any sort of civic engagement, or much less even knew that it was an avenue to improve their lot in life. Whereas before they just had their heads down, trying to survive. Now they view the cause as legitimate, and even consider carving out time to join in.

Throughout the interviews, I began to notice these bursts of confidence—or what we might again call cognitive liberation—and the feeling that they now had a small slice of political power. Consider the subtle ways this comes out in the conversations with the following folks from the low-income community, and the cautious sense of hope that it communicates. A cashier at a local supermarket, who immigrated to here when she was thirteen, and now has five children, espouses this growing confidence. "For people that are struggling, I think we can change if other people can help. . . . Again, join a rally and let the town know what things are missing in this town." Another respondent proudly told us of a recent rally he attended that gave him purpose and confidence. "I was in a rally to bring up the issue of housing . . . we had close to 100 people . . . they came with a purpose and the purpose is to improve the community." Others have also heard about rallies, and other community organizing opportunities. "I would like to change something, but I don't know how to change it. Maybe joining one of those rallies, maybe that would change it a little bit," remarked one cashier.

Even if people had not attended a rally, just seeing these sorts of public demonstrations gave people hope, because it very publicly ruptures the veneer of authentic community, and gives voice to the silent suffering. "We should just get our voice out there. . . . I know they did the [protest] march. . . . That put people to be aware of it. . . . I didn't go to the march, but I saw in the newspaper and it made me really happy for some reason because people were actually doing something." The protest publicly clarifies what is at stake, who is at fault, and what must be done. "The American or Anglo community is stronger than ours," says one young man, "but I think we have time to change this."

Another gentleman, who came from Mexico City, feels his confidence growing each day. "When I first arrived here, many years ago, I felt a bit shy. When I went to events with different cultures, I did feel shy. As years went by, I stopped feeling that. I can go with anyone. I don't feel more or less than any person. . . . I like giving people a 'slap with a white glove response' [Mexican saying] . . . when someone comes to me and wants to make me feel less, I let them talk, and I think 'they don't even know who they are talking to.'"

Some realize that they need to enter formal politics in order to make change. Even newcomers to this country like Jose Cortez-García, who came with his three children seventeen years ago, is planning to run for office. "I am going to go into politics. I am going to talk about myself," he says excitedly, alluding to his story of hard work and perseverance, and the barriers he's experienced firsthand. "In my family, my wife and I work, and we work hard, we pay a lot of taxes, we pay a lot. I am killing myself to earn $3,000, and then there is this other person that earns $500,000, but this person is going to get all these privileges, so then I wonder, how is this possible?"

Eroding Veneer

In this critical and final chapter, I journeyed deeper into the world of ultra-wealth, but from an entirely different perspective. As I've argued, we cannot fully understand ultra-wealth in isolation, especially when their way of life so heavily influences, and is influenced by, the folks we heard from in this chapter. With people like María Guadalupe Flores, Carmela Lopez, David Toledo, Margarita Dixon, Gabriel Lucas, Gloria Del Yando, Elias Sutton, and so many others letting us into their lives, we are given a truly unique window into life on the ground in the richest and most unequal community in the United States.

Amid our modern culture of sound bites and partisan politics, the real value of this "paired" approach is that the working poor's views of ultra-wealth are forged from decades of personal experience living with and working for the rich, caring for their kids, building their homes, tending their gardens, serving them food. These are hardwon views, with integrity and reliability rarely seen in the caricatures and clichés of the rich that are often slung carelessly from a distance.

From these firsthand experiences, the working poor called into question many of the positive perceptions ultra-wealthy people have of themselves as environmentalists, employers, friends, and more broadly as authentic, deserving people. They pointed out the irony and empty virtue of affluent environmentalism, and link it to the ongoing suffering of the working poor.

Likewise, they confronted the powerful myth that ultra-wealthy philanthropy sustains the community—a myth that has arguably pacified more powerful political changes to wages and taxes that are often silently opposed by the wealthy, even if by omission. Or in the words of Margarita Dixon, "you see a lot of charity but very little justice."

And last, they exposed a community veneer that masquerades behind a façade of "normalcy" and the mirage of authentic bonds.

I documented the extent to which the ultra-wealthy adopt working-class tastes and working-class friends as a way to reconcile their wealth with their personal insecurities and the social stigmas of greed, elitism, and savage ambition. And when it comes to the community, folks in this chapter note that these attempts are also a way for the ultra-wealthy to camouflage their wealth and erase outward signs that this community is gravely fractured. Yet, these attempts ring hollow to the nonwealthy. The old-time rural sense of community that the ultra-wealthy profess to love is simply a veneer—a patina that quickly eroded with every interview we conducted.

Remember that the most important pillar of this community, as emphasized by the ultra-wealthy, is the idea that everyone, rich or poor, gets along here because of the purity and simplicity of nature. In the words of the hedge fund executive from chapter 7, "It's not about money here! We are all just deeply in love with Wyoming." In Teton County, the awe-inspiring nature is an escape from the snares of careerism and ladder-climbing, and everyone is just able to relax. Billionaires befriend waiters. Nannies aren't just employees, they are part of the family. Oil-and-gas executives go backcountry camping with bohemian environmentalists. It's not about the money.

The problem is that these feelings aren't mutual. The authenticity of these relationships proves to be a mirage because, according to the working poor, the ultra-wealthy are confusing their servants for their friends. Beneath this façade, the relationships are merely based on economic exchange and services rendered. Second, the working poor point out that authentic friends do not ignore suffering, especially when they have immense economic and political power to alleviate that suffering. Third, this veneer glosses over the harsh reality of living as an immigrant and a person of color in this community, where exclusion and discrimination are all too common, yet rarely discussed because it is a buzz-kill that threatens to unmask both the veneer of community and the veneer of affluent environmentalism.

But as the working poor have become more informed in recent years, they have gone on the offensive about the ways that this community veneer does real damage, because similar to the veneer of environmentalism, this veneer of community—especially its claim to "normalcy" and authentic friendship—hides the suffering of the working poor in plain sight, and perpetuates political acquiescence. Cracks in the veneer are beginning to show, and people are moving out of the shadows to participate in grassroots mobilization. As we were reminded by one working-poor interviewee, if you "own a 10-million-dollar home, it is easy to look away . . . you don't see the families living in the shadows."

The hope, according to María Guadalupe Flores, and the many others from this chapter, is that exposing people to the reality of life beneath the veneer is the only avenue through which those at rarefied heights can actually achieve the authentic community they so desire, and genuinely begin to "see the workers as human beings, as people, as friends."

Epilogue

THE FUTURE OF WEALTH AND THE WEST

This story is far from over. In many ways, it is just beginning, because the findings uncovered here point to a much larger drama unfolding in similar communities across the Western United States—communities adjacent to desirable natural areas and public lands that have seen a recent influx of wealthy migrants who love nature and emulate the rural idyll. Millions of wealthy and ultra-wealthy folks like Julie and Craig Williams, whose luxurious environmental fundraiser opened this book, are increasingly settling in the likes of Bozeman, Montana; Portland, Oregon; Boulder, Colorado; Taos, New Mexico; Bend, Oregon; Boise, Idaho; Reno, Nevada; Salt Lake City, Utah; Lake Tahoe, California; and the outskirts of the San Francisco Bay Area, Seattle, and Denver, to name just a few places in this wild "New West."[1] While these trends are occurring at very different rates in different communities, taken together they represent an enormous and ongoing social, economic, and environmental transformation—often unbeknownst to many Americans in other regions who still overlook small and mid-size rural communities, especially in the West.

As I've argued, when it comes to the rich, we too often lose our way by fixating on simplistic questions about their moral merit as individuals. Instead, we should give more attention the contours of the *communities* in which they are increasingly choosing to live so that we can move beyond our hasty desire to brand them individually as either saviors or monsters, good or evil, deserving or undeserving, environmental heroes or destroyers of nature. And, given the major barriers to accessing the ultra-wealthy, examining the features that draw them to the rural West provides an easily accessible entry into the social and cultural makeup of this immensely powerful group, including how they see themselves, how they relate to their nonwealthy neighbors, and the ways that they strengthen or damage the fabric of communities and ecosystems.

With their unique blend of natural amenities and rural culture (and a splash of cosmopolitan comfort), *scenic Western locales provide a remarkable setting for the rich to resolve two underlying predicaments in their lives.* As we learned, the first is largely *economic*: how best to enjoy, share, protect, and multiply their great wealth. The second is largely *social*: how to respond to the cultural stigmas of wealth, assuage personal guilt, confront feelings of inauthenticity, and resolve their precarious standing in the community.

Each chapter of this book traced my journey in this Billionaire Wilderness and described in great detail the ways in which the rich wrestle with and resolve these two major tensions in their lives. Now it is time to step back and consider what the findings mean for the future of such communities and what the paired experiences of wealthy folks like Julie and Craig Williams and financially struggling residents like Hector and Dolorita Padilla can tell us. Last, I will end by cautiously suggesting some evidence-based solutions that might help to peel back the environmental and community veneers that shroud communities in this new wild West.

———

As revealed in part 2, the first predicament the ultra-wealthy attempt to resolve relates to their unique economic position. How do they attempt to enjoy this wealth? And how do they protect and multiply it? With regard to these dilemmas, I found that, whatever their good intentions, those at the very top of the socioeconomic ladder leverage nature to climb even higher. They transform wild settings into ultra-exclusive enclaves for enjoying wealth, multiplying wealth, and gaining social prestige through environmental conservation. Regrettably, these pursuits—described as "Compensation Conservation," "Connoisseur Conservation," and "Gilded Green Philanthropy"— often happen under the guise of environmental concern, philanthropic altruism, commitment to ecological science, and an uncritical use of nature as a therapeutic and spiritual tonic.

These affluent uses of nature can be quite regrettable because they perpetuate an *environmental veneer* that creates the appearance that protecting nature is a common good for all, yet in reality it helps to morally justify vast natural-resource consumption, deepens inequality, and bestows social rewards on individual philanthropic acts that tend to serve the environmental interests of a select few, ultimately reinforcing the larger economic and political trends that are making it almost impossible for folks like Hector and Dolorita Padilla to continue to make ends meet in a community that they love deeply and to which they have long contributed.

Many Americans, including the people we interviewed from the low-income community, understand and accept the fact that other people have more money than they do. Even the existence of a noticeable income gap is not a problem for most. As one popular economic argument goes, and as some of our low-income respondents echoed: If everyone is getting wealthier, then why should we care if the rich are getting much richer? The problem for many people, though, is that an income gap as large as Teton County's also creates a sizable *opportunity gap*. In such settings, folks at the bottom are no longer justly rewarded for the work they perform (services for the wealthy, in many cases); no longer have fair opportunities to improve their lives, or even keep a roof over their heads; and no longer enjoy the security of knowing they will be able to afford living in their own communities.[2] As we heard in chapter 10, scores of low-income people are working two or three jobs, yet they are facing major setbacks including sudden eviction, overcrowded living conditions in which children sleep on the floor, rock-bottom wages, and a host of other difficulties that are a major consequence of extreme wealth concentration. Thus, for many people the problem is not with an income gap itself, but with the ways in which it can lead to diminishing opportunities and unjust recompense.

Solutions to these problems are within reach. But not the kind of solutions that currently prevail—namely, what I have called "Gilded Green Philanthropy," which creates an overdependence on charitable acts by the wealthy, who as we have seen tend to restrict their giving to a small set of environmental and arts issues and tend to be motivated not by concern for equity so much as a desire to find salvation via nature and recapture what was lost in the climb to affluence. Duane Carrington's realization in chapter 6 summarizes this sentiment: "Oh my God, what have I sacrificed in my life to get to where I am?" This style of philanthropy serves to preserve the myths of the Old West, and allows donors to achieve "authenticity" and make a big splash akin to famous Western environmental heroes like John D. Rockefeller Jr. More basically, it allows the wealthy to fulfill their own social and emotional needs, because social integration into elite circles tends to happen within these exclusive philanthropic and environmental spaces.

This approach to philanthropy and selective environmental concern—which are largely assumed to be altruistic and morally *good*—takes precedence over addressing the more pressing "buzz-kill" issues that the wealthy moved to rural paradise to avoid. In their own minds, the perceived goodness of their philanthropy overshadows and even nullifies any harm they might inflict. But does it? As a handful of the working poor put it in chapter 10, the rich are "flying around in a jet and talking about how much [they] wanted to save the moose," and yet it seems that they "take care of the wolves more than the Latino workers in this community." Another lamented that the wealthy feel good about being "busy fighting for the elk or the moose," but they forget that "the other things that you're doing *are harmful* to other people." In other words, band-aid philanthropy does little to prevent structural harm.[3] Remember that Margarita

Dixon summed up Gilded Green Philanthropy this way: "You see a lot of charity, but very little justice."

Overreliance on gilded philanthropy also creates anxiety and desperation among the more than two hundred local nonprofits that must voraciously compete for wealthy folks' time and money, given the absence of a middle class and adequately funded public programs. Straightforward questions—*Who just moved into town? What is their net worth? How can we make contact? Are they already on a nonprofit board? Is it our competitor? Can we convince them of our mission? Wait, so-and-so left town?*—are ratcheted up here because the stakes are so high and major gifts tend to be few and far between. Some fundraising professionals say they fear that the newer wealthy folks are not as in tune with community needs as are the longer-term residents (I found anecdotal evidence to support these fears). Last, all of these concerns can create anxiety among the ultra-wealthy themselves, who feel pressured and overwhelmed by the number of nonprofits competing for their support.

While Teton County does boast many caring and generous ultra-wealthy benefactors—and many more outstanding nonprofit organizations—the reality is that even in what some nonprofit leaders described to me as the "Golden Age of Philanthropy" in Teton County, the social problems here seem to have worsened. Ironically, my research shows that the extreme concentration of wealth creates problems with its left hand that it then attempts to solve with its right. These problems originate in national systems of wealth creation and social inequality that span far beyond this little corner of the West, and thus the reliance on gilded philanthropy for solutions is just a small band-aid for much larger societal problems. Further, these gilded philanthropy solutions ultimately preserve the status quo, perpetuate these plutocratic systems, and at the same time create a status market in which wealthy philanthropists are not only esteemed but in some cases are also viewed as community saviors.

Importantly, the problems uncovered in this book did not happen by chance, but are the result of specific *policies* that overwhelmingly benefit the wealthy. For example, as noted in chapter 1, Wyoming is America's tax haven; Bloomberg calls it "America's wealth-friendliest state." This arrangement is made possible by the state's lucrative oil, gas, and coal industries and is spurred on by its proud antipathy toward government and taxes. Local real estate brokers have had an easy time selling this feature, convincing the rich to move themselves and their money under the sheltering skies of, ironically, "The Cowboy State." As one broker advertised, "Wyoming offers homeowners nearly as many financial benefits as it does outdoor activities and amenities. Learn about residency requirements in Wyoming so that you can take advantage of the state's shelter from income tax, corporate tax, estate tax, capital gains tax and trust tax, as well as some of the lowest excise, sales and property taxes in the United States."[4]

As a result of these policies, the number of affluent people moving to Teton County has skyrocketed, and with it the local accumulation of nonlabor investment income. In 2015, nearly *8 out of every 10 dollars in income earned* in Teton County came not from traditional wages or salary but from interest and dividends. Consider that in 1970, only $52 million in annual income here came from investments, but by 2015 this number had shot up 6,500 percent, to $3.4 billion. Compare this figure to wages or salary from an ordinary worker's job, which in 1970 paid $39,943. Forty-five years later, this figure had increased by only $1,109, to $41,052. Wage stagnation for those at the middle and bottom is part of a broader national trend: Since 1973, productivity among American workers has increased by 74 percent, while wages have increased only 12.5 percent, meaning that workers' productivity has risen six times faster than their pay.[5]

Despite the massive amount of wealth descending on this corner of the West, and despite now boasting the richest county in the country, this hardscrabble state has chosen to require very little from the scores of rich folks who have moved here to take advantage of its awe-inspiring natural resources, its tax shelters, and its plentiful population of underpaid workers.

In the face of these challenges, people (both wealthy and nonwealthy) and organizations that are genuinely interested in moving beyond the status quo and band-aid solutions should focus on using their money and power to reform policy and build more equitable institutions. Easier said than done, of course. Nevertheless, current local policies are simply inadequate to the task of responding to recent and dramatic wealth concentration, financialization of the local economy, population growth, middle- and low-income wage stagnation, and extreme housing insecurity that have come to define desirable locales across the West.

With regard to lack of proportionate ultra-wealthy taxation, extensive research shows that requiring more from multimillion-aires will not prompt them to pack up and leave.[6] This is likely more true in the rural West, with its captivating natural amenities. Thus, as fossil-fuel revenues in Wyoming continue to decline and the state desperately searches for new revenue to improve services such as education and technical skills training, politicians and community leaders would do well to reconsider their long-standing antipathy to tax revenue from the growing abundance of millionaire migrants—and more generally, to live up to its identity as "The Equality State" by enhancing the common good and ensuring a brighter future for *all* of its residents, not just its recent flood of ultra-wealthy transplants.

The first step in such a transformation is to wrestle with these deeper questions about what makes an authentic community in this new Gilded Age. How we answer this question will determine the types of specific policies that need to be pursued if we are to inch closer to the romantic version of old-time "community" where folks look after one another—a version that the ultra-wealthy now wrongly assume exists, and that the working poor and many rural Westerners now only wish existed.

———

This brings us to the second main dilemma the ultra-wealthy have sought to resolve, which concerns social stigmas, guilt, and feelings of inauthenticity. Remember from part 3 that the ultra-wealthy use nature and rural people as a vehicle for personal transformation, creating versions of themselves that they view as more authentic, virtuous, and community-minded. The lives of the working poor in the rural West are especially attractive to the rich because they provide a romantic model that allows the wealthy to escape the snares of high-profile, urban rat-racing by living closer to nature and rural people—people who often took the popular form (via art, dress, and other forms of ultra-wealthy material culture) of the dusty cowboy, the noble native, or the penniless nature lover, to each of whom they attribute ruralized values such as pastoral simplicity, material contentment, frontier authenticity, nature-oriented adventure, and reverence for untouched wilderness.

As I showed throughout, this use of nature and rural people can create a veneer of community where it *appears* that all's well in Paradise, yet in reality it romanticizes the ugly reality of modern rural poverty, confuses servants for friends, typecasts rural hardship as an idyllic choice (best lived by iconic rugged cowboys and noble natives), stereotypes modern poverty to be a mythic white ski-bum and nature-loving bohemian rather than the actual immigrant family hanging on by a thread, deliberately conceals outward indicators of racial, ethnic, and class-based inequities, and generally disguises the need for fundamental policy changes to address local social problems.

Solutions to this community veneer are not as straightforward as the economic policy solutions suggested earlier, yet I believe that buried within the rich's professed love for, and romantic appropriation of, nature and rural working-poor culture is a genuine longing for human relationships, therapeutic experiences in nature, and yearning for acceptance from those who may judge them. No doubt, this longing expresses itself in peculiar ways. In chapter 7, I noted the infatuation with working-class styles of dress, art, and having "normal" friends, and in chapter 8 I showed how self-transformation and integration into rural "normalcy" actually numbs and mutes the ultra-wealthy's feelings of guilt, shapes what they see and *don't* see, and masks the truth about who is doing the most harm to their penniless friends and to the fabric of the community.

When considering solutions, one good-faith approach is to take (as I do) the rich's search for authenticity and efforts at personal transformation to be sincere, despite their peculiar and sometimes regrettable side effects. As scientific research has shown, having great wealth creates unique social and psychological predicaments. Excessive money does not bring excessive happiness, and in some cases, quite the opposite.[7] Moreover, humans are social animals whose flourishing is tied to the quality of our relationships and our sense of purpose—both of which take on their fullest meaning within a community. As Colin Stewart, the Yellowstone Club member we met in chapter 2—who paternalistically claims to have many "very close" working-class friends—sums it up, "What makes a man happy? Relationships!"

Rich folks' common desire for relationships, belonging, acceptance, and a sense of community in the rural West—even if it is based on a romanticized and condescending version of a bucolic dusty cowboy, noble native locked in time, or modern pop iconic figure like Alexander Supertramp, rather than the reality of the Mexican immigrant who works for them—provides an opportunity to improve the community in two ways. The first is by *building trust*. Throughout the book, and especially in chapter 2, I showed how chronic paranoia can condition wealthy people to feel isolated and distrustful, and in some cases, feel like they are being unfairly targeted or exploited. These feelings harm the fabric of the community because they lead the rich to circle the wagons to ensure self-protection and self-interest, thus reinforcing rigid group boundaries, preventing more empathetic politics and policies, and isolating themselves from genuine community integration. But there is a unique opportunity to diffuse this paranoia if community leaders, politicians, and civic and religious institutions can tap constructively into wealthy folks' deep attraction to nature-oriented places and rural culture.

Which leads to the second opportunity: *increasing empathy*. If community leaders, politicians, and leaders of institutions can again find ways to cultivate greater openness among wealthy and powerful residents—an openness that the ultra-wealthy likely did not have to the same degree in their less romantic urban or suburban areas from which they came—and to harness their peculiar desires for intimate connection to rural and Western culture, it may also increase the empathy they feel for neighbors, employees, and "friends" who are struggling nearby.

Further research from neuroscience and psychology has shown that having money and power can make a person more self-absorbed, less generous, and less empathetic to suffering. But all hope is not lost, because additional research using "poverty simulations" has shown that empathy skills can be improved when people visualize themselves lower on the social pyramid.[8] Similarly, as I showed in chapter 7, the ultra-wealthy obsession with a certain rural, working-class, and nature-oriented culture involves a process of adopting this culture as their own. And in the same way, as described in chapter 4, their relationship with nature involves a process of stepping outside their everyday roles and *physically entering* a realm beyond the snares of money and power. Each of these processes, which together represent their efforts at personal transformation, has the potential to instill greater empathy.

But just as throwing a bit of money at local environmental projects might be done with good intentions, or might just help you sleep better at night, or might be a trivial attempt to apply a small band-aid to the global ecological problems perpetuated by your wealth creation activities, or might improve your property value, or might protect your spiritual experience of nature, or might just be an in-vogue story to tell at an elite cocktail party, in the same way, mustering up empathy to see and feel the experiences of those struggling in the shadow of your superabundance will ring hollow if it does not lead to actively *doing less harm*—both locally and globally—to the people you proudly call friends, the community you proudly call home, and the natural environment that you proudly revere.

This process of doing less harm can begin with a personal transformation and a journey away from superficial temptations of high society toward these more authentic and romanticized ideals of nature and rural life. But make no mistake, these alone are not enough—and in the words of our struggling low-income friend earlier—can perpetuate the appearance that all is well in paradise when in reality the "things that you're doing are harmful to other people." The next step is to minimize harm, move off the comfort of the sidelines, and begin to *strip away this veneer by actively supporting policies* that defend the rural people and the natural world you've come to love so much.

Methodological Notes

This appendix details the methodological process that underwrote this project from beginning to end. While I include methodological footnotes where appropriate throughout the chapters of the book, this appendix systematically reports the study's measurement, sampling, recruitment, observation, interviews, and coding. Compared to other projects—including my own and those of others in the field—this study was an extremely burdensome undertaking given its focus on (1) an exceptionally difficult to access population that is high profile and sacralizes privacy; (2) a vulnerable low-income community made up mostly of recent immigrants; and (3) all taking place within a small rural locale, creating more difficulty relative to issues of privacy and anonymity. Together, this created many serious challenges, but in what follows I demonstrate in detail how I sought to overcome these conceptual, methodological, and ethical complexities.

Anonymity

Great care has been taken to fully protect the anonymity of all persons in this study. All names and specific locations of the ultra-wealthy—as well as anyone they discuss during the interviews or participant observation—have been changed to ensure anonymity. Because of the uniqueness of this study, the high profile and more easily identifiable nature of many people, and the small-town locale, I also modified a great deal of personalized information that could possibly lead to individuals being identified. This meant multiple layers of anonymity that included altering any of the following:

profession, company, board membership, public office, major charitable contributions, job description, location (for example, specific city in which they had lived or from which they moved), estimated net worth, and specific neighborhoods or hotels known to be associated with certain individuals. *I always and everywhere erred on the side of anonymity.* Overall though, this process of deep anonymization affected only how I presented some of these individuals in the text, but as much as possible did not affect the actual interpretation or substantive findings as they are reported in the book. When alterations were made, I either abstracted to a higher level (for example, mentioning their state or region rather than their specific city; using more general descriptions of their profession) or used a comparable concept (for example, comparable pseudonym; similar company; similar industry or profession).

I took equally great care to protect the identity of the low-income interviewees. I never obtained the name of any low-income interviewee, and thus every name in the book is a pseudonym that reflects the respondent's gender and ethnic background (for example, many were first- or second-generation Mexican immigrants). Anonymity was especially important because a portion of these interviewees were undocumented immigrants. As I explain in the following, I worked closely with a local social services organization—which requested to remain anonymous for fear of retribution from wealthy donors—to conduct these fifty interviews with anonymity in mind. This organization provided me with exhaustive socioeconomic and demographic information on each interviewee, and we used ID numbers in lieu of names.

Statistical Profile of Semistructured Interviews

Table A.1 reports detailed aggregate statistics on each set of interviewees. Data are presented in the aggregate to ensure complete anonymity. The twenty-five pilot interviews are not included in these final data because they were aimed to test out the interview guide and were often much shorter interviews.

TABLE A.1. Descriptive Statistics for 205 Interviews

ULTRA-WEALTHY	
White (non-Hispanic)	93%
Female	24%
Male	76%
Married or partnered	86%
Profession: CEO or similarly high profile	29%
Profession: Finance	32%
Age (average years)	61
Education: College degree	95%
Tenure: Fewer than 10 years	21%
Tenure: 10–20 years	40%
Tenure: 20+ years	39%
LOW INCOME AND WORKING POOR	
Spanish speaking	86%
Housing insecure	68%
Female	48%
Male	52%
Married or partnered	58%
Profession: Services or housekeeping	56%
Profession: Construction	20%
Profession: Community nonprofit	10%
Age: 20s–30s	52%
Age: 40s–50s	40%
Age: 60s+	8%
Education: Less than high school	30%
Education: Only high school	34%
Education: College degree	36%
MIDDLE CLASS	
White (non-Hispanic)	82%
Nonwhite	18%
Female	52%
Male	48%
Married or partnered	60%
Age (average years)	41
Education: College degree	68%

Note: I interviewed 155 ultra-wealthy individuals, but the total interview count across all categories (N = 205) and the descriptive statistics here do not include 25 ultra-wealthy individuals who participated in the initial pilot interviews. The low-income and working-poor sample includes 50 individuals. The middle-class sample includes 25 individuals. Middle-class professions included architect, schoolteacher, full-time parent, conservation nonprofit, human services nonprofit, property manager, realtor, rancher, fundraiser, hotel manager, federal land manager, construction, and upscale restaurant manager.

Conceptual Definitions and Measurement

There is no scholarly or popularly agreed upon definition of what counts as "rich," "wealthy," or of "high," "very high," or "ultra" net worth. As with any social category that we fix upon the world, their characteristics and boundaries are often subjective and in flux, but ascribed with the aim of accurately representing the social category in question. A wide variety of different terms have been used to describe people in society who have much more wealth and income than others, monikers that include "super-rich," "super-wealthy," "economic elite," "ultra-high-net-worth," "very-high-net-worth," "high-level-of-wealth," and here in this book the "ultra-wealthy."

The fact that there is no agreed upon term also means that the financial thresholds that define these categories can vary widely. For example, a recent Harvard Business School study on millionaires defined "high levels of wealth" as those who have in excess of $8 million (and in another study they used $10 million as their threshold).[1] Using this cut-off, they then conduct a comparison between ordinary millionaires who do not fall within their "high level" group. Other researchers, especially in the wealth consulting sector, have similarly wrestled with how to define different categories that make up the millionaire and billionaire class. Wealth-X uses a category they term "high-net-worth" as those whose net worth tops $5 million, whereas their "ultra-high-net-worth" are those whose net worth tops $30 million.[2] The number of people in both of these categories has grown in recent years. According to their research, there are now 73,110 ultra-high-net-worth people in the United States, including 8,350 in the New York metropolitan area alone.[3]

All of these categories are at the same time arbitrary, and yet critically important. Furthermore, the information that makes up such categories can be extremely difficult to obtain. The researchers behind the Forbes 400 describe the inherent difficulty of such a measurement and definitional process, noting that, "Though we've been at it a long time, it's always a challenge . . . uncovering their fortunes required us to pore over thousands of SEC documents, court records, probate records and Web and print stories. . . . Of course, we don't pretend to know what is listed on each billionaire's private balance sheet."[4] For my study, knowing *exactly* what is on their balance sheet is less important. Because, as I launched the study, I was (and still am) less concerned about specific gradations *within* the social category I call "ultra-wealthy." Whereas Forbes needs this information to create a ranking system, I (similar the Harvard study earlier) was concerned with a basic threshold of who belongs to my social category in question and who does not. Thus, aside from a few notable exceptions, this study lumps together the $200 million person with the $50 million person. Both are simply "ultra-wealthy" as I define it here, sharing the same characteristic of having extreme wealth.

Furthermore, as a sociologist, I was as concerned with (1) ultra-wealthy *institutions* and (2) Teton County as an ultra-wealthy *community* as I was with specific ultra-wealthy individuals. Simply put, ultra-wealthy individuals only *in isolation* mattered very little to the study. Teton County is an ultra-wealthy *community* with characteristics that are not reducible to the individuals, and thus my research examined much more than the individuals whose quotes are littered throughout this book. Ultra-wealthy individuals were one piece of a much larger puzzle, pieced together by a variety of sources of data on the structure of the community and its institutions, including social network interactions over two decades' time, data on philanthropic giving, board membership, environmental conservation, real estate development, and demographic and socioeconomic change, as well as compiling large amounts of digitized text for computational machine learning.

Thus, while I certainly relied heavily on interviews with these individuals, I focused a great deal of attention on related institutions and the contours of this unique community. In some cases, these were what we might call total "ultra-wealthy" institutions, such as the Yellowstone Club in chapter 2 (and to some degree Shooting Star in Jackson Hole), but in other cases—such as the Jackson Hole Land Trust—institutions were less totalizing, made up of a mixture of different levels of wealth. In other words, I do not define the Jackson Hole Land Trust as an ultra-wealthy institution, yet as I show throughout the book, it is intimately connected to—and influences and is influenced by—this ultra-wealthy world.

As I've described this project to other researchers, NGO folks, and everyday people, I encountered a tendency to focus too narrowly on my interviews with the ultra-wealthy individuals. I certainly understand this tendency and the seemingly timeless curiosity people have about the rich, but my emphasis on institutions—and the qualitative and quantitative insight at the *community level*—are as important for learning about this unique social class as were the discussions I had with individuals from this class. What's more, we can glean great insights about one group of people by asking *others* about them, and thus the low-income and middle-class interviews provided another angle with which to examine the ultra-wealthy, their institutions, and this community defined by its immense wealth.

With all of this in mind, and turning to the individuals themselves, this study combines two different measures to define the boundaries of the social category of individuals I call "ultra-wealthy": (1) estimated net worth, and (2) estimated income. First, in terms of a net worth threshold, this study falls between the two thresholds noted earlier from the Harvard Business School study ($8/$10 million) and the wealth consulting sector, to define "ultra-wealthy" individuals as those with a minimum estimated net worth of at least $15 million. It is worth noting that most interviewees had an estimated net worth much higher than this, often in property assets alone. For example, a mountain home in Teton County or in the Yellowstone Club can very easily top $10–15 million. Using the conservative figure of $15 million as a general guide, I was able to include folks at these lower levels closer to $15 million, who still have much more wealth than they will likely spend in their lifetime, but do not have hundreds of millions like several other folks I interviewed. A 2017 U.S. Federal Reserve report also provides some context for this threshold, noting that $10.3 million is the net worth cutoff for the 1 percent in the United States.[5]

Of course, there exists no publicly available database to easily see another person's net worth, so in the following I describe in detail the diverse set of publicly available databases (for example, real estate holdings, SEC filings, aircraft registration) to triangulate and reliably estimate, especially in rare cases if there were doubts that a person did not meet the general $15 million threshold. In addition to triangulating using multiple databases, I was in some cases able to ascertain a self-reported estimate of their net worth by simply asking them.

Second, net worth estimates—calculated as the value of all assets minus liabilities—do not necessarily capture a person's recurrent income. Thus, estimates of income were particularly useful if in rare cases I was not certain that their net worth was north of $15 million. I calculated an estimate of their earned income based on comparable compensation data and commensurate with their profession and position. These estimates are derived from data collected and made public by reputable sources (for example, UPenn Wharton "Execu-comp" Executive Compensation Database 1992–present, BoardEx, AFL-CIO Executive Paywatch, S&P Global Market Intelligence, and reputable news articles). This adds another dimension to how I define "ultra-wealthy" because one person might appear to have relatively modest real estate holdings (for example, less than $5 million), yet they've very likely built a substantial amount of income and investments over the course of their lifetime to well exceed the $15 million threshold. Thus, these general estimates of earned income are especially useful for cases where a person appears to have (relatively) lower net worth but high compensation. While I rely primarily on estimates from the earlier databases, in some cases I was able to glean information from the interviews themselves about substantial salary or lifetime earnings, based on our in-depth conversations about their professional successes (for example, selling a medical supply company; cashing out a tech startup; decades of work as a CEO of a well-heeled global financial services company).

Table A.2 is the list of publicly available and curated database resources I used throughout the course of the research to estimate net worth or income if it was not clearly above the threshold, or if they did not self-report during the interview.

I am confident that every interviewee qualified as ultra-wealthy, but as with any study there is the potential for some error. Of course,

TABLE A.2. Sample of Available Data Sources to Estimate Net Worth and/or Income

Record Type	Additional Details
Property records	Homes, land, other property assets
Vehicle registrations	Auto and other
Inheritances	Probate filings
Private foundations	Via IRS filings
Divorce filings	Info on assets, retirement, etc.
SEC filings	Executive stock options, holdings, etc.
Small business retirement funds	IRS 5500
Uniform commercial code filings	Via secretary of state, assets of debtor
Civil litigation	Assets from lawsuit or settlement
Patents and trademarks	Can reveal monetary estimates
Aircraft registrations	Federal Aviation Administration
Watercraft registrations	State registrations, larger vessels via U.S. Coast Guard
Personal funds campaign contributions	If running for office, not subject to limits

Sample of Curated Databases	Additional Details
Compensation estimates:	Wharton "Execucomp" database 1992–present
	BoardEx
	ALF-CIO Executive Paywatch
Major charitable gifts:	Chronicle of Higher Education—$1 million or more
	OpenSecrets databases
	DonorSearch.net
Other financial:	S&P Global Market Intelligence
	Forbes databases
	Reputable journalism containing reliable estimates

the goal is to identify where error might exist and minimize it when possible through careful measurement and intentional sampling and recruitment, as I have done. But even still, a person could own a $10 million home in Teton County, a private aircraft, and another multi-million-dollar home in Greenwich, Connecticut, yet unbeknownst to me be $50 million in debt. Even though, in the words of Forbes earlier, it is ultimately impossible to know exactly what is listed on each person's private balance sheet, my two-pronged strategy (1—estimated net worth; 2—estimated income), the large size of my sample, the purposive and snowball sampling methods described here, and the deep insights from participant observation in the community all ensured that there was little to no error in my ultra-wealthy sample.

And last, while these data sources were used to estimate wealth and income at the individual level (rather than at the household level), wealth is often a household phenomenon that can include a spouse who themselves may be a full-time parent or not working, but I still considered to be part of the ultra-wealthy class. Thus, I included spouses and partners of ultra-wealthy individuals in my ultra-wealthy sample as long as they resided in the same household. Previous sociodemographic research on the wealthy shows just how skewed it is along the lines of gender. For example, only 12.5 percent of the Forbes 400 list are women,[6] and in a separate census of ultra-high-net-worth individuals, Wealth-X found that 87 percent are male and 93 percent are married.[7] It is no surprise then—and even expected—that the large majority of the nonearning spouses I included in my interview sample were women.

Low-Income Sampling and Recruitment

I paired with an established local social services organization—which requested to remain anonymous for fear of retribution from wealthy donors—that works very closely with the local working-poor and immigrant population to interview a representative sample of fifty people. Because this organization is so well connected in the community, it proved relatively straightforward to recruit interviewees. Working with a trusted third party *from within this community* also provided an anonymity buffer between myself and the interviewees, so I never knew of their names. I provided flat-rate financial compensation to all fifty interviewees, given (as I describe in chapters 9 and 10) how overworked these individuals are, and how valuable their time is to their survival. I worked closely with this organization as individuals were recruited to ensure that—like the ultra-wealthy interviews—this sample remained representative according to the socioeconomic and demographic traits of this particular community (see table A.1).

Sampling and Recruitment: Purposive and Snowball

The most time-consuming aspect of this study was recruiting and scheduling the interviews with the ultra-wealthy sample, who for reasons described in the introduction of the book are extremely difficult to access for up-close research. This process was guided by two established qualitative sampling techniques that were implemented using (1) my measurement framework outlined earlier in this appendix, (2) participant observation that began ten months before the interviews, (3) my background knowledge from many years of research in this community for a previous book as well as my own family's multigenerational presence in the region, and (4) the small body of research on known demographics of the wealthy, which assisted with creating a representative sample.

First, I used a *purposive sampling* method based on my primary definitional criteria of who counts as ultra-wealthy. This was an iterative process, which began by first casting a very wide net. To do this, I used the publicly available land records (the 2014 Teton County tax roll in conjunction with Zillow) to identify the 500 highest valued properties. I prepared a letter (figure A.1) explaining the study, which was then mail-merged with these real estate data to personalize each letter. In some cases, these letters were sent to their permanent resident outside Teton County, often in New York, Texas, or California. This letter was prepared and mailed in late 2014 and early 2015. I used the same process for the Yellowstone Club sample, mailing letters to every property within the club, which were also obtained using publicly accessible land records.

In addition to explaining the aim of the study in very general terms (for example, community change, in-migration, natural areas), I invited them to go to a custom website that I created called YaleYellowstone.org.[8] Most importantly, this website included a form that they could fill out that would send their information straight to my

Yale

Justin Farrell, Ph.D.
Sociology Professor
Yale University
New Haven, CT 06511

Dear (FIRST-NAME),

I am writing to request your participation in a new book about the greater Yellowstone area. Over the course of the next six months I will be talking with all sorts of folks, including homeowners, temporary residents, and vacationers. All conversations will be anonymous, and the aim of the book is to share the experiences of these different people, including yourself, who have come to vacation, work, and play in this magnificent area.

I am especially interested in the voices of folks like yourself who have a residence in the area, and this letter is a special invitation, in hopes that you or one of your family members might take a few minutes to chat with me over the phone or in person.

Even though the conversations are about non-controversial issues, no names will ever be used or made public. *Complete anonymity and privacy are guaranteed*, and taken very seriously in accordance with the legal and academic policies of Yale University.

Because many of the homeowners live away from the area during the year, it has been difficult to include their voices in the study. I am hoping that we can arrange a time to include your stories and experiences. There are no right or wrong answers, and I am not testing some scientific theory. Most people really enjoy the conversations, and they usually take about an hour.

I am happy to fly to meet wherever is most convenient for you. Or, if you prefer, we can arrange a time to talk over the phone. I've provided a few ways to connect. You can give me a call or shoot me an email. Or, you can head to the project website (**YaleYellowstone.org**) where there is more information and a short form to get in contact. I've only sent this letter to a handful of people, so your participation would be greatly appreciated. Please don't hesitate to give me a call (cell phone below) with any questions.

Thank you,

Justin Farrell, Ph.D.
Sociology Professor
Yale University
Cell phone: (307) 200-XXXX
Justin.Farrell@Yale.edu

e-mail, allowing them to inquire with questions or to set up a time to be interviewed. The form captured their name, e-mail, phone number, and comments/questions. In the letter, I also provided my personal cell phone number and e-mail address; some participants were more comfortable using these instead of the online form. The first response I got from the letters was a call on my cell phone from a banker in London while I was gassing up my car at a remote gas station on Interstate 80 in Wyoming.

On the website, I included photos of popular spots in the region (for example, Grand Tetons, Elk Refuge, Yellowstone's Old Faithful, Gallatin River) as well as favorite recreation activities that are prevalent within their social class (for example, resort skiing). Throughout this process, I reinforced over and again in the letter, on the website, and in initial phone conversations the guarantee of anonymity.

Response rates for difficult to access populations like this tend to be much lower, and this study was no exception. The response rate for this initial purposive sample from the letters and website was 18 percent. Not all who responded ended up being interviewed. Because I know the names of all of the people to whom I sent letters, as well as the value of their property (as an initial proxy for wealth that would later be improved), I have information on who responded and who did not respond, giving me traction on nonresponse bias that may be present. Relative to property value, there were no patterns to indicate systematic nonresponse bias—those who responded were evenly distributed among property values and the key demographics shown earlier in table A.1. Importantly, and as I noted earlier, property value is just one piece of the puzzle, albeit important. I paid careful attention to the representativeness of my sample as I moved through these spaces conducting ethnographic observation, and as I compiled qualitative and quantitative data on ultra-wealthy institutions. My doctoral student Katie McConnell assisted me with promptly following up and scheduling after we had received contact and verbal agreement to participate.

This initial purposive sample proved successful, resulting in fifty-one interviews, and more importantly, created a solid foundation for my further participant observation, as well as my second interview sampling method: snowball sampling.

Snowball sampling was an appropriate and effective second step because once I had established connections and built reciprocal trust within this world, I was able to at the end of every interview ask the respondents to suggest names of two or three of their peers who might also participate. Paired with the letters and website, I found that, in the end, snowball sampling proved to be the most effective means of reaching this population. And, as I describe in detail in the introduction, my twofold identity as a Yale professor and ignoble Westerner/native Wyomingite was novel for many of my interviewees, and is even indicative of some of the main findings as outlined in the introduction chapter. (See the introduction for more on how I used this strategy to build a presence within this community, and created the trust needed for them to refer me to their peers.)

In addition to these methods, I also met people during the course of my participant observation—at clubs, conservation events, and around town—who became part of the interview sample.

Last, snowball sampling techniques also aided in knowing when to conclude recruitment and interviews, and as is standard, I concluded when there was very little new information emerging, indicating that I had reached the point of saturation and redundancy.

Representativeness of the Ultra-Wealthy Sample

Prior research on the demographic makeup of the wealthy suggests that my sample (see table A.1, earlier) is largely representative. I did, however, oversample on females, interviewing about twice as many as is representative: Wealth-X reports that 86 percent of ultra-high-net-worth individuals are male and 13.7 percent are female (which happens to be a historical record high).[9] In New York, 95 percent of ultra-high-net-worth individuals are male. Coinciding with the Wealth-X data, 12.5 percent of the Forbes 400 are women. In oversampling on women, my sample resulted in 24 percent of ultra-wealthy respondents being female. I also aimed to align my sample with known figures about marital status, achieving representativeness with 86 percent of my sample being married or partnered, resembling previous research that puts this number around 90 percent.[10]

My sample is also representative of the racial/ethnic makeup of the ultra-wealthy, at 93 percent white (non-Hispanic). In addition to gender, marital status, and race/ethnicity, I also sought to achieve representativeness concerning profession. Data on profession are harder to come by, but Wealth-X reliably estimates that about 14 percent of ultra-high-net-worth globally are from the finance industry. In New York City, about 52 percent of ultra-high-net-worth are from finance. A large literature on financialization of the economy (see chapter 1) suggests that this number is growing nationwide, as more and more individuals make millions from finance-related work. Landing between the global estimate and the New York City estimate, 32 percent of my sample worked in the finance industry. Last, the average age of my sample (61.3) is also representative, within about 2 percentage points of the best available data.[11]

Conducting the Participant Observation and Interviews

I first began conducting participant observation in this region nine years ago for my first book *The Battle for Yellowstone*. As I recount in chapter 1 in this new book, my family has also been in the region for several generations, and I grew up watching wealth move in and the community and environmental change that followed. I launched the participant observation for this particular study in fall 2014, in both Teton County and in the counties within and adjacent to the Yellowstone Club (Gallatin and Madison). Over the course of the project, participant observation ranged from several months at a time (for example, summer 2016) to several weeks at a time throughout the year.

Yale generously granted me a one-year leave, during which I was able to spend extended time in the field. Furthermore, I was able to align my teaching schedule with this research project, bringing students from Yale out to Wyoming during the spring semesters. As

I describe in the introduction, I fully immersed myself in the world of the ultra-wealthy, spending time at their exclusive clubs, homes, ski resorts, breweries, art shows, conservation gatherings, fundraisers, political meetings, recreation areas, houses of worship, watering holes, restaurants, and other haunts. This routine observation informed every aspect of this book. Chapter 2 on the Yellowstone Club is particularly notable for its reliance on participant observation from inside the club, as well as just outside its walls in the town of Big Sky.

The fifty low-income interviews were all conducted in person by two leaders of the social service organization. They used my interview guide shown here, and we consulted regularly throughout the process to ensure that the interviews were conducted accurately and comprehensively. The interviews took place at the office of the organization or at the respondent's home. Interviews were then translated and transcribed. Per the Yale Institutional Review Board (IRB), and to protect interviewees, I have destroyed these recordings, but the social service organization retains a copy for their own use, in hopes that this information might allow them to better serve their community.

I conducted all of the interviews with the ultra-wealthy myself. I also conducted the twenty-five short pilot interviews and the twenty-five interviews with those I broadly call "middle-class" individuals (see table A.1, earlier, for a sample of professions). The ultra-wealthy interviews were conducted in person and via phone, with the majority of in-person interviews taking place in Teton County, often at a club, coffee shop, breakfast cafe, their home, or before/after an event. I also conducted interviews in New York City and nearby in Connecticut.

The interviews were semistructured, following a script but leaving plenty of flexibility for me to creatively probe when necessary, and for the respondents to talk at will. The duration of the interviews averaged about one hour and fifteen minutes, with three hours being the longest, and fifteen minutes the shortest. Shorter interviews were often due to terse answers or sudden interruptions where the respondent had to tend to a work or family issue. In some instances,

I conducted interviews with both spouses present. Fewer than half of the interviews were tape-recorded. Having conducted hundreds and hundreds of interviews over the years, beginning in graduate school with rural farmers for Princeton University Professor Robert Wuthnow's research, I am able to simultaneously conduct the interview and take detailed notes. These notes were typed on my computer if I was interviewing via phone or written on a notepad if the interview was in person. I paid particularly close attention to accurately capturing quotes relevant to the research questions and hypotheses, which became more and more clear as the research went on as I approached empirical saturation.

Per Yale IRB, and to protect research subjects' anonymity, all recordings, transcriptions, and written notes during interviews were destroyed.

Coding Process

This multiyear data collection process resulted in a massive amount of data, made up primarily of my participant observation field notes and interview notes and transcriptions. I used MaxQDA software to systematically code these data according to my research questions and hypotheses. Informed by prior research—including my own—I began the coding using six overarching categories: (1) Socioeconomic Status and Demographics, (2) Community Topics, (3) The Culture of Wealth, (4) Income Inequality, (5) Race and Ethnicity, (6) Environment and Conservation. Within these main categories, 492 total subcodes emerged, which were applied for a total of 5,163 coded segments.

Interview Guides

The following two sections show the two separate interview guides used for the ultra-wealthy and the low-income interviews, respectively. The interviews were semistructured, following a scripted rubric with specific questions, yet worded and presented to the respondent in a way that would make them feel comfortable, encouraging them to provide thoughtful answers or spark further conversation. Michèle Lamont (Harvard University) was kind enough to share her interview guide for her book *The Dignity of Working Men*, from which I adapted some of these questions, especially because I drew heavily on Lamont's boundary work approach to empirically studying social class, wealth, and morality. Many of the questions from these interview guides served as an entry point into the specific topic, and from there would often take on a life of their own, depending on the person and depending on the topic. The Yellowstone Club interview guide was nearly identical to the general ultra-wealthy guide shown here, but with questions tailored toward the club. The topics covered, and the wording of the questions remained identical.

Ultra-Wealthy Interview Guide

INTRODUCTION

First, can you tell me a little bit about yourself?

Where you grew up?
Where is "home" now?
Married or no? How long?

I am interested in hearing people's stories about how they got involved in the line of work they are in, whether that means their work, or homemaking, or what they used to do if they are retired. Could you tell me your story, maybe starting with when you were young?

Tell me what the main reasons are that your life has turned out in these ways?

COMMUNITY AND CHANGE

Next are some questions about your opinions and experiences in the greater Yellowstone area . . .

Now, are you the first in your family to have a place in this community, or did earlier generations live here as well?

[If yes] So tell me the story. Which of your family came here first? Where did they come from? When did they come? And why did they settle here?

[If no] Tell me the story of how you came to live here? When did you come? Where had you been before? And why did you come here?

I'd like you to take a typical day for you in the area—and walk me through it. Start in the morning and go through the day for me. [Probe by asking what happened next and whether anything else happened.]

Compare the satisfaction you get from the things you do for a living with the satisfaction from enjoying the Yellowstone area. Does one give you more satisfaction than the other? How do they compare?

Other than the natural beauty, what would you say the best thing is about living in this community (even if for only short periods of time)?

Can you give me an example—something that would illustrate what is really nice about living here? Why is that special to you?

And what is the worst thing about living here (even if for only short periods of time)? Or something you would change if you could?

Give me an example about that?

How has the community changed in recent years? If someone had left several years ago and came back today, what would be the main changes they would notice?

What are some of the main reasons for these changes? Have these changes been good for the community, or not so good?

There are people in most communities who kind of keep to themselves. What kinds of people in your community keep to themselves, or sort of fly under the radar?

Why do they keep to themselves?
Is this good or bad for the community?

How important would you say religion or spirituality is in your community?

Which religious congregation (if any) are you associated with? Back home?
If any: What tradition or denomination?

Would you say that Jackson Hole has a strong sense of community?

What is a concrete example that might illustrate this?

Stepping back a bit, how would you personally define "community"?

Geographic proximity?
Or shared values?
Anything else that comes to mind?
What does an "ideal" community look like?

COMMUNITY MEMBERS

Some questions about your opinion of folks who live in Jackson Hole. Again, we are just interested in your own confidential opinion . . .

In most communities there are people who are looked up to and respected. In your view, what kinds of people are these?

Can you give me an example (without naming names)? Why?

And then there are also people who shouldn't be respected as much. In your view, what kinds of people are these?

Can you give me an example (without naming names)? Why?

A somewhat different question: Whether we admit it or not, we all feel inferior or superior to some people at times. In relation to what types of people do you feel inferior?

Why? Can you give me concrete examples?

And of course, we can sometimes feel superior to some people . . . what types of people would you say?

Why? Can you give me concrete examples?

What kinds of people are you particularly sympathetic for? Why?

What kinds of people would you rather avoid in your day-to-day life? Why?

Some have said that Jackson is very laid back and casual—do you find that to be true?

How are things financially for people in the community these days? Are people pretty well off, having difficulties, or what?

Without mentioning any names, can you give me an example of somebody who has been having difficulties lately?

Some communities have a large gap between the "haves" and "have-nots," while other communities do not. In your experience, does it seem like this gap exists, or not so much?

Why do you think this (is or is not)?

For people who are struggling, what might they do to improve their situation?

Concrete example?

Stepping back a bit, in your view, why do some people in society struggle financially and yet others do so well?

ECONOMIC GROWTH IN THE AREA (AND MORAL DILEMMAS OF WEALTH)

A couple of questions about recent economic developments in the community. Remember, there is no right or wrong answer, but only your opinions . . .

Recently, I've read a bit in the local newspaper where some folks who have been critical of all of the wealth that has accumulated in Jackson Hole (not my intention in this book). Some have condemned it as morally wrong. Have you ever encountered this sort of thinking?

> [If yes] Can you give me a concrete example? How did this make you feel?
>
> [If no] How do you think this would make you feel?

What kinds of people tend to criticize wealth?

> Why?
>
> What do these people tend to have in common with each other?
>
> Have people ever criticized you directly?

Some longtimers (for example, ranchers) I've talked with are especially critical of the amount of wealth that has accumulated in the area. It doesn't seem to be pure envy or jealousy, but something else that I'm trying to put my finger on. In your opinion, what might be behind these feelings?

Some say that jealousy is all relative. Consider a hypothetical example: a homeless person in destitute poverty might express resentment and jealousy about someone that you and I might still consider to be living in poverty (despite having a great deal more than that homeless person).
So, are the negative feelings that outsiders express about Jackson wealth an example of relative jealousy, or something qualitatively different?

Have you ever felt criticized or judged concerning wealth?

> Why? Concrete example?

It seems that some people have tried to make wealthy people feel guilty . . . have you ever personally felt this way? Explain?

> [If yes] Is it temporary or ongoing? How do you deal with or soothe this guilt?

Some talk about responsibility . . . that the wealthier should have a higher responsibility? Be held to a higher standard. Or how would you put it?

> In your view, should the wealthy have to justify the morality of their choices to others?
> [If no] Why not?
> [If yes] What sorts of reasons might justify it? Explain.

This area is often referred by people as a "playground for the rich." In your view, what do people mean when they use this phrase?

> What kinds of people tend to use it?

In your view, does the increase in wealth have a positive or negative effect on the area?

> In what specific ways?
> Environmentally? (Ask them to reflect.)
> On the types of people in the area? (Ask them to reflect.)
> On cost of living? (Ask them to reflect.)

A lot of these questions have to do with debates about what it means to be a good person. And different definitions of that. More generally (to get philosophical on you), what makes a person "good"?

> Why? Concrete examples?

In your view, what makes an act right or wrong?

> Is it rules or laws? Consequences? How it feels? God's will?
> What kinds of "feelings" do you mean?
> Where do those feelings come from, in your view?
> What kinds of "consequences"?
> How clear is right and wrong?

NATURE

Last, a few questions about nature . . .

Just in general, how would you describe your relationship to
nature?

Can you describe for me your ideal natural area? Why this, but
not another area?

What sorts of ways do you enjoy nature?

What sorts of knowledge skills does this require?
How did you come to learn such skills?

If you pick up a newspaper on a given day, there has been a
lot of talk about right and wrong with regard to the natural environment. How do you personally determine what is
right or wrong for the environment for a given issue?

Have you been involved in philanthropic efforts in the area,
especially relating to the environment?

[If yes] Tell me about these efforts. Concrete example?
How did you get involved? Are friends of yours also
involved?
[If no] Do you feel a responsibility to get involved? Why or
why not?
Are you involved in any other nonenvironmental
philanthropy efforts?

If you were to get more involved, what sorts of environmental
efforts might interest you most?

[Ask all of these:]
Buying green products?
Protecting land from development?
Serving on the board of a local organization?
Giving money privately? [If yes, to which sorts of causes?]

If you could, would you hit the pause button on
development?

While there is not much land left, population and land
development are increasing. In your view, how important is it to protect nature by limiting further land
development?

[If yes] Why? What are most important? Limiting
residential development? Commercial? Recreational?
[If no] Why not?

One recent issue that has been in the news is the building
of low-income housing in and around Jackson Hole.
Proponents say that building new neighborhoods is
necessary to accommodate growth, while opponents say
that it threatens wildlife and Jackson's small-town character.
What are your thoughts on this?

Why? Explain.
On what bases should decisions about low-income housing
be made? (For example, science about environmental
impacts, preserving small-town character, human rights
needs for worker housing, ostensibly they could build a
high-rise.)

I've heard some say that it's just a fact of life that not everyone
can live there. People can simply commute (like people do
in other cities) if they want to work there. What are your
thoughts on this solution?

Why is it such a big issue in Jackson if commuting is normal
in other cities?

Many people who need affordable housing in the area are
immigrants from Mexico. Have you by chance interacted
much with this population?

In your view, what are the impacts of Jackson Hole growing
more diverse?

Others to talk with (snowball sampling)
Those are all my questions. Is there anything else you would
like to add?
Can you name two or three others you know well who would
be good to talk with? Contact info?

Low-Income Interview Guide

INTRODUCTION

First, can you tell me a little bit about yourself?

Where you grew up?
Where is "home" now?
Married? Kids?

Can you explain to me what kind of work do you do?
How did you happen to get into this line of work?
If you would compare how things are now at work to how they were ten years ago, have things changed? How?
Do you have someone you really like at work? What are the qualities you like in this person?
How would you describe your boss? How do they treat you? What do you like about them? What *don't* you like about them?

Can you give an example?

How do you get to work? What is commuting like? Can you describe it?
More generally, what would you define now as your goals in life? Do you consider yourself to be successful? Why?

COMMUNITY AND CHANGES

Next are some questions about your opinions and experiences in the area . . .

Are you the first in your family to come to this community, or did earlier generations live here as well?

[If yes] So, tell me the story. Which of your family came here first? Where did they come from? When did they come? And why did they settle here?
[If no] Tell me the story of how you came to live here? When did you come? Where had you been before? And why did you come here?

How do you like living and working in this community?

I'd like you to take a typical day for you in the area—and walk me through it. Start in the morning and go through the day for me. [Probe by asking what happened next and whether anything else happened.]

What kinds of things do you like to do when you are not working? (Leisure time, activities?)

What would you say the best thing is about living in this community?—Can you give me an example—something that would illustrate what is really nice about living here?— Why is that special to you?

And what is the worst thing about living here? Or something you would change if you could?—Give me an example about that?

Do you feel that you know most people around Jackson Hole? How could you get to know more people?

Do you feel that you are part of this community? In what ways? If not, why don't you feel part of this community? How does this make you feel?

Would you say that Jackson Hole has a strong sense of community?

What is a concrete example that might illustrate this? If not, why?

How could the sense of community in the Jackson area be improved?

How would you personally define "community"?

OTHER COMMUNITY MEMBERS

Some questions about your opinion of people who live in the Jackson area. Again, we are just interested in your own private and confidential opinion . . .

Do you think there are similarities and differences in the cultures of the various groups that live in your community? What differences? What similarities?

If you think about the culture of Latino people and the culture
of non-Latino people generally, what would you say are the
positives and negatives of each culture?

If I asked you to describe to me in general the kind of people
you like, what are the qualities that are most important to
you?

Is there someone you admire a lot? Do you have a hero?
Someone you look up to, whom you can use as a role
model?—What qualities do you particularly admire in this
person?

Could you tell me, in general, what kind of people you don't
like? In life, how would you describe the kind of people who
get on your nerves?

Does it happen to you sometimes that you feel inferior or
superior to certain people? What kind of people make you
feel one way or the other? Concrete example?

How are things financially for people in Jackson these days?
Are people pretty well off, having difficulties, or what?—
Without mentioning any names, can you give me an
example of somebody who has been having difficulties
lately?

Some communities have a large gap between the "haves"
and "have-nots," while other communities do not. In your
experience, does it seem like this gap exists, or not so
much?

Why do you think this gap exists?

For people who are struggling, what might they do to improve
their situation?—Concrete example?

More broadly, in your view, why do some people in
society struggle to make ends meet, and yet others do so
well?

What is your general opinion about very wealthy people?—Do
you think about them a lot? What comes to mind?—Can
you give an example of a specific interaction?

In your view, are very wealthy people deserving of all their money?

In your view, do wealthy people in Jackson generally have a positive or negative effect on the community?—In what specific ways? Concrete examples . . .

What ways do they affect the community positively? Concrete examples . . .

What ways do they affect the community negatively? Concrete examples . . .

What ways do they affect the natural environment? Concrete examples . . .

How would you describe the local Latino community's relationship to wealthy people?—How often do you interact with very wealthy people?

Other than having a large house, how can you tell if someone in Jackson is wealthy? If no answer, ask about clothing, dress, style, activities.

NATURE

Last, a few questions about nature . . .

Just in general, how would you describe your relationship to the natural environment?

What sorts of ways do you enjoy nature?—What specific activities, hobbies?

How often do you get to enjoy nature in these ways?

In general, how do you feel about conservation or preservation?

Explain.

What are your opinions about restricting construction in order to protect the natural environment?

Why? Explain.

What are your thoughts about building more affordable
housing?

How does the affordable housing issue relate to the natural
environment?

Those are all my questions. Is there anything else you would
like to add?

Notes to Introduction

1. Wealth-X (2017a, 2017b, 2018). See chapter 1 for much more on the recent rise of the ultra-wealthy class.

2. Bureau of Economic Analysis (2014), https://www.bea.gov/newsreleases /regional/lapi/lapi_highlights.pdf. According to the Bureau of Economic Analysis, "Per capita personal income—personal income divided by population—is a useful metric for making comparisons of the level of personal income across counties." Note: Defined as per-capita income.

3. Economic Policy Institute (2016). Also see Schiller (2016).

It is important to note that economic inequality can be measured in a variety of complex ways (for example, including wages, income, wealth, and living standards), but any way you slice it, there is a widening gap between the rich and poor that began in earnest in the 1970s. For more on this topic, see the research of Claude S. Fischer (2017), including this recent insightful discussion of these issues in the *Boston Review* article, "Inequality Is about Access to Public Goods, Not Income."

Throughout this book, I use the phrase "wealth inequality" because it includes people's assets and thus is a more robust measure. I use the phrase "income inequality" when specifically discussing income data. Income is also a common measure, but as Claude S. Fischer and others note, income is far less stable over time and not a holistic indicator of a person or family's economic well-being.

4. To reiterate, my goal here is intellectual honesty and a depth of careful reasoning and critique, in contrast to the hasty and shallow intellectual climate in which we live, where the swirling chaos of information has left us with a case of moral and intellectual vertigo, dizzied by hasty and shallow thought, confined to our tribalistic echo-chambers, and reliant on thoughtless caricatures of the cultural and political Other. The facts speak for themselves—and in this case, the facts are much more interesting than overly simplistic and dehumanizing clichés of contempt, resentment, or dismissal.

An important note on terms used throughout the book: The term "ultra-wealthy" is used very specifically in accordance with the definition and measurement bounds laid out in the appendix (also see the following note 7). So as not to be repetitive with the term "ultra-wealthy," I at times also employ the word "rich" and "affluent" in similarly specific ways *to refer to this same ultra-wealthy group* who are the focus in this book, rather than some other vague group of people who might have money but are not "ultra-wealthy." All similar monikers denote the ultra-wealthy. As such, the term "rich" is not meant to be pejorative, despite some of its popular connotations.

5. In the following, I introduce and discuss the very small—yet excellent and recently growing—body of research on the ultra-wealthy.

6. Additional interviews and observation were conducted at the Yellowstone Club and its surrounding communities (i.e. Big Sky, Bozeman). As the subject of chapter 2, the Yellowstone Club is one of the most exclusive private clubs in the world, counting among its members many prominent CEOs (e.g., Microsoft founder Bill Gates, Google's Eric Schmidt).

7. Importantly, see the appendix for details on all components of this research project.

1. Most critically, the protection of anonymity for all research subjects. For quotes or attributions from interviews or conversations during fieldwork, I use pseudonyms in all cases to protect the identity of respondents. Any descriptions of persons use multiple layers of security to ensure anonymity, while preserving the substantive meaning of who they are relative to the particular topic being discussed in the text. See the appendix for an extended discussion on this important process.

2. How I defined the social groups "ultra-wealthy" and "working poor," and descriptive statistics on each interview sample set.

3. Sampling and recruitment methods (i.e. Purposive and Snowball), as well as information on the representativeness of the sample.

4. Fieldwork and interview coding processes.

5. Interview guides used.

8. My paired approach here is inspired by an important line of work with similar labor and class dynamics at play, beginning with Judith Rollins's (1987) pioneering study of female domestic workers, Pierrette Hondagneu-Sotelo's (2007) study of immigrant workers in Los Angeles, Corey Dolgon's (2006) study of class struggle in the Hamptons, and Rachel Sherman's (2007) inside look at hotel workers who cater to wealthy patrons.

9. As I note in the introduction to part 4, Michèle Lamont and Charles Tilly have both, in different ways, paved the way for this type of paired approach. Lamont et al. (2014: 583), a leading expert on the culture of inequality, reminds us that "cultural processes do not solely depend on the actions of dominant actors . . . subordinates often participate in the elaboration of cultural processes as much as dominant agents do (e.g., in self-racialization through self-identification or self-stigmatization). Furthermore, the sorting can result from intentional actions or as an unintended consequence."

And, similarly, the novel work of Charles Tilly suggested that future research investigate in more detail these "paired" groups of people, rather than just those at the top or those at the bottom. Most notably, see his influential 1998 book *Durable Inequality*.

10. For example, the upscale Shooting Star club prominently displays this on their homepage. See http://www.shootingstarjh.com.

For more on these Bloomberg rankings, see Shooting Star Jackson Hole (2017), "Wyoming Tax Benefits," and, Business Journal (2004), "Wyoming Ranked No. 1 as 'Wealth-Friendly' State."

11. I replaced the name of this new development with a pseudonym to protect the identity of Hector and Dolorita. And because of their undocumented status, I have also slightly edited a few other details about them that are not pertinent to the facts presented in the chapter. As with the ultra-wealthy, this ensures that they will not be identified.

12. In chapter 8, I incorporate valuable neuroscientific work that, while not focused narrowly on the *ultra*-wealthy, still provides valuable insight into the psychological and moral effects of having money—for example, Dietze and Knowles (2016); Varnum et al. (2015); and Varnum et al. (2016).

13. Even though this center is now defunct, its website contains previous research reports and articles. Boston College University (2015), "Center on Wealth and Philanthropy.

14. Ostrander (1984); Kendall (2002).

15. Khan (2012); Howard and Gaztambide-Fernández (2010); Gaztambide-Fernández (2009); Stevens (2009); Armstrong and Hamilton (2015).

16. Lindsay (2007).

17. Kroch (1996); Zweig (2004).

18. Page and Gilens (2017); Suhay et al. (2018).

19. For a few excellent recent pieces in this literature, see Hahl et al. (2017); Johnston and Baumann (2007).

20. Ho (2009).

21. This is a huge body of research; for a recent example by leaders in the field, see Pinçon-Charlot and Pinçon (2018).

22. Rivera (2015).

23. Schor (1998).

24. Farrell (2016a); Farrell (2016b); Farrell (2019); Farrell et al. (2019).

25. For an overview, see Khan (2012). For methodological avenues, and several examples in a special issue on elites, see Cousin et al. (2018).

26. Sherman (2017).

27. Schimpfössl (2018).

28. Kuusela (2018); Kantola and Kuusela (2019).

29. Desmond (2016: 317). Later, in an interview about *Evicted*, Desmond expands upon this point, "There is a larger point here about the way we think about poverty. With books about single mothers, gang members, or the homeless, social scientists and journalists have a tendency to write about poor people as if they are cut off from the rest of society. These accounts exclude rich people— or, at least, non-poor people—who wield enormous influence over the lives of low-income families and their communities. I've always wondered why we have

documented how the poor struggle to make ends meet without asking why their bills are so high or where their money is flowing." Link to interview: https://www.penguinrandomhouse.com/books/247816/evicted-by-matthew-desmond/9780553447453/.

30. Piketty and Goldhammer (2014); Volscho and Kelly (2012); Young et al. (2016); Hacker and Pierson (2011).

31. Hochschild (2016: 5). Also see Musa al Gharbi's (2018) article examining how left-leaning biases shaped academic studies of the 2016 presidential election.

32. An excellent example is the study of social movements, which had been plagued by a singular focus on left-wing movements, with the civil rights movement being the paramount case. For many years, scholars were much less likely to conduct research on right-wing, and other so-called awkward, movements because they were less ideologically appealing than progressive movements, it was more emotionally taxing to encounter a challenging worldview, and in the end they provided less practical payoff relative to the left-leaning personal views of the researcher. This took a toll on the discipline because not only did it limit the types of people and movements that were being studied, but also it limited the types of difficult questions being asked, limited the unexpected puzzles that might arise, and most importantly, limited our general scientific knowledge about how movements work.

33. For more on this topic, see Cousin et al. (2018); Hertz and Imber (1995); Van Pelt (2013).

34. Harrington (2016); Kahn and Katz (2018).

35. As I describe throughout later chapters, I am guided in this research process by the thinking of sociologist Michèle Lamont, through her boundary-work approach to community and culture.

36. Grusky et al. (2015).

37. A major exception to this point is the field of rural sociology. Despite its rich history and important legacy, mainstream sociology has—to its own detriment—not integrated contributions from rural research into primary discussions in the discipline. For excellent examples of recent rural research, see Brown (2003); Lichter and Brown (2011); Smith and Tickamyer (2011); Smith and Krannich (2000); de Sherbinin et al. (2008); Smith et al. (2001).

38. Park and Pellow (2011).

39. Pellow and Brehm (2013); Park and Pellow (2011); Taylor (2016); Mohai et al. (2009).

Notes to Chapter 1

1. Scores of books and articles have crunched the numbers and provided the economic facts about the U.S. takeoff in wealth inequality. There's no need here to rehash all of the national numbers that have already been crunched. For that, see the following citations. But what we lack is a firsthand look into the everyday experiences of people—especially the ultra-wealthy. What do people like Jim actually think about this massive concentration of wealth, in which they play the leading

role? And how do people like Jim understand and deal with the environmental and social problems that some say extreme wealth is responsible for creating?

See Piketty and Goldhammer (2014); Volscho and Kelly (2012); Young et al. (2016); Hacker and Pierson (2011).

2. White et al. (2018).

3. U.S. Bureau of Economic Analysis (2014). For state-level income data, see the helpful Grusky et al. (2015).

Median family income in Teton County is $96,113, putting it in the top 2.6 percent of all U.S. counties. For more, see U.S. Census Bureau (2015, 2016).

4. Wealth-X (2017a, 2017b, 2018).

5. This is part of a broader national trend in the stagnation of worker wages, despite increasing productivity. One source of the problem is that workers are receiving smaller shares of the corporate income pie, especially since 2000. Worker productivity continued to rise, while compensation stagnated. The Economic Policy Institute (2015b) notes in a report that "Between 2000 and the second quarter of 2015, the share of income generated by corporations that went to workers' wages (instead of going to capital incomes like profits) declined from 82.3 percent to 75.5 percent. . . . This 6.8 percentage-point decline in labor's share of corporate income might not seem like a lot, but if labor's share had not fallen this much, employees in the corporate sector would have $535 billion more in their paychecks today. If this amount was spread over the entire labor force (not just corporate sector employees) this would translate into a $3,770 raise for each worker."

For data on the increase in worker productivity and the stagnation of wages, see Economic Policy Institute (2018). For data on the declining share of corporate-sector income by workers, see Economic Policy Institute (2015a).

6. For an overview of research on what has come to be called the "New West," see chapters 1 and 2 in Farrell (2015a) and Burow et al. (2019). Also see the excellent work of Ray Rasker and Headwaters Economics for the most up-to-date socioeconomic findings on New West communities, including the cities and counties that are experiencing the greatest influx of wealthy migrants, and the role that natural amenities and public lands play in this process. To understand the important ways that gender influences family and migration in the New West, see Schmalzbauer (2014). After completing this current book, I came across the two excellent articles that similarly examine rural gentrification by middle class in-migrants within the theoretical paradigm of shifting regimes of production/consumption in capitalism and modernity: Hines (2007, 2012).

7. See Hancock (2016). In addition to this investigation, I had a handful of ultra-wealthy folks proudly tell me about their friends' success in creating corporate shells in Wyoming. Also see Swanson (2017).

8. For example, the upscale Shooting Star club prominently displays this on its homepage. See http://www.shootingstarjh.com; also see Shooting Star Jackson Hole (2017), "Wyoming Tax Benefits," and the Business Journal (2004) article, "Wyoming Ranked No. 1 as 'Wealth-Friendly' State.

9. This quote is a representative example, taken from Linton Properties in Jackson Hole. See http://lintonbingle.com/.

10. For more on this, including a visualization of this discrepancy over time, see the Charture Institute and Jackson Hole News and Guide (2017), *Jackson Hole Compass*.

11. Internal Revenue Service (2015). Also see Scheiber and Cohen (2015).

12. For more on this topic, see pages 47–48 in Hacker and Pierson (2011).

13. For example, see page 67 in Farrell (2015a).

14. Economic Policy Institute (2015a).

15. For data behind these figures, see Grusky et al. (2015). Other data are based on 2013 tax returns: Economic Policy Institute (2019). I focus here on local indicators, but there are innumerable studies on income inequality at the national level. For starters, see the seminal, and wide-ranging work, of economists Thomas Picketty and Emmanuel Saez. For more on the national politics behind income inequality, see the work of Jacob Hacker and Paul Pierson. These should serve as introductions to what is a huge field of study. My goal here was not to get lost in this field of study, but to keep our focus on the local community level, which as I've argued throughout this book, has been neglected in work on income inequality.

16. Volscho and Kelly (2012).

17. Buffett (2013).

Notes to Chapter 2

1. I use real names in this paragraph because their membership (current or past) is widely known public information and because I did not conduct interviews with any of these individuals. As laid out in detail in the appendix, I take great care to protect the anonymity of all respondents who participated in this study.

2. Missoulian (2007).

3. Yellowstone Club (2016).

4. Cohan (2008).

5. There are dozens of articles about the early years. These two are particularly good because they include early conversations with Tim Blixseth and members, such as Cohan (2008); Dolan (2004).

6. Clifford (2016).

7. See "Fact Sheet: Dues and Assessments," in Yellowstone Club (2018).

8. Yellowstone Club (2016).

9. Flowers (2010).

10. Steiner (2009).

11. For example, see Park and Pellow (2011); Nelson and Nelson (2011); Pager (2007); Sachs et al. (2014).

12. Note: Colin used "socialism" and "communism" interchangeably, despite their significant historical and conceptual differences. Following Colin's lead, I make no distinction between the two in the text.

13. As mentioned earlier, the member names were collected via public tax and real estate records.

14. Fortunately, by this time I had completed enough interviews and observation that these cancellations did not affect the validity of my sample. In fact, the

timing of these events was fortunate, because I was able to conduct interviews after the club had contacted members attempting to sow seeds of distrust about my intentions. Thus, the interviews in the wake of these events provided insight into how members sought to guard the privacy of the club, mostly through giving basic "company-line" answers. These cases provided interesting data that led to insights about the construction and maintenance of ultra-wealthy privacy and paranoia in this case.

Note to Part II

1. There is a huge literature on "environmental justice" that examines the underbelly of environmentalism, but there is much less work about those at the top, which is why I describe this story as "alternative," "new," etc. See my discussion of literature on environmental justice and environmental privilege in the introduction.

Notes to Chapter 3

1. This is not unique to the ultra-wealthy. I see its effects regularly among the students (and faculty colleagues tasked with training them) during my day-to-day life teaching in an environmental studies department, full of students who are the future leaders of environmental conservation.

2. The exception being the last section of this book, where I examine those at the bottom of the socioeconomic ladder in Teton County, based on exhaustive interviews. Even still, this section reflects on their views of the ultra-wealthy, viewing these groups as interconnected through "linked migration," rather than separate. Their dependence on each other means that they *cannot* be analyzed separately or understood apart from each other.

3. Hunter et al. (2005); Headwaters Economics (2017, 2018); Pennsylvania Land Trust Association (2012).

4. See "Tax Implications" in Jackson Hole Land Trust (2016).

5. Merton (1968). The title of Merton's seminal *Science* article refers to the New Testament biblical passage Matthew 25:29, "For to everyone who has, more shall be given, and he will have an abundance; but from the one who does not have, even what he does have shall be taken away." New American Standard Translation. DiPrete and Eirich (2006); Willson et al. (2007); Angle (1986).

6. U.S. Census Bureau (2018). Also see the Western Greater Yellowstone Region Housing Needs Assessment from Rees Consulting et al. (2014).

7. McMullen (2016).

8. Anecdotal analysis on the prevalence of this phrase shows that it has exploded on the scene in popular and academic discourse alike. For example, explore "income inequality" on Google Ngram Viewer, http://books.google.com/ngrams/, and Google Search Trends, http://www.google.com/trends/.

9. Chapters 5 and 6 examine this relationship in great depth.

10. For these data, and more on this topic, see Charture Institute and Jackson Hole News and Guide (2017).

Notes to Chapter 4

1. Of course, there are centuries of work on this topic. For a quick summary relative to environmental issues, see the introduction in Farrell (2015a).

2. For more on this, see the large and diverse body of work within environmental sociology, beginning with Allan Schnaiberg's seminal "Treadmill of Production" theory and paradigm.

3. See chapter 3 for more on the impact of the Jackson Hole Land Trust.

4. *New York Times* columnist David Brooks has similarly written about what he calls "Cell Phone Naturalists." While I am focused on the ultra-wealthy in particular, there are commonalities about the obvious (and largely ignored) contradictions between consumerism and the natural experiences people seek.

5. For more on this, see Pellow and Park's "Aspen Logic," Park and Pellow (2011).

6. Of course, there is a long history of the study of modern rationalization, beginning most prominently in the work of Max Weber. With regard to the natural environment, I will not go into too much more depth here, as I have written at length about these processes of rationalization and science in my previous book (Farrell 2015a). Lamont and colleagues (2016) have recently written about cultural processes related to rationalization and "standardization," showing how they can become *cultural* processes of inequality.

7. Much has been written about a similar phenomenon with regard to corporate responsibility, and so-called greenwashing. Albeit different context and issues, what I am describing here has similar qualities, and certainly has a lot in common with this literature.

8. Griskevicius et al. (2010).

Notes to Chapter 5

1. Italic emphasis added to match vocal emphasis of George, stressing ultra-wealthy philanthropy as the answer to the stated problems in the first part of the quote.

2. As I will explain later in the chapter, philanthropy in Teton County has taken on qualities akin to what Peter Buffett—son of billionaire Warren Buffett—has called the "Charitable-Industrial-Complex." See Buffett (2013).

3. Conover (2015: 53).

4. Farrell (2015a).

5. Conover (2015: 53). For more on these issues of turnover, as well as definitions of nonprofit "success" in the Greater Yellowstone Ecosystem, see these two excellent works: Clark and Rutherford (2014); Cherney (2011).

6. All text is directly from Willow Street Trust Company website; see Willow Street Group (2019).

7. Given that I am using pseudonyms throughout this book to protect the identity of my respondents, the quoted name of this foundation uses the same pseudonym for George and Annie Butler.

8. U.S. Bureau of Economic Analysis (2014).

9. The Community Center for the Arts was missing a single entry in 1999, and the Latino Resource Center was missing a single entry in 2003. In both cases, I imputed data using a calculated mean from the year before and the year after.

10. To increase efficiency and secure the future functioning of health and human services offerings in Teton County, three of the most prominent organizations merged in 2016: the Latino Resource Center, El Puente, and the Community Resource Center. This organization is now known as One22.

11. Social network analysis is a common form of social scientific analysis, and I do my best here to describe the methods and findings in nontechnical terms.

12. Full-size vectorized images of these graphs are available at www.JustinFarrell .org.

13. Influence ranking is calculated based on betweenness centrality on a one-mode graph of organization to organization ties (e.g., organizations are linked by virtue of a shared board member).

14. This graph is a one-mode version of the bipartite graph displayed in two previous figures (see figures 5.4 and 5.1).

15. Influence is operationalized using the standard Betweenness Centrality measure from network science. This measure is especially useful for my purposes here because I am quantifying which organizations have the most power within the network with regard to flows of information and resources, which often amounts to influence.

16. See "View22 Project Continues and Expands in 2014," in Jackson Hole Land Trust (2014).

17. This is a one-mode graph of all person-to-person connections, based on their shared connections to an organization. The graph is plotted using the Fruchterman-Reingold algorithm.

18. As with everyone in this book, these are real people, but I use a pseudonym.

Notes to Chapter 6

1. For excellent examples, see Giridharadas (2018); Callahan (2017); Smith and Davidson (2014); Ostrander (2010). Also see Francie Ostrower's classic study of elite benefactors from New York City, Ostrower (1995). For an insightful review of sociological work on philanthropy, see Barman (2017). For influence of elite philanthropists on science and environment, see Farrell (2015a, 2016a, 2016b, 2019) and Farrell et al. (2019). On the financial industry takeover of nonprofit boards, see Jenkins (2015) and Aldrich (1997). For many more resources, see the excellent Lilly Family School of Philanthropy at Indiana University.

2. Data are from the nonpartisan Congressional Budget Office, and their "Trends in Family Wealth, 1989 to 2013" program. See U.S. Congressional Budget Office (2016).

3. Part 3 of this book explores these themes of interclass contact in considerable depth.

4. In this section, I use the phrase "nature" instead of "natural environment" to emphasize the cultural meanings that have been layered onto the physical properties that make up ecosystems.

5. These themes are explored in much more detail in the part 3 of this book on how the rich use nature and rural culture to solve their social problems. But, as I have shown in the four chapters that make up part 2, nature plays a central role in this process, and is not easily disentangled from ideas about, and the use of, rural culture.

6. For a masterful analysis of racial and ethnic dimensions of nativism, see Park and Pellow (2011).

7. Wyoming State Historical Society (2014).

8. For an excellent overview focused on the processes inherent to large-scale conservation, see Clark et al. (2014).

9. See especially chapter 4, on what I define to be "Connoisseur Conservation."

10. Emphasis added to highlight the passive inflection in his voice. This emphasis is telling because he did not say "I got involved" but that people he met in the community "*Got me* involved."

11. There is a massive literature in sociology at the intersection of residential segregation, poverty, and race/ethnicity. The field is too broad and deep to offer a single citation here, but I point the reader toward the discipline of sociology in particular, on these issues, for quantitative and qualitative insight. Relatedly, also of interest is the transdisciplinary "contact hypothesis" that has been explored in psychology, criminology, and sociology, testing the importance of intergroup contact for awareness and reducing group conflicts.

12. For example, we see this in other arenas of environmental politics. In other research, I have written about how private giving created a national movement to spread misinformation about the facts of climate change, and manufactured widespread doubt within the American public where none had existed before. Climate change went from being a bipartisan issue with widespread support (e.g., George H. W. Bush and majority of Republicans) to being one of the hottest-button and most polarizing issues of the day. This dramatic shift was no accident, but rather was due to an incredibly successful movement underwritten by wealthy foundations. See Farrell (2015a, 2016a, 2016b, 2019); Farrell et al. (2019).

13. Callahan (2017: 7).

14. Buffett (2013).

Notes to Part III

1. But see this book's introduction for a review of the small, but growing, body of research on the ultra-wealthy.

2. For example, Marx's classic theory of a "ruling class" elite, who control the means of material production; Thorstein Veblen's "leisure class," made up of wealthy individuals who gain status and exert social control through conspicuous consumption and public displays of leisure; C. Wright Mills's classic "power elite," who deploy interwoven military, political, and corporate channels of power to

control society from the top-down; E. Digby Baltzell's concept of the WASP; and William Domhoff's classic studies of the upper-middle-class power elite in his book *Who Rules America?* My book shares a lot in common with these approaches and their underlying theory of plutocratic and elite social control, as I have demonstrated in the chapters leading up to part 3.

Notes to Chapter 7

1. There is a huge literature on cultural omnivorousness as a way to understand the intersections of consumption, culture, power, and social class. The debate began in earnest in the early 1990s, led by sociologist Richard Peterson. This literature is certainly relevant here, and the ultra-wealthy are certainly engaging in cultural omnivorousness, but the issues at stake go well beyond taste profiles, to much deeper moral and existential issues about the impact of wealth on a person, how that person struggles to reconcile wealth with the type of person they think they should become, and how the nonwealthy are used by the ultra-wealthy as a source for regeneration, but also the source of social stigmatization and gatekeepers for social recognition.

2. My main finding in this chapter fits within a larger and active body of work investigating how certain high-status groups overcome feelings of authenticity-insecurity brought on by outsider denigration. Most notably, see the excellent article by Hahl et al. (2017). Also relevant is a recent study of cultural elites in Norway (Ljungren 2015). See a related analysis of the valorization of authenticity and exoticism, using the case of gourmet food, by Johnston and Baumann (2007). Last, the Pulitzer Prize–winning book *The Radicalism of the American Revolution* (Wood 1991) touches on the historical use of the term "friends" among unequal groups in early American colonies, which is relevant to this chapter, as many ultra-wealthy desire "friendships" with moneyless people in the community. Those interested in the historical lineage of the meaning of "friendship" between different social classes should refer to this book.

3. In this chapter, I refer to both the "working poor" and the "working class," which are two different socioeconomic groups, but their romanticized cultural styles, *and the shared way that they are idealized by the ultra-wealthy*, mean that they share many similarities in this specific case. I employ both terms throughout the chapter (in addition to "low-income") based on their relationship to the ultra-wealthy, and the way they are romanticized and often lumped together in oversimplified ways.

4. This is not the first study to identify elite attempts to become "normal." For example, see the recent excellent work by Sherman (2017).

5. Stellar et al. (2012); Varnum et al. (2015); Dietze and Knowles (2016); Varnum et al. (2016). Also see the following journalistic piece by two religious studies scholars, Charles Mathewes and Evan Sandsmark, who cite much more research on this topic (Mathewes and Sandsmark 2017).

6. Paraphrased quotation from Baer (2017).

7. Chua and Zou (2009); Mathewes and Sandsmark (2017); Marsh (2012).

8. Lamont et al. (2014: 17) proposes a few different definitions of "stigma," beginning with Goffman's "an attribute that is deeply discrediting."

For an excellent example of recent research on the relationship between stigmas and maintaining moral worth, see Cohen and Dromi (2018).

9. Farrell (2014).

10. Marsh (2012).

11. Much ink has been spilled about Ronald Inglehart's "post-materialism" theory, which has some similarities with what I am arguing here about the ultra-wealthy. Both Inglehart as well as Maslow's own hierarchy of needs theory have value here insofar as the material needs of the ultra-wealthy have been thoroughly met (and far-exceeded), so now they are indeed looking to satisfy these "higher" needs of self-actualization, intellectual curiosity, self-fulfillment, and so on.

I do not, however, buy whole cloth into either of these theories, especially the ways the arguments have been universalized to any developed culture that has attained material needs, assuming a linear process and progress of post-materialism (or Maslow's theory) will necessarily follow. Surely, I did find that the ultra-wealthy are seeking self-fulfillment, but as I showed in part 2 of this book, they are also continuing to seek material gain, and are not that seriously concerned with raising the standard of living for the rest of the world. Furthermore, the attempt at what I call "regeneration" or "self-fulfillment" is part of a larger effort to gain social acceptance among the nonwealthy, and the community at large, rather than regeneration just being a higher end in itself.

12. The following discussion and labels of the four stages of wealth in American culture are heavily indebted to Fluck (2003).

13. Ibid., 69.

14. Lamont et al. (2014).

15. The dynamics explored here, and throughout this chapter, inform and are informed by large bodies of research from several different fields of study. Ones that are especially relevant, and no doubt play a role in shaping ultra-wealthy worldviews, include the following: the romanticized idea of primitive "Noble Savages," who are viewed as innately good because they live beyond the corrupting reach of cities and civilization; Edward Said's concept of "Orientalism," which describes a condescending attitude that one culture can hold for another, often rooted in the view that the inferior culture is fixed in time as simplistic and static; and last, notions of cultural appropriation and/or "xenocentrism," meaning the predilection and adoption of a different culture's tastes, ideas, and way of life.

16. One prominent example in recent years is the emergence of the twenty-first-century "hipster." The modern hipster might be an example of the cultural omnivorousness described in the part 3 opener notes, rather than the type of moral and cultural refashioning I'm describing here, which has its roots in stigmatization and the struggles that immense wealth presents for becoming the type of person you envision.

17. Here, I've adapted the sardonic narrative of Paris-based writer Cody Delistraty. See Delistraty (2013); this insightful article also informed the vehicle for escapism theme discussed in the following.

Notes to Chapter 8

1. Guilt itself can take various forms. We may feel guilty for an act we've committed (e.g., lying, stealing, smoking, drinking), or we may feel guilty about something we didn't do (e.g., making time for someone who is suffering), or we may feel guilty about our success in life compared to others (e.g., making it out of poverty when others are left behind; surviving a tragedy when others died). Guilt is a common theme in psychology, beginning with Freud's own thinking on the subject. No doubt, guilt is also closely related to the general concept of "sin" that pervades many major religions, especially Judaism, Christianity, and Islam, which is itself informed by Ancient Greek (especially Platonic) concepts of honor, fault, moral culpability, and guilt.

2. See chapter 7 for more on the growing criticism of wealth, as well as some of the inherent contradictions in this criticism relative to popular modern mass consumerism and consumption.

3. Interestingly, and somewhat paradoxically, their view of income inequality (vague/not local) was the polar opposite of their interaction with environmental issues explored in part 2 (specific/local). The broader (and sometime more vague) environmental issues like climate change rarely were mentioned as a problem. In other words, when it came to societal problems, there was a tendency to pick and choose which local problems to see as important.

4. Stellar et al. (2012); Varnum et al. (2015); Dietze and Knowles (2016); Varnum et al. (2016). Also see the following journalistic piece by two religious studies scholars, Charles Mathewes and Evan Sandsmark, who cite much more research on this topic (Mathewes and Sandsmark 2017).

5. To be clear, however, I am not a psychotherapist, and thus I proceed with caution here, being careful not to exaggerate this finding or get out ahead of my skis relative to this defense mechanism I encountered.

6. Grusky and Kricheli-Katz (2012: 5–6).

7. Emphasis added.

8. In psychology, see, for example, Rothschild et al. (2012). In sociology, the recent and excellent work of Rachel Sherman (2017) has revealed how affluent New Yorkers wrestle with these issues, and the work they do to deal internally with guilt, in order to maintain their vision of themselves as morally worthy people.

9. For a recent historical account of how this has happened, see the book by a similar name, *Winner-Take-All-Politics*, by Yale political scientist Jacob Hacker and Berkeley political scientist Paul Pierson (Hacker and Pierson 2011).

Notes to Part IV

1. Lamont et al. (2014: 11).

2. Most notably, see his influential 1998 book *Durable Inequality* (Tilly 1998).

3. A handful of other interviews included leaders who have emerged from within this community, or who are working directly on many of the issues that affect this working poor community (for example, housing, wages, political representation).

Notes to Chapter 9

1. As unpacked in more detail in chapter 1, the average income for the top 1 percent in Teton County is $28,163,786. This is by far the highest for all counties in the United States. Average income is obviously skewed by billionaires, but in some ways that is the point, and as I show in this chapter, median income is similarly sky high. See chapter 1 for comprehensive figures of income and income inequality in Teton County. For more on living situations among the local working poor, see Latino Resource Center (2015); Schrank (2015); Barber (2016).

2. It is not until chapter 10 that I unpack the growing chorus of criticism, and accusations of ultra-wealth hypocrisy and injustice, that has begun to spring up from within the working-poor community in Teton County.

3. For example, see Beyerlein and Hipp (2006); McAdam (1986); Wilson and Musick (1997).

4. Emphasis added.

5. Interestingly, these scripts and ideas about wealth are beginning to shift, as will be seen in chapter 10. The working-poor community has carved out more time for education and civic engagement, and they are speaking out about the political and economic policies that they view as unfairly favoring the ultra-wealthy.

6. U.S. Census data do not accurately reflect the total population. The 2017 U.S. Census recorded 25.3 percent in the town of Jackson, but this figure is likely at least 30 percent as of the writing of this book. The percentage is slightly less in Teton County.

7. See Chadwick (2016).

In 2016, The Latino Resource Center merged with the Community Resource Center and El Puente to make a stronger and more unified organization called "One22." (22 is the Wyoming county designation number for Teton County. These county numbers are prominently displayed as a number prefix on all Wyoming plates.)

8. See Latino Resource Center, (2015), *Latino Community Assessment: Teton County, Wyoming*

9. See years 2009–13 in the American Community Survey (U.S. Census Bureau 2015). Importantly, the figures reported in the census are much lower than reality, because of the number of undocumented people in Teton County. A local study in Teton County conducted by a professional suggests that "The U.S. Census reports an average poverty rate in Teton County of 8%. This looks positive until we break out the numbers by ethnicity. Even in the hardest years, during the recent recession, the percentage of white residents living in poverty never reached double-digits. Conversely, the percentage of Hispanic residents remains over 10%, even as our economy recovers. We know that data on Hispanic population is likely low, due to the inconsistencies in census collection methods and how our local immigrants live and report. This means that the actual numbers are closer to 20- 30% of our Hispanic populations living in federally-qualified poverty and a much larger percentage experiencing poverty, such as difficulty finding housing, food, and healthcare. This

estimate is supported in client data in other parts of this report." Latino Resource Center (2015: 38).

10. Latino Resource Center (2015: 46–47).

11. For more on this dynamic, see the fascinating and important literature on "Linked Migration." Some examples include Nelson et al. (2014); Nelson and Nelson (2011); Marcouilleret al. (2011). Also see Park and Pellow (2011).

12. Latino Resource Center (2015).

13. Ibid.

14. 2014 Western Greater Yellowstone Area Housing Needs Assessment (Rees Consulting et al. 2014; Latino Resource Center 2015).

15. The following three quotes are from The Awareness Project Jackson Hole, a powerful collection of stories of eviction in the area. Contrary to the rest of the names in this book, the names used in these quotes are not pseudonyms, but were taken directly from the project's website (now defunct), which also included more on their stories as well as photographs and videos.

16. This issue was widely publicized in local newspapers and was an ongoing event during the writing of this book. A minimum thirty-day notice for evictions was passed, but the outcome of this political and moral struggle may change by the time of this book's publication.

17. See the 2014 Western Greater Yellowstone Area Housing Needs Assessment (Rees Consulting et al. 2014; Latino Resource Center 2015).

18. Park and Pellow (2011).

19. See chapter 1 and chapters 4–6 for evidence of this claim.

Notes to Chapter 10

1. McAdam (1982).

2. The findings from this chapter are based on evidence from interviews with mostly working-poor people, yet we also interviewed a handful of middle-income folks from this community who are working on these issues full time (often through a social service organization) and who can provide a bird's-eye view of the issues through their direct involvement.

3. Journalists have documented similar dynamics in similarly progressive mountain communities. For example, Boulder, Colorado, is on the face of it one of the most progressive cities in the country, yet people of color describe experiences that tell a much different story (Castle 2018).

4. See the appendix for the full interview guide. A special thanks to Michèle Lamont for sharing her interview guide with me.

5. Park and Pellow (2011: 23).

6. My goal here is not to unpack in great detail, or consider the merits, of the myriad different macro-level economic and political theories. Instead, my goal is to present the views of the low-income population about how and why wealth is accumulated. These necessarily involve specific economic theories, ranging from forms of laissez-faire capitalism to forms of socialism, all of which I do not have space to fairly engage here.

7. For more on this, including a visualization of this discrepancy over time, see pages 16–17 of Charture Institute and Jackson Hole News and Guide (2017).

8. The academic study of social movements and collective behavior offers useful tools for understanding dynamics in this chapter. I make use of some specific concepts (e.g., cognitive liberation), but also avoid getting caught up considering all of the different factors that birthed this movement, or the lessons that might explain whether or not it will be successful in the future. That is not my intention in this book. My focus is on the ultra-wealthy, and the general response to them by the working poor. As such, I do not have space to fully devote to applying various theories from social movements that are no doubt at play in this case (e.g., deprivation theory, resource mobilization theory, political process theory, and of course, the large literature on framing).

9. McAdam (1982).

10. More and more folks from the low-income community are beginning to attend and speak at town council meetings on these issues. As just one example, see the video of a recent town council meeting regarding affordable housing and exploitation housing insecurity among this community, Town of Jackson (2017), Item VI—Ordinance Z.

Notes to Epilogue

1. See chapter 1 text and notes for discussion of what has come to be called the "New West."

2. For an extended discussion of the relationships between economic inequality and opportunity inequality, see the work of sociologist Claude S. Fischer, especially his excellent and approachable 2017 article in the *Boston Review*, "Inequality is about access to public goods, not income." (Fischer 2017).

3. This theme of "doing harm" was reiterated by many low-income respondents. See chapter 10, as well as chapter 5. After writing the manuscript, I also came across Anand Giridharadas's excellent book that digs much deeper into issues relating to elite philanthropy and the imperative of doing less harm. This notion of doing less harm was raised by many of our low-income interviewees in 2016 prior to the release Anand's wonderful book in 2018, and should be taken as further evidence for his important conclusions (Giridharadas 2018).

4. This quote is a representative example, taken from Linton Properties in Jackson Hole. See http://lintonbingle.com/.

5. For data on the increase in worker productivity and the stagnation of wages, see Economic Policy Institute (2018). For data on the declining share of corporate-sector income by workers, see Economic Policy Institute (2015a).

6. Young (2017).

7. For example, Boston College's Center on Wealth and Philanthropy has decades of empirical studies on these topics. Also see Sherman (2017) and Wood (2011). Relatedly, see relevant neuroscientific research discussed and cited in chapter 8 of this book.

8. Stellar et al. (2012); Varnum et al. (2015); Dietze and Knowles (2016); Varnum et al. (2016). Also see the following journalistic piece by two religious studies scholars, Charles Mathewes and Evan Sandsmark, who cite much more research on this topic (Mathewes and Sandsmark 2017).

Notes to Appendix

1. See Donnelly et al. (2018).

2. See Wealth-X (2017a, 2017b, 2018).

3. Ibid.

4. See Kroll (2017).

5. For example, see this report that uses Federal Reserve data to estimate net worth brackets and percentiles of the top one percent: https://dqydj.com/net-worth-brackets-wealth-brackets-one-percent/.

6. See Au-Yeung (2017).

7. See Wealth-X (2016).

8. See http://YaleYellowstone.org.

9. See Wealth-X (2017a, 2017b, 2018).

10. Ibid.

11. Ibid.

REFERENCES

Abbink, Jan, and Tijo Salverda, eds. 2013. *Anthropology of Elites: Power, Culture, and the Complexities of Distinction.* 1st ed. New York: Palgrave Macmillan.

Aldrich, Nelson W. 1997. *Old Money: The Mythology of Wealth in America.* Expanded ed. New York: Allworth Press, 1997.

al Gharbi, Musa. 2018. "Race and the Race for the White House: On Social Research in the Age of Trump." *American Sociologist* 49, no. 4: 496–519. https://doi.org/10.1007/s12108-018-9373-5.

Angle, John. 1986. "Surplus Theory of Social Stratification and the Size Distribution of Personal Wealth." *Social Forces* 65, no. 2: 293–326. http://www.jstor.org/stable/2578675.

Armstrong, Elizabeth A., and Laura T. Hamilton. 2015. *Paying for the Party: How College Maintains Inequality.* Cambridge, MA: Harvard University Press.

Au-Yeung, Angel. 2017. "America's Richest Women 2017." *Forbes.* Updated October 17, 2017, https://www.forbes.com/sites/angelauyeung/2017/10/17/richest-women-2017-forbes-400/#32a8b6e57f24.

Baer, Drake. 2017. "Rich People Literally See the World Differently." *New York Magazine.* Updated February 14, 2017, http://nymag.com/scienceofus/2017/02/how-rich-people-see-the-world-differently.html.

Barber, Megan. 2016. "Unequal City." *Curbed.* Updated July 6, 2016, https://www.curbed.com/2016/7/6/12101006/jackson-hole-real-estate-tourism.

Barman, Emily. 2017. "Social Bases of Philanthropy." *Annual Review of Sociology* 43, no. 1: 271–90. https://doi.org/10.1146/annurev-soc-060116-053524.

Beyerlein, Kraig, and John Hipp. 2006. "Two-Stage Model for a Two-Stage Process: How Biographical Availability Matters for Social Movement Mobilization." *Mobilization: An International Quarterly* 11, no. 3: 299–320. https://doi.org/10.17813/maiq.11.3.8p1758741377684u. https://mobilizationjournal.org/doi/abs/10.17813/maiq.11.3.8p1758741377684u.

Boston College University. 2015. "Center on Wealth and Philanthropy." Updated August 31, 2015, https://www.bc.edu/research/cwp.html.

Brown, David L. 2003. "Introduction: Rural America Enters the New Millennium." In *Challenges for Rural America in the Twenty-First Century*, edited by David L. Brown, Louis E. Swanson, and Alan W. Barton, 1–16. University Park: Pennsylvania State University Press.

Buffett, Peter. 2013. "Charitable-Industrial Complex." *New York Times*. Updated July 26, 2013, https://www.nytimes.com/2013/07/27/opinion/the-charitable-industrial-complex.html.

Burow, Paul, Kathryn McConnell, and Justin Farrell. 2019. "Social Scientific Research on the American West: Current Debates, Novel Methods, and New Directions." *Environmental Research Letters*. https://iopscience.iop.org/article/10.1088/1748-9326/ab4030.

Business Journal. 2004. "Wyoming Ranked No. 1 as 'Wealth-Friendly' State." Updated May 21, 2004, http://archive.businessjournaldaily.com/wyoming-ranked-no-1-wealth-friendly-state-2004-5-21.

Callahan, David. 2017. *Givers: Wealth, Power, and Philanthropy in a New Gilded Age*. 1st ed. New York: Alfred A. Knopf.

Castle, Shay. 2018. "Boulder Prides Itself on Being Welcoming to All, But Its Citizens of Color Tell a Different Story." *Denver Post*. Updated July 29, 2018, https://www.denverpost.com/2018/07/29/boulder-diversity-civil-rights/.

Chadwick, Patrick. 2016. "El Voto Latino." *Planet Jackson Hole*. Updated July 12, 2016, https://archive.planetjh.com/2016/07/12/feature-el-voto-latino/.

Charture Institute and Jackson Hole News and Guide. 2017. "IRS vs. Census Population Estimates." *Jackson Hole Compass*, 16–19.

Cherney, David. 2011. "Environmental Saviors? Effectiveness of Nonprofit Organizations in Greater Yellowstone." PhD Dissertation, University of Colorado at Boulder. https://scholar.colorado.edu/envs_gradetds/7/.

Chua, Roy Y. J., and Xi Zou. 2009. "Devil Wears Prada? Effects of Exposure to Luxury Goods on Cognition and Decision Making." *Harvard Business School*. Updated November 25, 2009, https://www.hbs.edu/faculty/Publication%20Files/10-034.pdf.

Clark, Susan G., Aaron M. Hohl, Catherine H. Picard, and Elizabeth Thomas, eds. 2014. *Large-Scale Conservation in the Common Interest*. New York: Springer.

Clark, Susan G., and Murray B. Rutherford. 2014. *Large Carnivore Conservation: Integrating Science and Policy in the North American West*. Chicago: University of Chicago Press.

Clifford, Hal. 2016. "Mount Millionaire." *SKI Magazine*. Updated December 13, 2016, https://www.skimag.com/uncategorized/mount-millionaire.

Cohan, William D. 2008. "Paradise Lost." *Fortune Magazine*. Updated February 6, 2008, http://archive.fortune.com/2008/02/04/lifestyle/paradise_lost.fortune/index.htm.

Cohen, Andrew C., and Shai M. Dromi. 2018. "Advertising Morality: Maintaining Moral Worth in a Stigmatized Profession." *Theory and Society* 47, no. 2: 175–206. https://doi.org/10.1007/s11186-018-9309-7.

Conover, Katharine. 2015. *Jackson Hole Compass*, 53. https://issuu.com/jhnewsandguide/docs/compass_full.

Cousin, Bruno, Shamus Khan, and Ashley Mears. 2018. "Theoretical and Methodological Pathways for Research on Elites." *Socio-Economic Review* 16, no. 2: 225–49. https://doi.org/10.1093/ser/mwy019.

Delistraty, Cody. 2013. "Why It's Still Terrible to Be a Hipster." *Thought Catalog*. Updated September 9, 2013, https://thoughtcatalog.com/cody-delistraty/2013/09/why-its-still-terrible-to-be-a-hipster/.

de Sherbinin, Alex, Leah K. VanWey, Kendra McSweeney, Rimjhim Aggarwal, Alisson Barbieri, Sabine Henry, Lori M. Hunter, Wayne Twine, and Robert Walker. 2008. "Rural Household Demographics, Livelihoods, and the Environment." *Global Environmental Change* 18, no. 1: 38–53. https://doi.org/10.1016/j.gloenvcha.2007.05.005. http://www.sciencedirect.com/science/article/pii/S0959378007000398.

Desmond, Matthew. 2016. *Evicted: Poverty and Profit in the American City.* 1st ed. New York: Crown Publishers.

Dietze, Pia, and Eric D. Knowles. 2016. "Social Class and the Motivational Relevance of Other Human Beings: Evidence from Visual Attention." *Psychological Science* 27, no. 11: 1517–27. https://doi.org/10.1177/0956797616667721.

DiPrete, Thomas A., and Gregory M. Eirich. 2006. "Cumulative Advantage as a Mechanism for Inequality: A Review of Theoretical and Empirical Developments." *Annual Review of Sociology* 32, no. 1: 271–97. https://doi.org/10.1146/annurev.soc.32.061604.123127.

Dolan, Kerry A. 2004. "Private Powder." *Forbes*. Updated March 1, 2004, http://www.forbes.com/forbes/2004/0301/112.html.

Dolgon, Corey. 2006. *End of the Hamptons: Scenes from the Class Struggle in America's Paradise.* New York: New York University Press, 2006.

Domhoff, G. William. 1967. *Who Rules America? A Spectrum Book.* Englewood Cliffs, NJ: Prentice-Hall.

Donnelly, Grant E., Tianyi Zheng, Emily Haisley, and Michael I. Norton. 2018. "Amount and Source of Millionaires' Wealth (Moderately) Predict Their Happiness." [In English.] *Personality and Social Psychology Bulletin* 44, no. 5: 684–99. https://doi.org/10.1177/0146167217744766.

Economic Policy Institute. 2015a. "Decline in Labor's Share of Corporate Income since 2000 Means $535 Billion Less for Workers." Updated September 10, 2015, https://www.epi.org/publication/the-decline-in-labors-share-of-corporate-income-since-2000-means-535-billion-less-for-workers/.

———. 2015b. "Increasingly Unequal States of America: Income Inequality by State, 1917 to 2012." Updated January 26, 2015, https://www.epi.org/publication/income-inequality-by-state-1917-to-2012/.

———. 2016. "Income Inequality in the U.S. by State, Metropolitan Area, and County." Updated June 16, 2016, https://www.epi.org/publication/income-inequality-in-the-us/.

———. 2018. "Productivity–Pay Gap." Updated August 2018, https://www.epi.org/productivity-pay-gap/.

———. 2019. "Unequal States of America: Income Inequality in the United States." May 22, 2019, http://www.epi.org/multimedia/unequal-states-of-america/.

Farrell, Justin. 2014. "Moral Outpouring: Shock and Generosity in the Aftermath of the BP Oil Spill." *Social Problems* 61, no. 3: 482–506. https://doi.org/10.1525/sp.2014.12163.

Farrell, Justin. 2015a. *Battle for Yellowstone: Morality and the Sacred Roots of Environmental Conflict.* Princeton Studies in Cultural Sociology. Princeton, NJ: Princeton University Press, 2015.

Farrell, Justin. 2015b. "Echo Chambers and False Certainty." *Nature Climate Change* 5, no. 8: 719–20. https://doi.org/10.1038/nclimate2732.

Farrell, Justin. 2016a. "Corporate Funding and Ideological Polarization about Climate Change." *Proceedings of the National Academy of Sciences* 113, no. 1: 92–97. https://doi.org/10.1073/pnas.1509433112.

Farrell, Justin. 2016b. "Network Structure and Influence of the Climate Change Counter-Movement." *Nature Climate Change* 6, no. 4: 370–74. https://doi.org/10.1038/nclimate2875.

Farrell, Justin. 2019. "Growth of Climate Change Misinformation in US Philanthropy: Evidence from Natural Language Processing." *Environmental Research Letters* 14, no. 3: 034013. https://doi.org/10.1088/1748-9326/aaf939.

Farrell, Justin, Kathryn McConnell, and Robert Brulle. 2019. "Evidence-Based Strategies to Combat Scientific Misinformation." *Nature Climate Change* 9, no. 3: 191–95. https://doi.org/10.1038/s41558-018-0368-6.

Fischer, Claude S. 2017. "Inequality Is about Access to Public Goods, Not Income." *Boston Review*. Updated April 24, 2017, http://bostonreview.net/class-inequality/claude-s-fischer-inequality-about-access-public-goods-not-income.

Flowers, Patrick. 2010. "FWP Letter to Yellowstone Club." *Bozeman Daily Chronicle*. Updated August 24, 2010, https://www.bozemandailychronicle.com/news/fwp-lette-to-yellowstone-club/pdf_2c69e724-aed8-11df-960b-001cc4c002e0.html.

Fluck, Winfried. 2003. "What Is So Bad about Being Rich? Representation of Wealth in American Culture." *Comparative American Studies: An International Journal* 1, no. 1: 53–79. https://doi.org/10.1179/147757003X327266.

Gaztambide-Fernández, Rubén A. 2009. *Best of the Best: Becoming Elite at an American Boarding School.* Cambridge, MA: Harvard University Press.

Giridharadas, Anand. 2018. *Winners Take All: The Elite Charade of Changing the World.* New York: Knopf.

Griskevicius, V., J. M. Tybur, and B. Van den Bergh. 2010. "Going Green to Be Seen: Status, Reputation, and Conspicuous Conservation." [In English.] *Journal of Personality and Social Psychology* 98: 343–55. https://doi.org/10.1037/a0018589. https://research.vu.nl/en/publications/546ac1ef-ca5b-43c6-b6f9-521c164417c9.

Grusky, David B., and Tamar Kricheli-Katz. 2012. *New Gilded Age: The Critical Inequality Debates of Our Time.* Studies in Social Inequality. Stanford, CA: Stanford University Press.

Grusky, David B., Charles Varner, and Marybeth Mattingly. 2015. *State of the States: Poverty and Inequality Report.* Stanford, CA: Stanford Center on Poverty and Inequality.

Hacker, Jacob S., and Paul Pierson. 2011. *Winner-Take-All Politics: How Washington Made the Rich Richer and Turned Its Back on the Middle Class.* 1st ed. New York: Simon & Schuster.

Hahl, Oliver, Ezra W. Zuckerman, and Minjae Kim. 2017. "Why Elites Love Authentic Lowbrow Culture: Overcoming High-Status Denigration with Outsider Art." *American Sociological Review* 82, no. 4: 828–56. https://doi.org/10.1177/0003122417710642.

Hancock, Laura. 2016. "Panel to Look at Wyoming Shell Company Laws." Updated May 9, 2016, https://www.wyomingnews.com/news/panel-to-look-at-wyoming-shell-company-laws/article_4683ac8c-15a5-11e6-bce7-6798a513adbf.html.

Harrington, Brooke. 2016. *Capital without Borders: Wealth Managers and the One Percent.* Cambridge, MA: Harvard University Press.

Headwaters Economics. 2017. "Federal Lands in the West: Liability or Asset?" Updated February 2017, https://headwaterseconomics.org/public-lands/federal-lands-performance/.

———. 2018. "Economic Impact of National Parks." Updated May 2018, https://headwaterseconomics.org/public-lands/protected-lands/economic-impact-of-national-parks/.

Hertz, Rosanna, and Jonathan B. Imber. 1995. *Studying Elites Using Qualitative Methods.* Sage Focus Editions. Thousand Oaks, CA: Sage Publications.

Hines, J. Dwight. 2007. "Persistent Frontier and the Rural Gentrification of the Rocky Mountain West." *Journal of the West* 46, no. 1: 63–73.

———. 2012. "Post-Industrial Regime of Production/Consumption and the Rural Gentrification of the New West Archipelago." *Antipode* 44, no. 1: 74–97. https://doi.org/10.1111/j.1467-8330.2011.00843.x.

Ho, Karen Zouwen. 2009. *Liquidated: An Ethnography of Wall Street.* Durham, NC: Duke University Press.

Hochschild, Arlie Russell. 2016. *Strangers in Their Own Land: Anger and Mourning on the American Right.* New York: New Press.

Hondagneu-Sotelo, Pierrette. 2007. *Doméstica: Immigrant Workers Cleaning and Caring in the Shadows of Affluence.* Berkeley: University of California Press.

Howard, Adam, and Rubén A. Gaztambide-Fernández, eds. 2010. *Educating Elites: Class Privilege and Educational Advantage.* Lanham, MD: Rowman & Littlefield Education.

Hunter, Lori M., Jason D. Boardman, and Jarron M. Saint Onge. 2005. "Association between Natural Amenities, Rural Population Growth, and Long-Term Residents' Economic Well-Being." *Rural Sociology* 70, no. 4: 452–69. https://doi.org/10.1526/003601105775012714.

Internal Revenue Service. 2015. "The 400 Individual Income Tax Returns Reporting the Largest Adjusted Gross Incomes Each Year, 1992–2012." Updated February 26, 2015, https://www.irs.gov/pub/irs-soi/12intop400.pdf.

Jackson Hole Land Trust. 2014. "View22 Project Continues and Expands in 2014." Updated June 23, 2014, https://jhlandtrust.org/artists_partners/view22-project-continues-and-expands-in-2014/.

———. 2016. "Tax Implications." Updated June 29, 2016, http://jhlandtrust.org/land-protection/conserve-your-land/tax-implications/.

Johnston, Josée, and Shyon Baumann. 2007. "Democracy versus Distinction: A Study of Omnivorousness in Gourmet Food Writing." *American Journal of Sociology* 113, no. 1: 165–204. https://doi.org/10.1086/518923.

Kantola, Anu, and Hanna Kuusela. 2019. "Wealth Elite Moralities: Wealthy Entrepreneurs' Moral Boundaries." *Sociology* 53, no. 2: 368–84. https://doi.org/10.1177/0038038518768175.

Kendall, Diana Elizabeth. 2002. *Power of Good Deeds: Privileged Women and the Social Reproduction of the Upper Class.* Lanham, MD: Roman & Littlefield Publishers.

Khan, Shamus. 2011. *Privilege: Making of an Adolescent Elite at St. Paul's School.* Princeton Studies in Cultural Sociology. Princeton, NJ: Princeton University Press.

———. 2012. "Sociology of Elites." *Annual Review of Sociology* 38, no. 1: 361–77. https://doi.org/10.1146/annurev-soc-071811-145542.

———. 2019. "Subpoena of Ethnographic Data." *Sociological Forum* 34, no. 1: 253–63. https://doi.org/10.1111/socf.12493.

Kroch, Anthony S. 1996. "Dialect and Style in the Speech of Upper Class Philadelphia." In *Variation and Change in Language and Society: Papers in Honor of William Labov*, edited by Gregory R. Guy and William Labov, 23–46. Amsterdam: J. Benjamins.

Kroll, Luisa. 2017. "Forbes 400 2017: Meet the Richest People in America." Updated October 17, 2017, https://www.forbes.com/sites/luisakroll/2017/10/17/forbes-400-2017-americas-richest-people-bill-gates-jeff-bezos-mark-zuckerberg-donald-trump/#222bfaaa5ed5.

Kuusela, Hanna. 2018. "Learning to Own: Cross-Generational Meanings of Wealth and Class-Making in Wealthy Finnish Families." *Sociological Review* 66, no. 6: 1161–76. https://doi.org/10.1177/0038026118777698.

Lamont, Michèle, Stefan Beljean, and Matthew Clair. 2014. "What Is Missing? Cultural Processes and Causal Pathways to Inequality." *Socio-Economic Review* 12, no. 3: 573–608. https://doi.org/10.1093/ser/mwu011.

Lamont, Michèle, and Graziella Moraes Silva, Jessica S. Welburn, Joshua Guetzkow, Nissim Mizrachi, Hanna Herzog, and Elisa Reis. 2016. *Getting Respect: Responding to Stigma and Discrimination in the United States, Brazil, and Israel.* Princeton, NJ: Princeton University Press.

Latino Resource Center. 2015. *2015 Latino Community Assessment—Teton County, Wyoming.* Jackson, WY: Latino Resource Center.

Lichter, Daniel T., and David L. Brown. 2011. "Rural America in an Urban Society: Changing Spatial and Social Boundaries." *Annual Review of Sociology* 37, no. 1: 565–92. https://doi.org/10.1146/annurev-soc-081309-150208.

Lindsay, D. Michael. 2007. *Faith in the Halls of Power: How Evangelicals Joined the American Elite.* Oxford: Oxford University Press.

Linton Properties Jackson Hole. 2019. "Linton Properties—Home Page." *Linton Properties Jackson Hole*, May 23, 2019. http://lintonbingle.com/.

Ljunggren, Jørn. 2015. "Elitist Egalitarianism: Negotiating Identity in the Norwegian Cultural Elite." *Sociology* 51, no. 3: 559–74. https://doi.org/10.1177/0038038515590755.

Marsh, Jason. 2012. "Why Inequality Is Bad for the One Percent." Updated September 25, 2012, https://greatergood.berkeley.edu/article/item/why_inequality_is_bad_for_the_one_percent.

Mathewes, Charles, and Evan Sandsmark. 2017. "Being Rich Wrecks Your Soul. We Used to Know That." Updated July 28, 2017, https://www.washingtonpost.com/outlook/being-rich-wrecks-your-soul-we-used-to-know-that/2017/07/28/7d3e2b90-5ab3-11e7-9fc6-c7ef4bc58d13_story.html.

McAdam, Doug. 1982. *Political Process and the Development of Black Insurgency, 1930–1970.* Chicago: University of Chicago Press.

———. 1986. "Recruitment to High-Risk Activism: Case of Freedom Summer." *American Journal of Sociology* 92, no. 1: 64–90. http://www.jstor.org/stable/2779717.

McMullen, Troy. 2016. "Low Inventory and High Demand Drive Real Estate Prices Higher in Jackson Hole." *Forbes.* Updated June 3, 2016, https://www.forbes.com/sites/troymcmullen/2016/06/03/low-inventory-and-high-demand-drive-real-estate-prices-higher-in-jackson-hole-wyoming/#2793590d74bf.

Merton, Robert K. 1968. "Matthew Effect in Science." *Science* 159, no. 3810: 56–63. https://doi.org/10.1126/science.159.3810.56. http://science.sciencemag.org/content/159/3810/56.abstract.

Missoulian. 2007. "Blixseth Building 'World's Most Expensive Home.'" *Missoulian.* Updated January 29, 2007, https://missoulian.com/news/state-and-regional/blixseth-building-world-s-most-expensive-home-posted-on-jan/article_a3bb8b1f-692c-58cf-9687-0208ed335b60.html.

Mohai, Paul, David Pellow, and J. Timmons Roberts. 2009. "Environmental Justice." *Annual Review of Environment and Resources* 34, no. 1: 405–30. https://doi.org/10.1146/annurev-environ-082508-094348.

Nelson, Lise, and Peter B. Nelson. 2011. "Global Rural: Gentrification and Linked Migration in the Rural USA." *Progress in Human Geography* 35, no. 4: 441–59. https://doi.org/10.1177/0309132510380487.

Nelson, Peter B., Lise Nelson, and Laurie Trautman. 2014. "Linked Migration and Labor Market Flexibility in the Rural Amenity Destinations in the United States." *Journal of Rural Studies* 36: 121–36. https://doi.org/10.1016/j.jrurstud.2014.07.008. http://www.sciencedirect.com/science/article/pii/S0743016714000965.

Ostrander, Susan A. 1984. *Women of the Upper Class.* Women in the Political Economy. Philadelphia: Temple University Press.

———. 2010. *Money for Change: Social Movement Philanthropy at Haymarket People's Fund.* Philadelphia: Temple University Press.

Ostrower, Francie. 1995. *Why the Wealthy Give: The Culture of Elite Philanthropy.* Princeton, NJ: Princeton University Press.

Page, Benjamin I., and Martin Gilens. 2017. *Democracy in America?: What Has Gone Wrong and What We Can Do About It.* Chicago: University of Chicago Press.

Pager, Devah. 2007. *Marked: Race, Crime, and Finding Work in an Era of Mass Incarceration.* Chicago: University of Chicago Press.

Park, Lisa Sun-Hee, and David N. Pellow. 2011. *Slums of Aspen: Immigrants vs. the Environment in America's Eden.* Nation of Newcomers: Immigrant History as American History. New York: New York University Press.

Pellow, David N., and Hollie Nyseth Brehm. 2013. "Environmental Sociology for the Twenty-First Century." *Annual Review of Sociology* 39, no. 1: 229–50. https://doi.org/10.1146/annurev-soc-071312-145558.

Pennsylvania Land Trust Association. 2012. "Economic Benefits of Land Conservation." Updated April 6, 2012, https://conservationtools.org/guides/94-economic-benefits-of-land-conservation.

Piketty, Thomas, and Arthur Goldhammer. 2014. *Capital in the Twenty-First Century.* Cambridge, MA: Belknap Press of Harvard University Press.

Pinçon-Charlot, Monique, and Michel Pinçon. 2018. "Social Power and Power over Space: How the Bourgeoisie Reproduces Itself in the City." *International Journal of Urban and Regional Research* 42, no. 1: 115–25. https://doi.org/10.1111/1468-2427.12533.

Rees Consulting, WSW Consulting, Frontier Forward, and RRC Associates. 2014. *Western Greater Yellowstone Area Housing Needs Assessment.* Driggs, ID: City of Driggs.

Rivera, Lauren A. 2015. *Pedigree: How Elite Students Get Elite Jobs.* Princeton, NJ: Princeton University Press.

Rollins, Judith. 1987. *Between Women: Domestics and Their Employers.* Labor and Social Change. Philadelphia: Temple University Press.

Rothschild, Zachary K., Mark J. Landau, Daniel Sullivan, and Lucas A. Keefer. 2012. "Dual-Motive Model of Scapegoating: Displacing Blame to Reduce Guilt or Increase Control." [In English.] *Journal of Personality and Social Psychology* 102, no. 6: 1148–63. https://doi.org/10.1037/a0027413.

Sachs, Carolyn, Patricia Allen, A. Rachel Terman, Jennifer Hayden, and Christina Hatcher. 2014. "Front and Back of the House: Socio-Spatial Inequalities in Food Work." *Agriculture and Human Values* 31, no. 1: 3–17. https://doi.org/10.1007/s10460-013-9445-7.

Scheiber, Noam, and Patricia Cohen. 2015. "For the Wealthiest, a Private Tax System That Saves Them Billions." *New York Times.* Updated December 29, 2015, https://www.nytimes.com/2015/12/30/business/economy/for-the-wealthiest-private-tax-system-saves-them-billions.html.

Schiller, Ben. 2016. "Places in the U.S. Where Income Inequality Is Off the Charts." *Fast Company.* Updated July 22, 2016, https://www.fastcompany.com/3061025/the-places-in-the-us-where-income-inequality-is-off-the-charts.

Schimpfössl, Elisabeth. 2018. *Rich Russians: From Oligarchs to Bourgeoisie.* New York: Oxford University Press.

Schmalzbauer, Leah. 2014. *Last Best Place?: Gender, Family, and Migration in the New West.* Stanford, CA: Stanford University Press.

Schor, Juliet. 1998. *Overspent American: Upscaling, Downshifting, and the New Consumer.* 1st ed. New York: Basic Books.

Schrank, Aaron. 2015. "Inequality in the Equality State: Disparities Abound in Wyoming's Renowned Ski Town." *Wyoming Public Media.* Updated January 9,

2015, https://www.wyomingpublicmedia.org/post/inequality-equality-state-disparities-abound-wyomings-renowned-ski-town#stream/0.

Sherman, Rachel. 2007. *Class Acts: Service and Inequality in Luxury Hotels*. Berkeley: University of California Press.

———. 2017. *Uneasy Street: The Anxieties of Affluence*. Princeton, NJ: Princeton University Press, 2017.

Shooting Star Jackson Hole. 2017. "Wyoming Tax Benefits." May 25, 2017. http://www.shootingstarjh.com/wyoming-tax-information.html.

———. 2019. "Jackson Hole Golf at Shooting Star—Home Page." *Jackson Hole Golf Real Estate*, May 23, 2019. http:// www.shootingstarjh.com.

Smith, Christian, and Hilary A. Davidson. 2014. *Paradox of Generosity: Giving We Receive, Grasping We Lose*. New York: Oxford University Press.

Smith, Kristin E., and Ann R. Tickamyer, eds. 2011. *Economic Restructuring and Family Well-Being in Rural America*. Rural Studies Series. University Park: Pennsylvania State University Press.

Smith, Michael D., and Richard S. Krannich. 2000. "'Culture Clash' Revisited: Newcomer and Longer-Term Residents' Attitudes toward Land Use, Development, and Environmental Issues in Rural Communities in the Rocky Mountain West." *Rural Sociology* 65, no. 3: 396–421. https://doi.org/10.1111/j.1549-0831.2000.tb00036.x.

Smith, Michael D., Richard S. Krannich, and Lori M. Hunter. 2001. "Growth, Decline, Stability, and Disruption: Longitudinal Analysis of Social Well-Being in Four Western Rural Communities." *Rural Sociology* 66, no. 3: 425–50. https://doi.org/10.1111/j.1549-0831.2001.tb00075.x.

Stanford Social Innovation Review. 2015. "Wall Street Takeover of Nonprofit Boards." Updated Summer 2015, https://ssir.org/articles/entry/the_wall_street_takeover_of_nonprofit_boards.

Steiner, Christopher. 2009. "Yellowstone Club Files for Bankruptcy." *SKI Magazine*. https://www.skimag.com/adventure/yellowstone-club-files-for-bankruptcy.

Stellar, Jennifer E., Vida M. Manzo, Michael W. Kraus, and Dacher Keltner. 2012. "Class and Compassion: Socioeconomic Factors Predict Responses to Suffering." *Emotion* 12, no. 3: 449–59. https://doi.org/10.1037/a0026508.

Stevens, Mitchell L. 2009. *Creating a Class: College Admissions and the Education of Elites*. Cambridge, MA: Harvard University Press.

Suhay, Elizabeth, Marko Klašnja, and Gonzalo Rivero. 2018. "Ideology of Affluence: Explanations for Inequality and Political Attitudes among Rich Americans." Paper in Progress—Presented for 2018 APSA Class and Inequality (Section 45).

Swanson, Ana. 2017. "Ultra-Rich Are Hiding Way More Money Overseas Than Anyone Realized." *Washington Post*. Updated June 1, 2017, https://www.washingtonpost.com/news/wonk/wp/2017/06/01/researchers-are-figuring-out-just-how-much-wealth-the-super-rich-are-hiding-overseas/.

Taylor, Dorceta E. 2016. *Rise of the American Conservation Movement: Power, Privilege, and Environmental Protection*. Durham, NC: Duke University Press.

Tilly, Charles. 1998. *Durable Inequality*. Berkeley: University of California Press.

Town of Jackson. 2017. "Ordinance Z—an Ordinance Adding Chapter 5.80 to the Jackson Municipal Code Regarding Residential Rental Property Regulations (Presented for First Reading) (Audrey Cohen-Davis, Town Attorney)." Updated October 16, 2017, https://jacksonwy.swagit.com/play/10162017-1554.

U.S. Bureau of Economic Analysis. 2014. *Personal Income Summary: Personal Income, Population, Per Capita Personal Income.* Washington, DC: Bureau of Economic Analysis, 2014.

———. 2018. "Local Area Personal Income: New Estimates for 2017; Comprehensive Updates for 2001–2016." Updated November 15, 2018, https://www.bea.gov/news/2018/local-area-personal-income.

U.S. Census Bureau. 2015. "American Community Survey (ACS): 2009–2013 ACS 5-Year Estimates." Updated May 18, 2015, https://www.census.gov/programs-surveys/acs/technical-documentation/table-and-geography-changes/2013/5-year.html.

———. 2016. "American Community Survey: 2012–2016 ACS 5-Year Data Profiles." https://www.census.gov/acs/www/data/data-tables-and-tools/data-profiles/2016/.

———. 2018. "Annual Estimates of Housing Units for the United States, Regions, Divisions, States, and Counties: April 1, 2010 to July 1, 2017." Updated May 2018, https://factfinder.census.gov/.

U.S. Congressional Budget Office. 2016. "Trends in Family Wealth, 1989 to 2013." Updated August 18, 2016, https://www.cbo.gov/publication/51846.

Varnum, Michael E. W., Chris Blais, and Gene A. Brewer. 2016. "Social Class Affects Mu-Suppression During Action Observation." *Social Neuroscience* 11, no. 4: 449–54. https://doi.org/10.1080/17470919.2015.1105865.

Varnum, Michael E. W., Chris Blais, Ryan S. Hampton, and Gene A. Brewer. 2015. "Social Class Affects Neural Empathic Responses." *Culture and Brain* 3, no. 2: 122–30. https://doi.org/10.1007/s40167-015-0031-2.

Volscho, Thomas W., and Nathan J. Kelly. 2012. "Rise of the Super-Rich: Power Resources, Taxes, Financial Markets, and the Dynamics of the Top 1 Percent, 1949 to 2008." *American Sociological Review* 77, no. 5: 679–99. https://doi.org/10.1177/0003122412458508.

Wealth-X. 2016. "Demographics of UHNW Donors." Updated February 10, 2016, https://www.wealthx.com/featured/2016/uhnw-giving-demographics/.

———. 2017a. *Billionaire Census 2017.* New York: Wealth-X.

———. 2017b. "Exclusive UHNW Analysis: The World Ultra Wealth Report 2017." Updated June 27, 2017, https://www.wealthx.com/report/exclusive-uhnwi-analysis-world-ultra-wealth-report-2017/.

———. 2018. "Ultra Wealthy Analysis: World Ultra Wealth Report 2018." Updated September 5, 2018, https://www.wealthx.com/report/world-ultra-wealth-report-2018/.

Willow Street Group. 2019. "Willow Street Group—Home Page." May 23, 2019. http://willowstreetgroup.com.

Willson, Andrea, Kim Shuey, and Glen Elder Jr. 2007. "Cumulative Advantage Processes as Mechanisms of Inequality in Life Course Health." *American Journal of*

Sociology 112, no. 6: 1886–1924. https://doi.org/10.1086/512712. http://www.jstor.org/stable/10.1086/512712.

Wilson, John, and Marc Musick. 1997. "Who Cares? Toward an Integrated Theory of Volunteer Work." *American Sociological Review* 62, no. 5: 694–713. https://doi.org/10.2307/2657355. http://www.jstor.org/stable/2657355.

Wood, Gordon S. 1991. *Radicalism of the American Revolution.* 1st ed. New York: Alfred A. Knopf.

Wood, Graeme. 2011. "Secret Fears of the Super-Rich." *Atlantic.* Updated April 2011, https://www.theatlantic.com/magazine/archive/2011/04/secret-fears-of-the-super-rich/308419/.

Wyoming State Historical Society. 2014. "Establishment of Grand Teton National Park." Updated November 8, 2014, https://www.wyohistory.org/encyclopedia/establishment-grand-teton-national-park.

Yellowstone Club. 2016. "Summer 2016 Real Estate Guide." https://yellowstoneclub.com/wp-content/uploads/2016/07/2016_YC_Summer_Real_Estate_Guide-1.pdf.

———. 2018. "Fact Sheet: Dues and Assessments." Updated January 2018, https://yellowstoneclub.com/wp-content/uploads/2018/01/Dues-and-Assessments-2018-1.pdf.

Young, Cristobal. 2017. *Myth of Millionaire Tax Flight: How Place Still Matters for the Rich.* Studies in Social Inequality. Stanford, CA: Stanford University Press.

Young, Cristobal, Charles Varner, Ithai Z. Lurie, and Richard Prisinzano. 2016. "Millionaire Migration and Taxation of the Elite: Evidence from Administrative Data." *American Sociological Review* 81, no. 3: 421–46. https://doi.org/10.1177/0003122416639625.

Zweig, Michael. 2004. *What's Class Got to Do with It?: American Society in the Twenty-First Century.* Ithaca, NY: Cornell University Press.

INDEX

f denotes figure

A NOTE ON THE TYPE

This book has been composed in Adobe Text and Gotham.
Adobe Text, designed by Robert Slimbach for Adobe,
bridges the gap between fifteenth- and sixteenth-century
calligraphic and eighteenth-century Modern styles.
Gotham, inspired by New York street signs, was designed
by Tobias Frere-Jones for Hoefler & Co.